WORDS HAVE A PAST

The English Language, Colonialism, and the
Newspapers of Indian Boarding Schools

For nearly one hundred years, Indian boarding schools in Canada and
the United States produced newspapers that were read by white
settlers, government officials, and Indigenous parents. These newspapers were used as a settler colonial tool, yet within these tightly
controlled chronicles there also existed sites of resistance. Illuminating
and often deeply moving, this book traces colonial narratives of
language, time, and place from the nineteenth century to the present
day, post–Truth and Reconciliation Commission.

JANE GRIFFITH is an assistant professor in the School of Professional
Communication at Ryerson University.

D0723215

WORDS HAVE A PAST

The English Language, Colonialism, and the Newspapers of Indian Boarding Schools

JANE GRIFFITH

UNIVERSITY OF TORONTO PRESS
Toronto Buffalo London

© University of Toronto Press 2019
Toronto Buffalo London
utorontopress.com
Printed in Canada

ISBN 978-1-4875-0161-7 (cloth)   ISBN 978-1-4875-2155-4 (paper)

∞ Printed on acid-free, 100% post-consumer recycled paper with
vegetable-based inks.

Library and Archives Canada Cataloguing in Publication

Title: Words have a past : the English language, colonialism, and the
    newspapers of Indian boarding schools / Jane Griffith.
Names: Griffith, Jane, 1983–, author.
Description: Includes bibliographical references and index.
Identifiers: Canadiana 20190049626 | ISBN 9781487501617 (hardcover) |
    ISBN 9781487521554 (softcover)
Subjects: LCSH: Indian students – Canada – Intellectual life. | LCSH: Indian
    press – Canada – History. | LCSH: Student newspapers and periodicals – Canada –
    History. | LCSH: Indian students – Press coverage – Canada. | LCSH: Indians of
    North America – Languages – Social aspects. | LCSH: Sociolinguistics – Canada. |
    LCSH: Discrimination in education – Canada – History. | CSH: Indians of North
    America – Canada – Residential schools. | Indians of North America – Canada –
    Residential schools – Newspapers.
Classification: LCC PN4883 .G75 2019 | DDC 071/.108997 – dc23

This book has been published with the help of a grant from the Federation for the
Humanities and Social Sciences, through the Awards to Scholarly Publications Program,
using funds provided by the Social Sciences and Humanities Research Council of
Canada.

University of Toronto Press acknowledges the financial assistance to its publishing
program of the Canada Council for the Arts and the Ontario Arts Council, an agency of
the Government of Ontario.

**Canada Council
for the Arts**

**Conseil des Arts
du Canada**

**ONTARIO ARTS COUNCIL
CONSEIL DES ARTS DE L'ONTARIO**

an Ontario government agency
un organisme du gouvernement de l'Ontario

Funded by the   Financé par le
Government   gouvernement
of Canada   du Canada

Canada

MIX
Paper from
responsible sources
FSC® C016245

Contents

Illustrations

Figures

Tables

Acknowledgments

I would first like to thank residential school survivors and families who have shared their words.

Because this is an archival project, I also have many archivists and institutions to thank: Krista McCracken and the Residential School Survivors Centre at Algoma University; the Provincial Archives of Alberta; the British Columbia Archives; Archives of Manitoba; the Provincial Archives of Saskatchewan; Glenbow Archives; the Anglican General Synod Archives; the Esplanade Archives of Medicine Hat; the Archives Deschâtelets, Oblats de Marie Immaculée; the Chicago Newberry Library; Ceridwen Ross Collins and the Salt Spring Island Archives; Barbara Landis and the Cumberland County Historical Society; Rebecca Murray at Library and Archives Canada; and the Haskell Cultural Center and Museum in Kansas – huge thanks especially to Rhonda LeValdo and Karen Gillis. I also wish to thank the interlibrary loan staff at the University of Michigan, the University of Toronto, and York University. Thanks also to Desmond Wong.

I received generous support from Fulbright, the Social Sciences and Humanities Research Council of Canada, the History Education Network/Histoire et éducation en réseau, and the Faculties of Graduate Studies and Education at York University. Thanks also to the International Council for Canadian Studies, the Canadian Studies Network, the Robarts Centre for Canadian Studies, and the Canadian History of Education Association. I am grateful for feedback received at many conferences, including the Association of Canadian College and University Teachers of English, the Canadian Society for Studies in Education, the Indigenous Literary Studies Association, the International

Association of Genocide Scholars, and the Native American and Indigenous Studies Association. Thanks also to the Awards to Scholarly Publications Program through the Federation for the Humanities and Social Sciences.

Big thanks belong to the many scholars who have read this work, inspired this work, or provided support in other ways: Lee Airton, Funké Aladejebi, Jill Andrew, Donna Ashamock, Paul Axelrod, Abigail Bakan, Jeff Bale, Andrea Bear Nicholas, Sean Carleton, Brenda Child, Boyd Cothran, Warren Crichlow, Susan Dion, Susan Doyle, Gregory Dowd, Lisa Farley, Theodore Fontaine, Rubén Gaztambide-Fernández, Celia Haig-Brown, Maureen Niwa, Jennifer Jenson, Janelle Jenstad, Randy Kapashesit, Mary-Ellen Kelm, Aparna Mishra Tarc, Judith Mitchell, Mary Leigh Morbey, Ian Mosby, Nicholas Ng-A-Fook, Nikole Pascetta, Lisa Surridge, Cheryl Suzack, Coll Thrush, and Eve Tuck.

Thanks especially to Phil Deloria for my Fulbright research year at the University of Michigan, as well as to the Spolums, Austin McCoy, and Meryem Kamil for making the year much warmer. Thanks also to Dwayne Donald for going on an archival road trip with me. Deep thanks also to Martin Cannon during my postdoctoral fellowship at the University of Toronto. Karen Stanworth: thanks for so much, but especially for insisting on the importance of negative evidence, visual culture, and the archive.

To my new home in the School of Professional Communication at Ryerson University: thanks to my colleagues and to the Dean's Office of the Faculty of Communication and Design.

Thanks to the University of Toronto Press, in particular Len Husband, Dilia Narduzzi, Janice Evans, and Margaret de Boer.

And some warm thanks for warm friendships: Travis Allan, Rebecca Beaulne-Stuebing, Diane Bhalla, Audrey Hudson, Stephanie Matchiwita (who also contributed two of the photographs in this book), Maren Spolum, and Kim Tavares. Thanks to Brett, Mel, Chel, Kel, Ham, Sara, and Bronwyn. Particular praise belongs to Cristyne Hébert for basically everything. Thanks to my family: Joan, Dave, Janessa, Joanne, Dean, Mary Ann, Ken, Ruby, and Nana for their encouragement along the way. And most importantly dear Scott – you are many things, but most of all you are kind. Thanks to Sarah Leslie for the gift of life.

To our baby: we make up songs every day for you, and then forget them. But one song keeps sticking: *Alexander! We love you so much, we love you so much, we love you so much ...*

Parts of chapters 1 and 2 are derived, in part, from an article published in the journal *Paedagogica Historica* (2017).

Any profits made from this book will go to the Eyē? Sqâ'lewen Language Tables, based at Camosun College and led by Indigenous students and teachers. The tables support Indigenous language development for Indigenous students whose families experienced language loss as a result of colonization. Thanks to Eyē? Sqâ'lewen leaders for supporting this work. Thanks to Janice Simcoe and Dianne Biin.

Carlisle School Print Shop, c. 1900. Hoover Collection, H-006, Cumberland County Historical Society, Carlisle, PA. Courtesy of Cumberland County Historical Society, Carlisle, PA.

WORDS HAVE A PAST

The English Language, Colonialism, and the
Newspapers of Indian Boarding Schools

1 Bury the Lede: Introduction

Prospectus: This little paper is our own. It holds our School news and is to come out once a week. When we get it we shall know all that is going on in and near the school. Our officers will use it to tell us news from afar. For this we have to thank the Government.

– First page of the first issue of Battleford Indian
Industrial School's newspaper, *The Guide*, 1891

These records will lie. That's the strongest word I can tell you.
– Statement by former student Theodore Fontaine, 2014

The first epigraph above displays the first words of a newspaper printed at Battleford School in Saskatchewan in 1891. Fashioned as the voice of students, the prospectus positions the newspaper as "our own" filled with "our School news." In the second epigraph Theodore Fontaine, who attended two Manitoba Indian boarding schools in the 1950s, provides an alternative perspective: at a conference on genocide studies at which he spoke in 2014, he reminded those in attendance that the archives of boarding schools "will lie." This tension between a school's voice and a lie permeates the history of school newspapers produced at Indian boarding schools.[1]

Indian boarding school newspapers from the late nineteenth century – the focus of this book – were powerful political tools. They were touted as an avenue for communication between the school and interested parties, especially benefactors, who would read the newspapers and be encouraged to donate; government officials, who held the ability to give and withhold funds; and white settlers interested in the Other.[2]

Indigenous people read these newspapers, too, though other than alumni their readership was largely unexpected, to borrow the language of Philip J. Deloria (2004).[3] Schools mostly produced a newspaper as part of a larger industrial printing program. That students in the nineteenth century were the labour behind newspapers was important – often, newspapers announced directly under the newspaper's masthead that students had operated the school's press themselves. Why? Indian boarding schools and their newspapers trafficked in notions of assimilation, transformation, and the binary of savage/civilized. Schools that had printing programs, in contrast to other industries taught such as carpentry or farming, combined two elements of "civilization" that schools purported to offer: English literacy and technology, both of which Indigenous peoples were seen to lack. What is more, the fruit of a printing program – the newspaper – was meant to be disseminated, unlike industries used to sustain the school (e.g., a dairy). These publications featured mostly writing from principals, teachers, and reprinted articles from Christian, government, and proto-anthropological tracts of the day: a patchwork of often uncited white settler colonial echoes. School newspapers were legitimizing sources, which sought to influence settler opinions on Indian boarding schools and Indigenous peoples more generally.

School leaders knew the power a newspaper held for highlighting successes and couching failures. Richard Pratt, who in 1879 founded the flagship American Indian boarding school in Pennsylvania, ran an extensive printing program with a wide circulation of newspapers that unequivocally praised his efforts. He attempted to control outside media, too: when a reporter reviewed the school unfavourably, Pratt forced him off the premises (Eastman, 1935, p. 174). Pratt offered his US experiences to the principal of Shingwauk Home in Ontario: "Start the secular press at work in your favor" (*Our Forest Children* 1.4:19),[4] Pratt advised. School newspapers broadcasted political opinions of schools and showcased the labour and literacy of supposed assimilation.

Yet to dismiss school newspapers as only propaganda is too simplistic. Students contributed to these newspapers and while we cannot know whether students freely wrote every article attributed to them, these texts speak to either what students felt or what schools wished readers to believe students felt. These newspapers have the potential to contain institution-imposed narratives *as well as* the possibility of a veiled poetry of resistance. How can we read both? Robert Warrior (2005) argues for reading against the grain in his close readings of

Native non-fiction, invoking the theories of Edward Said (1994). The idea is that English literature has often been understood aesthetically rather than as propagating British imperialism and colonialism. Said's work claims that imperialism operated not just through legal, political, and economic realms but also through education, literature, and art. For this reason, Said reads texts contrapuntally – for surface-level narratives *and* those narratives that challenge the dominating discourse (p. 51). Warrior has applied these concepts to texts produced at Indian boarding schools in the US.

As an example of such contrapuntal reading from a Canadian context, here is an Indian Affairs Annual Report from 1889: "Many Indians cannot be induced to send their children, who are still wandering about on the reserves. Indian children like to enjoy their liberty, and their parents have not sufficient authority over them to make them attend school ... they object to the distance from the reserves, to their children, being obliged to work, and to not being allowed to use their own medicine on the children when sick ... They say they would rather have their children work at home than at the school (Department of Indian Affairs [DIA], p. 185). Reading against the grain here challenges the report's view of children merely "wandering about on the reserves," aimless and in need of rescuing. It also understands the parents not as lacking "sufficient authority" but rather provides a site for resisting the colonial attempts to remove their children, indoctrinate them in schools, and prohibit them from using their own health care. Other parts of these newspapers require what Ann Stoler (2009) describes as reading *along* the grain. Rather than searching for "hidden" meanings, she instead makes a case for studying what was known and assumed. Reading along the grain means studying carefully what these newspapers and their readers expected from schools and held as unquestioned assumptions – what *wasn't* hidden and was taken for granted.

Today, residential school history is commonly taught (when it is taught) in Canada as a timeline, exemplified in the book to study for the Canadian citizenship test. The timeline is as follows: Schools operated for over one hundred years across Canada. They were a partnership between government and various churches. Nearly 150,000 children were removed from their families and communities, sometimes for years. At school, children were forced to speak French and English and to practice Christianity. At many schools, children were physically, sexually, and emotionally abused and thousands died. In 2008, the prime minister apologized and former students received compensation. The

Truth and Reconciliation Commission of Canada (TRC), mandated to investigate the history of residential schools in Canada as part of the Indian Residential Schools Settlement Agreement, concluded in 2015. This timeline is tidy but avoids complicity and ends with resolution. Nearly twenty years before the TRC, Roland Chrisjohn and Sherri Young (1997) criticized such "standard accounts" of residential school history, stating that:

- residential schools were part of Canada's larger goals of genocide;[5]
- these attempts were and are hidden and rationalized as help, not genocide;
- many people knew the consequences of these attempts at the time;
- survivors' "symptoms" are natural responses to oppression; and
- pathologizing survivors avoids accountability (p. 3).

Today, scholars and former students continue to complicate the standard account, particularly after the conclusion of a state-sponsored commission of redress.[6] Glen Coulthard (2014) argues that in a settler colonial context, state-sanctioned forms of reconciliation typically situate abuse in the past instead of as structural and ongoing (p. 22). Jeff Corntassel, Chaw-win-is, and T'lakwadzi (2009) also make the case that reconciliation is neither an Indigenous concept nor one that is likely to disrupt the asymmetry of colonial relations (p. 145). And as Mario Di Paolantonio (2000) notes, TRCs may claim to master knowledge about genocide instead of rightly leaving it as imponderable (p. 163). It is significant that, when the commissioners of the TRC associated residential school history with the current reality of thousands of murdered and missing Indigenous women and girls upon the release of the final report, Bernard Valcourt, former minister of Aboriginal Affairs and Northern Development, remained seated while everyone else stood. The doors to boarding schools may have closed, but the legacies and ongoing violence against Indigenous peoples and their land is in the here and now.

Patrick Wolfe (1999) and others distinguish settler colonialism from colonialism. Examples of colonialism elsewhere required some colonizers on the ground but mostly depended on the labour of those indigenous to the land. The goal was rarely for vast numbers of colonizers to remain in the colony and consider it their own. Settler colonialism, in contrast, never completely depends on Indigenous labour, rather it requires land. The ultimate fantasy of the settler colonizer is that

Indigenous peoples disappear, permitting a narrative in which settler colonizers, not Indigenous peoples, are the original, rightful inhabitants. This is why Catherine Parr Traill's (1987) classic *Canadian Settlers' Guide*, originally published in 1855, only lists the word "Indian" in the table of contents in relation to rice and corn. Tied to such settler colonial erasures is a denial of violence, which promotes an image of national innocence. Yet at the same time, settlers simultaneously appropriate what they see as Indigenous to bolster these claims. The newspapers of Indian boarding schools both erased and appropriated what settlers saw as Indigenous, and this book traces these complicated and ostensibly incongruous rhetorical moves, always with an eye to how such practices continue today.

Scholarship is scant on Canadian examples of Indian boarding school newspapers, which are sometimes used as sources but rarely as objects of study in themselves.[7] Examples from the US on the other hand have been read in several ways. Some of this research reads newspapers for what they reveal about colonialism (Emery, 2012; Fear-Segal, 2007; Pfister, 2004) as well as literacy practices (Goodburn, 1999; Katanski, 2005; Spack, 2002). Some of these studies view school newspapers, particularly those from the late nineteenth and early twentieth centuries, as censored puff pieces selling the achievements of the school. Brenda Child (1999) rightly warns that school newspapers must be read with scepticism because they were published under the scrutiny of the larger school administration (p. xii). For this reason, some studies of Indian boarding schools in the US privilege interviews with former students (Ellis, 1996; Vučković, 2008) because, as K. Tsianina Lomawaima (1995) writes of Chilocco School in Oklahoma, student life "barely crept onto the margins of the printed pages of federal records and correspondence" (p. 159). Warrior (2005), in contrast, reads newspapers from Nebraska and Pennsylvania as indeed published under administrative eyes but also as examples of early Native non-fiction.

In Canada, some of the most urgent information school newspapers offer today is for former students and families. Attempts at archival access have been mired in controversy, from access limits to missing, redacted, forged, and destroyed documents (Ghaddar, 2016; Griffith, 2018). Survivor Bev Sellars (2013) describes in her memoir how she found fake documents attributed to her family members that were not written by them, including letters home, in the national archives (p. 68).[8] As of March 2013, over fifty thousand survivors received less than what they claimed in the Indian Residential Schools Settlement Agreement

(IRSSA) because of missing documents that could not verify attendance length (Barrera, 2013a, 2013b). The TRC itself faced barriers accessing archival documents from Library and Archives Canada as well as the Ontario Provincial Police, necessitating a court case to receive access (Canadian Press, 2013; Truth and Reconciliation Commission of Canada, 2012b, pp. 13, 16; Truth and Reconciliation of Canada, 2015, p. 27). School newspapers may be a place for survivors and families to find writing, art, and details that evaded archival destruction.

There could be many reasons why one document is archived, and another disappears. Verne Harris (2002) observes how archives are never a reflection of reality because when a document finally arrives in an archive, it has already passed through the hands that created it, the hands that managed it, the archivists who gathered it, and the researchers who read it (p. 65). In the case of Canada, another step would include at least three government-ordered culls of Indian Affairs archives, destroyed files that included attendance records, medical accounts, diaries, accident reports, and documents from inspectors and teachers (Sadowski, 2006). Archives are not neutral repositories – they are charged sites of power.[9]

These school newspapers were not easy to access, and my research included eleven archival sites across Canada and the US, each with different protocols (Griffith, 2018). Some archives were church run, while others were private or government based.[10] In the beautiful example of Haskell Indian Nations University in Kansas, formally a boarding school and now an Indigenous post-secondary institution, its community-controlled archive holds a complete collection of the country's oldest Native American student newspaper *Indian Leader*, which Indigenous journalists in the making still produce today.

Despite missing issues and publications spread across several different archives, many newspapers were archived. Why? Some (not all) archivists I encountered considered the newspapers as proof of the "lighter side" of boarding school, evidence of picnics, swimming, skating, football matches, and quilting sessions. For some, the newspapers and photographs may have confirmed a preferred reading (to use the language of Stuart Hall [2007]) of boarding schools. Sunny, beneficial, or banal experiences of boarding school existed and cannot be dismissed (Child, 2014b). Yet Andrew Woolford's (2014) framing is helpful here. He conceives of settler colonialism as mesh nets layered atop one another. Some are wider nets (e.g., the economy, education, and religion) and some are smaller (e.g., a specific principal or parent). For Woolford, even in places where a previously tight net loosens – a nice teacher, a kind Indian agent, a fun picnic – the nets still exist (pp. 31–2). Perhaps one reason these newspapers were, with some effort, available unlike many other files was that on their surface they represent no threat.

My reading of these newspapers engages with many of these seemingly contradictory perspectives: that the newspapers are examples of Indigenous media, that they are propaganda, that they are ideologically complicated, that they provide facts about the day-to-day, that they quash students' voices, and that they reveal resistance. In some places, I consider what newspapers offer in terms of new knowledge about boarding schools: newspapers as repositories. In other places, I seek to uncover what the newspapers reveal about student experiences: newspapers as resistance. And elsewhere, I read these newspapers for what they reveal about what Dwayne Donald calls "excavating the colonial terrain": newspapers as propaganda. Excavating the colonial terrain as I understand it means exposing the practices of settler colonialism. Reading the newspapers as repositories, as resistance, and as propaganda helps to consider a publication's different authors, audiences, receptions, and purposes. To ignore resistance is also to participate in what Eve Tuck (2009) calls "damage-centered research," which "looks to historical exploitation, domination, and colonization to explain contemporary brokenness" but in the process pathologizes (p. 413). Desire-based research, instead, accounts for despair but is also "concerned with understanding complexity, contradiction, and the self-determination of lived lives" (p. 416).

One archivist told me these newspapers had no access restrictions because they were originally published, unlike letters and medical records. These newspapers were certainly meant to be read from the perspective of *some* – teachers, school administrators, the government, church, and donors. Several articles attributed to students also mentioned excitement at writing for the newspaper, revealing a possible awareness on the part of students that their work would be published. But not all student writing was originally composed for the newspaper, and its original context is unknown. I have not casually concluded, as the archivist did, that this work was published in the same way as a daily newspaper and therefore free for academic consumption. I am informed by Laura L. Terrance (2011) and her concept of "Native feminist archival refusal." Although Terrance studied the unpublished, archived autograph journal of a boarding school student, Terrance ultimately writes only about the published memoir of Zitkala-Ša. Terrance does not tell her readers the name, community, or school of the autograph journal's author and never mentions the name of the archive (p. 621). Instead she discusses Zitkala-Ša because she (rather than the autograph journal's author) chose what to share (p. 624), which is similar to Linda Tuhiwai Smith's (2012) criticism of how who gets to study and gets studied has a long colonial history. For this and other reasons, I have largely not written about twentieth-century newspapers in this book. Newspapers from residential schools after the First World War, unlike nineteenth-century newspapers, often had more student writing and the writers are sometimes still alive. Where possible, I have tried to connect communities and families to the newspapers' whereabouts, inspired by the long-lost student artwork from Alberni School in British Columbia that was recently repatriated (Steel, 2012).

Some fellow settlers may claim they or their ancestors were not directly involved in residential schools, that their family was never even *in* what we call Canada at the time. But non-Indigenous people such as myself live here because of colonialism. As Roxanne Dunbar-Ortiz (2014) makes clear, "Whatever historical trauma was entailed in settling the land affects the assumptions and behavior of living generations at any given time, including immigrants and the children of recent immigrants" (p. 229). I grew up on W̱SÁNEĆ land on Vancouver Island, which had five residential schools. Five![11] I cannot claim non-complicity even though my parents moved there after the last one closed; my white settler family and I benefited from the schools being there earlier. We were able to call Vancouver Island home (and even call it "Vancouver Island") because of colonial tactics, including but not limited to residential schools, that eased the theft of land.

Unlike South Africa's Truth and Reconciliation Commission, which had subpoena power and could offer amnesty to perpetrators who provided testimony, there was no similar motivation for the people and representatives of the institutions directly responsible in residential schools to participate in Canada's commission.[12] And because Canada's commission investigated crimes over an extended period, unlike other truth and reconciliation commissions that focused on shorter and more recent periods, many of those directly responsible are now dead. The commission collected over 6,750 statements from survivors and families but only 96 from staff and their children (Truth and Reconciliation of Canada, 2015, pp. 25–6). As Martin Cannon (2012) writes: "It is routine to think about colonialism as having little, if anything, to do with non-Indigenous peoples. As such, it is typically Indigenous scholars, teachers, and populations who are left to explain the impact of colonization and residential schooling on our communities" (p. 21). Yet Sara Ahmed (2004) as well as Paulette Regan (2010) rightly question settlers who take up such a call, but in appropriative or voyeuristic ways merely to seek absolution (p. 47). I have attempted to avoid reading student writing in such ways or contributing to what Michalinos Zembylas (2008) calls "the violence of sentimentality" by instead exposing the actions of church and state, particularly the tactics of making colonialism appear natural, unmarked, and innocent. Reading these newspapers, in one small way, shines light on shadows left less exposed by the TRC: the voices of missionaries, inspectors, Indian agents, principals, teachers, and bureaucrats. Newspapers also feature the sentiments of a white settler public, another voice often unheard at the TRC.

Yet reading Indian boarding school newspapers only through a lens of settler colonial studies presents several limits. Corey Snelgrove, Rita Kaur Dhamoon, and Jeff Corntassel (2014) warn of how settler colonial studies as well as solidarity initiatives can recentre instead of expose settler colonialism (p. 4, 27). Settler colonial studies may also falsely paint such structures as totalizing, which ignores how former students were not, as Lomawaima (1995) states, "passive consumers of an ideology or lifestyle imparted from above by federal administrators. They actively created an ongoing educational and social process" (p. 167).

At most schools, students were the ones materially putting together the newspaper – laying type, rolling the press, inking the metal – even if they were not always allowed to write or edit it. As well, passages by students, or passages attributed to students, did appear in the newspaper. For this reason, I highlight the ways students may have used the newspapers in resistance. Throughout this book I turn to published accounts of life at school by former students even though they are from a period following the late nineteenth century.[13] While these sources cannot illuminate the specific conditions of a newspaper given differences in time and region, they offer perspectives unavailable within the censored space of the newspaper. I read these newspapers alongside the published accounts of former students – for instance, memoirs by Basil Johnston (1989), Isabelle Knockwood (1992), Theodore Fontaine (2010), and Bev Sellars (2013). Jo-Ann Episkenew (2009) writes that "Indigenous autobiography goes beyond catharsis. It is an act of imagination that inspires social regeneration by providing eyewitness testimony to historical injustices" (p. 75). I also read these newspapers alongside fiction and poetry, including work by Marilyn Dumont (1996,

2007a) and Richard Wagamese (2012). As Sam McKegney (2007) notes, literary boarding school texts "invigorate what survived, recreate what didn't, and re-imagine the place of the creative Indigenous individual in relation to her or his community" (p. 8). Some Indigenous literature that has greatly informed my understanding of these school newspapers has had direct connections to residential schools. Eden Robinson's novel *Monkey Beach* (2001) even names George Raley (p. 194), the principal of Kitamaat Home and editor of its newspaper, whom this book frequently discusses. Indigenous literature is helpful in reading these newspapers for what they confirm as well as what they counteract. And as Joanne DiNova examines (2012), Indigenous literature also contextualizes the nations and communities that school newspapers actively attempted to erase.

My reading of school newspapers is particularly informed by the poetry of Rita Joe, who attended Shubenacadie School in Nova Scotia. In her poem "I lost my talk" (1989), Joe writes that the addressee of the poem "snatched" her language from her at school, resulting in a "scrambled ballad, about my world." I interpret the concept of a scrambled ballad to mean holding those who snatched and scrambled responsible while also highlighting the existence of a ballad. As Susan Dion (2009) argues, "It was – and is – the violence of colonization that created conditions wherein Aboriginal people were deprived of the power to control the ways in which dominant society constructed and interpreted their images" (p. 20). Despite these conditions, Kathleen Buddle (2002) highlights how in the nineteenth century, Indigenous people still worked to control their own images at agricultural fairs, in the mainstream press, in museums, and by authoring their own books (p. 103). Indigenous parents also used newspapers and journalists to alert the public to treatment of their children in schools (Fournier and Crey, 2006, p. 42). Reading memoir and fiction provides counternarratives to these newspapers and "thirds" various binaries, including truth/fiction, now/then, and powerful/powerless. Not many other surviving texts from the nineteenth century offer how schools wished to be perceived *and* how students pushed back in the same source. Nineteenth-century Indian boarding school newspapers offer many opportunities for what Roger Simon (2005) views as learning from the past to unsettle the present (p. 106).

Read in this light, school newspapers reinforce how the horrors of a particular school were not the result of a bad teacher or bad apple. Boarding schools – across denominational lines, regions, time periods, and the colonial border between the US and Canada – were structural. As Eva Mackey (2013) observes, the apology of former prime minister Stephen Harper continues with the myth of residential schools as an anomalous, dark chapter (p. 54). School newspapers were an avenue for reinforcing colonial systems among Canadian schools; bolstering also happened through churches, the public, and governments in the US, Canada, and England. The communication by way of school newspapers between Indian boarding schools in the US and Canada is particularly striking and urges us to think of the two settler colonial systems as connected. School newspapers also speak directly to the white settler myth of non-complicity because they were written to be read by a public. For Benedict Anderson (1991), newspapers create an "extraordinary mass ceremony" because although we read newspapers privately, we are aware everyone performs the same ceremony (p. 35). Moreover, printing settler ideas in a newspaper in ink meant a permanence of ideas, or "typographical fixity" (Eisenstein, 2005), and also made dissemination possible. These newspapers, then, both constituted and reflected a settler colonial community.

School newspapers further help to expose the myth that the English language in North America is natural and neutral, taking cues from scholars such as Lorena Sekwan Fontaine (2017) and Andrea Bear Nicholas (2011) who work with the concept of linguicide – killing the language, not (necessarily) the speaker. While terms such as loss and disappearance vacate the doer, terms such as linguicide shine an accusatory light on the processes, policies, and people responsible. Rather than language loss or spread, the chapters of this book turn to the newspapers and ask *how, why,* and *by whom.* School newspapers help to expose the tactics and techniques Indian boarding schools used to teach English and to denigrate Indigenous languages. It may appear that a focus in this book on theft of language serves as a screen allegory for land restitution. As Eve Haque importantly asks in regard to the Royal Commission on Bilingualism and Biculturalism (1963–9), which led to Canada's Official Languages Act: "How, in Canada, did language come to be the site for articulating exclusion which can no longer be stated in terms of race and ethnicity?" (p. 4). But many insist language *is* land. They are not separate. As Jeanette Armstrong powerfully remarks: "The land constantly speaks. It is constantly communicating. Not to learn its language is to die" (p. 176). Such understandings both include and expand beyond understandings of restoring place names.

In the nineteenth century, newspapers were generally coded as a civilizing tool. Indian agents would sometimes use newspaper subscriptions as a barometer of Indigenous "progress." For instance, in 1904 the Indian agent for the Sioux of Birtle in Manitoba wrote: "To give an idea of the advanced condition of some of these Indians, I have only to state that I found in several houses copies of weekly newspapers, subscribed for by the occupants. This is surely keeping abreast of the times" (Department of Indian Affairs Annual Report [DIA], p. 108). The Indian Affairs report for Manitowaning in Ontario of 1886 listed newspaper subscriptions as an avenue for expanding readers' worlds, because "hitherto the world outside their own reserve has been a sealed book to them. By the agency of a newspaper they will acquire broader views of life" (DIA, p. 78). An Indian agent in 1896 at Fort Alexander in Manitoba observed that "the Indians of my agency are a law-abiding people. No strangers from a foreign land need be afraid to come among them. Many of them subscribe to newspapers, and are sure to read all matters pertaining to their race" (DIA, p. 112). The only way offered in these reports to understand Indigenous reading practices was as evidence of assimilation. In similar ways, school newspapers reframed and even forcibly excluded threats or challenges to such settler colonial narratives.

Major Canadian and US newspapers from the nineteenth century (and still today) both created and reflected stereotypes about Indigenous peoples and "progress" (Anderson and Robertson, 2011; Coward, 1999; Weston, 1996).[14] Buddle's (2002) research uncovers that the real barrier to Indigenous participation in nineteenth-century media was not incompetence but colonial blockades. Legislation such as the Act to Encourage Gradual Civilization of the Indians (1857) declared that any Indigenous man who was "able to speak, read and write either the english or the french language readily and well" and who had a basic education, good character, and no debt would "no longer be deemed an Indian" (p. 2), indicating death by language. Demonstrating English literacy at this time could have attracted added surveillance and meant the possibility of losing Indian status in the eyes of the state (p. 109).[15]

Newspapers have an additional colonial context considering that some of the white settler men responsible for the most devastating colonial policies of the nineteenth century cut their teeth in media. Egerton Ryerson, whose guidance helped direct the future of boarding schools in Canada, was editor of the country's first religious newspaper, the *Christian Guardian,* and later the *Journal of Education for Upper Canada*

(Gidney, 2003). Nicholas Flood Davin, though from a different political background than Ryerson, also helped shape the Indian school system in 1879 when he was commissioned by John A. Macdonald to travel to the US and report on boarding schools. He, too, was a journalist with the *Toronto Globe* and the *Toronto Mail* and also founded the conservative publication the *Regina Leader* (Thompson, 1994). Davin's newspapers attempted to quash instances of Indigenous resistance; he was therefore the only writer permitted at Riel's execution (Buddle, 2001, p. 150). Clifford Sifton, the minister of the interior and superintendent general of Indian Affairs from 1896 to 1905, owned the *Manitoba Free Press*, the *Morning Leader* in Regina, and the *Star Phoenix* in Saskatoon. Sifton's successor Frank Oliver, who served from 1905 to 1911, originally worked for the *Winnipeg Free Press* (Donald, 2004, p. 36). He started the first newspaper in what is currently known as Alberta, the *Edmonton Bulletin*, and used it to successfully advocate for the removal of the Papaschase people from their territory despite their resistance (Donald, 2004). Oliver also established the first formalized Canadian Jim Crow law, which attempted to dictate the movement of Black people (Mathieu, 2010, p. 57).[16] David Laird, Indian commissioner (1876–9 and 1898–1909), oversaw the creation of the Indian Act as well as many treaties (Titley, 2009); he was also a newspaper editor in Prince Edward Island. J.A.N. Provenchar, as Indian commissioner from 1873 to 1878, was also involved with several numbered treaties after a career in French language newspapers. Richard Pratt, founder of the Carlisle Indian School, grew up working on newspapers (Pratt, 2003, p. 19). These links are unsurprising given that in nineteenth-century Canada, "behind every successful politician was a newspaper doing his dirty work; behind every proprietor or editor, a politician, or a group of politicians, offering support" (Fetherling, 1990, p. 79). Journalists were often rewarded for their support with political posts (p. 93), and Ottawa awarded printing contracts to presses that favoured the party in power (p. 217).

The late nineteenth century – the focus of this book – was a period of great change in Canada. There was mass immigration, due in part to new governmental policies, the Yukon gold rush, and railroad completion. The year 1885 in the Northwest saw major acts of resistance by Cree, Métis, and Assiniboine peoples. The year also saw the largest mass hanging in Canada's history, which included the killing of politician and Métis leader, Louis Riel.[17] From 1881 to 1905, various amendments to the already devastating Indian Act included bans on ceremonies, laws restricting on-reserve trade, and increased powers to Indian agents. James Daschuk's (2013) work shows how government policies resulted in death, suffering, and tuberculosis epidemics triggered by immune suppression from famine among Plains peoples (p. 124). The late nineteenth century also comprised a shift in white perceptions of Indigenous peoples after a century of other shifts. The years following the War of 1812 revealed white settler understandings of Indigenous peoples less as sovereign allies and more as wards. The 1850s saw European artists such as Paul Kane catalogue Indigenous ways of life because they were thought to be vanishing, while at the end of the nineteenth century the narrative began to change with increased colonial expansion. As the nineteenth century closed in on itself, the view of Indigenous peoples as a threat to white claims to land intensified. School newspapers reflect this, finding new attempts to contain Indigenous resistance.

The nineteenth century also saw the cementing of Indian boarding schools as a *system*. The Bagot Commission of 1842 concluded that no progress had been made in civilizing Indigenous peoples since 1830 (Milloy, 1999, p. 13), and in 1846 the superintendent of Indian Affairs met with chiefs and missionaries at a conference in Orillia to pitch manual labour schools as the answer (J.R. Miller, 1996, p. 83). In 1847, the Chief Superintendent of Education for Upper Canada Egerton Ryerson proposed what these schools might look like. Despite advocating for secular education in the Common School Act the year before for non-Indigenous children, Ryerson (1847) believed Indigenous children could not be assimilated without Christianity (p. 73). The Common School Act also did little to ensure Black children could freely learn, despite the myths of educational egalitarianism in Canada West (McLaren, 2008). Though church-led instruction for Indigenous children has existed in what is currently known as Canada since 1620 (J.R. Miller, 1996b, pp. 39–60), the nineteenth century was a time of further entrenchment. By 1884, the federal government had funded the first three industrial schools (previously, the government had only provided limited funds to largely church-driven and less ambitious boarding schools) (TRC of Canada, 2015b, p. 197). Another change was the introduction of the disastrous per capita funding system in 1892, which resulted in schools recruiting and retaining unhealthy children, serving even unhealthier food, and requiring more student labour (J.R. Miller, 1996, pp. 128–33; Milloy, 1999, pp. 61–7). Another change to the Indian Act in 1894 included regulations with regards to attendance (and therefore parent-child separation). A new statute in 1894 permitted that "the

Governor in Council may make regulations ... to secure the compulsory attendance of children at school" (Venne, 1981).[18] Though such legislation was passed, it was not administered uniformly by all Indian agents or commissioners, and it was only in 1920 that the language changed to state that attendance was mandatory across the board. Still, the end of the nineteenth century saw increasing powers extended to the government with regards to schooling.

A different trajectory was taking place in the US. By 1890, the US had a standardized program of study for American Indian boarding schools (Adams, 1995, p. 62). Although attendance at US schools became compulsory around the same time, by 1893 superintendents in the US required consent from parents to send children to off-reservation schools (pp. 63–5). This law was often disregarded, but it would be decades before Canada adopted similar legislation. The US also phased out religious partnerships by 1900, which only happened in Canada in 1969. As well, an annual report in the US came out in 1901 deeming American schools a failure (p. 307), with a sweeping overhaul recommended by the Meriam Report in 1928.

Settler newspapers were also changing in the late nineteenth century. The 1880s and 1890s saw the first Linotype machine, which enabled quickly set type (Fetherling, 1990, p. 64). Photographs in newspapers were also introduced at this time (p. 66). As well, in 1893 the Associated Press signed a deal with Reuters to sell news exclusively to the Canadian Pacific Railway's telegraph department (Allen, 2014, p. 18). This recognition was significant because the Associated Press treated Canada as sovereign, unlike Cuba and Mexico (p. 19). A newspaper's purpose was also changing with the rise of "independent journalism," a misleading term that meant editors grew increasingly more powerful in dictating political outcomes instead of being mere pawns of politicians (p. 96). Paul Rutherford (1982) describes how in the 1890s newspapers existed "almost everywhere Canadians gathered – in taverns and stores, in mechanics' institutes and public libraries, in clubs and associations, on street corners and in railway stations" (p. 3). Rutherford attributes this explosion to three factors: the growth of big cities, changes in class and community, and increased literacy rates (p. 9). This frenzy meant changes within the church, where the clergy found their power newly threatened by journalism (p. 197). Newspapers also became increasingly commercialized at the end of the nineteenth century with the rise of press barons and the opening of new markets (Sotiron, 2005).[19]

Indian boarding school newspapers differed from commercial media at this time. Their circulation was nowhere near the major dailies of the late nineteenth century, and they were normally issued only once a month. In 1892, for instance, the *Globe* had a circulation of almost twenty-seven thousand (*McKim's Directory*), whereas most Canadian boarding school newspapers had only a few thousand subscribers. Advertising funded two-thirds of dailies (Rutherford, 1982, p. 7), but school newspapers were funded by the school (and therefore government) as well as donations and subscriptions (not to mention that the labour was almost entirely underwritten by Indigenous children). Dailies also operated under the threat of work stoppages (p. 95), which did not affect a boarding school's indentured student workforce. Despite these differences, the context of nineteenth-century media helps to frame the publications of Indian boarding schools specifically because schools with newspapers conceived of their printing programs as workplace preparation.

This book focuses on six newspapers written in English[20] and published at five boarding schools: Shingwauk Industrial Home in Ontario (*Our Forest Children*, 1887–90 and the *Canadian Indian*, 1890–1); Battleford Industrial School in what would later be called Saskatchewan (*Guide*, 1891–9); Rupert's Land Industrial School in Manitoba (*Aurora*, 1893–5); Regina Industrial School in what would later be called Saskatchewan (*Progress*, 1894–1910?); and Kitamaat Home in British Columbia (*Na-Na-Kwa*, 1898–1907).[21] More schools had printing programs and newspapers, but I focus on these six publications because they featured news on their schools as opposed to just the neighbouring settler town.[22]

Four of these five schools were industrial, meaning in theory they accepted older students and taught a trade.[23] I include Kitamaat Home's newspaper even though its school was neither industrial nor government funded because my scope includes any late nineteenth-century Canadian school for Indigenous children. Kitamaat Home was starkly different from other schools with newspapers because it boarded girls but not boys, who returned to their homes after each school day and could travel with their families depending on the season. The school was much smaller, and through the lens of the paper those operating it can be viewed as more personally involved with students compared to the larger industrial schools on the prairies and in Ontario. The newspaper depicted the school's principal George Raley welcoming donations of Indigenous food dropped off by parents (*Na-Na-Kwa* 20.9), decrying new government regulations against Indigenous fishing rights (5.7), and hiring a Tsimshian language instructor whom he acknowledged in the newspaper (31.9), examples with no equivalent in newspapers from industrial schools. Kitamaat Home was also located in British Columbia, which has a colonial history in many ways different from the prairies and Ontario. And as Paige Raibmon (1996) notes, when the principal of Kitamaat Home later taught at Coqualeetza School in British Columbia he was able to use his power to ease some of the worst aspects of residential schooling (though these attempts often reinforced the system, and other elements went unchallenged) (p. 70). Kitamaat Home and Shingwauk Home are also unique in that the same principal oversaw the entire run of the newspaper, unlike other schools with more frequent turnover. I was also able to access all issues of both schools' newspapers. For these reasons, I write of Kitamaat Home's and Shingwauk Home's principals, George Raley and Edward Wilson respectively, more frequently than other schools. This book is also about more than just these five schools as it touches on other institutions and readers producing newspapers throughout North America. The settler echoes continue further in considering how much newspaper content was reprinted from around the world.[24]

The six nineteenth-century newspapers from Indian boarding schools in Canada that this book primarily focuses on were from Protestant schools. To my knowledge, no Catholic-run Indian boarding school in late nineteenth-century Canada *had* a newspaper. This absence could be for several reasons. For one, Protestantism and Catholicism emerge from different histories of literacy. In the sixteenth and seventeenth centuries, Protestant communities in Europe often had higher rates of literacy and promoted reading as sacred and a method for direct access to the Bible (Houston, 2014, p. 158). Though class and location influenced such generalizations, some argue that in early modern Europe Catholics remained at best ambivalent and at worst resistant to reading, accessing faith through more visual and oral methods (pp. 160–1). As Harvey Graff (1987) notes, such differences of course can be overstated. But the Reformation did promote individual Bible reading (Mosher, 2016). As well, Protestant missionaries in the nineteenth century sometimes had more exposure to the secular world than Catholic missionaries (Higham, 2000, p. 217). Given that school newspapers had wide audiences, this difference could explain less impetus or opportunity for Catholic-run schools to disseminate ideas outside of their church via a newspaper. The annual report for 1896 noted that Fort Alexander reserve in Manitoba had two day schools: one Roman Catholic and the other Protestant. The inspector noted that "there is a marked difference in the two schools in regard to speaking English" because at the Roman Catholic school, students were picking up French and using inferior textbooks (DIA, 1896, p. 153). While this comparison is from a day school, it could suggest that at Catholic-run institutions there was less desire or ability on the part of French-speaking teachers and staff to produce newspapers in English.

More than these contexts, though, whether a school had a newspaper in the late nineteenth century likely had more to do with if it had access to a knowledgable printing instructor, an enthusiastic principal, hand-me-down equipment, and some financial support for an expensive trade that the Department of Indian Affairs did not in principle support. The denomination of an industrial school was frequently determined by the churches that petitioned the government and the whim of the government, motivated by political gains (Milloy, 1999, pp. 54–61). When newspapers at schools for Indigenous children became more widespread in the twentieth century, many Catholic and Protestant institutions alike produced them, as they were cheaper to run and less dependent on the know-how of staff. Unlike the nineteenth century (the focus of this book), twentieth century newspapers were not the result of an industrial training program and were viewed more as an avenue for creative expression and communication with parents.

I discuss all six newspapers thematically rather than individually. The risk in doing so is that major distinctions among each school are flattened. Many studies of Indian boarding schools focus on an individual school and even a time period, such as Amanda J. Cobb's (2000) study of the Bloomfield Academy for Chickasaw Females in Oklahoma, K. Tsianina Lomawaima's (1995) work on the Chilocco School also in Oklahoma, or Celia Haig-Brown's (1988) focus on the Kamloops School in British Columbia. I instead pull from regionally and denominationally diverse contexts – a Methodist mission school in British Columbia; a Presbyterian industrial school on the prairies; and Church of England industrial schools in Saskatchewan, Manitoba, and Ontario. Each school had staff, principals, Indian agents, and government inspectors with varying attitudes towards policy enforcement and assimilation. These schools taught diverse groups of students as well, people with different languages, nations, cultures, spiritualities, polities, and economies. Kitamaat Home for instance taught students who were Haisla, Nuxalk, Heiltsuk, and Tsimshian. These nations are distinct from one another and from those in eastern schools. Sampling school newspapers thematically in some ways homogenizes these major distinctions and takes each newspaper out of its own specific setting. While I provide context where possible, this book is a reflection of the newspapers, which *did* homogenize students and actively worked to erase fundamental distinctions. What is more, because much of a newspaper's content was clipped or liberally inspired by other reading material circulating at the time, these newspapers are in many ways assemblages of settler colonialism and reading them thematically keeps this original flattening intact.

Reading thematically may also obscure change over time within specific newspapers. Because I am only reading newspapers from a short time period (1887–1910) the newspapers I had access to reveal only minor changes. Yet newspapers over a longer time span were not so predetermined by relations of settler colonialism. School newspapers after the First World War have far more student content and far less visible intrusion from principals. Many of these newspapers (more properly labelled newsletters given their limited circulation) were addressed to parents, created to provide updates on the goings-on of the school to a limited and mostly Indigenous readership. These documents mostly do not contain clippings from Christian, anthropological, or daily newspapers the way nineteenth-century newspapers did. As well, the denigration of Indigenous languages and parents is far subtler in twentieth-century papers produced at Indian residential schools. Some of these shifts can be attributed to changes in technology considering school papers produced in the twentieth century used mimeographs and other small-scale duplicating machines rather than the industrial trade of printing taught at nineteenth-century schools. But addressing parents rather than white settler "stakeholders" through twentieth-century newspapers was also in no small part due to the persistence and resistance of Indigenous parents and communities enforcing greater control over their children's education.

I have broken this research into six chapters aside from the introduction and conclusion. After this introduction, chapter 2 provides material contexts for printing programs in late nineteenth-century boarding schools in Canada. Chapters 3 though 7 are organized around three broad concepts: language (chapters 3 and 4), time (chapters 5 and 6), and place (chapter 7). Language, time, and place may seem to reify particularly entrenched colonial categories. Vine Deloria Jr (2003) famously notes the concern of time versus space as the key difference between Western Europeans and Indigenous peoples, respectively (p. 63). This book also separates, by chapters, English from Indigenous languages. This is a particularly fraught binary as some boarding school teachers spoke Indigenous languages and advocated for bilingual education, many parents wished and fought for their children to learn English and had their own purposes for doing so, and schools were not entirely devoid of Indigenous languages. Furthermore, Indigenous literary scholars offer far more nuanced understandings of English as both a language of dominance *and* of liberation (Harjo and Bird, 1997; Vizenor, 1999; Womack, 2008).

Jeannette Armstrong (1998) combines all three concepts – language, time, place – in one sentence: "I have heard elders explain that the language changed as we [Okanagan] moved and spread over the land through time" (p. 175). As we shall see, boarding schools created their own worlds of time and place, demarcating and patrolling the lines between what colonial institutions saw as oral and written, language and gibberish, progress and stagnancy, vanishing and futurity, and colonial place and Indigenous land. My divisions maintain these categories, while my analysis seeks to destabilize them.

These distinctions may appear as mild within schools infamous for violence. Recently, seventy unmarked graves were uncovered at the former site of Brandon School in Manitoba (Quan, 2015). Boarding schools could be violent and even deadly places, where students contracted preventable illnesses and starved. Survivors recount how they were beaten, sexually assaulted, electrocuted, disabled by machinery, and forced to eat vomit. Language, time, and place could seem like, as Michel-Rolph Trouillot (2012) calls it, attempts to "sweeten the horror or banalize the uniqueness of a situation by focusing on details" (p. 97).

But these categories reflect the *newspapers'* seeming non-violence. At the five schools on which I focus, all was not what was projected. During the same time period I investigate, Regina School's death rate prompted parents to withhold their children and demand a meeting, following Elders who believed that "the worst element on the reserve is to be found among returned graduates who in a year or two, drift down sadly" (J.R. Miller, 1996, p. 349, 350, 353). One incident explicitly contrasts the picnics and spelling bees of the newspaper: after a student in 1903 disclosed suicidal ideations, her teacher produced a gun. Though it was unloaded, she was not prevented from pulling the trigger (Milloy, 1999, p. 155). At Battleford School in Saskatchewan, which also had a newspaper, a government inspector described the institution as having "quite a heavy death rate" (p. 85) and recorded cases of sexual abuse the principal did not stop as well as years of general concerns by the department about the principal's ability to effectively run the school, leaving the school with a bad name among Indigenous families (J.R. Miller, 1996, pp. 106–12, 337). And Rupert's Land School in Manitoba, also a school with a newspaper that I discuss, had confirmed cases of "thrashings" (p. 155) that alarmed parents and authorities. Even Deputy Superintendent General of Indian Affairs Hayter Reed observed "the depressed bearing of the pupils" (p. 68) at this school. Parents demanded an investigation after finding bruises on their children. The principal finally admitted in 1889 that "he fed the children rancid butter and crept into the dormitories at night to kiss little girls" (p. 57). Unsurprisingly, none of these incidents receive mention in the school newspaper, nor does the ongoing resistance of parents.

Clearly, horrific scenes occurred at schools publishing a shiny newspaper each month. What newspapers leave out – negative evidence – is not what my research seeks to uncover. Schools appear to have known that sickness, death, parental resistance, and abuse were unacceptable to report. What this research instead reveals is what newspapers saw as reality. Rather than seeking the "hidden meaning" behind newspapers, I seek to understand what newspapers, *on their surface*, tell us. What was in the open, even celebrated? What did schools hope a wider audience might see, whether or not it was true? How did students resist or complicate the school's public face? And how does the writing of former students from today unsettle what otherwise seemed so assured?

While newspapers sought to theorize and metaphorize language, time, and place, survivor testimony reveals that attacks on Indigenous languages were and are purposefully planned, violently enacted, painfully endured, and forcefully resisted. Time may seem airy-fairy, but when newspapers depicted an Indigenous past and settler colonial future, the connections to violence are clearer. And though newspapers present settler acquisition of land as inevitable, newspapers demonstrate how theft began with theory. Considering the violence of language, time, and place asks non-Indigenous Canadians to be disturbed by this, too. Reading nineteenth-century Indian boarding school newspapers contributes to broader historical understandings of settler colonialism through their testaments to resistance of linguicidal attempts. School newspapers reveal settler colonial narratives of language, past, future, and land that we have inherited and presently have to grapple with.

Words Have a Past refers to the history of the English language on this continent. It is far too frequent, in the nineteenth century and today, for Indigenous languages to be thought of as dying, dead, and in the past. English, in contrast, is – then and now – portrayed as vibrant and the ticket to a bright future. The past of English is, like whiteness, viewed as apolitical and ahistorical; it is seen as natural and blank. This book seeks to challenge these problematic renderings by historicizing the violence of the English language in North America and by invigorating a responsibility on the part of settlers that translates to a tangible restitution of, at the very least, languages and lands.

2 Printer's Devil: The Trade of Newspapers

An 1898 issue of a newspaper produced at Battleford School in Saskatchewan recorded the delight of a student and printer named Louis on a visit to Winnipeg. The newspaper depicts a city that amazed Louis, with "cars running without horses on steam, men and women flying around on bicycles, [and] news boys" (*Guide* 7.1:1). His trip away from school, necessitated by an eye condition, included a tour of the *Winnipeg Free Press*. Until this visit, Louis was quoted as saying he had "never believed that presses like that could print every page and make it ready for mailing" or "how they can set the type with the machines." According to the newspaper, Louis concluded nothing was "more interesting than the Free Press Office" (7.4:1). Like all Indian boarding school newspapers, certain narratives are favoured. Here, Louis fits into a larger arc of students in awe – by the city, by machinery, and by medical treatment. Readers might even have imagined a continuum between Louis-the-student and a future Louis-the-employee.

Less favoured narratives exist in this scene, too. Louis must visit Winnipeg for an unnamed problem with his eye. While it is unclear whether his long hours on the school's printing press caused the problem, eye conditions such as trachoma and other illnesses were rampant. In invoking a connection between Louis's trade at school and his future in the workforce, the scene also silences the reality that systemic barriers usually prevented students, no matter how talented, from seeking employment that competed with white workers. We also hear little here from Louis. What is more, despite the perhaps surprise non-Indigenous readers may have felt at Louis in a city, Lisa Brooks (2008) notes how Indigenous peoples have always incorporated into their lives – on their own terms – media, English, and technology (p. xxxi).[1] Coll Thrush

(2016), too, notes how despite such colonial narratives, urban space is also Indigenous space (p. 14).

Students were almost always the labour behind nineteenth-century boarding school newspapers. For this reason, the material conditions under which these newspapers were produced matter just as much as what the text says – the labour, expenses, circulation, stated purposes, intended audiences, and machinery of the schools' printing programs. Material conditions further include people – the leaders, readers, students, and personae of the newspapers. As well, material conditions extended beyond a student's time in the printing program to their attempts at later employment in the printing trade. The conditions and people who actively shaped (and were shaped by) the newspaper help to contextualize later discussions on language, time, and place.

The Trade of Printing

Nineteenth-century Indian boarding schools offered many trades: sewing, cooking, baking, and laundry for girls; blacksmithing, carpentry, farming, and many other options for boys. Though far less common, schools also offered printing. At Rupert's Land School in Manitoba, printing students began on "plain newspaper composition from printed copy" and quickly moved on to manuscript (DIA, 1891, p. 114). From there, students advanced to printing circulars and notices. Junior boys, physically unable to do press work, learned to wash type and rollers. Printing programs were small. In 1897, for instance, Wikwemikong School in Ontario trained only two boys as printers compared to seventeen as farmers (DIA, p. 269); in 1892 Battleford School trained only three printers compared to fourteen carpenters, fourteen blacksmiths, and seventeen farmers (p. 246). Print shops often existed in shared space. At Wikwemikong School, the printing office and bakery existed together (DIA, 1897, p. 268). Rupert's Land School printed off-campus at a nearby rectory, and Washakada Home in Manitoba printed in town sharing space with a butcher, hardware store, and an assembly hall (Elkhorn and District Historical Society, 1982, p. 7).[2]

Printing programs at Canadian schools were modest in comparison to those in the US, which often had a purpose-built edifice and better equipment. Carlisle School in Pennsylvania had eight distinct newspapers, with circulation numbers far greater than Canadian schools. And US schools celebrated their printers elaborately. Haskell Institute in Kansas held an annual reception for its printers. At the party in 1911, the school feted printers with oyster soup and quince jelly while a teacher read aloud the first issue of the school's newspaper and passed out a poem called "the Haskell Printers" (*Indian Leader* 14.47:2). The superintendent read a speech about famous people who began as print-ers,[3] and students raced each other as they set up type as part of a cel-ebratory game.

Though humbler, Canadian printing programs were also charged sites of surveillance and labour. As an article from Battleford School's newspaper stated, "go into the printing office and look at the proofs; and the one who has the most mistakes in his type, is as a rule, the boy who is the fullest of mistakes, and must be watched" (*Guide* 5.8:2). The goals of teaching any boarding school trade were threefold: (1) to dem-onstrate boarding school success to outsiders; (2) to offset costs; and (3) to teach employable skills, a goal loaded with rhetoric about self-sufficiency and assimilation. Bounty from trades helped the bottom line: eggs, milk, and ham from student farmers supplemented an under-funded kitchen and student-created wares such as horse harnesses or broom handles could be sold in town.[4] The same went for printed goods. Boarding school print shops produced documents necessary for the bureaucratic functioning of the school. Alicia Fahey and Chelsea Horton (2012) ponder whether student printers in British Columbia could have even printed the written materials that sanctioned their own removal from family (p. 23). Schools also printed for profit. The Washakada Home in Manitoba advertised print items for farmers and merchants such as cards (for business, funerals, and weddings), voter lists, lien notes, and Sunday school materials – "promptly executed" for "fair prices" (DIA, 1895, p. 166). The following is the output of Rupert's Land School in just nine months:

- magazines (124-paged quarto): 4,525 copies
- magazines (12-paged octavo): 300 copies
- pamphlets and circulars: 900 copies
- envelopes: 35,000
- receipt books: 17
- prescriptions: 12,000
- letter, bill, note, and memo heads: 71,000
- subscription slips: 2000
- religious book (4000-paged octavo): 1000 copies
- program and wedding cards: 225
- tabular returns: 600

- vouchers: 500
- school rules: 175
- writing pads: 400 (DIA, 1895, p. 176)

In addition to printing the school newspaper, students at Rupert's Land School also printed the cover of the *Christ Church Parish Magazine* each month (the rest of the magazine was printed in Toronto [*Aurora* 2.16:3]). As this list suggests, much of what students printed – without yet considering school newspapers – helped to establish the settler town and propel its growth through religious, cultural, legal, economic, and political channels.

Students used hand-me-down equipment, typically a variety of foot-pedal letterpresses. Regina School had an Edison mimeograph, though in 1893 desired a "regular printing press" (DIA, 1893, p. 119) and later received a donation (*Progress* 3.81:5). It appears Regina School also purchased used equipment from the *Qu'Appelle Echo* (*Aurora* 2.17:2). Rupert's Land School used a challenge foot press (DIA, 1891, p. 156), while the Washakada Home used a small army newspaper press as well as a Gordon job press. The Kitamaat Home relied on a Golding and Company press (Fahey and Horton, 2012, p. 49) but received a Gordon press in 1900 by donation (*Na-Na-Kwa* 10.7).[5] Schools could also pass their donated presses onto other schools: when Battleford School closed in 1914, it bequeathed its press to a school in the Pas (Wasylow, 1972, p. 484). Other newspapers thanked readers for their generous donations of presses, paper, and type.

That schools relied on second-hand printing equipment may at first sound similar to Canada's agricultural policies of the time. Sarah Carter (1990) has debunked the myth that Plains people had difficulty farming in the late nineteenth century because of an inherent inability. Government would instruct Indigenous peoples about farming using purposefully outmoded methods and technology to ensure they only farmed by hand for subsistence rather than with the machinery of the day. This policy saved the government money, mitigated competition with white economies, and purported to promote self-sufficiency in a population the government considered lazy. But insisting that Indigenous peoples farm using rudimentary principles also accorded with the belief they should not skip over evolutionary stages – from savagery to barbarism to civilization (pp. 209–13; DIA, 1891, p. 193). Indigenous peoples should become like white people, but not too fast. Boarding school printing programs did not keep up with advances in newspaper production and taught skills fast becoming obsolete. But printing technology was rapidly advancing in the late nineteenth century, and cash-strapped schools could not be expected to have equipment that even cities could not always access. Though the old equipment may not have been a direct way of barring Indigenous peoples from the media, the state had other methods. As Kathleen Buddle's (2002; 2001) research reveals, actively quashing Indigenous participation in media more often came in the form of legislation.

School Newspapers: Purposes and Formatting

Most schools with a printing program produced a newspaper, but not all of these were *school* newspapers.[6] The newspaper of Washakada Home, the *Elkhorn Advocate*, as well as the first newspaper of Rupert's Land School, the *Rupert's Land Gleaner*, were settler community newspapers and rarely mentioned boarding schools. The *Elkhorn Advocate* was more likely to comment on whether the government should fund denominational schools (the Manitoba Schools Question) than the school printing its pages. Instead, these two newspapers discussed the growth of their towns, unlike newspapers consumed by educational matters – teachers, students, and activities. Such newspapers helped schools keep in touch with former students who had returned home, a source of great anxiety. An 1898 issue of Battleford School's newspaper pleaded with the government to (ironically) establish a colony for graduates so they could avoid being "contaminated by the evil influence of the reserve" (7.6:1).[7] School newspapers often updated readers on the narrowly defined successes of former students: marriage, employment, and home ownership. Alumni updates provided non-Indigenous readers with examples of supposed assimilation, as well as the promise that both the students and the newspaper itself were spreading their assimilative power back to the reserve. Updates also demonstrated how former students, now adults, were applying the skills, morals, and English language they learned at school.

In a time when reading materials were scarce and expensive, a pragmatic reason for a school newspaper was the "exchange" – a swap with the newspaper of a church, community, or other school. Some schools had as many as seventy exchanges (DIA, 1897 p. 309). They were built on reciprocated praise, which sometimes came in the form of a humble brag. When the Crowstand School in Saskatchewan launched its newspaper, Regina School ran an article in its own publication wishing it a "safe voyage on the sea of journalism" (*Progress* 18.4:4). The praise, though, included the fact that Regina School's had been "for some time the only paper in Canada edited and published in a Protestant Indian school [and] has been extremely lonesome." Such praise also fell upon denominational affinities – Crowstand and Regina Schools, for example, were both Presbyterian. Praise was usually returned in a hallway of mirrors. Both Battleford and Kitamaat Schools subscribed to *The Indian Advocate* from White Fish Lake, NWT, and made sure to praise it in their own pages. *The Indian Advocate*, in turn, praised the newspapers from Battleford and Kitamaat. These two schools then reprinted this praise in their own papers. Exchanges also added to the content of a school's newspaper. Schools would regularly clip from other newspapers, sometimes crediting the original and sometimes not. Occasionally such clippings covered news of the day, but far more clippings came from other school newspapers, establishing both a network and an echo chamber among boarding schools in Canada and the US.

By and large, schools used their newspapers as an avenue for showcasing supposed assimilation. Shingwauk Home promised to deliver news on "the training in white men's ways and the leading to the foot of the cross, of the ignorant and ill cared-for children of the forest" (*Our Forest Children* 3.1:45). Newspapers often framed their columns as answers to the "Indian problem,"[8] which Regina School's newspaper defined:

> The Indian problem is the world's problem; that is it is but a part of the great problem that meets the dominant race wherever it meets the conquered race. What shall we, the British people, do with the races of India? What shall we do with the millions of Negros and Kaffres in our settlements in Africa? What shall the United States do with her millions of Negroes? What shall Canada do with her Indians? Are all but parts of one great question. When we have answered this question and solved the problems appended to it; then we may be permitted to lay down "the whiteman's burden." (*Progress* 18.9:3)

The real problem, as many argue, was that Indigenous peoples all over the world stood in the way of colonialism, and their existence delegitimized settlers' claims to land. Framing Indigenous peoples, not the settlers and colonialism, as the problem exculpated settlers. Haskell Institute's newspaper suggested the solution was that an Indigenous person's "land should be treated as an estate given to him" (*Indian*

Leader 5.22.1). Edward Francis Wilson, the principal of Shingwauk Home, suggested that readers interested in the "question" keep issues of the school's newspapers "on file, [and] they will thus have a history of this movement from the beginning" (*Our Forest Children* 1.5:4). Sometimes, newspapers highlighted the government's failure to solve the "Indian problem." Regina School, for instance, argued that "those in the service are best qualified to indicate the strong and weak points in our Indian Policy" (*Progress* 3.72:6), not the government. Printing, more than any other school trade, demonstrated one answer to the "Indian problem" by proving students could now operate modern technology and read and write English; the colonial content of the newspaper complemented this evidence. While the success of trades such as farming or baking may have been known throughout a school's neighbouring community, newspapers reached audiences far and wide.

Newspapers also served as a fundraising tool. They did not hide schools' desperation for funds, frequently pleading for more subscriptions and donations. Such requests exemplify the severe underfunding of schools, which was even more acute in the late nineteenth century because the government introduced per capita funding in 1892 (Milloy, 1999, p. 63). This new model did not consider local needs of individual schools, forcing institutions to over-recruit and overcrowd. Because funding shortfalls were now the responsibility of churches, school newspapers became one way of drumming up alternative revenue. Shingwauk Home's newspaper went so far as to warn readers that donations through the Board of Foreign and Domestic would not reach the school, asking readers to donate to the principal directly (*Our Forest Children* 2.7:24). Kitamaat Home's newspaper asked both for funds as well as specific items for the community such as a stove (*Na-Na-Kwa* 15.10; 16.9; 17.7) or a wheelchair (20.10). Most schools also used their newspapers as a way to thank donors, usually listing a name and what or how much was donated – a printed acknowledgment could prompt more donations.

Schools also sent newspapers as a reward for donations. Shingwauk Home, for instance, would send twenty to thirty copies of its newspaper as a reward for anyone (and this was often a Sunday school) who donated fifty dollars a year to the institution (*Our Forest Children* 2.8:27), an amount that some schools noted was the per capita shortfall after government funding. The school would also send a letter from a student, so that the donor could "have an Indian pupil allotted to their care, to think of, to correspond with, and to pray for" (3.11:130). In one instance, a donor became irate that "P. was no longer our girl," and that the money had gone to someone new (2.12:44). Washakada Home, too, advertised that if readers were to supply fifty dollars, "contributors of this amount may be said practically to adopt a child" (*Elkhorn Advocate* 1.1.5). Though present-day international aid societies commonly invoke the metaphor of adoption in their fundraising campaigns, its use here resonates with the connections made by Cindy Blackstock (2007) and others between residential schooling, the Sixties Scoop where Indigenous children were adopted out to white families later in the twentieth century, and the present-day statistics on the disproportionate number of Indigenous children in government "care" compared to the rest of the population.

Schools had to dance a careful dance: despite the fundraising potential of a newspaper, its production could not be seen as a source of financial strain. Schools made it clear that newspapers were financially self-sufficient and in fact a revenue source. Kitamaat Home reported how its newspaper relieved the principal of "the burden of written correspondence" (*Na-Na-Kwa* 6.1). Schools also ensured their newspapers were sustainable by charging readers (see table 1). Though Washakada Home charged one dollar per year for its newspaper (a common rate), it also accepted goods such as vegetables, wood, butter, and mittens as payment (*Elkhorn Advocate*, January 4, 1893). Many schools supplied their newspapers free to Sunday schools. Boarding schools occasionally resorted to guilting readers who did not pay for their newspaper. Shingwauk Home published its fear that the newspaper would "never bring back to us even one cent to pay for their cost of production and transmission" (*Our Forest Children* 3.3:7). Regina School's newspaper described a reader whose entrance to heaven was denied because he owed two years' subscription fees. In the article, God reminds readers that "the paper was printed by Indian boys who never had very much money, and edited by members of the staff, who were developing gray hairs worrying over financial matters" (*Progress* 15.1:7).

During the 1890s, major dailies garnered two-thirds of their income from advertising and only one-third from subscriptions, whereas earlier in the nineteenth century major dailies in Canada depended far more on subscriptions to cover costs (Rutherford, 1982, p. 97). Other than the community-focused publications of Washakada Home and Rupert's Land School, school newspapers were mostly free of advertisements and therefore financially depended on subscriptions. One exception included later issues of Shingwauk Home's newspaper, whose issues ended with a page advertising pianos, church bells, and "Indian" books by non-Indigenous authors such as Helen Hunt Jackson's novel *Ramona*. Rupert's Land School's school newspaper, *The Aurora*, advertised Winnipeg services such as veterinarians and jewelers. But mostly school newspapers depended on subscribers. Having a subscription list also saved money: in Canada before 1897, a newspaper mailed from the place of publication to a regular subscriber did not require postage (Arfken and Pawluk, 2006, pp. 104–7).

Schools were smart to quash perceptions of their newspapers as an extravagance, as such criticisms came from the top. Clifford Sifton served as minister of the interior and superintendent general of Indian Affairs beginning in 1896. In 1897, Sifton commissioned a report from Martin Benson, a member of the education section of the department. Benson attributed the deficits of schools to church mismanagement. He also believed industrial schools were too "ambitious" (Benson, 1897, p. 12) and should teach only basic skills such as farming, carpentry, and blacksmithing (Benson, 1897, pp. 10–11). For Benson, teaching students shoemaking or printing wasted time, wages, and material; in addition, these trades had no job openings (Benson, 1897, p. 11). But Benson's criticism was also about appearance. As Benson saw it in 1897, "The chief ambition of an Industrial school is to possess a Brass Band and a printing press," which he saw as merely "for outward show and [to] help to advertise the school" (Benson, 1897, p. 11). Boarding school brass bands in the US and Canada instilled military-like discipline and showcased supposed assimilation through music, uniform, and line; but students also circumvented the designs of the schools, using music as resistance (Neylan and Meyer, 2006; Troutman, 2009; Warrior, 2005). Newspapers differed from brass bands in that they more ostensibly prepared students for employment. And as newspapers took great pains to explain, subscribers and exchanges offset costs. Benson's disapproval of showiness may have been for financial reasons and optics. It may also reveal the larger philosophy that Indigenous peoples were incapable of higher art forms and instead destined for only the simplest trades. Or, his distinction between basic and extravagant may be code for sites of creativity such as music and writing in which students could more likely undermine assimilative agendas. Benson's beliefs were echoed in 1905 by Indian commissioner David Laird, who stated he too had "to a great extent discouraged entering into such arts as printing, fancy carpentering, and blacksmithing" (Titley, 2009, p. 164).

Before a reader would have opened a school newspaper and learned of these stated purposes, they would have seen its title and masthead. Shingwauk Home's newspaper was titled *Our Forest Children (and What We Want to Do with Them)*. The pronoun "our" is still familiar today, appearing in editorials and political addresses across the country that praise, pity, or loathe "*Canada's* First Nations," or (said by a non-Indigenous person) "*our* Aboriginal people." In this title, the "forest children" *belong* to the reader, whom the newspaper largely assumed was non-Indigenous. The responsibility for transforming *them*, found in the newspaper's subtitle, rests with the reader too. So, both the perceived problem and solution are owned by the non-Indigenous reader. The second word of the newspaper's title is equally connotative. "Forest" suggests the wilds antithetical to the school's reforming mission, established as a space outside of civilization. Forest being aligned with Indigenous peoples would not have been uncommon to nineteenth-century readers, who would have encountered it in the first book published by an Indigenous person in Canada, George Copway's *Recollections of a Forest Life* (1847), as well as in Susanna Moodie's *Roughing It in the Bush: Or, Forest Life in Canada* (1852) and Eliza Morrison's *A Little History of My Forest Life* (1894). Shingwauk Home's newspaper figured itself as "this leaf from the Forest which has alighted at your door" (3.3:7), emerging from the same forest once seemingly home to students.

In addition to forest references of early books in Canada, students were occasionally coded as wood themselves. Wikwemikong School remarked that its teacher had skill in driving "the heads of the little Indians, as the wedge into the log" (DIA, 1892, p. 55). The violent analogy was also used in the US by the principal of Carlisle School, who compared students to "raw material in the forest" that needed "to be brought and put through the proper refining influences of our civilization mills of today" (qtd. in Pfister p. 40). Pratt, invoking Alexander Pope's commonly cited eighteenth-century phrase, also believed that a twig (implying a child) was "easier to bend than the bough, but that, too, may be bent if enough force is applied" (Eastman, 1935, p. 93). Battleford School's newspaper also printed that Indigenous peoples either "bend or break"; while older people were rigid, saplings could "be put into whatever shape may be required" (*Progress* 4.8:4). In these analogies, genocide, assimilative education, and resource extraction all conflate in one violent knot. The final word of *Our Forest Children* may appear innocuous: the students were indeed children. But the word extended to adults as well, who were seen as government wards.[9] All three words of this title are loaded.

The metaphor of children-as-wood continued in the newspaper's masthead, which included the newspaper's complete title in stylized wood with branches peeping behind it (see figure 2.1). A circle sits below, with a view of the school and a flag, as four men saw and axe wood amidst the clearing of the school. In the background of this circle are faint images of caricatured Indigenous people on a floor of ferns and a banner with text no longer created out of wood but capitalized: *And What We Want to Do with Them*. The declared transformation of these schools frames most issues of *Our Forest Children* through its opening image – the text changes from gnarly, comical wood-text to print, and idle, faint, images of Indigenous people lounging on a fern-upholstered floor become men who stand, work, and create. Bodies almost indistinguishable from wood become crisp figures in the foreground of a school with its flag and tools. Such distinctions between so-called progressive versus traditionalist Indigenous communities and people were common in the US and Canada. The image of wooden forest people transforming to men who create things with wood has an additional resonance with the paper on which *Our Forest Children* was printed. So, the forest is the source of Indigenous people, timber, and the newspaper itself – raw materials requiring transformation. Compare these wood analogies to a poem by Marilyn Dumont (2007a) in which a woman "inhales through the roots of her spine" and "responds to light and air and clear water / like her mother before her," while she shelters saplings from storms (pp. 20–1).

Kitamaat Home's newspaper *Na-Na-Kwa* could be read initially as a nod of respect for the people it is about. Certainly, the title ushers in less derogatory and assimilative implications than *Our Forest Children*. To my knowledge, no other nineteenth-century boarding school newspaper from Canada used Indigenous words in its title, though some American (*Eadle Keatah Toh* at Carlisle) and later twentieth-century Canadian newspapers (*Chupka* from Cranbrook and *Oke Nape* from Cluny Crowfoot) do. Nineteenth-century non-boarding school missionary newspapers such as Kamloop's *Wawa* (Lowman, 2017) and the Nisga'a *Hağağa* (G. Edwards, 2001, pp. 217–20) did as well. But I want to guard against interpreting *Na-Na-Kwa* as any less concerned with transformation than other newspapers simply because its title is in the Tsimshian language. For one, the title *Na-Na-Kwa* appeared

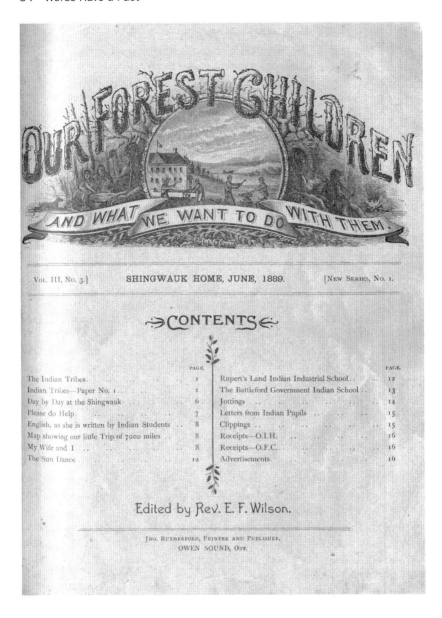

Figure 2.1. *Our Forest Children* masthead and contents list.

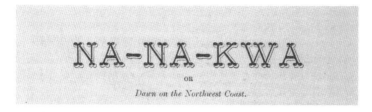

Figure 2.2. *Na-Na-Kwa* masthead.

Figure 2.3. *The Guide* masthead.

in a different font than its translation (see figure 2.2), almost exoticizing the language. Further, the translation of *Na-Na-Kwa* appears in the newspaper's subtitle, "Dawn on the Northwest Coast," whose font is instead italicized. The English translation is also the name of an eight-part origin story of how Christianity "arrived" at Kitamaat, featured in the first eight issues of the newspaper.[10] The serialized story describes how Christianity's light had difficulty "penetrat[ing] the darkness of heathenism" (1.1), concluding as a conversion narrative. For one missionary in the story, "the idea occurred to him if a teacher could only be obtained, the savage Kitamaats might be thus influenced by the gospel" (3.1). So, although the newspaper's title is in Tsimshian, its font and English translation begin to limit possibilities of homage.

The masthead of Battleford School's newspaper *The Guide* did without the lavish twists of *Our Forest Children* or *Na-Na-Kwa*, adopting instead a font of seeming simplicity, with a period at the end of its title to boot (see figure 2.3). For the newspaper's first four volumes, beneath its title was the motto "The Same Road Leads to Virtue and Success," which later changed to "In all the ways acknowledge Him, and he shall direct thy paths." Both mottos frame the word "guide" – less a manual and more a source of spiritual support. The title of Regina School's newspaper, *Progress*, perhaps requires the least amount of unpacking – or the most. The title implies that both the newspaper and its content represent a progression of the school's students along evolutionary lines. Nary a late nineteenth-century Indian Affairs report escapes using the concept. In these contexts, "progress" stands in for children who can read and write English, who can work on machinery, and who are well behaved. Unlike one-off articles or isolated scenes, a newspaper's stated purpose and formatting came at readers in every issue and helped to reinforce the general theme of assimilation present in all boarding school publications.

Printing on Display

"THE MECHANICAL WORK ON THIS PAPER IS DONE ENTIRELY BY INDIAN BOYS" – so announced most issues of Regina School's newspaper. Battleford School, too, boasted in each issue that "All the mechanical work in connection with THE GUIDE is performed by our pupils." Washakada School's stamp simply noted it was "published by the Washakada Indian Homes," but its occasional supplement devoted entirely to news on the school would read "THIS SUPPLE-MENT IS THE WORK OF OUR INDIAN BOYS" (29 March 1894). The newspaper of Rupert's Land School also declared in every instalment that "the mechanical work of printing this Magazine is entirely done by the pupils." Most of Carlisle School's publications exhibited a similar tagline. As well, annual reports would reiterate that in terms of school newspapers, "all the mechanical work, from setting the type to making up the forms, and correcting the proofs, [was] being done by the boys" (DIA, 1899 p. 362). The nature of the work ranged; for instance, at Rupert's Land School one student described how he was responsible for stoking the stove in the print shop, for taking out the ashes, dusting the office, and setting type and distributing it (*Aurora* 2.14:4).

Students contributed most of the labour, so much so that an article in Kitamaat Home's newspaper explained how "so useful are [the students] that without them Nanakwa could not exist" (17.6). Similarly, the labour for Regina School's paper was more than token: during the summer, publication would lessen or cease altogether without the boys' help (*Progress* 3.78:7–8). While not all newspapers featured such a line below the masthead, their articles would frequently discuss the labour of the children behind the newspaper. The newspaper itself stood as proof students were transforming from supposedly unskilled and illiterate boys to those capable of working a machine and printing in English. Advertising that students were the labour, who readers would assume were unpaid, perhaps also quelled assumptions that the newspaper symbolized excess spending and reminded readers that lapses in payment were on the backs of unpaid boys. In his analysis of school newspapers in the US, Robert Warrior (2005) postulates what these authenticating stamps, which appeared on the front of many American Indian school newspapers as well, may have meant: one, the printers sneakily wrote these phrases, "injecting a bit of Native agency into a document that otherwise spoke for the students and about them"; or two, that the printers asked for permission to include the phrase, demanding their acknowledgment (p. 98). Warrior, though, considers neither of these scenarios probable. A more likely scenario, he proposes, is that an instructor constructed the phrase but "those students in the print shop who could read were probably happy to see themselves and their work highlighted."

Despite labour attributed to a homogenous group of "OUR INDIAN BOYS" in its masthead stamps, individual printers frequently received attention. Though homogenizing labour and yet highlighting specific people appear in opposition, Joel Pfister (2004) argues that boarding schools in the US sought to "individualize" students – a core construct of US identity. But before schools could attempt to instil the tenets of American individualism they first had to homogenize them as "Indians," which meant attempting to eradicate spiritual, linguistic, and visual markers that differentiated the diverse nations represented at any given school. Vine Deloria Jr (1988), too, observes how "Indians must be redefined in terms that white men will accept, even if that means re-Indianizing them according to a whiteman's idea of what they were like in the past and should logically become in the future" (p. 92). Both of these forces were at work in school newspapers: a homogenous mass of "OUR INDIAN BOYS" responsible for labour mingled with profiles of individual printers.

Printer boys were individualized both for their skill in the trade but also because they were typically top of their class. At Regina School, chief printers Jack Muchahoo and Fred Peters received specific attention in their school newspaper. John Kasto was also a celebrated printer, who moved on from Regina School to the prestigious Hampton Institute in Virginia (DIA, 1902, p. 423), a historically Black college originally established for freedmen after the Civil War.[11] Though many students contracted measles, John's case received mention in the newspaper (*Progress* 3.84:6). Similarly, Washakada Home highlighted the work of Miles Cochrane, Angus Prince, and Fred Pratt, who were described as "expert at the case," "expert compositors," (DIA, 1895, p. 166), and able to "set up a job tastily" (1896, p. 362). At the beginning of 1896, two new printers named Samuel Pratt and James Flett joined the crew and quickly learned to "set type, run off the paper," and showed "great adaptability in the business" (p. 362). The school's print shop also included a Blackfoot "deaf mute" named Nap-ia-mo-kin-ma but also referred to as "Dummy." He printed for at least three years (1895, p. 166) until he went to Brandon Hospital for tuberculosis in his knee (1896, p. 362). Despite his derogatory nickname, annual reports described him as "next to" the other printers in "expertness in type-setting and running the presses." Teachers considered him "a marvel, being a deaf mute" and a "fine, strong, intelligent lad of fine physique" who was able to "read, write, [and] do sums" (1895, p. 166). Printing was not uncommon in the nineteenth century for people who were deaf. Prior to the industrial revolution, they were often limited to teaching at deaf schools. But with increased literacy rates and industry, printing as an occupation in the US "predominated for deaf men" (Haller, 1993, p. 44). Deaf schools in both Canada and the US often produced newspapers because they, like Indian boarding schools, had printing programs for students to prepare for employment (Haller, 1993; Iozzo, 2015). Like other printers – and perhaps even more so because the school had limited expectations of his abilities – Nap-ia-mo-kin-ma was both homogenized and yet singled out.

At Battleford School, Gilbert Bear and Louis Laronde were in such a league: printers yet also academic all-stars, receiving individualized attention throughout the newspaper. So too at Rupert's Land School, where Arthur Cochrane and Maurice Sanderson comprised what was considered the "management" of the shop (DIA, 1895, p. 11). Robert Stevenson received particular attention as one of the junior printers because "while playing with the press had his hand caught and hurt. It has progressed favorably and will, we hope, soon to be well" (*Rupert's Land Gleaner* 1892, p. 32). Accidents from children operating machinery intended for adults were frequent, and, as Robert's injury exemplifies, the print shop was no exception.[12] That the newspaper mentions the accident at all – albeit nonchalantly, almost blaming the child for "playing" – reveals the gravity of the injury, for school newspapers were experts at burying all too commonplace deaths, diseases, and injuries. Its mention may also expose how valued printers were.

Like other school newspapers, that of Kitamaat Home isolated and praised particularly adept printers, the only difference being that the printers were girls at this all-female school.[13] Printing programs in Canada were typically reserved for boys, as the trade was outside of the domestic skills girls learned. Girls at Indian boarding schools typically learned domestic skills such as sewing and cleaning, while boys learned such skills as carpentry, farming, and printing. What constituted male versus female tasks often had to do with demarcated lines of indoor/ outdoor work as well as dexterous/physical, in addition to broader societal ways of viewing such divisions of labour and gender. Indeed, a key element of boarding school assimilation included inculcating settler understandings of gender and sexuality. Printing was more broadly considered a male task outside of schools at this time: women were not formally apprenticed as journeymen printers in the nineteenth century (Raible, 2007, p. 60). Male printers went on strike at the *Globe* in the mid-nineteenth century in part because newspaper founder and editor George Brown hired non-unionized women as compositors ("Brown's harem"), who were let go after the strike. Exceptions included women trained in family-run presses as well as Mary Ann Shadd, the first Black female publisher in North America (Rhodes, 1999). Nonetheless, printing was a skill typically reserved for boys at Indian boarding schools.

An exception in addition to Kitamaat Home existed at Carlisle School, where printing was co-ed. While one student at Carlisle School wrote in 1888 she hoped "girls will learn to print. I don't think printing is any harder than washing" (*Red Man* 8.7:8), a later photograph of printers from 1895 shows girls included as printers. Besides the girls, labour also came from female staff: the principal's wife and two teachers (15.2).[14] The girls may have been compensated for their labour, at least during holidays, as one teacher lists work on *Na-Na-Kwa* as a source of "profitable employment," on par with other duties such as tending the school's garden and creating pinafores (18.8). Like the boys of other newspapers, Kitamaat Home's described one printer named Minnie as "a bright child and capable" (14.11). The newspaper recognized Flora as able to "do any part of the mechanical work, in fact is indispensable" and "Nancy is very useful and obliging" (13.1); she was later described as someone who "understands thoroughly the mechanical work of Nanakwa and is a good compositor" (17.11). Besides typesetting, Kitamaat Home's printers also wrote for the newspaper occasionally. Their celebrated role as printers was a frame through which to read their essays, as their connection to printing prefaced their compositions. As well, their frequent mention in the newspaper would have made their names familiar to readers. Though the plan was never realized, the newspaper promised "to give a short sketch of the two junior printers" (17.11), revealing a similar attention to male printers in other newspapers.

Besides printers, school newspapers attempted to convert real children into characters. One issue of Kitamaat Home's newspaper offered a chart with students' Anglo names, Indigenous names with a pronunciation guide, and ages – for use "as a reference for the children are often referred to in Nanakwa" (7.6). The chart serves as a legend, as if found in a complicated novel. Regina School also treated real children as characters, most notably "Little Joe."[15] The newspaper records him as looking "cuter than ever now in a little Buster Brown suit made for him by Miss Johnstone. He is specially proud of the real pocket in his blouse that has a real handkerchief in it" (*Progress* 17.9:3). In one scene, the newspaper remarked that "it is very amusing to see baby Joe with No10 skates on skating around the kitchen yard" (18.2:5). When he is older, the newspaper paints Little Joe as "always saying smart things" (19.2:6). The newspaper poked fun at the character of Joe for asserting himself. In one scene, he takes issue with the matron on duty who wishes to control his money when he attends a fair. As the newspaper frames it, "this arrangement did not quite suit little Joe, and he announced to her as they were on their way to the grounds, 'I think I could take care of five cents my own self'" (18.9:6). In another, Little Joe allows two girls to go ahead of him as they entered the school, remarking "ladies first" (19.2:6). Part of the violence these newspapers represent is how they transformed real children into caricatures, which non-Indigenous readers consumed while the children's parents had little or no contact.

Newspapers also displayed their printing at fairs and in parades. Regina School reprinted an article explaining the practice as a way to prove to a wider public – beyond just readers – that "the children of the red man have mental and mechanical ability equal to any race" (*Progress* 8.13:1). Schools went further than just exhibiting the products of printing to the public: they also exhibited students themselves. As Sadiah Qureshi (2011) notes, the end of the nineteenth century represented a change in scale of human display at exhibitions (p. 2). Students at Haskell Institute in Kansas, for instance, displayed their trades in a Fourth of July parade in 1902 (*Indian Leader* 6.18:6). Female students operated sewing machines atop a float adorned by the motto "work that is half done is always asking to be done again." Printers "lifted high the case, immense 'stick,' press roller, rolls of papers" and advertised their newspaper. Carlisle School printers also paraded as part of the quad-ricentennial of Columbus, carrying printing equipment and copies of newspapers (Pratt, 2003, p. 296).

Besides parades, fairs were another venue for displaying the trade of printing. Indigenous peoples were often featured prominently, par-ticularly at the 1893 Chicago's World Fair because of its celebration of Columbus's "arrival" four hundred years prior. According to Edward Francis Wilson's journal, he was hired by the Smithsonian in 1891 to conduct research in advance of the fair, "taking scientific measurements of the persons of Indians of various ages and of different tribes, the color of their eyes, specimens of their handy work, implements, weap-ons, canoes, carts, sleighs, etc." (p. 98). This is just one example of how Indian boarding schools served as a major part of the fair. Boarding schools across North America capitalized on the opportunity to show-case student "transformation" to the world. Some of the showcasing included student wares. For example, Rupert's Land School submitted student creations for display in Chicago such as a cabinet, church door hinges, a carved model of the school itself from the original building plans, crochet work, knitting, and moccasins (*Aurora* 1.3:3). The print-ing shop sent sample work, too, such as its school's annual report and municipal lists. Canadian Indian boarding schools – including Rupert's Land School, Shingwauk Home, Elkhorn School, and Battleford School – won several awards for examples of school work at the fair, as did the Department of Indian Affairs (2.16:2).

Schools also sent students themselves, displaying them sitting at desks and operating machinery, including printing. Pratt sent Carl-isle students, and in Canada the Department of Indian Affairs rotated its display among eight schools, sending students to work in a mock schoolroom for fair visitors to observe (Raibmon, 2005a, pp. 40–1). One display included student printers, who operated a press and created pamphlets called *The Canadian Indian: The Work of a Few Years among the Indians* (DIA, 1893, p. 106). The sixteen-page booklet detailed everything from treaties to reserves and schooling. So, while many trades were presented at the Chicago World's Fair, the printing displays included souvenirs visitors could bring home. Circulating at the world's fair was also a birchbark tract created by Potawatomi storyteller Simon Pokagon, which rebuked the US for its treatment of Indigenous peoples (C. Walker, 1997, pp. 200–2; 212–20) and perhaps could have served as a counternarrative to *The Canadian Indian* for fairgoers.

One of the printers at Rupert's Land School, Maurice, wrote back to a friend about Chicago, and his school newspaper reprinted the letter. The letter reveals mild criticisms of the set-up in Chicago – that "the press is a very small one, the chase is only about one foot long and about eight or nine inches wide; and the paper cutter stands only about one foot and a half high. There are about thirteen fonts of type. I have to get half of the money I make here" (*Aurora* 1.10: 2). The letter was also critical of a fellow student printer:

> That printer who was there from Battleford, when he left off work that evening left the rollers on the plate, didn't take off the forme from the press, and left the press closed; and the next day when I went there, the type was all in pie [slang for jumbled type] on the floor, and I had to take it up and put it in the case. When he locked up the forme, he only put furniture on the sides and front and none on the back, and put it in the press like that, and I don't think he had any quoins [a device to lock type down] either. (1.10: 2)

Despite criticizing the technology of the press, the letter also revealed the thrill of walking around Chicago, seeing the Manufacturers' Building of the Fair, and viewing an Egyptian mummy. A letter from a female student visitor to the fair from Battleford School discussed the excitement of fireworks and of visiting the Fishery Building, where she saw crocodiles, crabs, and oysters (*Aurora* 1.11:2). She only saw lions from afar, as admission to this part of the Fair cost fifty cents. Her letter states that she and the other students leave their lodging in a suburb of Chicago at eleven o'clock in the morning and then work from one to four in the afternoon, overseen by a man who scares her but does not scold her. She states the students were paid twenty-five cents extra the previous week for working an hour longer.

Robert A. Trennert explains how the American Indian boarding school displays at the Chicago World's Fair backfired on organizers, failing to satiate fairgoers who did not desire to see boys writing English and operating machinery but instead wanted to see "traditional" Indigenous peoples. School displays like those put on by Carlisle School and the Department of Indian Affairs in Canada competed each day with Buffalo Bill shows on neighbouring fairgrounds, which Pratt vehemently opposed and would blast in Carlisle's newspapers for undermining the message of "progress" (Pfister, 2004, p. 71). Raibmon (2005a), too, provides an account of resistance by Kwakwaka'wakw performers at the fair, who pushed against the designs of boarding school displays and the larger colonial message of the fair.

Another example of resistance in Chicago included a printer. Gilbert Bear, an all-star student and printer at Battleford School, spent three months operating a press for visitors to the fair. Annual reports stated Gilbert "performed some very excellent work" (DIA, 1893, p. 121) and "conducted himself in a most becoming manner whilst there, and did a greater part of the mechanical work in connection with the printing of the *Canadian Indian*." According to the report, "the change greatly improved the lad, in both appearance and manner" (p. 174). The *Battleford Herald* (qtd. in *Manitoba Morning Press*, March 23, 1894, p. 3) reported that Gilbert was "one of the lucky boys and saw Chicago last year during the fair," gaining "a little knowledge of civilized life." So while Gilbert was already an exceptional student, the fair changed him even more according to media. Despite reports and articles explaining Gilbert was "lucky" to be on display in Chicago, Gilbert's own words offer a different perspective. An 1894 article in the *Battleford Herald* quotes Gilbert, when asked if he liked the fair, as replying "No; too hot and too many people." The newspaper chocks Gilbert's response up to him having "not much to say about this visit" (*Manitoba Morning Free Press*, 1894, February 28, p. 8). I read this quote as saying something significant: despite pressure to go along with the narrative of the newspaper, which frames Gilbert as "lucky," he said "no." It *would* have been hot, and there *were* many people at the world's fair – almost twenty-eight million visitors.

Gilbert could have meant more, too, when the newspaper quoted him saying "no." Did he oppose the assimilative goals of the fair? Was he paid for his three months? Did he contest being put on display, viewed by disappointed fairgoers unable to see a "real Indian"? Was he happy to meet with other students and printers? Proud to have his talents recognized? Did he have time to gripe with other students on display about barriers to employment? Was he able to network? Did Gilbert have occasion to sneak off and spend time with other Indigenous people at the fair or outside of it at the Buffalo Bill shows? One can only wonder. An inquiring newspaper wanted Gilbert to say, "I was lucky to have a further opportunity to be civilized at the fair. I was able to show the rest of the world how civilizing our school is in Saskatchewan"; instead, Gilbert said "no."

Yet another way schools displayed their printers was through photography. Many have theorized how boarding school photographs served as propaganda (Brady and Hiltz, 2017; Malmsheimer, 1985; J.R. Miller, 2003; Racette, 2009; Warley, 2009). Images of students staged before their time at school paired with images of them after, with short hair and school uniforms, were particular examples of boarding school photography. Another perspective may be informed by Susan Sontag's *Regarding the Pain of Others* (2003). Sontag insists that viewing a photograph of someone's pain cannot ever fix suffering, it can only invite a viewer "to pay attention, to reflect, to learn, to examine the rationalizations for mass suffering offered by established powers" (p. 117). These newspapers help to shed further light on boarding school photography because they both mentioned how students (or rather how teachers thought students) felt about school photographs and also printed photographs and advertised their sale to readers. Regina School wrote in its newspaper that "there was a quite a bit of excitement at the School" because a photographer took a group shot, minus the older boys who were away threshing. The newspaper explained it was "a lot of work getting such a big crowd into position, but it was done, and we are all quite pleased with the result." The newspaper also stated that "some of the girls, who were wearing extra fancy hair ribbons for the occasion, were wishing they could have the back of their heads taken as well as the front" (*Progress* 17.8:3). One student wrote that she was sad because it looked like she had two faces in a school photograph since she was chewing gum and did not remain still (4.6:1). These comments perhaps suggest an interest or even excitement in photography on the part of students, adding an additional layer to their role. These behind-the-scenes stories usher in a sense of motion to the stillness of the photographs – the big, moving crowd; the boys not in the shot because they were threshing; the desire for simultaneous front and back photographs of hair ribbons; and the girl chewing gum. But in another article from Carlisle School, Pratt describes his attempts to collapse such motion. He explains that he orchestrated a clear photograph of the entire school by telling the children to keep "motionless as if instead of a harmless camera they had been looking at Medusa's head and had really turned to stone," a stillness the newspaper saw as demonstrating "the effect of generations of drill in that immobility of muscles upon which the Indian prides himself" (*Redman* 8.7:5). *Progress* revealed that parents received such photographs, who were "always delighted to receive these mementoes which are carefully laid aside and frequently scanned" (Progress 3.71:8). Here, the camera is far from what Pratt calls "harmless" or objective, continuing to exclude and frame his version of school experiences, which he further narrates in the newspaper. Yet photographs – if what *Progress* states is true – may have also been a way for parents to see their children.

Newspapers also displayed and advertised photographs of students, including images of printers, which is strange given how few students printed. Pictures of children working figure prominently in government reports, serving as the "visual embodiment of [the schools'] momentous project" (Racette, 2009, p. 54). Carlisle School was the leader in boarding school photographs and used them as incentives for subscriptions.[16] Carlisle School's newspaper *Morning Star* had a standing offer: if readers were to supply three new subscribers, they would receive a nine-by-fourteen-inch photograph of the whole school; for two new subscribers, before-and-after photographs of either Pueblo or Navajo students; and for one new subscriber, an eight-by-five-inch photograph of the newspaper's printers. These images of printers, in their school uniforms, are group portraits rather than candid. Nothing about their poses, clothing, or the background of the portraits indicates they were printers. Though not as valuable as a shot of the whole school or a before-and-after image, the photograph of printers (rather than any other trade) was offered as a reward for new subscriptions. Why? These images may have achieved several goals. They display the before-and-after without the before: students in uniforms and short hair, with a caption explaining that they now are printers and therefore able to read and write English as well as operate machinery. Readers may also have been keen on receiving these images because printers' names appeared frequently. Printers would have known this since they were the ones laying the type that advertised their pictures.

Photographs of printers were not offered in Canadian newspapers as incentive, but they still existed. One such photograph appeared in Battleford School's annual report for 1896. Seven boys look straight at the camera, their teacher standing authoritatively in the middle with one of his hands on his hip and the other on a chair (see figure 2.4). Three of these children appear too young for the dangerous work of printing, even by schools' low standards. Everyone wears a suit, posed in a studio with a painted background of columns, potted plants, and drapes as if they were in a European sitting room. Like the Carlisle photographs, nothing here points to the trade of printing save for the report's caption, but they do communicate the "momentous project" in their short hair and suits.

CLASS OF PRINTERS WITH INSTRUCTOR, REGINA INDIAN INDUSTRIAL SCHOOL.

Figure 2.4. A class of printers with instructor, 1896. R-A1877 (1), Saskatchewan Archives Board.

Other images displayed printers in action. A photograph of Regina School's printers shows three boys operating a hand press in work clothes and hats (see figure 2.5). Two of the boys appear engaged with the press, though still posed; the third boy stares straight back at the camera, standing behind the press with an expression perhaps of indifference or defiance. Haskell Institute's newspaper, too, published an image of its printing office as students operated machinery (2.19.2). So did Carlisle: figure 2.6 is a group portrait of boy printers and three students who present as girls, with the female printing instructor Marianna Burgess in the middle. Brian Hochman (2014) remarks on the 1920s in situ photography taken of Indigenous peoples in *National Geographic*. He notes that despite attempts to display action, the stillness of these images remains. It is as if the photographs were meant to mimic a display in a museum. For Hochman, such stasis was "both a function of

Figure 2.5. Regina school boys operating a hand press, 1896. R-A2679, Saskatchewan Archives Board.

evolutionary ideology and a product of mechanical necessity" (p. 168). Decades earlier, the photographs of the student printers – both action shots and posed – convey this similar freezing, whether in a studio or the workshop.

Kitamaat School's newspaper also published a photograph of its students in 1902, praising in particular the three students – Martha, Minnie, and Nancy – who were printers (17.8). While some students smile, others appear upset. Yet the newspaper closes down any negative interpretations readers might have had: the article accompanying the photograph states that the girls are a "happy group" and some only

Figure 2.6. Group of printers, 1895(?). CIS-001, box 2, folder 1, Dickinson College Archives and Special Collections.

appear "somewhat distressed by the sun shining in their eyes" (see figure 2.7). The newspaper states it hopes to destabilize stereotypes of Indigenous peoples as "stoical, immobile races, in whom there is no sense of humor." But the article reinscribes other stereotypes, explaining that these girls are "longing for the freedom of the tribes" and are "true daughters of nature." The article also attempts to further contain a significant example of resistance. The girls wear blankets even though schools typically showcased uniforms. The article explains that the girls are only wearing blankets because they "dearly love to play 'old woman.'" In this form of play, the girls would wear shawls, "their bodies bent at precisely the same angle" with a handkerchief around their head as they pretended to gossip using "the favourite phrases of their grannies with perfect intonation" (17.8–9). In stifling the threat

GEIGABOA. (Some Home Girls.)

Figure 2.7. "Geigaboa (Some Home Girls)." *Na-Na-Kwa* 17.1: January 1902.

that the blankets may represent an unfinished process of assimilation, the article reveals more.

This photograph reveals how students may have been remembering their grandmothers, openly embodying memories of their clothing, posture, gossip, language, and intonation. Maybe the girls played what the paper called "old woman" (rather than "grandmother") because they desired to be grandmothers one day and by definition survive school. Maybe they weren't playing. Perhaps they missed their grandparents. Or, they were just having fun. Maybe they wished to openly defy the school's attempts to make them forget. Whatever the reason, the newspaper permits only the narrowest explanation, calling their play "laughable." The accompanying article states the girls regard cloth as "one of their most coveted treasures" but does not recognize the cloth as a tool of memory. Sontag's words extend here: the photograph frames and therefore excludes, while the accompanying text attempts to further negate possibilities of Indigenous resistance.

Leaders and Readers

Children were not the only people who created school newspapers: the students had teachers. Sometimes a printing program depended on a professional, as was the case at Regina School with J.K. McInnis, the editor of the *Regina Standard* (*Progress* 3.77:7). Battleford School had the assistance of P.G. Laurie, who was the founder and editor of the *Saskatchewan Herald*. Laurie created the newspaper after walking 650 miles from Winnipeg next to an ox-cart carrying his printing press (Hildebrandt, 1994). He appears to have set up the school's printing program, leaving a boy in charge upon his departure (DIA, 1892, p. 245). Laurie would continue to praise Battleford School's printing shop efforts in his own newspaper years later. As Walter Wasylow (1972) points out, Laurie wrote critically of the school in the *Saskatchewan Herald*, describing bored and starved children (*Herald*, 5.19). He questioned to what extent the state even had authority over Indigenous children (17.10) and he may have acted as a watchdog, reporting on runaways and fires at the school (7.1). But Laurie also viewed Indigenous peoples as "an obstacle to white settlement" (Hildebrandt, 1994) and assured his readers the state was not starving Indigenous peoples on the plains, blaming famine on Indigenous peoples themselves (Carter, 1990, p. 72). Laurie also printed an anti-Riel proclamation, resulting in Riel putting a price on Laurie's head (Fetherling, 1990, pp. 47–8). These contexts complicate Laurie's motivations for helping Battleford School's printers.

Most schools did not have the benefit of consulting established editors. The principal at Kitamaat Home reminded readers he had "never seen inside a press room" (*Na-Na-Kwa* 2.1), noting that he created the newspaper "very often when the missionary is weary at the close of the day" (6.1) and "in the midst of washing dishes, and all sorts of work" (8.4; 12.4). Sometimes, schools hired an instructor briefly until students got the hang of the trade. At Birtle School in Manitoba, the print shop was "without any permanent instructors" (DIA, 1897, p. 310), while students at Battleford School "proved equal to the task of all type-setting without further aid from an instructor" (DIA, 1895, p. 397). At Rupert's Land School, students learned under a James Lawler and then a J.T. French (DIA, 1893, p. 126). This changed the following year, when both the blacksmith and printer instructors were discharged and replaced with "trained pupils." Rupert Land School's newspaper also announced that "on account of the heavy school expense, the Government has discharged our printing Instructor; he went to the *Free Press* in Winnipeg, and the two senior printer boys were promoted to the role of 'sub-editor'" (*Aurora* 2.24:3). The annual report frames the instructors' dismissals as symbolic of the students "getting used to their business" and "gaining more self-reliance" (DIA, 1895, p. 110). Students at Regina School had an instructor for only four months before he was replaced by "two of the boys who had no previous training in typesetting" but "were competent to take full charge of the work" (DIA, 1895, p. 176). Though letting a printing instructor go was more likely to do with the schools' financial distress, annual reports framed these discharges as symbolic of a student's transformation into a skilled worker.

Editors also varied. The second issue of Battleford School's newspaper claimed its students were the editors (*Guide* 1.2:1), and Rupert's Land School stated its newspaper was "edited by a committee of the pupils" (DIA, 1892, p. 245) who were called "sub-editors." Washakada School admitted its printers did "a little editing" (DIA, 1895, p. 166). Students *did* contribute more for each newspaper than just manual labour. In addition to their writing, some newspapers pointed to students' roles in gathering news (*Guide* 1.2.1; DIA, 1895, p. 166). Battleford School had a way for students to submit ideas to a "News Box" (1.2.1). But editorial control appears to have remained largely with the principal. Though the teacher D.C. Munro of Regina School was called the editor of *Progress*, his student successor years later did not receive the same moniker (14.7:6). Every issue of the *Indian Helper* published by Carlisle School stated it was "PRINTED by Indian boys, but EDITED by The-Man-on-the-Band-stand who is NOT an Indian" (3.1:2). Though newspapers attempted to distinguish the labour from editorial control, it would be wrong to assume students were merely cogs in the wheel. It is unclear how much students were suggesting ideas and writing behind the scenes.

Students and teachers were not the only people involved considering that each newspaper typically reached a few thousand readers (see table 1 for self-reported circulation rates). Furthermore, school newspapers appear to have been passed around, which was typical for nineteenth-century reading material. As one reader in Ontario wrote of Battleford School's newspaper, "After reading my copy I send it to a friend of mine who, in turn, passes it on to someone else and everyone enjoys it" (*Guide* 6.8:1). Readers lived throughout Canada, the US, and England, and papers were sometimes listed in both Canadian and British currency. As early as 1899, Kitamaat School's newspaper boasted of a readership "in all parts of Canada," as well as "the British Isles and more remote parts of the Eastern Hemisphere" (*Na-Na-Kwa* 5.1). Shingwauk Home's newspaper reprinted letters of praise in its 1888 issue from Ontario, Nova Scotia, Bermuda, and Scotland; from a member of the British Association; a superintendent of a boarding school in Nebraska; the editor of the magazine *Science* in New York; both a Baptist and a Presbyterian missionary; and members of the Indian Department in the Northwest Territories, the Geological Survey Department in Ottawa, the Bureau of Ethnology in Washington, and the Library of Parliament in Ottawa (2.4:12–16). In addition to such a wide-ranging readership, newspapers sometimes addressed teachers with advice on pedagogy (4.10:2). School newspapers also reached out to other missionaries, both at home and "in the field." Regina School's newspaper saw itself as explaining for readers in the East what missionaries were doing in the West (*Progress* 15.1:8). Battleford School's newspaper regularly asked for contributions from within the church. Kitamaat's newspaper aimed to reach "those who contribute, and pray for the success of our Indian Work" (*Na-Na-Kwa* 3.1). Its readers included members of the Women's Methodist Society and the Epworth League (a Methodist youth club), as well as the principal's friends (15.2) – supporters of the school. Readers also included settlers in nearby towns. For example, the principal of Shingwauk Home advertised *Our Forest Children* in the local newspaper of Medicine Hat, Alberta, where he was planning a future school.

Though newspapers were not directly addressed to Indigenous readers beyond students, newspapers enjoyed an Indigenous readership over and above alumni. One Joseph Hawk from Saskatoon was described as "an intelligent Indian and an old subscriber" who had paid the Regina School a visit (*Progress* 3.79.7). One issue of Carlisle's newspaper, entitled "A Red Man Wants the *Red Man*" (the name of the publication), published a letter from an Indigenous man who subscribed for one year to learn "all about my people back there so that I will know how they are getting along" (4.5:8). The occasional reference in *Na-Na-Kwa* points to a Kitamaat readership (4.1; 4.4), but these instances are rare. Newspapers generally disparaged parents in the third person and rarely addressed them. This does not mean parents weren't reading the

newspapers – just that newspapers did not intend, promote, or antici-
pate them.[17] One exception included Battleford School, which in 1892
began distributing copies to "each boy and girl in the school, and one
for each of their parents" (*Guide* 1.10). This could be because as Brenda
Child (1999) notes in the US, school newspapers could be used to persuade sceptical parents to send their children to school (p. 69). One
Indigenous reader Battleford School made sure to acknowledge was
John Ojijatekha Brant-Sero, a Mohawk celebrity, actor, interpreter, and
lecturer (S. P. Petrone, 1998). Brant-Sero wrote the newspaper asking
to become a subscriber and requesting back copies – ideally all issues
(*Guide* 5.3:4). The school published Brant-Sero's letter and below it ran
an article on his life under the heading "A Cultured Indian," impressing
upon readers the importance of his request. Brant-Sero also wrote a letter to Shingwauk Home's newspaper (3.11:140). Why Brant-Sero read
these two publications is unclear, though the schools take the requests
as praise. Did he approve of these schools? Was he keeping tabs? Communicating information back to parents?

The major Indigenous audience of school newspapers was children.
Articles spoke of how important the school newspaper was to students.
One boy who was sent home from Haskell Institute and later died was
reported to have slept on his deathbed with three issues of his school
newspaper (3.5.4). Many articles presumed a mixed audience. One
article from Battleford School stated its tips on health were for "all our
readers, white or red" (*Guide* 7.9:2). Regina School had a sporadically
published column aimed at both children in boarding schools as well as
non-Indigenous Sunday schoolers (3.71:11). Shingwauk Home's newspaper began dedicating pages to Sunday schoolers in early 1890, calling
the pamphlet a "Stray Leaf from the Forest" (3.11:129) because the pages
could either be read as part of the original publication or separately
distributed.[18] Shingwauk Home's principal had a strict understanding
of how his newspaper would be taken up: he suggested that one copy
should belong to the head of the Sunday school and a second copy be
kept in the library, with copies bound after one year for reference.

Other articles only addressed students at Indian boarding schools.
One issue of Battleford School's newspaper announced how meals
would now be served simultaneously to staff and students, leaving
the job of monitoring to students. The newspaper suggested that "the
older boys and girls ought to be very pleased to be placed in a position
of trust like this" (*Guide* 4.3:1). A later issue explained, "we trust that
the boys who have been appointed to positions of trust in the School

will feel a sense of the honour and responsibility" and will "fulfill their duties and promote the best interests of the School which is their home" (6.7:1). The newspaper of Rupert's Land School, too, introduced the peer monitoring system to readers, which appeared "to work well, and the pupils appreciated the confidence placed in them. Only two minor punishments have been inflicted during the past three months" (*Aurora* 2.13:1). At this school, student monitors were identified with gold stripes and badges on their uniforms (1.12:3). Unlike more general articles that could apply to all children, pieces such as these directly cautioned Indigenous students not to take this new responsibility lightly, massaging out changes in the school's surveillance in print. Despite the direct address to boarding school students, non-Indigenous readers would also glean from such an update that discipline would still be upheld in the face of shifts in routine.

Our Forest Children featured a column authored by the persona of "Barbara Birchbark," who would answer questions posed by settler Sunday schoolers. The character of Barbara told "all the ins and outs of a pupil's life at the Indian Homes under Mr. Wilson's control" (3.11:129), acting as a fly on the wall for outsiders. Barbara would typically outline a seasonal event, such as Christmas or the beginning of summer holidays. She would then present an individual student who usually did something funny, such as the child who used a parasol to keep the moonlight off her skin (4.5:1) or the child who thought the devil lurked under her table and whom Barbara "could not help laughing at" (4.3:194). Non-Indigenous Sunday schoolers were encouraged to pose questions to Barbara about life at Shingwauk: Do they play sports? Mimic their teachers (4.3:194)? In her first article, Barbara implied boys at Shingwauk (who were only permitted to visit their sisters at the girls' school on Christmas day) lied about having a sibling there (3.11:143). Barbara described how students were "generally very home-sick and unhappy when they first arrive; they don't see any sense in their being taken away from their teepees and their own free prairie life. Probably they think the white people very unkind and unjust, and very meddlesome into the bargain" (3.12:158). Barbara went on to describe how the children "really are very affectionate, these poor, wild, little boys and girls" (3.12:158). While much of the newspaper appears directed at a mixed-child audience, Barbara's column was directed at white students curious about life at an Indian boarding school.

The persona of Barbara Birchbark finds its nearest equivalent in Carlisle School's newspaper and its personae of "Mr. See-it-all" and

"Mr. Man-on-the-Band-Stand" (MOTBS). The personae are speculated to be aliases for Marianna Burgess, superintendent of printing at Carlisle for fifteen years. MOTBS would panoptically comment on small infractions that Burgess spied, mostly concerning students' appearance and behaviour. MOTBS even claimed the power to see inside children's homes after leaving school. For Jacqueline Fear-Segal (2007), MOTBS "combined the characteristics of God, Uncle Sam, and grandfather with those of prison officer, spy, and dirty old man" (p. 207). In his first 1885 appearance in the *Indian Helper*, MOTBS addressed students: "You can't see me but I can see you." Fear-Segal (2007) maintains that the persona "attempted to control, intimidate, and manipulate the children" through surveillance (p. 210).

When Shingwauk Home's principal Edward Francis Wilson visited Carlisle School, he was also struck by the symbol of the bandstand and wrote about it once home: "I mention the band-stand first because the band-stand stands in the centre of the grounds ... [It's] the headquarters of the editor of the little weekly paper called the *Indian Helper*. The *Indian Helper* is edited by 'the man on the band-stand.' And 'the man on the band-stand' is supposed to be surveying from his elevated position everything that takes place at Carlisle" (*Our Forest Children* 3.4:28). Wilson places the bandstand for his readers at the centre of campus, which was the perch of MOTBS. No schools I surveyed had an equivalent to MOTBS, which lasted for fifteen years. The *Indian Leader* from Haskell Institute in Kansas, though, comes close: "Uncle John sometimes takes a tiny notebook from his pocket and begins to write when the children are naughty and call each other names. Afterward he reads aloud to them what he has written. They do not like to hear it, although they know it is true, every word of it. 'For somehow,' as Bess declares, 'it wouldn't have been so dreadful if it hadn't been written down.' Now, whenever Uncle John begins to write in his little book they run to him and say: 'Please don't write it down; we'll not say nay more naughty words'" (1.4.3). Though Uncle John was not incessant, he carries similar elements of surveillance in the figure of a paternal yet threatening male watcher. Battleford School's newspaper ran one article in a similar vein named "Weesarkachark," which is a Cree trickster figure: "Weesarkachark says the loafers on the bridge ought to starve. They work so little that they do not deserve to eat. Weesarkachark sees many holes in boots that might be mended. He does not like to see a lot of Half-breed boys playing baseball on Sunday on the hill. They would be better at Sunday school, like our boys and girls ... Weesarkachark was at church with us last Sunday evening. He was sorry to hear the boys and girls so little" (*Guide* 1.2.1). Like MOTBS, Weesarkachark commands an all-seeing view: from the school's bridge, to a hill off-campus, to inside the church. Weesarkachark prints in the newspaper what he was able to see, including infractions related to religious sloth, appearance, and behaviour. But unlike MOTBS, Weesarkachark only appeared once. As well, MOTBS's persona is that of an old, white man, while Weesarkachark takes its name from Cree traditions and twists this reference to support the school.[19]

Barbara Birchbark lasted only one year. Moreover, Barbara never overtly proclaimed panoptic control like MOTBS did. This is not to say surveillance in newspapers was non-existent, just that it was not issued through a persona. Newspapers often called out particular students for their successes and failures. MOTBS also adopted the persona of an older man; Barbara's persona was of a matronly teacher. Where similarities can be drawn is in how both columns reported the goings-on to readers. Both columns also asked readers to submit questions for personae to answer, locating both the authority to answer and privilege to ask with non-Indigenous readers.

Personae of the Paper

In addition to leaders and readers of newspapers, school newspapers themselves took on personae. As stated, a school newspaper would highlight that living, breathing students created it; at the same time, one of the newspapers' key techniques (and the schools' more largely) was to *de*humanize students. Yet newspapers would extend the category of human to themselves through a persona. When much of the colonial project was bold and bombast, school newspapers represented themselves diminutively. The newspapers of Rupert's Land School, Battleford School, and Kitamaat Home all referred to themselves as a "little paper." Shingwauk Home's publication, too, called itself a "humble little" newspaper (3.1.1) and analogized its beginnings to "launching our frail craft – our Indian bark canoe" (3.3.7).[20] The first issue of Haskell Institute's newspaper explained it debuted "modestly, even shyly" (1.1:2). Its second instalment wished that "by the next issue its modesty will be so far over come that some of the many compliments may be printed" (1.2.2). But in its second year, it still called itself "a timid, modest little two-year-old" (2.19.2). Kitamaat Home's newspaper called itself a "modest enterprise" (9.7) and "an amateur production" (24.3).

Regina School, too, explained it could never "compete with The London Times in editorials, with the great dailies" (15.1:8).

But in the same breath, school newspapers would signal what set them apart: original content rather than "common place matter, culled carelessly from other papers" (*Our Forest Children* 3.3:7). Despite setting themselves up as slapdash, school newspapers such as *Progress* would distinguish themselves from most "local newspapers in the West," which merely derived articles from "some central City office," resulting in a "ready made appearance and warmed-over flavor" (15.1:8). In addition to a persona both denying its quality and yet distinguishing itself from bigger outlets, school newspapers charted their own perceived success by drawing attention to how they grew, for instance from a four- to a sixteen-page paper, and by circulation. Part of this humbling may have been to assure readers the newspaper was not at the expense of other missionary duties. At Kitamaat Home, for example, the principal assured readers the newspaper was not produced at the expense of "more important mission work" (3.1) or the "duties pertaining to Mission life" (24.3). But such a persona – at once humble and innocent yet expanding and powerful – mirrors the persona of settler colonialism more generally.

The personae of newspapers also took literal turns. At a celebration of Haskell Institute's newspaper, the superintendent's wife Ruth Peairs attended wearing a hat and dress constructed of the newsprint. Students would also sometimes dress up as a "printer's devil." The term means both a young printing assistant as well as an invisible scapegoat for errors. A contemporaneous literary guide offers one etymology of the term: a fifteenth-century printer named Aldo Manuzio, credited with developing italic type, the semicolon, and the comma, had employed a "little black boy" who "was believed to be an imp of Satan, and went by the name of the 'printer's devil'" (Cobham Brewer, 1896, p. 860). This anti-Black etymology bears on Haskell students, who would dress up as printers' devils. One came to a reception celebrating printers in a "suit of flaming red" and face paint (*Indian Leader* 2.4:2). At a Fourth of July parade, another student also dressed as a printer's devil "in bright red with horns and tail." The school newspaper reported, "He attracted a great deal of attention and some excitement among small children, who did not wish to be on the same street as 'the bad man'" (6.18:6).

Inverse examples also existed, in which the newspaper was personified and given human traits. Regina School's newspaper stated that it "sometimes grieves 'If anything inanimate e'er grieves'" over former students who "do not seem to have courage enough to embark on the matrimonial sea." *Progress*-the-newspaper, not the voice of a principal or teacher, advises such students to "be courageous" (*Progress* 15.6:4). Inducing students to marry aligns with schools' larger anxieties about students returning to the reserve, and adopting the voice of the newspaper makes the advice sound almost omnipresent, as if through the newspaper the gaze of the school could reach ex-students. Though *Progress* adopted the voice of the newspaper minimally, and most newspapers spoke through the voice of the editor-principal, Kitamaat Home's newspaper *Na-Na-Kwa* consistently adopted the persona of a child. The persona began using the third person: "NANAKWA is no longer an infant of days, as this issue commences its second year. For a young baby it has seen much of the world … As this missionary letter is printed chiefly in the interest of the children's Home, we send it forth in the name of that Saviour who welcomed little children to his bosom" (5.1). Here, the child/newspaper is a baby. Three groups of children get entangled in this passage: the newspaper-as-child, Indigenous children in the school, and the biblical children Jesus was said to have welcomed. There is also a possible allusion to the verse that to enter heaven requires becoming humble like a child (Matt. 18:4).

As the trope continues in a later issue, the voice transforms from the third to the first person, as if to mimic the child/newspaper's ability to now speak for itself: "I am only two … 'one of our younger children' … My publisher has sometimes had to look sadly and almost reproachfully at me, because of a lack of careful arrangement and trimness in my appearance. The truth is, his supply of type has been so meager that it was impossible for me to appear before you in smart attire. But thanks to a donation of type just received, and acknowledged elsewhere, I hope to be more presentable" (9.7). This passage reveals the newspaper's function of acknowledging donations, but in the voice of a child. The newspaper compares itself to students ("one of our younger children") and its type to clothing. Such donations increase the child/newspaper's "usefulness," aligning with the importance schools placed on clothing as symbolic of transformation (Milloy, 1999, p. 124). After a delay, the persona returns:

> I have not been "shut in" but unavoidably "laid aside" for awhile. Now my master is taking me up again and he says I still have a mission to accomplish and so I am going forth once more to visit every continent in this world. It is a far cry "to the ends of the earth" and I am very young to

take such journeys, only 8 years old, but I have a lot of friends. My ocean passage and railway fare are paid. The Post Office Officials take care of me and arrange for my journey and see I reach my destination in safety ... Though I am but a small child brought up in a very lone land and isolated hundreds of miles from my own kith and kin yet I will try and please you and when I see you, tell you what you want to know about my home, the missionary, his family and his friends. (29.2)

Beyond the use of the persona to excuse the delay, the context of the newspaper's production by children cannot be ignored. The persona explains that the delay in the newspaper is not because the child/newspaper has been "shut in," which was a regular occurrence because of sickness, punishment, and estrangement from parents. Similarly, the child/newspaper claims to have grown up "in a very lone land and isolated hundreds of miles from my own kith and kin," not unlike boarding school students. The "age" of the newspaper is eight, a common age for children to be forced to attend school.[21] The persona of the child fits with the humbling and modest tone of newspapers that veils an expansionist, colonial motive underneath. *Na-Na-Kwa* invokes the realities of children dressed inappropriately (culturally and weather-wise) and separated from their families; however, while the children of boarding schools were often denied their humanity, the newspaper's is freely granted.

Barriers to Printing Jobs

In addition to demonstrating progress and offsetting costs, schools boasted how printing prepared students for jobs. But as was the case for Gilbert Bear, who worked at the Chicago fair, these promises were seldom fulfilled. Carlisle School boasted its program could prepare a student to become "an accurate copyist, a careful clerk and a general all-round business man" (qtd. in *Indian Leader* 6.30.4). The school further emphasized its print shop as a site for employment training: "[The student printers] are all learners. To get the work done, is the smallest part of the duties of the advanced printers and instructors. To show how to work takes longer and requires more patience and tact than to do the work oneself. We are a school printing, learning how, from the beginning steps in type setting, and press work up through all the stages" (*Red Man and Helper* 6.30.4). Student printers in the US found work both on- and off-reservation. Daniel F. Littlefield and James W.

Parins (1984) list many successful boarding school printers, including those who established "periodicals that were attempts at Indian unity and were voices for reform in Indian policy" (p. xvii-xviii). K. Tsianina Lomawaima interviewed one such printer named Coleman praising his 1930s training at Chilocco School in Oklahoma: "When I went to [college] I worked in the print shop. Well I felt I was just as good as the next guy. So many times the Indian people feel degraded when they go out and try to mix with the non-Indians, but to me, printing and Chilocco gave me a crutch to adjust" (Lomawaima 1995, p. 162). His observations point to an even bigger benefit than employability – confidence. In Canada print training also led to jobs, as was the case for several students from Birtle and Regina Schools, who found work for "good wages" at the *Regina Standard* (DIA, 1897, p. 310; 1909, p. 385; *Progress* 3.71:7; 3.78:7) and the *Saskatchewan Leader* (14.7:4).

But systemic barriers blocked students wishing to apply what they learned in school. As Washakada School's report for 1897 explained, its two senior printers were "now quite sufficiently advanced to take positions in other offices and to earn their own living, and in fact are only waiting for suitable opportunities to do so" (DIA, p. 275). Why did they have to wait? For one, politicians such as Frank Oliver in 1897 believed the government was "educating these Indians to compete industrially with our own [white] people, which seems to me a very undesirable use of public money" (qtd. in D. Hall, 2009, p. 190). The 1895 annual report for Rupert's Land School also considered the blacksmith and print shop "handicapped" because the tradespeople in the same town "complain that it interferes with their business" (DIA, p. 11). The school attempted to prevent direct competition by distinguishing its printing output from services offered by white townspeople (DIA, p. 11), but inevitably the school could print "very little owing to much opposition from local tradesmen," who did not feel it fair to compete with "government-fed people" (DIA, 1895, p. 366). The threat appears double: such competition included not only a government institution but also one that attempted to lift the "buckskin curtain" (Cardinal, 1999) between Indigenous and white workers. Whatever jobs Rupert's Land School organized for students, it had to "cancel their engagements, as their [white] men will not work beside an Indian any more than beside a Chinese" (DIA, 1895, p. 367), a bold statement considering anti-Asian sentiment at this time. This report came only ten years after the Chinese Immigration Act of 1885, which was an attempt to curtail Chinese immigration through a head tax. This racist legislation appeared in the same year the Canadian Pacific Railway was completed, primarily by poorly paid Chinese labourers initially beckoned to work in Canada until deemed expendable (Cho, 2013, p. 87).[22] The report from Rupert's Land School makes sense through the lens of Iyko Day (2016), whose work expands the binary of white settler and Indigenous person by considering how "mixing alien labor" – which included Black slaves and Asian migrants – "with Indigenous land to expand white property was the basis and objective of settler colonialism" (p. 31). What is more, David Goutor (2011) explains that nineteenth-century Canadian trade unions viewed neither Indigenous nor Black people as significant competition over jobs; this "safe distance" therefore resulted in regarding Chinese labourers in particular as "unfair competition" (p. 44). In her memoir, residential school survivor Bev Sellars also writes of how she uncovered archival letters from businessmen in the 1930s, who complained that they could not compete with the prices underwritten by the free labour of children at the school for such products as harnesses, tack, and vegetables (2013, p. 203). For printing, such "safe distance" appears not to have existed. Washakada Home, however, stated in 1895 that both its shoemaking and printer shops were successful for the same reason Rupert Land School's print shop failed: at Washakada Home, "the town offer[ed] no competition" (DIA, p. 412).

Another context for these employment barriers includes the history of Canadian organized labour. Printer unions are the country's oldest (Forbes, 2012). And though unions were illegal until 1872, "the printing trades had special status based partly on prior existence" (Fetherling, 1990, p. 35). Printers were leaders: the Toronto Typographical Union went on strike in 1872, advocating for a nine-hour work day and legalized unions. As Rutherford (1982) notes, "the militancy of the printers meant the ever-present threat of a work stoppage" (p. 95). By the turn of the century, this power weakened with new technologies that eliminated a need for typesetters (Fetherling, 1990, p. 65). But both the union's power and later weakened position meant nothing for Indigenous printers.

Gilbert Bear provides an example of these barriers to employment as a printer. Gilbert's name appeared often in his school's newspaper, highlighting his superior academic and athletic achievements (see figure 2.8). Before he worked at the world's fair, Gilbert had "sole charge" of the school print shop and seems to have been at times printing the newspaper single-handedly (DIA, 1893, p. 121). Gilbert was so adept at printing, the editor of the *Saskatchewan Herald* called him as "the

Figure 2.8. Gilbert Bear and the Battleford School football team, 1897. Gilbert Bear: Front row, left. NA-299-7, Glenbow Archives.

smartest boy he had ever seen in learning the art of type setting" (qtd in Wasylow, 1972, p. 129). After his three-month stint in Chicago, Gilbert returned to Battleford School as an employee, heading the print shop (DIA, 1894, p. 174; 1895, p. 282). Gilbert later gained a printing job in Ottawa (*Guide* 4.4:1), perhaps because Prime Minister Mackenzie Bowell learned of his work ("After the rebellion," 2012). Eighteen years after Gilbert left school, annual reports still held him up as a great success. A 1913 report continued to cite Gilbert, who made "the most progress, as he has quite a nice trading post, and makes a lot of money" (DIA, 1913, p. 130).

But the school newspaper avoided mentioning Gilbert's fate. Benson's internal 1897 report used the case of Gilbert to prove printing programs were wasted government money. Benson relayed what Battleford School's newspaper also relished to say: Gilbert was a star pupil, had worked in Chicago, and later worked as foreman on the school's press. And, like everyone else, Benson also described Gilbert's job with the *Ottawa Citizen*. But Benson's report went further and noted that for two years in Ottawa, Gilbert had been restricted to working nights and earning only $3.50 per week. Despite a $0.50 raise, Gilbert was unable to pay for lodging or clothing. The 1898 annual report lists that Battleford School still paid Gilbert's living expenses: $6.00 for board, $25.00 for a suit and overcoat, and $5.00 for a Young Men's Christian Association membership (DIA, 1898, p. 679). Benson contended that despite Gilbert's talents, he could not earn more because Gilbert was excluded from the union and was "merely a printer's devil."

During Gilbert's time working at the *Ottawa Citizen*, an ironic employer name given Gilbert's precarious citizenship according to Ottawa, he was fired after a fight with the foreman regarding overtime. The foreman argued Gilbert could not take orders, a suspicious claim given Gilbert's previous success and survival in a boarding school. Gilbert maintained he was being unfairly treated and sought support. Benson intervened twice, negotiating with the proprietor of the *Citizen* to accept Gilbert back. But Benson's report explains that "since the close of the [parliamentary] Session printers are plentiful," and Gilbert was able to return only because Benson was able to pull some strings. Benson predicted that "trouble is likely to occur again as Gilbert is dissatisfied, hates the night work, and if the truth were told, would rather be back home on the Reserve and end his brilliant career of letters" (Benson, 1897, p. 19). Whether or not "brilliant career" was meant sarcastically, Benson's report paints a grim picture of Gilbert's life post-school.

Benson cited Gilbert's life in his report to expose the larger failure of boarding schools, though Gilbert's life was more than that. But the facts remain: Gilbert was the best student a boarding school could possibly produce in all realms – academics, athletics, and trade. He must have been equally personable to be sent as one of few student representatives to the world's fair. Teachers, workers, and even the prime minister recognized Gilbert as the cream of the crop. And yet such talents and hard work could not shatter the larger white supremacy Gilbert faced in Ottawa. He went all the way to Ottawa only to work nights and receive unpaid overtime as a lowly assistant, still having his life paid for by the school. Gilbert's life also reveals how curated reports and school newspapers were: he still received attention in their pages, but the systemic barriers he faced and ultimate failure of the boarding school system to prepare students for work went unmentioned. Even in

Benson's internal report, Gilbert's story is only used to make his more sweeping point that schools should just teach basic skills rather than printing, which prepares students to compete with white workers who will use whatever means necessary (e.g., legal, economic) to ensure such threats were quashed. Benson's report does not highlight Gilbert's story to expose white supremacy, but rather to maintain it. Gilbert's inability to find work represents the broader story of settler colonialism, where the ultimate goal was that Indigenous peoples vanish, not compete for jobs with white workers.

Conclusion

Some of these newspapers lasted only a few years. Printing programs were not even the most significant trade taught at school, often employing just a handful of students. The trade of printing also failed the two principal reasons for teaching a trade: to offset costs of the school and provide future jobs to students, goals thwarted by white workers who had the power to eliminate competition. Even the government, as Benson's report demonstrates, disapproved of printing at schools because it – like a brass band – was only for show. And yet printing programs and their newspapers reveal much about nineteenth-century boarding schools. Newspapers both homogenized and individualized printers. Sometimes such individuation worked against what the newspaper intended: at Kitamaat Home, for example, an article and photograph of its female printers in fact revealed how students still remembered and embodied their relations. For Gilbert Bear, the newspapers were willing to individualize him but only in ways that excluded his resistance: his firm "no," as quoted by local newspapers in their response to his question of whether he enjoyed the fair; his desire to leave Ottawa; and his fight with the foreman. Individuation also extended to the personae of newspapers produced by schools that attempted to dehumanize students. Among leaders and readers, Indigenous printers were leaders themselves, although the newspapers attempted to quell this fact and reduce them only to labour, further foreclosed by white tradespeople and unions. In spite of this history, students had success with printing at school and actively shaped their newspapers.

3 Indigenous Languages Did Not Disappear: English Language Instruction

In his memoir, former student Theodore Fontaine (2010) recalls a teacher's reaction to speaking his language at boarding school in the 1950s. He remembers playing on the floor and acting out a movie he and his friends had seen. When he "inadvertently said something in Ojibway," the nun threatens to wash his mouth out with soap and then pushes him into a closet, where he remained for what "seemed like an eternity" (p. 107). In his desperation, Fontaine does several things: "I clenched my eyes to visualize my cousin Dee and me frolicking at Treaty Point ... I sobbed for a while, to no avail. Eventually [the nun] let me out. Her first word was 'Tiens! (Take that)!' followed by a warning not to speak my 'savage' language." Fontaine portrays the nun's brutality – yelling, washing his mouth, locking him in a closet, and denigrating his language – as well as his mechanisms of survivance.[1] He also reveals the school's policy on language: English mattered more than literacy, which Fontaine demonstrated by replaying the plot of a movie and his ability to speak and understand Anishinaabemowin, English, and the French abbreviation for "tiens, ça t'apprendra!" meaning "There! That will teach you!" The scene further complicates the supremacy of English as the Oblate nun, whose first language was probably French, reprimands Fontaine for not using English by committing the same infraction.[2]

Survivor memoirs and testimony recall bans on and denigration of Indigenous languages at boarding schools throughout the nineteenth and twentieth centuries. Before Canada's Truth and Reconciliation Commission (2008–15), the Royal Commission on Aboriginal Peoples (1991–6) also documented sanctions against Indigenous languages in Canada. Discipline often came in the form of corporal punishment, and frequently at the physical site of language – the mouth and tongue. Some US schools demoted students' "rank" or charged fines for not speaking English, while Shingwauk Home used the *jeton* system in which students began the week with buttons and lost one when they spoke an Indigenous word. Those who retained their buttons each week competed for nuts (Milloy, 1999, p. 39). For survivor Isabelle Knockwood, she had her Mi'kmaw language referred to as "mumbo jumbo" (1992, p. 98).

At the same time schools punished and denigrated Indigenous languages, they vehemently promoted English as a far superior substitute. In addition to classroom-based English instruction, schools also saw trades as an additional way to learn English. Shingwauk Home, inspired by Carlisle School, advised every industrial shop to have a blackboard so students could learn to spell and pronounce names of tools (*Our Forest Children* 3.5:46). Carlisle School even offered courses in industrial English, household English, and farm writing (Carlisle Indian Industrial School, 1915, p. 55). Amanda J. Cobb (2000), in her research on the Bloomfield Academy for Chickasaw Females in Oklahoma, also identifies industrial English as a form of literacy promoted in domestic trades (pp. 14–15).

Out of all trades, some schools saw printing as particularly instructive. Regina School believed that "the printing office is useful in connection with the class-room work, as the printer boys are found to make the greatest progress in spelling and English composition" (DIA, 1910, p. 452). The principal of Battleford School, Thomas Clarke, also saw the school newspaper as "an excellent educator" and a "means of inducing children to write, read and think in English. This is absolutely necessary in order to make 'English' the language of the institution" (qtd in Wasylow, 1972, p. 103). Haskell Institute in Kansas, too, shared this belief in printing as fundamental to English. An article in its school newspaper titled "Printing Helps to Educate" argued that students who learned printing "improve much more rapidly in their language and spelling after they enter the printing class" and learning English while printing "can not be avoided for any advance made in the art educates the boy unconsciously, whether he will it or not" (*Indian Leader* 5.21.4). The article suggests printers learned English almost by osmosis, and printing programs benefited broader literacy goals. Schools could have claimed this to ensure funding for a trade attacked for its showiness, or they could have believed in earnest that printing offered a form of embodied literacy, that laying type, inking, rolling, and assembling a newspaper could transform students into English speakers. Either way, school newspapers accorded with the larger premise of their schools: English *only* rather than English *in addition to* Indigenous languages. That said, newspapers also reveal that students resisted, resignified, and repurposed English in their own ways.

The Ideology of English Only

At most boarding schools, English reigned supreme.[3] So important was English that in 1895 Deputy Superintendent General Hayter Reed went so far as to say Indigenous people were "permanently disabled" without it (DIA, p. xxii-xxiii).[4] The primacy of English had been codified in 1857 with the Act to Encourage Gradual Civilization of the Indians, which held that an Indigenous man who could read and write either French or English was considered to have lost Indian status.[5] Men unable to read or write English but still able to speak were placed under a three-year period of probation, formalizing language training as the cornerstone of assimilation. Of further importance is how "enfranchisement" was crystallized: notice in a newspaper, for all readers to see.

Later in the nineteenth century, English in boarding schools continued to stand in opposition – not in addition – to Indigenous languages. Borrowing terminology from linguist Wallace Lambert, Ruth Spack (2002) notes how in American Indian boarding schools, language acquisition was subtractive (English only) instead of additive (English *and* Indigenous languages). One reason schools taught English was usually not made explicit in newspapers or annual reports; that is, it was meant to sever ties among generations. When students returned home after years of separation, they sometimes could not speak with family. While schools restricted contact between children and their parents, English served as a long-term strategy for breaking family ties. Battleford School's newspaper provided an account of one of its students, who "would reply to his mother in English when she addressed him in Cree – although he was only six, and could talk Cree fluently" (*Guide* 6.3:1). While schools and churches praised the importance of family, while principals discussed their own children in school newspapers, linguistic estrangement was celebrated as an achievement in school newspapers.

The underlying purpose of English existed outside of schools' own stated justifications. School newspapers did not ever state, as Nuu-chah-nulth publisher Randy Fred does today, that attempting to eradicate an

Indigenous language "has always been a primary stage in a process of cultural genocide" (qtd. in Haig-Brown, 1988, p. 15). Nineteenth-century texts did not explain that with the loss of a language goes a world view and culture, resulting in "widespread social and psychological upheaval in Aboriginal communities" (Battiste and Barman, 1995, p. viii).

In particular, school newspapers veil participation in what Robert Phillipson (2013) calls "linguistic imperialism" – when language denigration coincides with other forms of oppression yet appears natural and legitimate (p. 2). If language denigration becomes language death, scholars such as Lorena Sekwan Fontaine (2017), Phillipson, Tove Skutnabb-Kangas (2013), and Andrea Bear Nicholas (2011) refer to the term "linguicide," which is killing a language but not necessarily the speaker. This term emphasizes an agent, whereas terms such as language spread, death, or loss do not. Linguicide as a term and concept is particularly useful given the history of language within the United Nations definition of genocide. In the 1948 draft of the Ad Hoc Committee on Genocide, Article III initially included that genocide also meant the prohibition of a people's language in everyday life, in schools, and in printed publications (Woolford, 2015, p. 25); settler colonial nations including Canada, though, called for Article III to be removed from the official UN definition of genocide.

Studies such as Elizabeth Stuckey's *The Violence of Literacy* (1991) and Catherine Prendergast's *Literacy and Racial Justice* (2003) offer important work on how literacy in the US has been demarcated as white property and denuded of race, class, ideology, and history. These and other studies, however, neglect the history of literacy on the land on which they were created. Other excellent examinations on the history of reading and literacy focus on the moral and political implications of English instruction, but they only minimally consider colonialism.[6] Perhaps such elisions are commonplace because, as Laura E. Donaldson (1998) notes, "English alphabetic writing has become so thoroughly naturalized that its function as a colonial technology has remained obscure" (p. 47). Alistair Pennycook (2002) names some of the typical justifications for teaching English in colonial states, from moral or religious obligations for spreading the gift of English to enforcing capitalism and governing nations better under one common language (p. 20). Carlisle School's principal Richard Pratt (2003) reveals all of these reasons in one sentence: "the sooner all tribal relations are broken up, the sooner the Indian loses all his Indian ways, even his language, the better it will be for him and for the government and the greater will be the economy to both" (p. 266).

School newspapers participated in this narrative of English innocently spreading. In 1897, Battleford School's newspaper featured an article called "The Growth of the English Language." The piece never draws attention to the colonial contexts of the countries sampled – South Africa, India, Canada, and the US – but instead it praises English as like no other language for its "rapid progress" and ability to "absorb" speakers (*Guide* 6.4:2). Newspapers and their schools depicted the "spread" of English, uncomplicated by colonialism. So, if Regina School called English "the language of the country" (1893, p. 98), how did this happen?

One way was through English-only policies at schools.[7] Canada did not have a nationally enforced policy of language instruction in its nineteenth-century boarding schools. In 1894, the Department of Indian Affairs offered a "Programme of Studies for Indian Schools," which provided a basic curriculum similar to public schools (TRC of Canada, 2015b, pp. 300–7). Each grade, called a standard, included departmental expectations for a variety of subjects. Standard I in English, for instance, named skills such as recognizing words, creating sentences, sounding out the alphabet, and copying words. By Standard VI, students were expected to analyse simple sentences, identify parts of speech, and write letters and compositions. In addition to the subject of English, the program of studies also included language-based subjects such as general knowledge, writing, reading, and recitations. School newspapers would often identify students by the standard they were in and discuss activities within standards. Yet enforcement of standards at a federal level was minimal. Instead individual schools developed their own policies, resulting in "a patchwork of differing approaches shifting decade by decade, principal by principal" (Milloy, 1999, p. 185). This approach diverged from the US, which as early as 1880 directly tied government funding of schools to an ability to teach English (Spack, 2002, p. 91). By 1887, US Commissioner of Indian Affairs John DC Atkins went further and forbade Indigenous languages at government-funded schools. A Canadian report from 1897 lamented this lack of formal policy in Canada, praising the US and its "Syllabus of Language work" (Benson, 1897, p. 18). Though Canada never had a national approach, its nineteenth-century boarding schools were surprisingly unified. Most schools instituted English-only policies, which did not actually mean English-only considering that Latin and French were sometimes taught as well. Instead, English-only meant no Indigenous languages.

While most published accounts by survivors about life at school come from the twentieth century, Walter Wasylow's (1972) research includes rare interviews from students who attended Battleford School in the 1890s. While perspectives varied, the one constant is dissatisfaction with the English-only rule.[8] Peter Wuttunee, who began school in 1898, stated, "If there had been no restrictions as far as language is concerned – allowed us to talk our own language and so on, we could leanred [sic] English just as quickly without losing that language" (p. 479).[9] He took as an example the white children of teachers who attended the school too and learned Cree – sometimes "better than Indians." Wuttunee believed the English-only rule "was one of the worst things they can do. It's a blessed thing when you can talk two languages" (p. 463).

It was not just Battleford School that promoted an English-only policy. Government reports reveal schools across a newly forming Canada that proclaimed their enforcement of English and denigration of Indigenous languages, which were often reduced to the singular ("the Indian language") or referred to as dialects rather than diverse, distinct, numerous, fully formed languages. Schools emphasized that the English-only rule existed even during playtime, requiring "teachers and other employees to extend the English lessons beyond the walls of the class-rooms and [industrial] shops into the play ground and work fields" (1892, p. 202). Some schools enforced English most of the time but allowed certain off periods, such as Sunday (DIA, 1896, p. 386) or after supper (1898, p. 332). Kitamaat Home at first enforced English only during meals and sewing lessons (*Na-Na-Kwa* 2.3) but changed to English entirely after finding students "seldom spoke except to say their sentences and answer questions" (6.4). The rule was often impossible to enforce because most students who entered school did not know English and teachers did not usually know students' languages. Edward Metatawabin's (2014) memoir from school in the 1950s provides a first-day account: "'Thisissdalastofdem,' said Sister Wesley to the white man. He pointed to us. 'Kipkawayettverywonn.' I looked at her, panicked, wondering what she had said. The other boys had been murmuring to each other, but they too froze" (p. 36). On his first day, English words are just sounds. Some schools relaxed the English-only rule in response to such realities; others did not.

Schools had various stances on mixing English and non-English speakers. According to Battleford School's newspaper, "The school is divided into ENGLISH SPEAKERS and Indian speakers. Indian speakers eat by themselves and are treated differently" while "English speakers in the School have a Literary and Musical Society now" (*Guide* 1.1.1). Carlisle School formalized such mingling: each dormitory room had three to four children, who all spoke a different language, which helped "in the rapid acquirement of English" but also in breaking up "tribal clannishness" (Eastman, 1935, p. 206). Schools also depended on staff. At Birtle School in Manitoba all staff assisted "in suppressing the use of the Indian language amongst the pupils" (DIA, 1897, p. 285), and at Qu'Appelle School in Saskatchewan teachers were expected to "mingle with the children and to converse with them" (1892, p. 203). Both Battleford and Regina Schools appointed student monitors to police language (DIA, 1889, p. 142; 1898, p. 316). Schools were quick to point out success in English, which meant proving what it had replaced. Battleford School boasted, "The English language is the only one spoken both amongst Cree and Stony pupils. Days together pass at the school without hearing a word of Indian spoken" (DIA 1892, p. 244). The school maintained that many students "never make use of the Cree at all now, although it is their mother tongue" (1898, p. 316).

Schools praised English as a lingua franca, a common language capable of bridging linguistic divides. Shingwauk Home's newspaper quoted the US commissioner of Indian Affairs: "No community of feeling can be established among different peoples unless they are brought to speak the same language" (*Our Forest Children* 2.1:3–4). Regina School similarly observed, "The substitution of the common English language for the multitudinous tribal dialects is establishing among them a bond of unity" (*Progress* 3.83:3). Battleford School believed that because it taught both Cree and Assiniboine speakers, English was "the natural, in fact the only medium of communication" (DIA, 1887, p. 102). One of Carlisle School's newspapers elaborated:

> Here before me are twenty or thirty different tribes of Indians represented, each having a separate language. To compare theirs with the use of English is something like a boy living in a house with one small window. He can see out of the window, but he sees very little of the great outside world; whereas, if he lived in a large house with large windows he could see much more of the world. The boy who speaks only an Indian language, is like the person living in the small house, but the boy who can speak the English language is like the one who lives in the large house. (*Morning Star* 5.9:5)

Battleford School's newspaper, too, presented English as "a new pair of eyes seeing into new worlds" (*Guide* 5.6:4). School newspapers claimed English as an innocuous solution for the supposed problem of diversely lingual Indigenous peoples. But as Phillipson (2013) notes, English is not a true bridge because it "serves the interest of some much better than others" (p. 28). Furthermore, the lingua franca narrative of school newspapers denied the possibility that Indigenous nations had their own solutions to perceived communication barriers. When Carlisle School first opened, Pratt observed the Cheyenne and Kiowa students were learning Sioux, prompting him to institute more strict English-only policies (Eastman, 1935, p. 206). If Pratt desired a true lingua franca, he would have learned Sioux, too.

Schools elided the violence of English that survivor testimony would later reveal. Instead, English is described as natural and painless. Schools claimed students were "giving up their own dialect to adopt the English language" (DIA, 1892, p. 296) and seemed to "have entirely forgotten the Indian language" (1894, p. 149). Other schools attested, "The Indian language is a thing of the past: English is the order of the day" (1894, p. 186). One school made it clear, "No rewards or punishments have been necessary to encourage the English language and abolish the Cree" (1899, 334) and students "seem to prefer English now" (1897, p. 301). Reports stated that schools refrained from "severity" (DIA, 1889, p. 144), "sheer force" (1896, p. 386), and "the fear of the teacher." Instead, schools professed only to have "induced" English with "mere persuasion" (1897, p. 293). Schools framed English as something students voluntarily, naturally adopted and preferred, while they forgot or "gave up" Indigenous languages.

Though these declarations contradict survivor accounts from later boarding school history, they line up perfectly with definitions of settler colonialism. As Lorenzo Veracini (2010a) notes, settler colonialism requires a denial of violence (pp. 75–7). As Audra Simpson (2014) contends, "These nation-states have the gall, the mendacity, and the hyperbolic influence to call and then imagine themselves as something other than dispossessing, occupying, and judicially dubious" (p. 112). The same can be said in terms of how English was taught in nineteenth-century boarding schools. According to school reports and newspapers, English language acquisition just *happened*, without any violence required. But the totalizing fantasy of an English-only school was never so complete, and schools had explanations at the ready. Schools blamed too many new students arriving at once (DIA, 1896, p.

433) and even the students themselves, who were thought to be "rather dull, slow in discarding their native tongue, and show but little interest in the improvement of the mind" (1895, p. 55). Other schools blamed the slow progress of English on proximity to the reserve (1896, p. 303; 1895, p. 388).[10]

School newspapers sometimes chalked up language "deficiencies" to sex. Schools themselves were notoriously segregated so that in co-educational spaces, boys and girls – including siblings – were typically separated from one another in their quarters and industrial training. Other schools were all-boys or all-girls. School newspapers reflected such segregation, grouping student writing by sex and printing articles whose content espoused the heteronormativity and patriarchy of white settler society more broadly. Such articles defined how "the ideal boy is a boy; not a girl boy, nor sprig, but a genuine boy, as nature intended him to be" (*Progress* 3.70:11). Other articles expressed a particular concern about Indigenous girls, whom outside of schools allegedly lived in positions of "servility and degradation," disrespected by Indigenous men (3.71:4). *Na-Na-Kwa* went so far as to say Indigenous girls were "neglected and often ill-treated and tortured. They are not considered equals of men [and] when married become literally slaves" without missionary intervention (8.1). The narrative that white men at schools saved Indigenous girls from Indigenous men extended in school newspapers to English language learning as well. One article reprinted in Battleford School's newspaper quotes a Carlisle teacher who claimed girls could learn as fast as boys, but as they grow older began to plateau "due to the savage customs which force women more and more into the background as she grows in years, and makes her the uncomplaining drudge and slave of the Indian man," which would "tend to dull the intellect as she begins to take on the cares of an Indian woman's life" (5.6:4). Battleford School kept statistics on who spoke English based on sex (*Guide* 1.2.2). Many reports listed boys as faster at acquiring English than girls (1892, p. 203), who were thought to "not show so much willingness to comply with the rule prohibiting the use of the Indian language" (1895, p. 445) and "take no pride in being able to speak English" (1894, p. 186). Girls, according to a teacher at Kitamaat Home, could write English better, but in "work requiring reason and thought power the boys are noticeably more apt" (*Na-Na-Kwa* 12.4). However, because Kitamaat Home educated both boys and girls but only housed girls, the boys "[did] not understand English very well as yet" and had "to pick it up somehow" (29.7). Some of this perceived gap might be attributed to a lack of access to reading material; for example, at Mohawk Institute in Ontario, only the boys' reading room was supplied with the daily newspaper (DIA, 1905, p. 282). But what could have been students' resistance to disavowing their language was often explained away by inability.

Even when schools dubiously reported all students spoke English, they criticized *how*. One way of understanding this phenomenon is through Aileen Moreton-Robinson's (2015) concept of "possessive logics" – rationalizing "an excessive desire to invest in reproducing and reaffirming the nation-state's ownership, control, and domination" (p. xii). When schools emphasized the successes yet limits of students' acquisition of English, they display the logic that schools, not students, ultimately possessed English. Reports pointed out students' pronunciation was "defective" (DIA, 1892, p. 296) and "not yet perfect" (1894, p. 190; 1898, p. 339). Schools would frequently accuse students of not being able to "speak out and read distinctly" (1897, p. 266; 1898, p. 316) and of having a problem with "low speaking" (*Guide* 5.7:3). Battleford School's newspaper admitted, "It would be so much nicer if each [student] would try to read or recite much slower and more distinctly" (*Guide* 4.1:3). Shingwauk Home's newspaper called it "broken English" (*Our Forest Children* 2.4:34). Sources attributed such inability to pronounce English "properly" to students' shame. The inspector's report for Brandon School in Manitoba observed the following: "The only fault I found was the whispering style of reading and in answering questions. Pupils who, when outside, had lungs that could make themselves heard miles off; would only whisper when in school … They could write letters and from dictation very well, and seemed to understand the English, but would not speak it freely" (DIA, 1899, p. 441). Reports for St Joseph's and Qu'Appelle Schools, too, accused children of being ashamed to speak English (1889, p. 144; 1897, p. 303; 1897, p. 303) or too shy (*Na-Na-Kwa* 3.5; *Our Forest Children* 2.12:42; DIA 1889, p. 74; 1891, p. 73; 1899, p. 90). In reviewing a school concert, Battleford School's newspaper concluded, "Some of the children felt a little nervous, this is quite natural, and one of the reasons for encouraging these entertainments is to get every one to overcome this feeling" (*Guide* 4.2:1). Ruth Spack (2002) observes a similar tendency in US schools, which criticized students for being bashful, shy, and having "excessive reserve" (p. 64). One teacher at Carlisle School found students "won't talk! In school with white, English-speaking children, the teacher sometimes found them diffident or somewhat slow" (Eastman, 1935, p. 227).

Schools regulated not only what students read and wrote but also how they spoke.

Students certainly could have been nervous or shy, particularly given that they had to speak and sing in front of crowds, which included unsympathetic teachers. And these reports reveal more. For one, they suggest schools expected a certain kind of speaker, steeped in the rhetoric and style of British schoolchildren, recalling the refrain, "Speak up, child!" As well, labelling students ashamed or nervous denies their possible fear of or resistance to English. Furthermore, these claims reinforce the concept of "pure English." The school at Wikwemikong praised students for "speaking remarkably pure English and singing in a pleasing English accent" (DIA, 1889, p. 74). Yet Andrea Sterzuk's (2011) research disrupts the idea of "pure English." She takes aim at how Englishes (she avoids the terms "dialect" and "non-standard English") are spoken by contemporary Indigenous students in Saskatchewan, and at how white teachers view these language varieties as deficient and in need of correction. So English – in the nineteenth century and now – is not only *what* was spoken but how.

Such critiques of students' speech, blamed on slowness, nerves, and diffidence, accords with Frantz Fanon's (2008) "colonial situation." As interpreted by Eric Cheyfitz (1997), in Fanon's conception the "native speaker must speak like a native or, more precisely, like the master's conception of how a native speaks" (p. 126; Spack, 2002, p. 148). Visitors to Alert Bay School expressed "surprise that the children can converse in the English language" (DIA, 1897, p. 319). Regina School's newspaper, too, explained, "Visitors to school frequently ask concerning the pupils: 'Do they speak English?'" (*Progress* 13.3:5). Some schools adopted a pedagogy of humiliation when it came to reading aloud. Some newspapers reported how the "dialect" of students was "laughable" (*Our Forest Children* 4.6:242) and would "afford much amusement in [students'] attempts to speak" (*Na-Na-Kwa* 9.4). One former student wrote how he had failed twice to deliver a speech, and now as he attempted to write for the newspaper he felt "as though I were on the platform in the school room. and you all laughing at me" (*Progress* 14.4:6). Another student entry in the newspaper, though, noted that "if anyone laughs at you while you are reading, don't care much, but just try to do the best you can" (*Guide* 4.9:1). Students likely did speak English differently from their teachers since they were mostly new to the language. They also were possibly nervous and shy given the public arenas in which they had to speak. They also may have been resisting

speaking English, exhibited by silence and "low speaking," by scream-
ing in the schoolyard but refusing to speak to teachers. They may have
been making English their own. But according to Fanon, even if none
of this were true, the teachers and officials would likely still hesitate to
concede mastery given the English language's longer history as white
property.

Schools further decried students who merely memorized English,
blaming their supposed inability to "know" the language on intellect.
One internal report criticized "the slow progress in English made by
the pupils, who althoug [sic] able to repeat sentences in English off their
book, do not understand what they read" (Benson, 1897, p. 34). Koote-
nay School thought its students' writing was strong only because "some
are gifted with memory" rather than because of intellect (DIA, 1894,
p. 194). Peigan School, too, found that "writing, being purely mechanical, seems to be easily learnt," but reading and English were not (1895,
p. 388). Indian agent W.M. Laing-Meason, too, wrote that in terms of
writing, students had "a natural gift of imitation in this respect, far more
developed than in white children" (1892, pp. 248–9). The report further explained students' copybooks were clean and free of inkblots, but
that "their ignorance of the English language" kept them from understanding what was on the page. Kitamaat Home, as well, reported the
children's "especial talent is imitating" (*Na-Na-Kwa* 12.4). A journalist
who visited Rupert's Land School also remarked after viewing student
writing that "the tendency to imitate is strongly developed in the Indians" (*Aurora* 2.20:1). For schools, it was not enough for students to print
English and read it, they had to understand it too. However, schools
often attributed students' supposed lack to a biologically determined
ability of imitation, not intellect. Like speaking, schools regulated and
questioned whether students actually "knew" English. These ideologies behind boarding school language instruction help to frame what
school newspapers reported when it came to English.

Pedagogies, Tools, Technologies

School newspapers frequently shared with readers how students
were learning the English language at schools. Shingwauk Home, for
instance, published student examinations on the difference between
the possessive plural and the possessive singular. One exam that was
published in an annual report asked students to parse a sentence. In
this exercise, the answer required students to atomize the word "boys"

into a common noun, masculine gender, plural number, third person, possessive (DIA, 1887, p. 27). In addition to grammar, school newspapers condemned simple memorization of English. As an article originally published by Regina School and later reprinted by Battleford School put it, "Parrot like repeating must be closely guarded against" (*Guide* 5.7:3). The article promoted the "look and say" method (5.7:3), an approach popular in the mid-nineteenth century that advocated memorizing whole words as opposed to later developments in phonics (Pearson, Barr, and Kamil, 1996, p. 585). It also commented on better reading materials to prevent "sluggish minds and a famine of ideas." The article advised teachers to "use newspapers. Refer frequently to the library that should be in every school. Have everything reproduced in writing. Pressing necessities in the teacher were: An encouraging tone of voice, simple language and frequent and patient reviewing" (*Guide* 5.7:3). In this take on how to teach English, sight reading with constant review was best. But more than rote learning, students needed to be informed by bigger ideas from newspapers and the library.

School newspapers often specified the type of literature read at schools. The Bible is mentioned frequently, as are books donated to schools. Cherie Dimaline's novel *The Marrow Thieves* (2017) connects reading the Bible at residential school to attacks on Indigenous languages, describing the practice as "stories about a book that was like a vacuum, used to suck the language right out of your lungs" (p. 107). At Regina School, a teacher from Poole, Ontario, would "accumulate from week to week bundles of reading matter and then forward them to the school" (*Progress* 3.70:7). Readers of Battleford School's newspaper also donated bookmarks, books (*Guide* 4.9:1), Bibles, and newspapers (4.6:2). School newspapers also contained poetry by well-known writers such as E. Pauline Johnson (*Our Forest Children* 3.10:119), Alfred Tennyson (*Progress* 18.2:1), Owen Meredith (*Progress* 3.71:12), and Rudyard Kipling (*Guide* 6.4:2; *Progress* 3.80:1; 3.83:1). Newspapers also featured lesser-known poetry extolling Christian virtues (*Guide* 4.1:1; 4.2:1; 4.3:1; 4.5:1; 4.6:1) and colonialism, with titles in *Progress* that included "Clear the Way!" (3.71:1), "My Canada" (3.79:1), "A Glorious Land" (14.7:1), and "The Indian's Faith" (16.9:1). But what appears to be more frequently read were not books but newspapers. In addition to other school newspapers, students read the periodicals *Boys' Own* and *Girls' Own*, which at Mohawk Institute were listed as the students' favourites (*Our Forest Children* 2.13:13). These publications were relentlessly colonial in theme (Dunae, 1980), with articles named "The Red Man's Revenge" (1879),

"Adventures of a Boston Boy among Savages" (1880), and "Perched Up behind a None-Too-Clean Indian" (1892). One article (1880) attributes the decline of buffalo to Indigenous greed. Often, reading material not only didn't reflect Indigenous students' experiences, it also required their identification with white narrators to make any sense. To have an "Adventure with the Apaches" (1894) assumes you are not Apache; to have "My First Sight of Wild Indians" (1879) implies the anticipated reader is non-Indian. Importantly, we do not know from school newspapers how students were interpreting these texts.

In addition to reading materials, newspapers also reported how schools taught English through avenues such as literary societies. Schools conceived of the societies as an entertaining way for students to "express their ideas" and for teachers to see "in what direction their efforts should be exerted" (*Guide* 4.9:1). The clubs of Regina and Battleford Schools met every Friday night. About thirty boys and girls would gather to read essays on different subjects, including law and school, drinking, sleeping, and the police (*Guide* 1.1:1; *Progress* 3.73:7). Regina School incorporated music and students' own stories (*Progress* 3.70:7). Newspapers also promoted school debate clubs. Regina School hosted debates on whether "Indians were happier before the coming of the white man." Importantly, students were "affirmative, but not unanimous" (*Progress* 3.74:7). The most formalized debate club was the Onward and Upward Club at Shingwauk Home. As Sharon Wall (2003) describes it, "Political socialization, initiation into the democratic process and religious instruction were combined and represented in an entertaining atmosphere" (p. 12). The club had its own constitution and positions, such as chairman and secretary ("some Indian boy that writes a nice, clear hand"), all filled by students except the president, who was the principal (*Our Forest Children* 4.2:177–8). Meetings also included a "curator," who would "prepare the room." The club's committees crafted the weekly program and chose "handiwork" that members would create during the meeting (e.g., carving picture frames, netting, and woolwork), which the school would later sell (DIA, sessional paper, vol. 10, 1890, XXIII, p. 23). Each grade had its own membership card with responsibilities. It appears girls were allowed to participate given that the certificate of full membership addressed "our brother (or sister)." The club would occasionally throw socials for the public, and revenue would be put towards special purchases, such as instruments.

One of the Onward and Upward Club's main endeavours was to encourage English. Students were expected to "make acquaintance with useful literature," "learn the art of elocution," "carry on a debate," and "encourage self-reliance in speaking publicly in English" (DIA, 1888, p. 124). Other officers' roles included a correspondent, who would write and read letters from other branches of the club (i.e., Carlisle School). Another role included that of news reporter, who would bring forward "readings, speeches, dialogues, debate, general discussion." Then, the appointed "critic" would "criticise the Speeches, songs, etc. at the close of each meeting." At the end, the critic was "called upon for his criticism of the evening's performance" (*Our Forest Children* 4.2:178).

Barbara Birchbark's column described one Onward and Upward meeting for readers of Shingwauk Home's newspaper. One night, a boy read the Charles Mackay poem "There's a Good Time Coming": "There's a good time coming, boys, a good time coming. We may not live to see the day, but Earth shall glisten in the ray of the good time coming. Cannonballs may aid the truth, but thought's a weapon stronger: We'll win our battle with its aid – wait a little longer" (1892, p. 303). As the column reported it, one student began reading the poem but could not finish. Instead another boy, with the "most melancholy disposition possible" and who "always looked unhappy, no matter what was going on," joined in to ease tensions. From Birchbark's perspective, the first student "got on swimmingly for some time, then he faltered, got red[,] blurted out 'There's a good time coming, boys,' and stopped short. But the melancholy boy was equal to the occasion, and amid the profound silence, remarked in his usual doleful tone, 'He tell lie, that fellow'" (4.2:178). In this club, designed for students to practice English, one student could not continue. Birchbark can only narrate this scene as his failure – he falters, reddens, stops. She frames the "melancholy" boy, though, as successful because he punctured the "profound silence." But he did more than fill the room with English; he called the poem a lie, perhaps offering others a chance to contemplate the poem in relation to themselves. The newspaper chooses not to correct his grammar – "he tell lie" – undermining his boldness just as Birchbark writes him off as miserable. Regardless, his message remains despite the newspaper's larger focus on exhibiting the club's civilizing purposes. Students had their own reactions to and reasons for learning English.

Newspapers also reported various technologies that schools used to teach English. At Shingwauk Home, students practiced English by operating a telegraph. Up to six boys learned the telegraph as one of many trades at the school (*Our Forest Children* 3.2:6). Telegraph posts and wire connected the school's hospital to the principal's office and his bedroom, and students printed the messages on carbon paper. Students had frequent exchanges through the telegraph with one another and practiced both sending as well as receiving (4.3:195); they learned how to send telegrams "in proper form" (3.2:6) and how "to manipulate the key" (3.1:48). The principal, Edward Francis Wilson, wrote of one telegraphic exchange between him and the school captain, Albert Sahguj:

> The instrument is on a shelf just at my back, and I twist round on my screw-chair and respond … "I, I, I am here in my office waiting to hear what you have to say." The telegram delivers itself – From Albert Sahguj, Captain's room, to MR. Wilson. "Please, is there to be inspection to-day?" I repeat the question to shew that I understand it – which is the best way for amateurs. Sahguj says "O.K. sig. A.S., 7" – which means all right, followed by his signature and the number of words in the sentence. Finding it to be all right, I respond[,] "O.K., sig. E.F.W." Then I give him my answer "No, not to day; all keep at work." After "O.K.," again on both sides, and signature, I say "G.N." (good night), and Sahguj responds "G.N." That means, I am leaving the key; – "we always say 'good night'" on the telegraph – whatever time it may be. (3.3:6)

Though these descriptions of telegraph lessons represented for readers yet another trade being taught, they also exemplified new literacy skills. In the newspaper, Wilson details how he taught students – "amateurs" – to communicate over the telegraph using new phrases, signatures, and Morse code. Like the production of newspapers, the telegraph served as another way to learn English through technology.

Other technologies of literacy mentioned in school newspapers were distinctly visual. Rupert's Land School retold tales of Bo Peep, Blue Beard, and the Chinese Giant with Mrs Jarley's wax figures (*Aurora* 3.26:3). The classroom had posters from *Pall Mall Budget* magazine (3.27:2) and displayed donated posters that would "tell an interesting story[, which] stimulate eye and brain far more effectually than any abstract theme" (3.27:2). Rupert Land's School had students in Standard II write compositions based first on images (3.26:4). As one newspaper said, "the eye, telegraph Station No. 1, must be trained to see correctly" (3.25:2).

Another technology school newspapers discussed was the magic lantern, a seventeenth-century Dutch invention that was an early iteration of the slide projector and could project paintings and photographs

(Barber, 1989, p. 73). At boarding schools, magic lantern shows appeared to be a treat (*Guide* 6.5:1; *Na-Na-Kwa* 30.2) and seemed significant enough for students that they wrote about it in school newspapers. One student entry explained how "last Thursday we had Magic Lantern, we saw Elephants and Mr. Heron [the principal] has gone to File Hills to give a Magic Lantern. And all of us little girls have short hairs" (*Progress* 17.9:7). Here, the magic lantern was as worthy of mention as the girls' haircuts. As countless survivor testimonies reveal, schools were fanatical about cutting children's hair (J.R. Miller, 1996b, pp. 194–8), resulting in traumatic experiences for students whose hair had great significance. Sarah Soonias, who was five when she began at Battleford School in 1900, recalls in an interview decades later that the first punishment for speaking Cree was a strapping, but "when girls were very bad and persisted in speaking Cree, they had their hair cut short as a punishment" (Wasylow, 1972, p. 454). In this case, haircuts were a graver punishment than getting strapped.

The magic lantern shows at Regina and Battleford Schools appear to be of two categories: English and Others. In the English shows, students watched scenes from the Bible (*Progress* 4.8:1; 3.71:7), the royal family (*Guide* 4.8:1), and English architecture, of tales such as Cinderella and Dick Whittington, and "numerous views of natural phenomena [and] cities" (DIA, 1892, p. 243). In the shows of Others, students saw scenes of elephants (*Progress* 17.9:7) and the "customs of foreign lands" (DIA, 1892, p. 243). Students also watched "scenes of Indian sundances" (*Guide* 4.8:1). The Sun Dance was banned under the Indian Act from 1895 to 1951 (Pettipas, 1994), and this particular show was from 1897. I do not read the magic lantern show of the Sun Dance as evidence of an inclusive curriculum or a challenge to legal sanctions. Projecting images of the Sun Dance and discussing it in the school newspaper reiterated who had the power to discuss and showcase Sun Dances – not Indigenous peoples, who were prosecuted for doing so, but boarding schools. Furthermore, the shows exhibited a ceremony alongside scenes of entertainment, such as Cinderella. The magic lantern attempted to render the Sun Dance as foreign, like an elephant, instead of intimate and familiar, which it may have been for Indigenous students on the prairies. It appears, though, on at least one occasion at Regina School that two students were permitted "to explain in their own language the meaning of the pictures" from a magic lantern show "to our Indian visitors" (*Progress* 18.1:7). It is unclear how common such an occasion would have been or what the students and "Indian visitors" discussed concerning the images.

Schools further promoted an English-only environment by showcasing student writing in their newspapers, often in glowing terms. As the newspaper at Rupert's Land School stated, "the penmanship of youthful Indians is nearly always superior to that of white children who have had similar advantages" (*Aurora* 1.12:1). One recurring form of writing was the home letter. Many former students recount how letters were written as a class exercise and never made it home, were redacted, and were forged (Cobb, 2000, p. 87; Hare, 2009, p. 255; Johnston, 1989, p. 138; Lomawaima, 1995, p. 24; Pokiak-Fenton and Jordan-Fenton, 2010, pp. 60, 64; Sellars, 2013, p. 68). Brenda Child (1999) examines archival letters between parent and child at the Flandreau School in South Dakota. In Child's study, officials censored incoming and outgoing mail (p. 39) and cut off communication even when children were sick or dying (p. 67). Her research reveals, though, that parents were relentless, continuing to write letters threatening to report abuses to authorities (p. 42). For Child, these letters "speak for the deepest of bonds, able to survive separation and efforts to undermine American Indian families" (p. 100).

But school newspapers usually framed home letters as evidence of literacy skills rather than as a connection between parent and child. When home letters appeared in newspapers, they typically appeared with prefaces. These opening sentences assured readers "this letter was written by a little boy who has only been a short time in the Home, and could not speak a word of English when he came" (*Our Forest Children* 4.4:209), or that the "following is a specimen letter from a Kitamaat boy, who, until two or three years ago, spoke only Kitamaat" (*Na-Na-Kwa* 30.13). These statements directed readers to consider the letter not as content but as evidence of progress in English, no matter how emotional or private. Carlisle School reported, "In the 217 original home letters written by our students this month, some of which were good length, only 116 words in all were misspelled, showing that 101 of them were perfect in orthography" (*Morning Star* 4.10:3). One student's intimate published letter explained he was sick with a chest cold and thinks of passed away relatives, but the newspaper's preface only mentions that "the handwriting is clear, firm and distinct. The characters are well formed and the punctuation marks and capitalization correctly placed in most cases" (*Aurora* 1.8:3). In an extreme example, Kitamaat Home published a letter from a former student asking the principal, George Raley, for help: "Please sent, me milson [medicine] for me Because I am got sick all time and my wife got sick to an my In law mother to get sick every time, my heald sick and my heart sick and all my skin out side you sent me all sam Blood drink milson and all sam like my wife mil-son all sam you give him in Kitamaat that time he was sick like Black milson, and milson for that outside skin" (*Na-Na-Kwa* 4.2). The letter appears desperate. The writer as well as his wife and mother-in-law are all hurting in the heart, head, and skin. He asks Raley for medicine, a request Raley admits was "not uncommon." Other articles in *Na-Na-Kwa* present desperate situations, but Raley would typically summa-rize the problem rather than sharing personal communication, and he would directly ask readers for something specific, such as money for a wheelchair or a new woodstove. Raley prefaces the letter: "Consider-ing the fact that the young man who wrote the request had but little advantage in the way of school, it is very good." In this example, Raley published the letter not to advocate for help, not to demonstrate the damage of colonial policies, but as evidence of English usage for read-ers. Though it could have been published to seek donations, the let-ter deviates from other attempts that direct readers how to help. As well, other appeals to readers typically do not comment on the person's capacity to write English.

School newspapers published many examples of classroom work, including answers to grammar examinations. But I see the publication of home letters as a particular violation. These letters are addressed not to the newspaper, the principal, or to fellow students, but to parents – who were often not able to see their children and whose attempts to communicate with their children frequently were met with censorship and sanction, who may not have received these newspapers, and who may not have been able to read English. Though writing a letter to par-ents is a typical exercise in elementary school and summer camp, it is particularly cruel in this context given the enforced separation between parent and child. Why are these letters addressed to parents when sur-vivor testimony throughout boarding school history highlights a lack of communication? When the intended audience of these newspapers was not exclusively parents? Perhaps publishing these letters suggested to readers across Canada that children were hardly suffering and were not completely estranged from their families. I doubt this because sur-rounding content within the newspapers reinforced that contact with parents prevented progress. Maybe the letters were addressed to par-ents as a motivation for children to write more than they would to any other recipient. Or perhaps the parental addressee offered further proof of the letter's veracity, because students were likely to write more truth-fully about life at school.

Many letters praised the school. One to an uncle called Shingwauk Home "a very good place" (*Our Forest Children* 3.10:120). Letters highlighted academic success (2.9:20), band performances (4.4:210), and Christianity, as well as baseball, marbles, and swimming (3.7:75). One published letter declared "we are all happy, and enjoying ourselves." Kathleen Buddle (2001) suggests such uniformity could be attributed to students' limited vocabulary, but more likely it was censorship (p. 89). Students could have also been sincere, as Child's (2014b, pp. 274–5) work urges us not to dismiss. Other letters, though, deviated from the script. One student mentioned that school was "almost like home" (*Our Forest Children* 3.7:75), but not quite. Another student wrote, "When the school commenced it was hard for me to learn at first. While learning my lessons the thoughts would come to me of the good times that I had. I am all right now" (2.9:20). One published letter asked a parent to send apples and money, perhaps because of schools' notorious lack of food. Another student asked a parent to "please will you send me one dollar to spend in the winter, and sometimes I am quite lonesome … If you send me some money I will take my picture [to] send you" (3.7:76). Other student letters describe thoughts of parents and hopes for reunion (3.10:120). One letter stated: "Dear father: I am writing to you to let you know that I am quite well. I was very sorry to hear that Mary had a sour leg. I hope she is getting better. I can read Indian letter just as well as English letter, so you can write to me in Indian if you like … Everything is going on well in the Shingwauk Except P – is in the jail yet – Shingwauk jail, and I am the jailer. I will not tell you what he done as you know all about it. I must now close my letter, I am, your dear son" (3.10:120). In this letter, the student tells both his parents and the newspaper's readers that he has some communication from back home (he learns of Mary's leg and assumes his parents already know the news about P). He also refers to the school's jail. In an earlier issue, another student also referenced "one boy in jail" (3.7:75), and an additional letter detailed how two boys ran away, were caught eighty miles away, and the trial was soon to begin. The student explains, "Judges and jury are by the boys; no white people to be present" (4.4:210). In these instances, students allude to punishment at Shingwauk as well as student resistance in the form of running away. The student boldly announces he can still read and write his Indigenous language, and if his parents prefer, he will write them that way.

It is difficult to determine whether these published letters reached parents. Carlisle School wanted to minimize "the impression that all letters written by our pupils are carefully examined before they are allowed to go in the mail. This is not the case. All are free to write wherever they please and as often as they please." Instead, it maintained, the only letters examined were "those written at the close of each month as a school exercise" (*Morning Star* 5.7:7). Survivor testimony confirms letters were indeed censored, but it is possible letters published in the newspapers were never meant to reach parents. Regardless, these letters written to parents were made public, for everyone to read. They appear to have been fodder for the newspaper, evidence of English rather than a genuine concern for parent-child contact. In a school newspaper much later, in 1955, one student openly questioned the censorship of home letters, asking in the newspaper: "Why does the Father Principal read the letters sent out or received by the children?" (*Moccasin Telegram* 13.2). The principal defended the practice, answering that it was "to check the content, and in so doing, avoid trouble that may arise from certain letters to certain persons." The principal compares himself to "a vigilant father" who "should check his children's relations." He either missed or was aware of the irony – that his admitted censorship in fact disrupted relations. It appears that by the mid-twentieth century, censorship of home letters could be openly questioned by students but also admitted and defended by the school. In the late nineteenth-century, on the other hand, school newspapers denied any censorship and directed readers to focus on published letters as examples of English.

In addition to letters, school newspapers exhibited student compositions. These essays, too, were prefaced and were said to be "without any alteration" (*Na-Na-Kwa* 16.11; 17.7), were "first attempts" and "very crude" (1.3), reprinted "just as they are handed in" (26.3). As was the case with letters, newspapers directed readers to consider student work as evidence of "the difficulties which have to be surmounted by the native children in the study of English" (1.3). Many student essays published in the newspaper mirrored larger goals also expressed by government reports. One student piece compared the lives of two boys: one "wild and reckless" who later becomes a gambler, the other an "obedient" boy who attends boarding school and grows up to own a clean home, an example of those who "try to do right and take advantage of the Government's kindness" (*Guide* 6.9:1). Another essay explains Indigenous children have inherited from "the old Indians" a tendency to be cruel towards animals. According to the piece of writing, Indigenous children "like to see the things being hurt" and are "fond of doing it" (3.4:30–1). In contrast, the newspaper stated, "Not many white boys are cruel."

But other student essays resist the colonial narratives of the school newspaper. One composition from Kitamaat Home described how Indigenous Elders – the "Old People" – were lazy and only attended church for the singing. However, students also wrote, "The old people are very funny they always make us laugh when they go up [to] the home [at the school] and they want to tell a story to the girls" (*Na-Na-Kwa* 22.4). The humour and storytelling of the children's Elders likely *had* to be framed as evidencing their laziness, just as the students could not call them family or grandparents – only "the old people." Shingwauk Home's newspaper published student pieces on the "pleasures and hardships of life at the Shingwauk." Students wrote of pleasures such as playing, hunting, games, skating, and Christmas celebrations (1.12:3). Some student compositions detailed the hardships of misbehaving children and the shame of one fellow student going to jail (1.12:4); one student even claimed he "cannot tell anything about hardships I don't think there is any hardships at all" (1.12:3). Another student, though, declared, "The hardship of our life at the Shingwauk, is on account of sickness. One of our fellow pupils had a fever, and several others had another kind of sickness." Though the rest of the composition explains the biggest hardship is Wilson's in running the school, it does expose the illnesses rampant at school that newspapers often left unacknowledged.

Some shorter compositions in Battleford School's newspaper reveal lighter stories. One entry attributed to a student in grade 3 explained how a classmate had made a mountain out of sand and dug a hole in the middle. The teacher "put some stuff in this hole and it began to hiss and spit, and all at once a bright flame shot out. One of the boys shouted: Vesuvius! And I am sure it was like it" (*Guide* 6.9:1). Another entry detailed how two boys "went to kill rats on Battle River we could see the rats under the ice swimming in the water we did not get any of them but had plenty of fun the ice broke and Tom Crow got into the water it was deep enough to give him a good ducking and he just looked like a drowned rat himself" (7.4:1). One more note describes how when one student "went to [the] slide last night I saw a dog running by me and I ran after it and it ran away. The dog's tail was long and it ran fast" (7.7:1). *The Aurora* also published a short account attributed to a student in Standard IV, who described how she would "often carry about the little puppies. I cover mine with my apron. I come into the dining-room to get some food for him; I hold the piece of meat in my hand, and he jumps up and barks till he gets it. I sing to him till he shuts his little eyes. Once I put a piece of candy on my hand, and he licked it up. Sometimes we wrap them up in clothes, and nurse them like little babies. We like them very much" (2.21:4). These compositions were likely offered in the school newspaper as evidence of progress in English. Yet they also reveal humorous and sensitive writing by children under extraordinary conditions who poked fun at their classmates and wrote creatively, who may have learned English for the first time at school and used it to express something of their time as students.

Other compositions from Kitamaat Home focus less on school life and more on creative imaginings. These stories offered readers scenes of shape-shifting and metamorphosis. They often concluded with the lesson that things are not always as they seem, developed through tales of animals and humans alike. Student stories regaled readers with tales about bears that ate too much seaweed and a family who picked berries and encountered wolves. Essays described a king's daughter who was offered a brooch and a hand in marriage, but she later discovered the brooch was a crab claw and the suitor a bear. Students created stories about a man who was actually a serpent and a woman who was really a bear (26.3–4), as well as a "coast ghost story" (15.9). A piece of writing attributed to the chief's daughter described how to dry salmon (3.7). It is unclear whether children retold stories they heard from family or based them on their own experiences. Students may have also been inspired by reading materials from school. Regardless of how students came upon their ideas, these compositions depart from the rest of *Na-Na-Kwa* and its reports on colonial development and Christian missionaries. Though school newspapers prefaced writing by students as examples of progress in grammar and spelling, this work punctured the newspaper's more predictable storylines of assimilation.

English And

This final section distinguishes between how school newspapers represented English *only* compared to English *and* – English in addition to Indigenous languages. This differentiation critically separates the policies of government and school from the beliefs of many parents and children, who learned English for their own reasons but not at the expense of another language. Lisa Brooks (2008) observes how colonialism meant Indigenous peoples adapted their literacy practices: "Birchbark messages became letters and petitions, wampum records became treaties, and journey pictographs became written 'journals'" (p. 13). As Jan Hare (2009) writes, "Aboriginal people were very aware of the changing word, and Western literacy was seen to offer a gateway, indeed *the* gateway, to the newcomer's world" (p. 244). But schools dimmed this distinction, even as late as the 1970s when an article from the Halifax *Herald-Chronicle* quoted a mother who appreciated learning English at boarding school but did not want her children to lose Mi'kmaw. The headline and the rest of the article, though, interpret her perspective as English *only* rather than English *and* (M.C. Anderson and Robertson, 2011, p. 169). Nineteenth-century school newspapers also attempted to flatten the difference, though student entries often upheld it.

School newspapers reported students developing a love of reading English. Battleford School claimed its students exhibited a "strong desire" to learn English (DIA, 1892, p. 244). Regina School's newspaper reported how students read books until they became "somewhat dilapidated in appearance" (*Progress* 3.72:5) and that "our school libraries are used to advantage outside of school hours" (DIA, 1896, p. 349). One student entry explained,

> There are different ways of reading. In order to get some good out of what you are reading, you must read slowly, and get everything that you can squeeze out of each word, verse, or paragraph, into your head, before it runs away. Do not pass a verse just because it looks simple but study it carefully and you might get what you are looking for, or get something better than it. (17.11:6)

Another issue asked readers for donations of reading material, revealing students' love of books. The newspaper explained that at the school "there are awakened and hungry minds to feed as well as mouths to fill and bodies to clothe ... If people saw Indian pupils at night perusing and enjoying their books and papers they would be both pleased and surprised. They are surely getting ready for citizenship" (*Progress* 3.70:8). The rest of the article claims that the right kind of texts are capable of awakening and feeding the mind, laying a foundation for good character, increasing the efficacy of missionaries, and creating citizens. But it also exhibits the image of students voraciously reading. Though the literature supplied at boarding schools promoted a colonial agenda and reports asserted that the "love of reading" led to citizenship and good Christian character, Brendan Edwards' (2005) work reminds us that Indigenous peoples constantly negotiated how non-Indigenous literacy practices were to be incorporated (p. xii). With reports of students who love reading, spending nights in the library and wearing down books until "dilapidated," students were not necessarily reading for the reasons the school had in mind.

Students also wrote how learning English could benefit them and their communities. In 1892 the Oblate priest Father LeJeune wrote that Indigenous peoples learned English "too soon for their own good" and should not be taught English but should "learn it how they may, and as late as possible" (qtd. in Haig-Brown, 1988, p. 35). LeJeune implied English led to contact with white people, who would cause harm. But in a Carlisle School student's letter to his father, published in the school newspaper, the student entry cites English as both a great language and a method of protecting land rights. He tells his father: "Suppose any white man goes to your place and tries to drive you away, could you stay if you don't understand him or unless you can talk as well as he can?" (*Morning Star* 5.7:8). Unlike LeJeune, some children's perspectives in school newspapers suggested the answer to avoiding white manipulation was not to stay away from but rather to *learn* English.

Students' compositions in newspapers further cited English as helpful in learning about the rest of the world and gaining employment (*Progress* 17.11:5–6). One composition declared that when students learn to read, "they can read letters sent to them by their friends; never mind how far they may be." Students also explained that reading helped pass the time and if someone was "sad he can read some interesting story that will make him forget his troubles" (17.11:6). Another student entry stated the student liked "to learn the Alphabet so as when I go home and when some of my friends is sick and come to ask me to read to them out of the bible I can so" (*Our Forest Children* 1.10.13). Battleford School's newspaper printed that "one of the boys tried to impress upon the pupils how necessary it is for all of them to learn the English language properly for their own future welfare and usefulness" (*Guide* 4.8:1). Students may have even treated English language learning as the key to leaving the school and returning home. To this end, Regina School's newspaper stated: "One of our younger pupils is anxious for an early honorable discharge from the school. He says he has now 'caught on to the English language perfectly'" (*Progress* 3.83:7). Though the newspaper framed this tidbit as humorous, it reveals an understanding that knowing English meant being able to leave. It is impossible to know whether entries attributed to students were truly written by students; however, in these compositions, reading was less about the civilizing projects the school proclaimed in annual reports but instead a means of employment, for keeping in contact with those far away, providing spiritual comfort, and surviving school. One of the topics of Battleford School's literary society meeting was "English Speaking" (*Guide* 1.1:2). One student's speech urged his peers to try "not to speak Indian any more":

> It is for our own good, not for the good of the Principals, Masters, and the Government. Some of us can talk good English. We must try to make the Indian speakers talk English. We must teach them to help the Inspector, the Principal, and our masters. It is a good thing for us to speak English because if we were to meet an Englishman somewhere and he asked us something in English we would not know what he said or what he meant, but if we learn to speak English we can speak to any Englishman that comes across us … So, boys and girls, the best thing for us to do is to speak English all the time, not to speak one word of Cree, and I want you all to remember that. (1.2:2)

The student promotes English *instead of* Indigenous languages, but he had no space to say otherwise – not at the school, in the literary society, or in the newspaper. As well, he focuses on *speaking*, never on unlearning Cree. He pleas for his peers to learn English like him not, as government reports and schools insisted, to banish "heathen" tongues in the name of civilization. Instead, he promotes English to ensure his peers will always know what an Englishman is asking them, which could include grave questions they may face as adults on the law, child removal, treaties, employment, or land theft. The student insists learning English is not for "Principals, Masters, and the Government" but the good of the children themselves. Finally, he reveals that there remained "Indian speakers" at the school, contradicting school reports that claimed everyone had long forgotten.

At another literary club meeting, Battleford School students read essays on the importance of reading. Again, their responses differ from government mandates. One student entry explained how "our friends find it difficult to talk to white people and when we go among them they will expect us to help them; if we don't learn well now, this will be hard for us; and will cause them trouble" (*Guide* 4.9:1). Another student stated, "We must learn all we can about reading while we stay in the school, so that when we leave here we can still read good books, and so go on learning things as long as we live." Yet another noted, "We who can read can learn much if we try." One student declared that without knowing how to write, "We could not send our thoughts and wishes to our friends who live far away from us," possibly meaning her family. Still another student entry commented, "We cannot talk to people who are far away, but we can write to them, say what we want to, ask them questions, or tell them anything we wish, just as easily as I can talk to you now." These reasons included to avoid "trouble" with white people and to help non-English speaking Indigenous people to avoid it, too; to learn for life; and to communicate across distances. Such reasons depart from those typically cited by school and government – to progress away from heathenism.

Pratt at Carlisle School seemed aware of the distinction between English *only* and English *and*, appealing to it when attempting to convince a former student to send his children:

> Cannot you see it is far, far better for you to have your children educated and trained as our children are so that they can speak the English language, write letters, and do the things which bring to the white man such prosperity, and each of them be able to stand for their rights as the white man stands for his? Cannot you see that [your children] will be of great value to you if after a few years they come back from school with the ability to read and write letters for you, interpret for you, and help look after your business affairs in Washington? (2003, p. 223)

Pratt's justifications for English contradict what he wrote elsewhere, and the particular parent Pratt was attempting to persuade, Spotted Tail, could see through Pratt, who had just fired his son-in-law from his job as school interpreter. Spotted Tail in turn threatened to pull out not only his own but all Sioux children in attendance (p. 238). In this powerful example, Spotted Tail encouraged English in addition, not only. He forcefully resisted on behalf of his family and community against Pratt's designs, seeing through his duplicity.

Compare these sentiments – that Indigenous peoples could use English on their own terms, not at the expense of Indigenous languages – to a speech by Oneida student Dennison Wheelock at Carlisle School. Wheelock wrote the award-winning speech in 1887, answering the school's prompt, "Is it right for the Government to stop the teaching of the Indian languages in Reservation Schools?"[11] Wheelock, the school's prized pupil (and a printer), flatly declared, "The Indian language is one that few persons who wish to live as human beings can use." The speech was circulated in both Carlisle School's newspaper as well as Shingwauk Home's (1.10:8). Robert Warrior (2005) reads the speech contrapuntally, as both evidence of how "Pratt's ideology had succeeded, though not totally" (p. 123). Warrior contextualizes the essay with Wheelock's later commitments to the Oneida Nation, further noting how this essay appeared in 1887, at the height of Pratt's power (p. 125). Finally, Warrior relates this piece of writing to Wheelock's other endeavours such as music in which he had more freedom. Warrior imagines "the printer boys at Carlisle seeing the printed praises of Wheelock's exploits and resenting him and the administrators who extolled him with every turn of the drum of their printing press. But all of these students, from those sneaking a smoke behind the print shop to those trying desperately to please their teachers, are part and parcel of Native educational legacy."

Like Wheelock, student entries in Canadian boarding school newspapers also occasionally praised English to the exclusion of Indigenous languages. One student report in an 1897 issue of Battleford School's newspaper stated the student hoped new pupils would quickly learn English (*Guide* 5.8:1). Another student's writing explained, "It is better for us to talk English all the time. We come to this School to talk English like white people. Not to talk Indian"; after this student's quote, the newspaper observes she "seems to be thoughtful" (1.1:1). On the following page, the same student wrote she was "indeed very much pleased to hear the girls talking English when playing. Very little Indian is spoken now by anyone" (1.2:2). Regina School reprinted the account of an alumnus who complained that when students returned home, they did not speak English: "Sometimes our mother's tongue goes back into its place. We don't think in English. Thinking in English makes us talk English the better. I have followed it and it has worked well" (*Progress* 3.72:3). One of Carlisle School's newspapers features a man who asks a student to say "rock" in his Indigenous language; the boy refuses three times, admonishing the man by stating, "I am always talk English" (*Morning Star* 3.12:2). These instances operated as part of the school's larger system of pitting students against one another, particularly when it came to language. They also highlight Warrior's point that a simple binary framing the English language or praises of it as a mark of being colonized is dangerously simplistic. As Fanon states, interpreted by Cheyfitz (1997), in the revolutionary (as opposed to the colonial) situation, "The native speaker masters the master's language not to become white, not to assume the position of the eloquent orator, but to explode, or expose, that position. The native speaker, then, doesn't so much master the master's language as take possession of it, or, more precisely take up his rightful place in it" (p. 126). This "explosion" is more obvious in articles attributed to students on the benefits of English *and*, but it is also possible to recognize in moments seemingly praising English *only* (Spack, 2002, p. 148–9).

Scott Lyons's (2010) scholarship is helpful in ironing out the distinction further. He understands the x-mark – an Indigenous signature on a treaty – as a symbol for Native assent. Though Lyons acknowledges treaties involved coercion and misunderstanding, more generally x-marks symbolize people who carefully debated the implications (p. 127). The x-mark for Lyons signifies "more than just embracing new or foreign ideas as your own; it means consciously connecting those ideas to certain values, interests, and political objectives, and making the best call you can under conditions not of your making" (p. 70). Informed by scholars such as Craig Womack, Jace Weaver, and Simon J. Ortiz, Lyons discusses English as an "Indian language," a move that opens up the possibility to "'unbrainwash' people in Native communities who may feel a little less Native for having their languages taken away" (p. 158). Elsewhere, Lyons (2009) offers the image of a fence between English and Indigenous languages rather than the postcolonial concept of hybridity – "not to keep things out, but to keep important things in" (p. 79). Though school newspapers printed statements by students ostensibly advocating English-only beliefs, students may have established their own fences between languages. In this way, their defence against linguicide may have actually meant learning English.

Daniel Heath Justice (2006) asserts that Cherokee literature in English is "more than just a concession to the linguistic violence of an oppressive invader culture; instead, it – like the Cherokee language itself – is a powerful reflection of self-determination and agency" (p. 13). Consider these thoughts in one letter of a school newspaper attributed to a mother: "It came to my mind that our boy how he get along from this time. Are good health or not, and tell him we are well and I will try to send some apple for him. And I will to tell you what I want for to learn – to learn reading all about. If you bring him to be wise, might be useful for good interpreter or to work the minister. If you bring that way I shall be glad" (*Our Forest Children* 2.9:16–17). This mother desires her son "to learn reading all about" so he may be useful as a minister or interpreter – English in addition. As Joy Harjo and Gloria Bird (1997) submit, focusing on Indigenous languages as lost perpetuates the myth of vanishing. Whether students qualified their endorsement of English in newspapers as English *and* or appear at first to promote English *only*, the framing of Lyons, Justice, and Harjo and Bird creates space for understanding these occurrences as far more complicated. That these instances appeared in school newspapers with such a controlled English-only narrative, though, suggests that schools did not or could not understand the difference. For school newspapers, it appears they assumed any praise of English on the part of students meant English *only*, rather than the more complicated possibility of English *and*.

Conclusion

The chapter began with Theodore Fontaine's (2010) reprimand for Anishinaabemowin. But in other scenes of his memoir, English also represents another world for Fontaine:

> I'd watch my brothers read Dell and Marvel comic books and been intrigued by their intense focus on the bubbles above characters' heads. Sometimes they'd paraphrase the story in Ojibway for me, as all I could say and understand in English then was "hello," "good day, eh?," "yes, please" and "no, please" ... My brothers' translations were very exciting and brought a whole new world to my little "Indian" life. They instilled in me a strong desire to read ... Mom would say, in Ojibway, "When you go to school, you will be able to read comics." In my mind, this would be the greatest benefit of my schooling. (pp. 24–5)

Neither Fontaine nor his family opposes learning the "whole new world" of English. Basil Johnston's (1989) memoir of Spanish School in Ontario also recounts how his teacher would synopsize *Treasure Island* and *The Illustrated London News*, leaving students "spellbound" (p. 39). Schools sometimes subscribed to seventy newspapers and had libraries of "dilapidated" books, accessed by students who loved to read even outside school hours. Students wrote and spoke about their own reasons for learning English, including building (not destroying) relations, learning about the world, and outsmarting white attempts at manipulation.

But these uses of English and the attendant methods of survival and resistance do not excuse the bans on Indigenous languages or the official policies, practices, and pedagogies promoted in late nineteenth-century boarding schools. School newspapers instead reveal that ostensible communication between parent and child was offered up for the consumption of non-Indigenous readers, and that schools framed English learning as a voluntary, natural preference when the larger picture demonstrates the calculated and violent ways schools enforced English at the expense of Indigenous languages. This history offers at least three lessons: (1) it bolsters an obligation on the part of the state for supporting Indigenous language resurgence today, framing such support not as charity but as justice for historical and ongoing wrongdoings; (2) it denaturalizes the naturalness of the English language on this continent – that English just "happened"; and (3) it historicizes Indigenous peoples' resistance to as well as engagement with English. School newspapers operated as a way to disseminate to readers the techniques and progress of English in nineteenth-century boarding schools, yet they also reveal how students and parents even then were challenging the binary between English and Indigenous languages.

4 "Getting Indian Words": Representations of Indigenous Languages

In the "The Devil's Language" (1996, pp. 54–5), poet Marilyn Dumont juxtaposes Cree with the "lily white words" of English, challenging the denigration of Indigenous languages and the supposed superiority of English. Dumont's poem converts Cree from a violation, an anachronism, and a marker of the devil into a language of the land and her mother. The devil in her poem is not the homey images of bannock, tea, and lullabies but the linguistic estrangement from her mother, that the speaker "can't make the sound of that voice" as an adult. From a Kenyan context, Ngũgĩ wa Thiong'o (2005) similarly states that such linguistic disharmony stems from two simultaneous prongs: the elevation of English and denigration of an Indigenous language (p. 17). School newspapers deployed both tactics. Despite their English-only agendas, school newspapers featured Indigenous languages in instances that were both sanctioned and unsanctioned.

Most school newspapers denigrated Indigenous languages, espousing the ideology they represented a lower evolutionary stage and therefore were incapable of expressing all that European languages could communicate. Some school newspapers confirmed these beliefs in articles about how Indigenous languages lacked concepts such as gratitude (*Guide* 4.5.1; *Progress* 3.71:7). Others stated Anishinaabemowin lacked a rich vocabulary compared to English (*Our Forest Children* 1.12:2–3). One newspaper even associated an Alaskan language with the sound of chirping birds (*Progress* 3.83:1).

Such denigration flies in the face of how many Indigenous scholars centre language. For Okanagan author Jeannette Armstrong (1998), to speak is "a sacred act" (p. 183). For Nishnaabeg writer and scholar Leanne Simpson (2011), "Our languages house our teachings and bring the practice of those teachings to life in our daily existence" (p. 49). And for Mi'kmaw scholar Marie Battiste (2000), languages are how Indigenous consciousness, cultures, literatures, histories, religions, political institutions, and values have survived and are transmitted (p. 199). Such perspectives are in no way unanimous. Still, many cite Indigenous languages as key to survival and resurgence. The inverse, then, is true too: Daniel Heath Justice (2006) writes of how assimilationists targeted Indigenous languages because "a people who know their own stories are strong" (p. 46).

One might assume schools and their newspapers were devoid of Indigenous languages. But often they permitted Indigenous languages and even lauded them. Indian boarding schools were sites of both sanctioned and unsanctioned instances of Indigenous languages. Despite the techniques, policies, and pedagogies that – often violently – attempted to stamp out Indigenous languages, and despite the experiences of survivors as well as artists such as Dumont who testify to the lifelong consequences of such attempts, students defied the rules. In sometimes limited and prescribed instances, schools and their newspapers allowed Indigenous languages, though often for ulterior motives that contrasted with student forms of resistance.

Resistance: Unsanctioned Language

Though nineteenth-century school newspapers rarely shared with readers that students spoke Indigenous languages in spite of English-only policies, survivor testimony from the twentieth century uncovers frequent examples. Isabelle Knockwood (1992), who attended Shubenacadie School in interwar Nova Scotia, recalls learning one day that Latin was dead because no one spoke it any longer. She discovers for herself that "if we are not allowed to speak Mi'kmaw, it will die. So I'm juggling three languages here. I think in Mi'kmaw, talk and learn in English, and pray in Latin" (p. 54). Knockwood staves off the death of Mi'kmaw by continuing to think in it. The same phenomenon occurs in fiction. For example, Richard Wagamese's (2012) novel *Indian Horse* (2012) describes a ten-year-old character who dies after being punished for speaking Anishinaabemowin. The other children learn to speak in whispers or without moving their mouths, "an odd ventriloquism that allowed them to keep their talk alive" (p. 48). In Wagamese's novel, students develop techniques for not only avoiding the same fate as their peers but also for maintaining language.

Survivor Samuel Ross, who attended Prince Albert All Saints School in Saskatchewan in the 1940s and 1950s, explained that before students would speak Cree, they "had to look around first" (*Samuel Ross* n.d.). Mary Battaja, who attended Chooutla Indian Residential School in the Yukon in the 1950s, also recalls furtively maintaining her Northern Tutchone language by sneaking into the bush to meet with her brothers, who were otherwise separated from her (*Mary Battaja*, n.d.). Survivor Mabel Harry-Fontaine found sites both outside as well as within the walls of Fort Alexander Residential School in Manitoba in the 1950s:

> I used to speak my language anyway, with the other girls. I even know the places outside, when we were playing outside, where the Nun was far away. I still spoke my language. I remember under the stairs, the stairway, you know the stairs where there's a space. I remember speaking my language there every chance I got. And in the washroom ... They took away a lot from me but they could not take [Anishinaabemowin] away. Still yet today I speak my language and somehow I get a satisfaction out of that, that they couldn't take it away from me because they tried. God, did they ever try. Every day. And I had to fight that. (*Mabel Harry-Fontaine* n.d.)

Mabel makes clear that the school attempted to take her language and her maintenance of that language was a fight.

Predictably, school newspapers were not candid about strategies of language protection in the same way as survivor memoir, literature, and testimony. In the 1960s, a school newspaper from Gordon's School in Saskatchewan called *Peekiskwatan* reported that the night watchman wondered why "the girls who talk in their sleep, always speak Cree" (General Synod Archives, MM29.7 G59).[1] Yet nineteenth-century school newspapers rarely mentioned examples of students speaking Indigenous languages – unconsciously or otherwise. This absence may exemplify how school newspapers carefully created an English-only fantasy for readers, but it may also attest to the success of students' secrecy, since newspapers may not have reported that students still knew Indigenous languages because schools were unaware. An exception includes Regina School's newspaper, in which the laundress witnessed how one child "chatters away in Indian but he knows enough English to ask for a cookie" (*Progress* 16.9:6), implying children used English strategically. Government reports, if read contrapuntally, were more forthcoming in how students continued to speak their language, though they framed such resistance as failure. An Indian agent in Manitoba observed, "It is Cree, first, last, and always except a little parrot English in the classroom, Cree is the language of the country" (DIA, 1904, p. 110). This is a problem for the agent, but the sentence can be read in two ways: as proof of the school's or students' failure or that Indigenous people were not easily submitting to the suppression of their languages. Other reports highlighted how students would speak English in front of teachers and employers but speak Indigenous languages during playtime or at home (1892, p. 249; 1905, p. 2; 1896, p. 428; 1886, p. 141; 1899, p. 441). Reports framed children, who could be read as resisting the linguicidal goals of their institution, as instead "obstinate" and "diffident" (1890, p. 162; 1886, p. 141; 1889, p. 74). While reports interpreted such defiance as a problem, when coupled with survivor testimony and fiction they further indicate strategies students used to resist language denigration.

School-Sanctioned Indigenous Languages

The earliest boarding schools began as multilingual spaces, using both English and Indigenous languages. In the seventeenth century, European-run schools in North America for Indigenous children emphasized conversion to Christianity first and assimilation – linguistic and otherwise – second (J.R. Miller, 1996b, p. 451). Some missionaries believed the ideas communicated, not the language of instruction, mattered most. As Alison Norman (2017) notes, some schools were staffed by Indigenous teachers who were hired because of their ability to teach in Indigenous languages as well as in English. Some of this was strategic: Anglicans, Oblates, and Methodists saw how their knowledge of an Indigenous language made recruitment, retention, teaching, and Christianizing easier (pp. 199–204). But in the 1850s, the colonial government began insisting schools teach in English. This directive contradicted the philosophy of many churches, which had a long history of learning and publishing religious materials in Indigenous languages. Kitamaat Home, which was a mission school, demonstrated in its newspaper the continuation of this philosophy at the turn of the century, where kindergarten was taught "in the native language substituting English equivalents" (*Na-Na-Kwa* 12.4). The teacher claimed bilingual instruction was "of mutual benefit." As she saw it, the students "never let opportunity pass of correcting my jumbled Kitamaat, repeating it after me with a merry laugh to show me how much better they know it than I. It is only those attempting to learn this language that can understand how difficult it is. In fact they have a peculiar k' and h' sounds that I despair of my tongue and throat ever uttering properly, if it were not evident that Mr. Raley has done so, I would deem it impossible for English tongues." This teacher learned Kitamaat alongside her students, humbling herself in the shared challenge of learning. But the larger frame of the newspaper suggests the Tsimshian language was more commonly viewed at Kitamaat Home as a means to a Christian, English-speaking end. Niezen (2013) recounts how during his research at the Archives Deschâtelets, the librarian showed him a collection of bilingual dictionaries created by Oblate missionaries as if to say, "Why would the priests have gone through all this effort if their goal was to destroy these languages?" (p. 134). I had the same impression of this archive, where I was shown a syllabics-based typewriter.

To comprehend bilingualism in early boarding schools, consider the advice of Anglican missionary William Duncan to government in 1875. He suggested the most important intervention government could make was through surveillance. Without it, he argued, "no satisfactory relationship can ever exist between the Government and the Indians." Today this belief in the role of surveillance persists, as Indigenous academics and activists attest (Blackstock, 2014; Diabo and Pasternak, 2011; Proulx, 2014). Duncan saw Indigenous languages as a particular method of infiltrating communities and surveilling them. In his report he suggested the government appoint a "sub-agent" to each Indigenous language, which in British Columbia he estimated was between ten and twelve with four to five thousand speakers per language. The sub-agent, Duncan suggested, would "of course reside among his Indians and … it should be his aim, as soon as possible, to learn the language of his Indians" (DIA, 1875, p. lx). In this proposal, Indigenous languages serve two purposes: they are a more streamlined way to categorize First Nations and an avenue by which authorities could endear themselves to their respective groups so as to ultimately surveil communities. The possessive pronoun of "his Indians" reappears, too. Settlers may have also learned Indigenous languages for more altruistic or neighbourly reasons. Such moments as the teacher learning Tsimshian for "mutual benefit" with her kindergarten class may have provided moments of respite; however, such interventions did not alter the ultimate colonizing project.

The Santee School in Nebraska, founded in 1870, helps to contextualize Indigenous languages in the newspapers of otherwise English-only schools. In 1868, the superintendent of Indian schools in the US advocated bilingual language policies based on Friedrich Froebel's techniques, suggesting one language helps to learn another (Spack, 2002, p. 26). But as per the Commissioner of Indian Affairs Hiram Price, in 1881 English became mandatory in government-funded schools (p. 24), and by 1887, the rule extended to missions, much to the alarm of bilingual schools across the country (p. 33).[2] The policy hit particularly hard at Santee School, which had translated the Bible, dictionaries, grammar manuals, and schoolbooks and created a bilingual school newspaper titled *Iapi Oyae / The Word Carrier* (Fear-Segal, 2007, pp. 85–6).[3] Santee School's dedication to the Dakota language even in the face of government cuts was not, as Spack (2002) and Fear-Segal (2007) argue, out of respect for the language but "to penetrate and inscribe new parameters on the Dakota people in an unremitting campaign to establish their own version of an 'imagined community' of Christian Dakota" (pp. 89–90).

It could have been different. Luther Standing Bear (2006), who studied at Carlisle School when it opened in 1879, promoted bilingualism when he later became a teacher: "My pupils read first in English, then I asked them to read the same words in their own tongue to prove that they knew what they were reading about. They read the translations as well as they did English. Then I asked if the other [non-bilingual] classes would translate, but this they could not do. They had been merely drilled parrot-like to read some words out of a book" (pp. 241–2). Standing Bear developed this pedagogy after recalling how Carlisle's English-only rule had made him depressed and homesick. His students seemed to appreciate his techniques and according to Standing Bear learned English faster this way (p. 242).[4] A government report from 1864 documents how an Indigenous teacher of a day school in Cape Crocker, Ontario, taught English. He first had the children read in English. He would then translate the meaning for them and ask questions about the text in both languages, resulting in students who could "understand and speak a good many words in English." Importantly, parents expressed "their entire satisfaction with the progress the children had made" (DIA, 1864, p. 26). This instruction may have represented the spirit of what parents had expected from English training: namely, a trauma-free environment in which both languages were freely expressed and where English was taught in addition to, not at the expense of, Indigenous languages. Whether as a means to an assimilative end or for the reasons advocated by Indigenous teachers and parents, the larger history of boarding schools in North America reveals bilingual pedagogies.

Schools in the late nineteenth century may not have been as commonly bilingual as they were in the decades and centuries before, but many of their newspapers permitted isolated instances of Indigenous languages. For example, one 1895 issue from Battleford School described how Premier of the Dominion, Sir Mackenzie Bowell, visited. Long before ascending to the role of Canada's fifth prime minister, Bowell began as a printer's assistant for the *Belleville Intelligencer*, a publication he later owned (Waite, 1998). He both helped to found and served as president of the Canadian Press Association. During his visit to Battleford School as a politician, Bowell surprised students by "setting up and distributing some type, and displaying a thorough knowledge of all the details of a printing office" (*Guide* 4.3:1). Just prior to this visit, *The Aurora* highlighted Bowell's bill to amend the Indian Act, which would permit the department to "lease Indian lands to an aborigine without the tribal consent" and to provide "for the sale of Indian lands for school purposes" (3.30:1), among other encroachments. As a gift to acknowledge his visit, the print shop boys at Battleford School presented Bowell with copies they had created of Canada's national anthem – in Cree.[5] The boys then printed this encounter in their school newspaper (4.3:1).

In this scene, much remains to be unpacked. Bowell began a political career in a newly confederated Canada as a newspaperman. Producing and then owning a newspaper, which espoused the conservative and colonial values of the mid-nineteenth century, acted as a launch pad for a political career, where his policies continued to colonize. Bowell's interactions with the print boys of the Battleford School operate on two levels: he is not only a fellow newsie but also a political leader visiting industrial schools, making a grand tour and inspecting their progress in attempting to assimilate Indigenous children. Bowell could have received any document, even a copy of the school newspaper, for its effect would have been the same as long as it was printed by the boys' own hands, symbolizing their ability to write English and operate a machine. However, the students handed him the national anthem in Cree. This gift could be read several ways. The most obvious may be as a challenge to Bowell's policies and the school since the students are still able to speak, write, and understand Cree. But Bowell's visit is staged, condoned by the school and written in its newspaper for a larger audience. Students' knowledge of Cree is permissible because it bolsters national endeavours as an anthem. But if nationalism were all the gift was supposed to communicate, printing in English would make more sense. Possibly, then, the seeming *trace* of the students' Indigeneity mattered. Retaining Cree – on the schools' terms – might have signified that what the school considered the remnants of a language were now only good for assimilative purposes: the national anthem, gratitude for a politician, and proof of industrial competency via the printing press.

Besides Bowell's visit, newspapers also reported other instances in which the school permitted Indigenous languages. Elder Jacob Bear visited Regina School and "addressed the children in Cree; he has an earnest impressive way of speaking and all seemed to follow him with the greatest attention" (*Progress* 18.2:5). He also led a sermon in Cree. The newspaper described him "as a great orator among a people who pride themselves on their powers of speech-making. He has the orator's power, but he has more; he is on fire, and his words fall like blazing torches in the minds of the Indians. Many of the Indians said, after hearing him, Sunday morning 'That is the best Cree sermon I ever heard'" (18.3:1). The students also had visits from a chief in Mistawasis, who addressed them in Cree and who the students "listened to with the very closest attention" (18.10:2). The newspaper also reprinted an article about an Indigenous man named Thomas Walker. The article states, "To hear him pray is like a benediction as in his own tongue he calls down God's blessing upon a lost world. To hear him speak to the people is grand. His language flowing readily and his thoughts wide and liberal" (3.84:2). It appears that in these isolated examples, students and visitors could speak Indigenous languages at the school and this practice was accepted enough to publish in the newspaper. Such exceptions demonstrate how schools temporarily overrode English-only policies if an Indigenous language promoted Christianity or facilitated a visit from a prominent person like a chief or prime minister.

Some schools provided reading materials in Indigenous languages. Upon Queen Victoria's death, Kitamaat Home's newspaper proclaimed "Owmuskunnoxs Mudseilth," meaning "the Greatest Chiefess" (*Na-Na-Kwa* 14.1). An 1895 issue of Battleford School's newspaper featured "God Save the Queen" in Cree with the Roman alphabet (*Guide* 4.5:2; see figure 4.1). Far more of what newspapers translated was religious: Kitamaat Home translated the Lord's Prayer into Kitamaat (*Na-Na-Kwa* 1.3; 5.6) and Haida (6.2), and it did the same with Psalm 23 (3.7) and the Ten Commandments (11.3). Battleford School translated the Lord's Prayer and grace into Cree (*Guide* 7.12:4). Students also served as interpreters for Indian Agents (*Progress* 3.81:5), and Kitamaat Home's principal

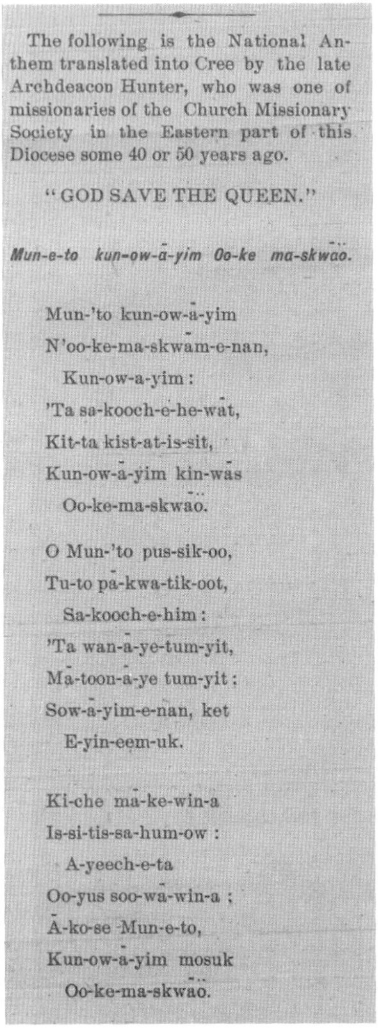

The following is the National An-
them translated into Cree by the late
Archdeacon Hunter, who was one of
missionaries of the Church Missionary
Society in the Eastern part of this
Diocese some 40 or 50 years ago.

"GOD SAVE THE QUEEN."

Mun-e-to kun-ow-ā-yim Oo-ke ma-skwao.

Mun-'to kun-ow-à-yim
N'oo-ke-ma-skwam-e-nan,
Kun-ow-a-yim :
'Ta sa-kooch-e-he-wat,
Kit-ta kist-at-is-sit,
Kun-ow-à-yim kin-was
Oo-ke-ma-skwao.

O Mun-'to pus-sik-oo,
Tu-to pà-kwa-tik-oot,
Sa-kooch-e-him :
'Ta wan-à-ye-tum-yit,
Ma-toon-à-ye tum-yit :
Sow-à-yim-e-nan, ket
E-yin-eem-uk.

Ki-che mà-ke-win-a
Is-si-tis-sa-hum-ow :
A-yeech-e-ta
Oo-yus soo-wà-win-a ;
À-ko-se Mun-e-to,
Kun-ow-à-yim mosuk
Oo-ke-ma-skwao.

Figure 4.1. "God Save the Queen" in Cree. *The Guide* 4.5:2: November 1895.

George Raley learned Tsimshian from the chief's wife, Kate Dudoward (*Na-Na-Kwa* 31.9). In these instances, schools, not Indigenous communities, dictated when and how Indigenous languages would appear, and that often happened in service of church and state.

Some school newspapers also discussed and printed Indigenous languages in syllabics, which are alphabets that better represent Indigenous languages than the Roman alphabet. Missionaries have been representing Indigenous languages using special orthographies as an evangelizing tool since the 1600s (Hochman, 2014, p. 14),[6] so their use in boarding schools run by missionaries is not altogether surprising. The principal of Kitamaat Home used the same press to print the school newspaper as well as publish work "in connection with the Kitamaat language" (*Na-Na-Kwa* 1.1), meaning his missionary translation work (Fahey and Horton, 2012, p. 49). Annual reports that mention the use of syllabics consider the alphabet a substitute for communities without a school or a skilled teacher (DIA, 1881, p. 102; 1897, p. 75; 78; 1905, p. 203; 1906, p. 237).

When school newspapers mentioned syllabics, it was typically to revere purported settler creators of the orthography. Rupert's Land School, for instance, provided an article on Bishop Horden of Moosonee, Ontario, after he died that describes his translation of the gospels into syllabics (*Aurora* 1.8:4). Though Horden had sent his proofs away to England to be printed, he received instead after a year of waiting only a printing press and type so that he could correct the proofs in Canada himself. The article almost elevates Horden's printing to an act of divinity. Most school newspapers, though, focused on syllabics and the Wesleyan reverend James Evans. He has been credited with inventing Ojibway and Cree syllabics while operating a mission in Manitoba in the mid-nineteenth century. One article published in Battleford School's newspaper explained how in 1895, students were now able to receive the gift of English at boarding school; however, Evans and his syllabics were worth remembering. According to the article, Evans was "privileged to confer the boon of a written language on the Cree nation" (*Guide* 4.1:3). The article continues:

> Was it possible to teach an Indian to read? It certainly was no easy matter. We all know how long it takes to teach most children to read even English. The spelling is the great difficulty, especially with the long words. But what are long English words compared with Cree words? Take the simple sentence, "God is love" – in Cree "Muneto sakihiwawiniwew." What hope was there that an untutored Indian, with opportunities of receiving instruction few and far between, could ever learn to spell out words of eight, 10 or 12 syllables? Some method other than the English must be devised.

The Roman alphabet is never seen as deficient here. Instead, the text indicates the problem remains with incapable students and too-long Cree words. Rupert's Land School also reprinted an article exclusively crediting James Evans with invention of Cree syllabics (*Aurora* 2.22:2) and advertising the sale of an 1890 tract titled *James Evans: Inventor of the Syllabic System of the Cree Language* (McLean, 1890). An Indian Affairs inspector in Manitoba also perpetuated the trope. He declared that Indigenous peoples owed "a debt of gratitude to the Rev. Mr. Evans for his invention of syllabic characters" (DIA, 1899, p. 100). The origin story of the syllabics almost mythologizes Evans, who first used melted lead from old tea boxes, ink from sturgeon oil and soot, and a repurposed jack-press originally used for bundling furs (B. Edwards, 2005, p. 51).

This Battleford School newspaper article attempts to foreclose at least three contexts. For one, Grenoble and Whaley (2006) cite many dangers of syllabic writing, where "traditional wordplay may disappear. The role of stories, and accordingly of the Elders or other authority figures who tell them, can be transformed, which has attendant effects on social hierarchies. The connection between speech and spirituality can be loosened" (p. 119). Also, Evans was accused of sexually abusing Indigenous women in 1846 while in Manitoba.[7] The mythologizing of Evans also excludes Indigenous oral history of collaboration and even sole invention, meaning that Evans took credit for something in fact created by Indigenous peoples themselves (Francis, 2011, p. 149). Evans collaborated with Ojibway missionaries Peter Jones and Henry Bird Steinhauer (B. Edwards, 2005, p. 51). Cree oral history goes further, claiming syllabics as in fact from the Creator, who bestowed the symbols to two Elders, Mistanaskowew (Badger Bull) and Machiminahtik (Hunting Rod) (p. 68). Winona Wheeler documents two oral histories on the origins of Cree syllabics, where missionaries learned from Cree people (Badger Call and Raining Bird). As Wheeler writes, Canadian history has mythologized supposed settler creation of Cree syllabics despite Indigenous oral histories that provide counternarratives (Stevenson, 1999, p. 24).

Haskell Institute's newspaper also printed an article on the Cherokee syllabary,[8] which was developed by a man named Sequoyah in the early 1800s. The Cherokee Nation released the first issue of its bilingual newspaper the *Cherokee Phoenix* in 1828, which required a special press to print Sequoyah's letters. Ellen Cushman (2011) argues the syllabary was a direct response to increases in white populations and English enforcements, and Margaret Bender (2002) understands the syllabary as both challenging and reinforcing nineteenth-century ideologies concerning written text and Indigenous peoples (p. 24). Daniel Heath Justice (2006) views the syllabary as a powerful tool used to resist and then rebuild after the Trail of Tears between 1836 and 1839, in which thousands of people died after their forced relocation to Oklahoma (p. 6). Unlike the reverence paid to Evans, Haskell's newspaper compared Sequoyah to Psalmanazar, an eighteenth-century imposter who created a fake alphabet (*Indian Leader* 3.4:3). The newspaper describes Sequoyah's invention as wholly inspired by white alphabets and that his barriers to creating the alphabet included "the old Cherokee tradition [that] constantly dinned into his ears." As Patrick Giasson's (2004) work indicates, though, the Cherokee syllabary is unique in terms of writing systems in that it did not mimic another system or develop over time but was solely invented by Sequoyah. For the school newspaper, Sequoyah invented the syllabary *in spite of* being Cherokee, not because he was. The newspaper also subtly dismisses syllabaries because they are allegedly easy to learn and inefficiently contain too many characters, unlike the Roman alphabet. In these two articles schools deployed tactics for discussing but also containing Indigenous languages, limiting the resistance of the syllabary.

School newspapers occasionally featured articles on Indigenous sign making, such as stories recorded on trees and rocks (*Progress* 3.71:3) as well as pictograms (*Our Forest Children* 4.6:241). Rupert's Land School dubbed communication with fire, smoke, mirrors, and blankets as "the telegraphic system of the natives" (*Aurora* 2.21:2). As Jan Hare (2009) argues, expanded definitions of Indigenous meaning-making challenge limited and colonial understandings of literacy (p. 261). School newspapers were largely uninterested in this expanded understanding; however, newspapers from both the nineteenth and twentieth centuries sometimes featured articles on Indigenous sign languages. Though schools falsely conceived of English as a lingua franca, these sign languages served as a bridge across a variety of mutually unintelligible Indigenous languages (Davis 2010, p. 1). Though there were many sign languages used by Indigenous peoples across North America, the Plains Indian Sign Language (PISL) is perhaps the most well documented and widely used, spanning over four million square kilometres (pp. 6–9). That schools published articles about Indigenous sign languages is unsurprising given the interest in them during the mid- to late nineteenth century. Proto-anthropologists in the 1860s considered sign languages as linguistic fossils (Hochman, 2014, p. 42). They believed PISL may have predated spoken language and was therefore a key to understanding evolution and how humans differed from animals. These beliefs were so strong that some educators in the

1860s and 1870s suppressed American Sign Language because of its supposed connections to "savagery" (p. 43). As Jennifer Esmail (2013) writes, "Victorians understood signed languages in multiple, often contradictory, ways: as objects of fascination and revulsion, as having scientific import and literary interest, and as being both a unique mode of human communication and an apparent vestige of our bestial heritage" (p. 4). When schools wrote about PISL, they did so either to praise preservation efforts by white philologists or to offer readers exoticized signs to try for themselves. Haskell Institute's newspaper claimed Indigenous peoples did not have historians ("no moccasined Macaulay nor copper-colored Gibbon"), necessitating the efforts of an H.L. Scott of the Smithsonian to preserve PISL before it died out (*Indian Leader* 6.9:1). The newspaper regarded Scott as "probably the best living authority on the sign language." Battleford School's newspaper, too, praised Scott's preservation efforts, citing his twenty-three years of study (in 1899) as putting him "in a position to speak authoritatively on the subject" (*Guide* 7.8:2). Such articles wrest authority of an Indigenous language away from Indigenous peoples and participate in the myth of the "vanishing Indian." School newspapers also discussed PISL as entertainment for readers. *Our Forest Children*, for instance, listed directions for over fifty signs (2.13:17–18) – from words such as "Sioux" and "white man" to "sunrise" and "sunset," and from "I am cold" and "he is fibbing" to "I hate you" and "I am ashamed." Students would have also read about sign language in *The Boys' Own Paper* (see figure 4.2), to which many boarding schools subscribed. The newspaper not only compared Indigenous sign languages to the gestures of Italian pantomime and Cistercian monks but also to monkeys, crickets, and the "insane" ("The Sign Language of the American Indians" 1890a, p. 492).

Compare this position to how Standing Bear (2006) considered sign languages in 1933. Signing represented an expanded rather than a lesser form of communication, a "beautiful and expressive use of the hands." He further alludes to the encroachment of anthropologists. Standing Bear considered sign language books "useless," the same as trying "to learn stage acting from photographs, or piano playing by watching someone play" (pp. 81–2). Standing Bear's views contrast with how newspapers appropriated PISL. His perspective also counters an article in Shingwauk Home's newspaper, which described how a staff member escorted a Blackfoot student, Daniel, from Washakada

Figure 4.2. *Boys' Own* magazine and sign language. "The Sign Language of the American Indians," 1890b.

Home in Manitoba to his family. The boy chanced upon a Cree woman, with whom he conversed by sign:

> The Cree asked Daniel what he had done with his hair, as a year ago he had long ringlets and wore a blanket; but now wears his hair short and has a good suit of English clothes. He informed the Cree that he was now a Christian and produced his Testament out of his pocket and told him he was going to his home on the reserve; but next spring was coming back on the staff of the new Industrial Schools at this place. All this took place by hand signs, which I am told are understood by all Indian tribes. (*Canadian Indian* 1.4:108)

The staff member would not have been able to confirm this is indeed what they said in its entirety. Standing Bear recalled how he and other students used sign language to defy the English-only rule at Carlisle School. For him, "Those of us who knew the sign language made use of it, but imagine what it meant to those who had to remain silent" (p. 242). While school newspapers placed Indigenous sign languages under the purview of anthropologists and framed PISL as amusement amid a larger belief that they were a "savage" form of communication, Standing Bear reveals how such depictions were wrong. Students who knew how to sign used it to communicate at school under the noses of administrators. Whether this scene from Shingwauk Home's newspaper happened this way or not, the newspaper offered readers an example of signing not to circumvent rules as Standing Bear describes but instead to discuss markers of assimilation and Christianity.

School newspapers also permitted Indigenous languages through story. Kitamaat Home's newspaper printed stories attributed to children who heard them from their chief. Stories include one about the first beaver (*Na-Na-Kwa* 20.8), which was "related by Chief Jessea" and "reported to Nanakwa by Martha Brown," a student and printer. Another printer, Minnie Amos, was also credited with "interpreting" the story of the beaver and the porcupine (18.3). Another story, "The Blind Chief Hantlekwelass" was "related by Chief Moses McMillan" and "translated" by the principal, Raley (22.11). Chief Jessea is also credited as the one who "related" a story about Whenath's bear hunt (11.3). The story "Abuks Tlalumkwaks" is also credited to Chief Jessea as well as to the missionary who translated it (6.3). Other stories are presented as authored by a chief, such as "The Story of Wahuksgomalayou" (3.3).

The author of "The Story about the Death of Chone" (25.5) is credited to Kin-da-shon's wife and "Frog's Revenge" is credited to Chief Jessea as well (29.6–7). Sophie McCall (2011) avoids the binary between Indigenous storytellers and non-Indigenous writers and editors: "Two or more mediators produce these composite texts, and their negotiations [are] shaped by contested relations of power" (pp. 41–2). These newspaper examples are between Indigenous storytellers (chiefs) and Indigenous writers and printers (the children) while Raley served as non-Indigenous intermediary, complicating McCall's points. Another layer emerges in how Indigenous languages are sustained within English: Dumont (2007b) describes this as how "in a few borrowed sounds of English / the nerve of Cree remains / in mouths that have tasted a foreign alphabet too long" (p. 1).

Students and chiefs may have shared these stories with the newspaper for their own reasons. It is not clear what role Indigenous readers, printers, and writers had in insisting that these appear in the newspapers or how they felt upon reading them. At the same time, school newspapers would frame such stories as entertainment. Some publications called Indigenous stories superstitions (*Guide*, 5.7:4), legends (*Progress* 3.80:4; 8.13:3), and curious traditions (3.5:41); they were considered by the newspapers as "fascinating" (5.10) and as "charming children's stories" (*Indian Leader* 15.30:3). As Dian Million (2011) explains, "Story has always been practical, strategic, and restorative" (p. 35). For Leanne Simpson (2011), "Elders tell us that everything we need to know is encoded in the structure, content, and context of these stories" (p. 33), which are a tool to envision new futures (p. 40). The inclusion of Indigenous storytelling within school newspapers may have been told and written within the same frame that McCall, Million, and Simpson outline, in spite of the larger frame of the newspaper.

Indigenous Languages and Ethnography

School newspapers also printed articles on Indigenous languages as part of a larger interest in ethnography, a discipline born out of colonialism. As Audra Simpson (2014) writes, colonialism is more than military occupation; colonial techniques also include "methods and modalities of knowing – in particular, categorization, ethnological comparison, linguistic translation, and ethnography" (p. 95). Importantly, increased interest in Indigenous peoples by settlers through such techniques coincided with expanded sanctions against Indigenous people for doing what was of such ethnographic interest; for instance, languages were banned in boarding schools and the Indian Act prohibited ceremonies. Rupert's Land School reprinted an article calling Cree "a euphonious and expressive tongue, systematic in arrangement and beautiful though complicated in the multiplicity of its forms" (*Aurora* 2.22:1), though likely the same students setting the type to reprint this article were not permitted to speak Cree at the school. It was as if settlers were communicating to Indigenous peoples, *You no longer are permitted to speak your language, wear your regalia, eat your food, or practice your ceremonies, but the newspaper/school/ethnographer can, and knows more.* One burgeoning form of ethnographic interest in the nineteenth century and in school newspapers was linguistic. Such desires to quickly record languages before they disappeared aligned with the larger efforts of salvage ethnography – the attempts of "civilized" scientists and artists in the nineteenth century to record what they thought to be unavoidably on the brink of extinction because their primitive existence could supposedly not survive in the modern world.

The seeming lament for "dying" languages accelerated in the nineteenth century, particularly with the influence of German philologist Max Müller's "diseases of language" theory in the 1850s. Müller believed that though the original meaning of a word might be lost, its linguistic prehistory could be recovered, a belief that accorded with Victorians' larger preoccupation with origins. School newspapers occasionally revealed this obsession; for example, issues of *Our Forest Children* questioned whether Indigenous peoples in North America were Antediluvian (3.4:21) or originally Egyptians (3.7:71), Israelites (3.13:171), or South American (3.9:111; 3.10:126; 3.11:141; 4.5:239; 4.6:242; 3.83:2). Patrick Wolfe (1999, p. 134) views philology as a text-based precursor to anthropology, where claims made about linguistic origins of the past served colonial claims to land of the nineteenth-century present. American scholars such as William Dwight Whitney (1867), Lewis Henry Morgan (1877), and John Wesley Powell (who wrote from the 1860s to the turn of the century) put forward theories about Indigenous languages, arguing they could reveal ancient secrets and help to position peoples on an evolutionary ladder. Such research was controversial: in 1866 the Société de Linguistique of Paris and then in 1872 the Philological Society of London banned further study on the origins of language, deeming such research unscientific (Davis, 2010, p. 66).[9] In the US, though, such study appears to have thrived. That boarding school newspapers published articles about Indigenous languages is in some ways explained by a larger historical milieu of ethnographic interest in them.

Battleford School's newspaper offers an example in its article, "Indian Languages Fast Disappearing." The article compares Indigenous languages to the buffalo, lamenting them without delving into the backstory of their "disappearance." It goes on to state that now most Indigenous children, when pressed to speak their Indigenous languages, are unable to articulate "even the commonest words or phrases" (*Guide* 7.1:4). Though the article praises the preservation efforts of the Smithsonian as well as the promise of the phonograph and Graphophone for recording languages, it cautions that "the machines of the day will record the language if it is talked into them, but the difficulty is to get Indians who can talk with the necessary degree of accuracy." The article then concludes by predicting that in twenty years, no more Indigenous languages will exist. This article ostensibly mourns the "disappearance" of Indigenous languages within a newspaper whose school was part of the problem. This supposed disappearance was not unconnected from colonial endeavours, but school newspapers packaged articles on "vanishing" Indigenous languages as seemingly respectful, scientific studies. Yet these ethnographies of supposedly dying or damaged words served as a foil to the perceived supremacy of English found in the rest of the newspaper.

Though most newspapers published articles on the ethnography of Indigenous languages, Shingwauk Home's two newspapers exhibited sustained devotion to the topic. The school's principal Edward Francis Wilson was an armchair anthropologist, a not uncommon crossover as the divide between the enthusiast and professional were hardly fixed in the late nineteenth century. Robert L.A. Hancock (2006) separates Canadian anthropology into four periods: the missionary era, amateur era, National Museum era, and university era. Wilson straddled the first two as he was a missionary yet adopted techniques common of the amateur era. When he wasn't operating the Sault Ste Marie school for twenty years (1873–93) as well as another boarding school in Manitoba, Wilson contributed to Canada's emerging anthropological scene. He founded the short-lived Canadian Indian Research and Aid Society in 1890, which had three interests: missionaries at Indian schools, the "plight" of Indigenous peoples, and the science and anthropology of Indigenous peoples (Nock, 1976, p. 32). The society's membership included clergy, Indian Affairs officials, museum workers and archaeologists, as well as the Mohawk actor and lecturer John Ojijatekha Brant-Sero and Ojibway reverend John Jacobs (*Canadian Indian* 1.1:1–2). When Shingwauk Home's *Our Forest Children* disbanded, Wilson switched to a new publication, *The Canadian Indian* (1890–1), which served as an organ for the society. Wilson began early ethnographic work with his book *The Ojebway Language* (original spelling) (1874), which included grammar, a dictionary, and exercises. The section on commands for use in school offers a taste of Wilson's pedagogy: *Go to your seat. Look at your book. Bring me your slate. Look (plural) at the black-board. You are late. You have been very idle. Your hands are dirty* (pp. 141–2). Many of the phrases relate to literacy: *Write nicely. Don't talk. Where is your pencil? Read louder. Read distinctly.* Others hint at violence: *That is what the master says. I must whip you if you do that. Do what I say at once.* Wilson advertised the manual for sale in the school's newspapers decades later.[10]

Wilson received praise for his ethnographic research from famed anthropologists Franz Boas and A.F. Chamberlain (3.10:127). As well, the American Antiquarian Society, one of the oldest learned societies in the US, praised *Our Forest Children* for offering "ethnographic and even linguistic articles, interesting correspondence and other *sound* reading matter" unlike the "temperance and total abstinence twaddle, devotional splurges and baby-talk" found in most other "Indian journals" (*Our Forest Children* 3.7:76). Marcus Tomalin (2011) posits that despite the view that anthropologists distanced themselves from the supposedly amateur work of missionaries in the century prior, the two groups in fact informed one another in this early period (pp. 151–2).

David A. Nock (1988) suggests Wilson changed his philosophy on Indigenous education after 1885 due to a new appreciation for ethnology, his interaction with Indigenous groups in the US, and his disillusionment with government (p. 4). Nock convincingly attributes a pseudonymous series of papers published in Shingwauk Home's newspaper *The Canadian Indian* titled "Fair Play" to Wilson, in which he confesses misgivings about boarding schools (p. 135). However, Sharon Wall (2003) takes a different tack. While conceding some ways Wilson rejected assimilationist practices, she ultimately concludes Wilson did so "to more surely secure [Indigenous people's] consent to the educational project" (p. 19). For Wall, Wilson's leanings suggest strategy, not transformation. Kathleen Buddle (2001) also highlights how because Wilson wrote the Fair Play papers under a nom de plume, he avoided political repercussions (p. 93). Moreover, Wilson states the following in the Fair Play papers: "We want the land. We cannot have Indian hunters annoying our farmers and settlers. If the Indian is to remain, we expect him to be a decent neighbour; and to be a decent neighbour, we expect him to accept our religion, our education, our laws, and our customs" (*Canadian Indian* 1.8). This passage could be read as advocating for the land to be shared, that Indigenous peoples and settlers could lay claim to separate land and be neighbours. Another way to read the quotation is that a neighbourly existence, according to Wilson, is contingent on spiritual, educational, legal, and social assimilation. As well, the phrase "if the Indian is to remain" is threatening, assigning control of Indigenous survival to white settlers. The excerpt further reveals how Wilson's insistence that "we want the land" demonstrates the inability or unwillingness of arguably thoughtful settlers to rethink entitlement to land.

Nock is correct that Wilson moved away from some of the beliefs of his contemporaries. Wilson often praised Indigenous languages, arguing they were "not rude barbarous tongues, as those who have never studied the subject might suppose, but are capable of giving expression to the most abstruse ideas" (*Canadian Indian* 1.2:25). In many places, Wilson counteracts the myth that Indigenous languages were inferior. But Wilson only valued Indigenous languages for him and his non-Indigenous peers to learn about and research, to the exclusion of Indigenous peoples' rights to their own languages. Wilson prioritized "the subject of collecting all the folk-lore and traditions of the Indians left amongst us, while yet there is time to do so, before they disappear or merge into the general community." Wilson does not frame these "disappearances" as connected to the institutions (boarding schools) and discourses (school newspapers and ethnographic publications) for which he was responsible.

Wilson's justifications for the importance of Indigenous languages in Shingwauk Home's two newspapers are revealing. The newspapers explain that first, Indigenous languages unlocked clues about evolution (*Our Forest Children* 3.5:43; *Canadian Indian* 1.2:25). Second, Wilson also appears interested in Indigenous languages because he thought they were going to be gone soon (1.2:25). These justifications are unified in their concern for power – to know languages and therefore all of humanity. Wilson also reinscribes power by confirming (albeit with seeming lament) that the colonial project was working – English was close to superseding Indigenous languages. The efforts to preserve may also contribute to what Eve Tuck and K. Wayne Yang call "settler moves to innocence." Building on the work of Janet Mawhinney, Mary Louise Fellows, and Sherene Razack, Tuck and Yang describe "those strategies or positionings that attempt to relieve the settler of feelings of guilt or responsibility without giving up land or power or privilege, without having to change" (p. 10). Wilson's concern for threatened languages is one such move.

The contradiction of school newspapers praising Indigenous languages on, say, page 6 but then calling for their eradication on page 8 is explained by school newspapers themselves, suggesting a link between knowing about Indigenous peoples so as to better lay claim to land. Wilson exemplifies this connection in his thought, "We must be content at the present stage to accumulate the needful materials to master the history of the races of our own Dominion" (1.2:26). Wilson understood a link between knowing all about Indigenous peoples – mastering the history – and laying claim to "our own" land. Battleford School's newspaper made this connection explicit: "We cannot deal with the Indian of to-day unless we know the Indian of yesterday" (*Guide* 7.9:3). This article claimed that knowing the history of Indigenous peoples ("the Indian of yesterday") would help in "dealing" with Indigenous people in the nineteenth century, which at the time meant mostly making land dispossession possible. A common way "to know the Indian of yesterday" in the nineteenth century meant ethnography. Yet school newspapers did not typically present knowledge about Indigenous peoples as connected to contemporaneous claims to land. Instead, school newspapers veiled such ethnographic interest as general, innocent quests for universal knowledge. While an individual article on ethnography in a newspaper might not mention the study's larger colonial context, the connection between land and knowledge emerges by reading other articles on other pages in the same issue about land and dispossession.

"Getting Indian Words"

Wilson published his illustrations and research on Indigenous languages in two columns, which appeared in both of Shingwauk Home's newspapers. The first column, "Indian Tribes," located Indigenous people and their languages in the past. Appearing on the first or second page, the column featured a different Indigenous nation in each issue. It would typically begin with an introduction to the nation, including the meaning behind its name, as well as linguistic and biological relationships to other nations and any migration history Wilson researched. He would assess the nation's placement on an evolutionary scale, using terms such as "wild," "heathen," "civilized," and "advanced." The column would also explain to readers the "habits of these people in the days that are past," listing marriage and funeral rites as well as legal practices and vignettes of famous people.

The only contemporary Indigenous people Wilson discussed in this column were students originally from the nation he was profiling who were now enrolled in his school or those who were statistics of a dwindling population, listing the number of those still living. Each issue, the column would feature a different Indigenous nation, listing Seminoles, Pacific Coast Indians, Ona, Tuscaroras, Chipewyan, Ottawa, Cherokee, Mohawk, Chickasaws, Pueblo, Assiniboine, and Mandan peoples. Unlike other parts of Shingwauk Home's and other school newspapers, this column praised Indigenous language, faiths, regalia, and values. Such information, at times, was painstakingly sought after for its accuracy rather than completely falsified. The column reported on (and did not always outwardly denigrate) Indigenous child-rearing, ceremony, marriage, clothing, homes, burial rites, and customs.

Considerable textual real estate of the "Indian Tribes" column was devoted to language. Wilson often used the past tense, as if the speakers no longer existed. The entry for Mandan is typical, describing Mandan territory, spirituality, creation stories, and burial practices. The passage offers "Grammatical Notes," highlighting what "letters of the alphabet are wanting" and thereby locating the Roman alphabet as the benchmark. The passage mentions linguistic terminology such as the dubitative case, as well as a pronunciation guide that used English, French, and German for comparison. The section then provides a list of words and translations. Nouns include people and animals (e.g., woman and snake), the environment (e.g., house and tree), and adjectives (e.g., little axe, bad axe, big axe). Such word lists, used often by missionaries, drew from vocabulary presumed to be basic or common to all peoples rather than words that were important to white settlers using the lists (Heller and McElhinny, 2017, pp. 49–50). These articles also included basic sentences: *It is good. Thou seest him. If I see him. Is he asleep?* (3.8:81–5). This section was less a learner's guide and more an opportunity for readers to compare all languages. One issue features Wilson's monthly instalments as a chart (1.4:106). The chart offered words for man, water, fire, and some numbers. It profiled fifty-six languages – from Apache to Zuni; Kickapoo to Omaha; Comanche to Seneca; Pima to Chickasaw; and Pawnee to Haida. The languages were separated into eight categories: Algonkin, Sionan, Pacific Coast, Iroquoin, Shoshone, Pima, Muskhog, Athabascan, Caddo, a group of unclassified languages (e.g.,

Pueblo languages and "Eskimo"), as well as Japanese and Ainu (the only non–North American languages on the chart).

While Wilson used the column "Indian Tribes" to present readers with the fruits of his research, he went behind the scenes of his ethnographic work in his second column, "My Wife and I." The column served as a shadow text to "Indian Tribes," revealing how Wilson learned about Indigenous languages. He describes the successes and pitfalls of his research – the speakers he interviews as well as the rainy horse rides, broken-down trains, and lost luggage he experiences during his travels. An advertisement for *Our Forest Children* in the local newspaper for Medicine Hat, Alberta (where Wilson was hoping to establish a new Indian boarding school), described the column "My Wife and I" as humorous. His wife, Frances, is every bit a part of the travel, and she sometimes stood in as a barometer for how "wild" things became. When Wilson travels to Pueblo territory and the Mexican border, he leaves Frances in Denver for three weeks. Suddenly, Wilson's descriptions of the landscape and people are wilder than when Frances was at his side (3.12:156). Unlike in "Indian Tribes," in "My Wife and I" Indigenous peoples are permitted to be in the present, but Wilson continues to rank and adjudicate them. This Indigenous presence served as amusement and narrative rather than as counter to the pastness of the "Indian Tribes" column. In these two columns, Wilson bifurcated his research findings by time. In "Indian Tribes," Wilson's findings are old stories, ancient customs, dead chiefs, and dying populations and languages; in "My Wife and I," we learn of these "findings" from living people who actively practice that which Wilson researches. "Indian Tribes" aimed for true objectivity, never discussing at any point Wilson's own subject position; in contrast, "My Wife and I" is written in the first person, filled with the quotidian of the Wilsons' lives. "My Wife and I" also differs from Wilson's "Indian Tribes" column in that he explains *how* he gathered his information. When such research is repackaged as "Indian Tribes," Wilson excludes himself and any discussion of colonialism whatever.

Wilson gathered his information on Indigenous languages for inclusion in school newspapers in several ways. For one, he consulted the dictionaries and grammar manuals of the Smithsonian's ethnological department in Washington, DC (*Our Forest Children* 3.5:42–3). He even sketched an image of himself, titled "Taking Notes," to accompany the description of his research at the Smithsonian (see figure 4.3). In this image, Wilson hovers over a book. In the background is a bookcase and

42   OUR FOREST CHILDREN.

TAKING NOTES.

America and the Mongolian of China, whether in language, habits, or tradition. There may be Chinese and Japanese blood in some of the coast tribes, brought about by intercourse with the survivors of ship-wrecked junks; but there seems to be little, if any, likelihood that the Indians as a people, from Hudson Bay to Cape Horn, sprang from such a source. Again, secondly, these people, although so scattered, and so *sparsely* scattered, all over the vast continents of North and South America, bear strong evidence of having been originally but one people. An Indian is an Indian, whether you meet with him in the far north or in the far south. There is the same brown skin, the same black straight hair, the same lithe figure and generally well-cut features, the same peculiar gait and posture, the same animal instincts and animal proclivities, the same curious mixture of rude courtesy on the one hand and utter oblivion to the rules of civilized society on the other, the same keen eyesight, the same stolidity, and the same cleverness and ingenuity in providing the necessities of life out of the rudest material; the same lack of ambition and indisposition to continued effort; the same love for a wild life, the same deeply rooted communistic principle, the same strong recognition of family ties. Thirdly, there are ancient remains, the old ruins and mounds which have never yet been satisfactorily accounted for. The ancient ruins of Nineveh and Babylon and the excavations in Egypt and Palestine, bring to our view objects which we have already read about in ancient history— they go to confirm things which we have already heard about. But not so with the ancient ruins of America. Before the discovery of that continent by Christopher Columbus, in 1492, it was not even known that there was such a country; still less was it conceived that there existed a people far away across the Atlantic, who dwelt in cities built of stone, and who understood the art of weaving and working in various metals. These ruins which are found in America are unique in themselves. Large stone buildings of excellent construction are there found, built not of great quarried stones, but of small sized leaf-like slabs laid one upon another in excellent form and united in one solid block with a mortar, in the composition of which lime, although found in the locality, had no part. And these buildings had many of them arched and vaulted roofs, the arches not built on the old-world principle, with a key stone in the apex, but each stone in the arch bevelled with the hammer and the arch built over a solid core which was afterwards removed.

were marked, so far as at present known, the original haunts of the various Indian tribes, and also to make all the notes I pleased from the many dictionaries and grammars in various Indian dialects with which their library was stocked. A little pamphlet gave me valuable information as to the various linguistic stocks to which it was adjudged the different Indian languages belonged. It was only a proof sheet, and not supposed to be entirely reliable, but still I found it of great value even in its suggestiveness. I can certainly never forget the great kindness and courtesy with which I was treated by the gentlemen of the Bureau of Ethnology in Washington—neither must I omit to mention that for two or three years past they have most kindly supplied me with copies of their many most valuable and expensive publications. I may say, indeed, that it has been the receipt of these valuable and interesting works that has spurred me on more than anything else to give a good part of my time and attention to the study of Indian languages and Indian history.

It may not be out of place here just to give briefly the reasons why I think the study of the Indian people of this continent so interesting.

First of all their origin is at present wrapped in such great uncertainty. The idea of their having come originally from Asia and to have crossed the Behring straits is, I believe, now exploded. And no more satisfactory is the theory that they have sprung from ship-wrecked sailors, belonging to the Chinese or Japanese nations. Except for the almond-shaped eyes, sometimes observable in certain of the Indian tribes, there seems to be little if any similarity between the Red Indian of

Figure 4.3. "Taking Notes" and surrounding layout. *Our Forest Children* 3.5:42: August 1889.

each shelf is dedicated to, one by one, a different Indigenous group. The bookcase almost appears as a language mortuary. Wilson also discussed the research of other settlers (3.72:5; 3.3:13) and was active in professional organizations such as the American Folklore Association (3.5:41).

Wilson additionally gathered his notes from a seven-thousand-mile trip that he took with his wife through the US, which he documented in his two newspapers. The trip was extensive, beginning from Shingwauk Home in Sault Ste Marie to cities such as Ottawa, Washington, Santa Fe, and Denver; through Nebraska and Minnesota; from Cheyenne and Arapahoe territory to the land of Pueblo and Zuni peoples; and finally, to so-called more "civilized tribes" such as the Cherokee (3.3:8–9). The trip's purpose was to learn about American Indian boarding school policies. But Wilson's other motivation was to fulfil his budding interest as an ethnographer.[11] Before the trip, Wilson had begun a comparative vocabulary of at least forty Indigenous languages, and on the trip he "wanted to be gradually adding to [his] stock." Part of the answer to why Wilson would praise English-only policies and yet seek knowledge about Indigenous languages lies in the word "stock." Wilson believed Indigenous languages were for him – not Indigenous peoples. Furthermore, Wilson saw these languages not in the way Indigenous scholars today cite, but as a relic to collect. Wilson frames Indigenous languages as a resource from which he extracts, mirroring the science and anthropology of his day as well as literal resource extraction in North America then and now.

The trip was not his first; two years earlier, Wilson visited three institutions, including Carlisle, and "formed a connection" (1.5:3). In October 1888, Wilson set off on his more ambitious venture. Though Wilson sold his trip as a chance to learn about American school policies, he also took the opportunity to interview children about their languages. The first school on his trip to the US was Lincoln Institute, a boarding school in Philadelphia. The institute began after a group of women saw Carlisle School students on parade to celebrate the city's bicentennial and were inspired to begin their own federally funded school. When Wilson writes about these school visits in his newspapers, he usually begins discussing the school's progress in English before documenting the children's Indigenous languages. For instance, upon first arriving at Lincoln Institute, he remarks that he and his wife "could hear the quaint talk going on – just the way the girls talk to each other, in imperfect English" at Shingwauk Home. Wilson also read aloud letters that his students had written in English for the children to hear at the

American Indian boarding schools. Wilson typically began his articles by providing some basic information about the schools' policies. It is as if Wilson wished for his readers to understand that these schools, like his own, were still very much dedicated to promoting English before devoting the rest of his articles to Indigenous languages.

But then Wilson shifts to his "business to attend to" – his desire to "get words and sentences from some of these girls in their various different dialects." The Lincoln Institute offered Wilson three or four girls who all spoke different languages to spend a few hours with Wilson and "give [him] all the information that they could." Wilson would spend the time in these sessions writing down "words and phrases in their different tongues" (*Our Forest Children* 3.4:24–5). From the Lincoln Institute, Wilson travelled to Carlisle School and painted a similar scene. He began describing the English used at the school – the songs and speeches the children delivered, the conversations he had with students, and the letters from students in Ontario that he read to the children at Carlisle. But like at Lincoln, Wilson shifts to his "business." He began Monday morning at nine o'clock in the office of Carlisle's disciplinarian (a role Wilson defines as "one who drills pupils, sees after their clothing, books, bathing, &c, and occasionally whips them"). Wilson sat at the disciplinarian's desk with a book and pencil and took down words. The following is his account of how he learned Indigenous languages from Carlisle students:

> For twenty-two minutes did I ply that Comanche Indian with questions, asking him to give me the Comanche rendering of a long string of words and sentences.
>   "What is the word for man?"
>   "Say it again please."
>   "Does that mean a white man or an Indian, or simply man?"
>   "Oh, that's it, is it?"
>   "Say it again, please."
>   "Te-ne-pa."
>   "Do I say it right?"
>   "Say it once more";
>   "Thank you."
>   "Now, woman."

Wilson's version of his business in the disciplinarian's office is a monologue. Even in Wilson's behind-the-scenes column of how he "got

Indian words," the Indigenous children are not represented as having a voice. Even in his self-reflective "My Wife and I" column, there was no space to reflect on how the method of "adding to a stock" foreclosed far more nuanced understandings of language. In this example, the question of how to say "man" and "woman" presumes gender in English and Comanche are the same. Instead, we hear Wilson's responses and methods of plying only. After the Comanche child, Wilson interrogates Cheyenne-, Kiowa-, Omaha-, and Onondaga-speaking children. Wilson boasts, "Seven languages are taken down now before lunch, and ten more in the afternoon." By Tuesday, Wilson claimed to have taken down twenty-five different Indigenous languages (*Our Forest Children* 3.4:27). Throughout his column, Wilson describes how he learned Indigenous languages from students. One exception was when he interviewed not students but a chief of police, who supplied Wilson with Ponca words while a boy named Charlie sat on the floor and "kept putting in a word or two now and then" (3.11:138). But for the most part, when Wilson visited a school he usually interviewed students on their Indigenous languages, prefacing the encounter in his writing by first highlighting how the school promoted English literacy.

Wilson explains how he "procured" interviewees by presenting photographs of Shingwauk Home. As Wilson explains, potential interlocutors initially regarded Wilson "curiously," but "their faces lighted up and they very quickly made friends" after he shared his photographs and situated himself as having lived for twenty years "among the Indians" (4.2:186). This example reveals an additional way boarding school photography was used besides its role in recruiting students, advertising the school, and reporting to government. Wilson would ask school administrators to connect him with students whose languages he required for his research. For instance at Genoa School in Nebraska, Wilson writes in "My Wife and I" that though the school head offers for Wilson to tour the classrooms and workshops, Wilson interjects that he was foremost interested in hearing students speak. Though the school's head tells Wilson he could "have any of these children that you wish, and procure from them such information as you need about their languages," Wilson did not require all students, as he already had many contributions to his "stock" over his research and travels (*Canadian Indian* 1.6:177). In other words, Wilson was not concerned with learning what students had to share; rather, he was only interested in filling the gaps of his "stock." The same was true for his visit to Chilocco School in Oklahoma, which was particularly hurried. The second thing

Wilson did at the school was tour the institution and its workshops with the superintendent. But "the first thing, after introducing myself to the authorities, was to interview some of the children of the Caddo, Oto, and Tonkawa tribes, and take down words in their languages" (*Our Forest Children* 3.2:138). Wilson directed which words he desired to know and from whom. He describes one Arapaho student, Gabriel, as having "a tongue that could talk." According to Wilson, Gabriel was "determined to tell [Wilson] every Shoshoni word he knew" and was "bound [that Wilson] should have them." However, the words Gabriel wished to share were not on Wilson's "list" (*Canadian Indian* 1.6:177).

While Gabriel appeared interested in sharing his language with Wilson, other students did not in more disturbing scenes. At Genoa School, Wilson met with "two little Flathead girls." Wilson describes them as "very shy" and noted that "it was long before I could even get them to open their mouths." Just when one of them was about to speak, Wilson states that a "dreadful" Sioux dusting boy came in the room. The boy came in, leaned his elbows on Wilson's desk, and "look[ed] intently into the little Flat-head's mouth to see what she was going to say." The boy's action caused the girls to come "to a dead stop," making Wilson doubt he would hear from either girl. Though Wilson directs the dusting boy to complete his other duties, the boy keeps his eyes on the "little Flat-head girl's mouth" and her "fast-closed lips." Wilson tries to get the boy to leave: "'Had you better go and clean your lamps then?' I said, 'I think these little girls are shy, and I want them to speak to me and tell about their language.' The dusting boy was evidently of the opinion that his lamps could wait; and he seemed bound he would see the Flat-head girl's mouth open before he went." Wilson believes the boy remains because he wants to hear the girls as well, as Wilson appears to so desperately desire. And perhaps the boy does defy the orders because he wishes to hear forbidden languages and encounter a space in which he, too, could safely speak his language. But Wilson may have been wrong. The boy could have stayed to take the heat off the two girls who appear unconsenting in Wilson's desire to hear them speak. Wilson realizes the boy will not leave:

I changed my tactics, and began asking the dusting boy the rendering of certain English words in his language, which was Sioux. I thought at first that this plan was going to prove a success, for both the little Flat-heads pricked up their ears and a flash of something like intelligence crossed their faces as they heard the dusting boy repeat the words I gave him in the Sioux language; the boy also evidently thought he was going to bring the girls out and make them speak, by taking his part in the play. But no, it was no good; the little Flat-heads were still mum; they had evidently made an inward resolve that they would neither of them utter a single word in the presence of the dusting boy. (1.7:208–9)

Though Wilson already "had" Sioux words, he asks the boy to speak so as to encourage the girls, whose language Wilson *is* interested in. Though he understands the boy to be "taking his part in the play," again this is unknown – perhaps the boy participated as a chance to speak a language otherwise forbidden. Or maybe he wanted to alleviate the girls' stress. It is also unclear what the "flash of something like intelligence" on their faces meant: Surprise to hear an Indigenous language? Relief they didn't have to? The school head then comes in and orders the boy to leave. Now, the girls are forced to speak:

A very low whisper came from the elder girl, giving, as I supposed, the Flat-head rendering of the English word which I had just repeated to her for the fiftieth time. "Thank you," I said, "that's just what I want"; and I wrote it down. I had not the least idea what the child had said, but I would not discourage her by letting her know that, so I wrote down something and gave her another word; and she whispered again, and I wrote again. At length, as I had anticipated, the child gained confidence and began to speak out; and I was able to get the words from her correctly, and to correct those which I had at first written down. (1.7:209)

Now unencumbered, Wilson "plies" the girls with an air of frustration. One girl responds in a "low whisper," a tone children were accused of using in the previous chapter. Wilson attempts to foreclose understanding the dusting boy or the girls' silence as resistance in this disturbing scene. But as Menominee poet Chrystos (1994) articulates, this may have been a moment where "no photograph or tape recorder or drawing can touch / the mountain of our spirits" (l. 24–5).

Besides documenting these interviews in his column "My Wife and I," Wilson also drew several pictures of how he learned Indigenous words. The sketch of his interviews at Carlisle School, titled "Getting Indian Words" (see figure 4.4), shows Wilson on the left in profile, his right hand holding a pen, as he looks at a boy whose arms are stretched out. Wilson sits at the desk while the boy does not, and above both of them is the corner of a framed map, with the Gulf of Mexico showing.

OUR FOREST CHILDREN.   27

The pupils, Indian boys and girls, ranging in age from 10 to 20, and upwards of 400 in number, filled the body of the building. There are nearly 600 pupils now belonging to the school, but a number of these are out on the school farm, which is some distance off, and about 150 have been placed out temporarily as apprentices with white people.

The evening's entertainment consisted in songs, readings, recitations, speeches, &c., all by the Indian pupils,—and was very creditably conducted. One young Indian gave us a temperance lecture, another took for his subject "Try, try again." Five or six little children, some of whom were white, sung an infant song, keeping time with their hands and feet. One of these was a little Apache, not long from the camp, and only about 6 years old. The little fellow was quite on his dignity and kept feeling his little stick-up collar and arranging his white cuffs. The prettiest thing of all was a something by a number of little Indian girls in dark blue dresses, white collars, and red sashes, who went through a number of evolutions threading in and out among each other to the time of the music; they each had a sort of baton with a red tuft at each end, in each hand, and sometimes they rattled their battons together; sometimes they seemed to aim them at the assembled audience; sometimes they pressed them to their breasts and put one foot forward, and leaned back, and turned up the whites of their eyes. It was all very pretty, and they were encored and had to do it again.

Then when the children's part was all over, the great, tall, towering form of the captain appeared on the platform. We expected to hear him speak in a big voice, but he didn't; he spoke rather low, but very clearly, and everybody listened while he was speaking. Then my turn came to speak, and I said a few words and read the two letters I had brought with me from the Shingwauk and Wawanosh Home.

Next day was Sunday. We had purposely planned to pass a Sunday at the Carlisle School. The Carlisle school is undenominational. On Sunday morning those pupils who have been baptised and joined some Christian body, are allowed to attend whatever church they have been received into; they are detailed off into squads, and, accompanied by an Indian serjeant or corporal, go to their own place of worship. In the afternoon is Sunday school, and preaching in the assembly room, and in the evening, a service of prayer or praise, generally led by the Captain himself. The Captain and Mrs. Pratt are Presbyterians.

At 10.30, the school herdic, with two horses (not the

one we arrived in) was driven up to the door, and ourselves and several of the teachers took seats in it and were driven to the Episcopal Church. Quite a number of the Indian boys were present in their blue United States uniforms, and several of them remained with us for Holy Communion. In the afternoon, the Captain asked me to assist the Rev. Mr. Rittenhouse, Congregational minister, in conducting service at the school. It consisted in hymns, prayers, and a missionary address by myself, in which I told the pupils something of the early history of our Homes at Sault Ste. Marie, and shewed how the work had from the first been carried on, by a simple dependence upon God. In the evening, I thought I would like a walk to the Episcopal church again, and, the night being dark and the church some distance off, I asked the Captain to allow two of his boys to go with me to shew me the way. As I was given the choice, I selected two little fellows twelve or thirteen years old, their homes a very wide distance apart—Saisena Nora, a Pueblo boy, from Laguna, New Mexico, and Henry Philip, a Thlinkit, from far Alaska. It was very interesting to hear the talk of these two bright, intelligent little fellows; they both told me about their homes, and the way in which their people lived.

*   *   *   *   *

I had come to Carlisle for business. The business began at nine o'clock on Monday Morning. It happened in the office of Mr. Cambell, the disciplinarian. (Disciplinarian, it should be explained, is an American term, meaning one who drills pupils, sees after their clothing, boots, bathing, &c., and occasionally whips them). I took my seat at the desk, a scribbling book before me, a pencil with a morsel of india rubber at the other end in my hand. On my right, close to me, sat a young Comanche Indian.—A Coman-

GETTING INDIAN WORDS.

che Indian, clothed in United States uniform, in his

TWO LITTLE FLATHEADS.

Figure 4.5. "Two Little Flatheads." *Canadian Indian* 1.7:208: April 1891.

In the image Wilson drew of his interviews at Genoa School (see figure 4.5), the scene is from behind. The dusting boy stands on one side of a desk, his eyes on the girls. Wilson sits on the other side of the desk in profile, staring at the two girls. The smaller one stands behind a taller girl. While both face Wilson, the taller girl lowers her head. In these images, it appears imperative that Wilson portrays for readers how he learned Indigenous words – both in text and in image. Remember that this behind-the-scenes column is in addition to the column where he presented his findings. What is curious about Wilson's sketches is that he includes himself – rather than illustrating a scene he views, he includes his own body as if someone else, not him, sketched his interviews. Both images are from behind Wilson and the children, all in profile (with the exception of the dusting boy), and both images feature Wilson as bigger than the children, who are in positions of almost supplication. Wilson's right hand is at the ready, vested with the authority of the desk, the pen and inkwell, books, and in one case a map.

Even Wilson's sketches may have been created under duress. In another episode of "My Wife and I," Wilson relates how in Santa Fe he visited the San Miguel Church. He decided the exterior was "too ugly" to sketch and moved inside (3.13:172). Wilson states that when a boy inside appears "disconcerted" by Wilson's presence, he proceeds anyhow because the boy "did not know enough English to express his feelings": "He seemed very uneasy, appeared to be afraid that a priest or some one would come in, – every now and then he sighed, shuffled his feet and said, 'better go now'; but I kept talking amicably to him till I got through, asked him about the pictures on the wall, ascertained that one was 700 years old, and two others each 400 years old. Then I replaced my drawing materials in my satchel, and continued my pilgrimage." The boy clearly knows enough English to tell Wilson about the church and order him to leave, but not enough that Wilson believes he has to. The scene represents how Wilson gleaned his information outside of formal institutions like the Smithsonian (which may have gathered research in the same way). In Zuni territory, Wilson lays out another way he created sketches, which appears against the will of interlocutors: "I also took several 'instantaneous photographs' – that is, I took a good look at an individual, and then sketched him down before he knew it. I can manage to take down these Indians now pretty well, without their being aware of it. If they think they are being sketched, they cover their faces, turn their backs, and move off; but I always pretend to be sketching the sky, or some distant object, when my model turns a suspicious eye to me, and that reassures him, and enables me to get another look at him before he moves off" (*Canadian Indian* 1.2:51). Like the boy in the church, the subjects of "instantaneous photographs" appear not to welcome Wilson's sketches. The boy shuffles his feet and directly tells Wilson to leave; the Zuni turn away and cover themselves. In both scenes, Wilson seems almost boastful of his techniques, which include distraction, feigned obliviousness to their discomfort, and deceit (in pretending to sketch the sky). But within these scenes may be what Audra Simpson (2007) calls "ethnographic refusal." Simpson's larger work understands how Indigenous people "interrupt anthropological portraits of timelessness, procedure, and function that dominate representations of their past, and sometimes, their present" (p. 68). People thwart Wilson's attempts at "instantaneous photographs." And when Wilson conducted research in Assiniboine, he stated, "These people do not seem to indulge much in tradition, their ideas as to their own origin and theories of the human race are very vague" (3.11:133). Leaving Wilson's treatment of tradition as an indulgence aside, we may also read his finding as ethnographic refusal.

Scenes in which Wilson learns Indigenous words are prefaced by the work of the school – children praying, singing, and speaking English.

These prefaces as well as Wilson's sketches show a controlled environment in which students are permitted, by Wilson and the school alone,
to speak their Indigenous language. As well, Wilson offers scenes in
which students do not or cannot speak any language but English:
"Some of the pupils had a somewhat imperfect knowledge of their own
language. Carlisle had done its work, and had in some instances succeeded in driving the native tongue almost entirely out of the Indian
head in the course of 4 or 5 years." Wilson describes an interview in
which a student professed only to know how to say "yes," and Wilson later discovered that even this was incorrect. He also interviews
a Shoshone-speaking student who "had forgotten a great part of his
mother tongue, and was obliged to withdraw after giving me a few
words in a rather hesitating manner" (*Canadian Indian* 1.6:177). In these
"failures," we may read the careful line Wilson had to walk: He wishes
to showcase the successes of these schools, which he is using as a model
for his own in Canada. But he also wants to satisfy his desire to hear
Indigenous words for his "stock." Students may indeed have forgotten, which would confirm for readers the success of an English-only
curriculum. Alternatively, their silence may be resistance to Wilson's
force, resulting in claims they have "forgotten" or are "hesitating" and
"vague" when they instead are refusing to participate.

When the trip concluded, Wilson prepared a pamphlet after "taking
down the words as pronounced from the Indians' lips" (*Our Forest Children* 3.1:47). The pamphlet included information on eighty languages,
though some of the information was partial. The pamphlet therefore
had blank space for readers of the newspaper, who could contribute
additional information. Wilson isolated such readers as people "living
among Indians, or interested in Indian linguistics" as well as "books
bearing on Indian history or Indian language" (3.1:47), not Indigenous
people themselves, perpetuating the belief that the languages (naturally, and in no way *because of* boarding schools) are dead or nearing
extinction.

Of course, Indigenous peoples had their own reasons for participating in ethnographic research in the late nineteenth century. As Hochman (2014) argues, "At a time when their collective future seemed
outwardly imperiled, native peoples sat for photographs, talked to
phonographs and performed in films, and they had their own motivations for doing so" (p. xxii). But in Wilson's ethnographic behind-the-
scenes column "My Wife and I," the child speakers do not appear as
willing participants. In a letter dated 3 April 1888 (six months before

Wilson embarked on his second American trip), Wilson suggested to Pratt they exchange two students each for six months to a year. Wilson wrote that it would do his students good, but he also explains he was "deep in the study" of "Indian languages and dialects" and could better study the Carlisle students if they remained with him for a considerable time (Wilson, 1887–8). Though the plan seems not to have actualized, the fact Wilson even thought a second removal of children from their land and families for his research was possible or ethical reveals how permeable the colonial border was according to heads of boarding schools. His proposition also suggests Wilson's thought process – namely, ethnography no matter the cost.

Conclusion

The word "sanction" denotes two contradictory meanings: as a verb, it can permit (the school *sanctioned* Indigenous languages), yet as a noun it can condemn (the school had *sanctions* against Indigenous languages). As this chapter has identified, schools and their newspapers had seemingly contradictory views on the role of Indigenous languages. The previous chapter reiterated what survivors have long testified, which is that at best, Indigenous languages were not encouraged or were denigrated, and at worst, students were violently punished. UNESCO outlines six levels of support for a local compared to national language: equal support, differentiated support, passive assimilation, active assimilation, forced assimilation, and prohibition (Grenoble and Whaley, 2006, pp. 11–12). Many nineteenth-century boarding schools edged towards the latter.

And yet this chapter has suggested how Indigenous languages were heard or read at boarding schools in certain instances. Many of these moments came from survivors such as Isabelle Knockwood, who realized if she no longer spoke Mi'kmaw it would die like Latin. Yet schools and their newspapers labelled children who continued with Indigenous languages as obstinate, diffident, and slow. Schools permitted Indigenous languages, but often as a method of teaching about Christianity or English. As well, schools – in particular Shingwauk Home and the ethnographic work of Wilson – participated in the larger nineteenth-century interest in Indigenous languages as exoticized curiosities, as remnants of the past, and as scientific keys.

As many linguists document, outsiders who seek to "save" a language will inevitably fail because community members will always be the most invested in revitalization (Grenoble and Whaley, 2006, p. x). But it was the school, church, and government who attempted to control when, where, how, and by whom Indigenous languages could make an appearance. Furthermore, many languages did not *need* revitalizing in the nineteenth century. Schools were largely in the business of eradicating, not preserving, Indigenous languages. UNESCO measures the vitality of a language by the "amount and quality of documentation," in which Wilson was certainly devoted. But this factor is last, preceded by government support and – the number one factor – intergenerational transmission (p. 6). As Standing Bear remarked, "A language, unused, embalmed, and reposing only in a book, is a dead language. Only the people themselves, and never the scholars, can nourish it into life" (2006, p. 234). We see in the case of Wilson a behind-the-scenes glimpse into *how* he documented languages – troubling scenes in which Wilson added to his stock, no matter the resistance from children. Recall the previous chapter, which detailed the almost limitless efforts of principals, including Wilson, to supplant Indigenous languages with English only – Wilson was the one who employed a *jeton* system at the school and incentivized children to speak English with bags of nuts as prizes.

Today, many think of language extinction without regard for the *how*. As Marie Battiste (2011) writes, the violence of English has been hidden by myths of literacy (p. 165). While school newspapers reveal the construction of some of these myths – that Indigenous languages disappeared naturally, and literacy is unquestionably a benevolent gift – they complement survivor testimony that insists schools were not devoid of Indigenous languages. Students still spoke them despite the rules, both accidentally and in resistance, in order to maintain their languages and sustain their spirits. School newspapers also reveal how Indigenous languages were permitted as ethnographic curiosities, as something principals – not Indigenous children and their families – got to catalogue and teach readers of a newspaper. Indigenous-led language resurgence projects today deserve support from many levels. Such support is justice and a debt owed, not charity.

5 Ahead by a Century: Time on Paper

In 1897, Battleford School printed an article in its newspaper by a Reverend P.L. Spencer titled "The Indian as a Factor in the Making Up of Future Canada." It begins by disputing the myth of "the vanishing Indian" with statistics of population booms. Because of this growth, Spencer argued that Canadians should try to make Indigenous peoples "good and useful members of the commonwealth." His article continues:

> If we take the liberty of pointing the camera towards them, we should do so not because we fancy that they will soon be "blocked out" of nature's picture, but because we see in them a people that have had a mysterious history in the past, occupy at the present time an interesting and remarkable position in the social vista, and are certain to exercise in the future no little influence for weal or woe in the formation of a Canadian nation ... The camera of the heart will be opened, and into it will be flashed the strong light of eternal truth, leaving as its impress the image of the Divine. (*Guide* 5.12:3)

It is not a coincidence Spencer leaned on the metaphor of the camera since he was an avid photographer in addition to a late nineteenth-century reverend and missionary in Ontario. Spencer wrote for the *Canadian Photographic Journal* of the ways he photographed Elders as well as Indian boarding school students, sometimes detailing how these images were not taken with consent. He would take these images and convert them into magic lantern slides and then bring them to England as a visual aid for explaining his work in Canada (Spencer, 1895a, p. 39; 1895b).[1] What was more, much of the nineteenth century's attempts to salvage the "vanishing Indian" came in the form of cameras. According to this excerpt Indigenous peoples were worthy of attention not because, as other sources of the day suggested, they were about to disappear and be "blocked out of nature's picture" but rather since they were examples of an exoticized past and a progressive present. The future included Indigenous peoples, but only those who would help to form Canada; anyone refusing to acknowledge the legitimacy of the nation-state was literally not in the picture.

Boarding school newspapers offered narratives of past, present, and future for readers as if these divisions existed outside of the settler imaginary.[2] But such narratives of time are constructed, not found. As Bruno Latour (1993) argues, "*it is the sorting that makes the times, not the times that make the sorting*" (p. 76). In other words, the way time is organized (sorted) constitutes it. Or as Cree/Métis poet Marilyn Dumont (2007a) writes, "time is a story we tell" (p. 35). The nineteenth century was a particularly intense period of European stories of time, with new technologies such as the telephone, telegraph, railroad, and cinema as well as time-based theories of evolution, religion, and ethnography (2003, p. 1). One consequence of such new technologies was that time became further naturalized, entrenching beliefs in positivist neutrality that, as Johannes Fabian (2014) notes, were hardly devoid of politics and led to classifications of civilized, primitive, and modern (p. 17).[3] Elizabeth Strakosch and Alissa Macoun (2012) cite time as a particular tool of settler colonialism, and in the time and place of these newspapers its wielding intensified. It was after all a Canadian in the nineteenth century, Sandford Fleming, who created world time zones (Creet, 1998).[4] Newspapers were largely uninterested in Indigenous conceptions of time (e.g., Lakota winter counts or Cree moon phases). School publications were not concerned with Scott Lyons's (2010) concept of "temporal multiplicity," which challenges the narrative of Indigenous peoples in the past and modernity as a time haplessly imposed by Europeans (p. 13). School newspapers actively foreclosed Mark Rifkin's concept of "temporal sovereignty," which considers Indigenous articulations of time and self-determination in spite of settler time and its aims to enfold Indigenous peoples into it (2017, p. 3). Missing from school newspapers were understandings of Indigenous futurisms, as defined by Grace Dillon (2012) and others. School newspapers attempted to contain examples of "temporal resistance," a concept Paul Huebener (2016) takes up in his work on time in Canadian literature. School newspapers deployed what Elizabeth Povinelli (2010, p. 30) calls "technologies of temporality" – time tools. Newspapers also naturalized linear time, which Vine Deloria Jr (2003) makes clear is a Western European construction (p. 63).

School newspapers established Indigenous peoples as foil to the speed, success, and industry of white settlers – traditional versus modern, indolent versus industrious, dying out versus population growth. School newspapers presented time, not the settler, as the inescapable culprit for genocide, poverty, displacement, forced removal of children, and linguicide. Time in these newspapers was another settler fantasy that located Indigenous peoples in the past while reserving the future for settlers themselves, all the while using humanitarian language to describe colonialism.[5] Besides the time of the newspaper itself (its frequency, special issues dedicated to Christian holidays, and the milestones of Queen Victoria), newspapers along with other media and technologies of time displayed a mostly non-Indigenous future. While Shingwauk Home in Ontario had hoped to offer watchmaking as one of its trades (*Our Forest Children* 1.9:4), far more frequently school newspapers used time theoretically. Some articles in these newspapers explicitly spell out the problem with "Indian time," praising policies to correct such supposed signifiers of savagery. In other instances, time was tacit and was represented in articles on the day-to-day of classes, the schoolyard whistle, and railroad expansion. These techniques attempted to locate Indigenous peoples in and out of time depending on what narrative best suited settler needs.

Time to Change

One way school newspapers foreclosed temporal multiplicity was by blaming genocide on the unstoppable force of time. Regina School in Saskatchewan summarized this belief in one disturbing poem it reprinted titled "Departure of the Indians," which depicts Indigenous peoples' destiny to march sluggishly, sit down, weep, die, and "give to the white man all!" (*Progress* 3.70:2–3). Newspapers referred to students and their families as "these great people of the past" (*Our Forest Children* 3.5:34), as part of a "vanished race" (*Progress* 3.79:2, 11), and belonging to a "past tribal greatness" (*Na-Na-Kwa* 12.5).

But more often newspapers sought to counteract the myth. Perhaps more accurately, newspapers took the myth as given but claimed their schools helped to thwart this fate. Regina School reproduced an article from a Scottish newspaper predicting Indigenous peoples would be wiped out, but the school newspaper discredits the article in a preface by stating "the writer's knowledge of the facts is not re-Markably accurate" (3.80:3). Battleford School, too, denied claims of "decline or gradual disappearance" (*Guide* 5.12:3). Regina School reprinted an article dispelling the myth, claiming that Indigenous populations were in fact increasing (18.2:7). School newspapers presented their institutions as mitigating the inevitable damage of time. Kitamaat Home's newspaper asserted that "the Indians in the Dominion would have been extinct had it not been for the good offices of those who do not believe it is to the credit of the white man to see the Indian disappear entirely" (*Na-Na-Kwa* 30.12). It further declared that a dying-out was not the school's aim: "It is not to our credit to see the Indians dying out, we do not wish it, it behooves us to use all means in our power to prevent it, and to save the remnant of a powerful nation" (2.2). Shingwauk Home's newspaper considered education "the wisest and most just and humane course for us in Canada to pursue" because "either we must despoil them of all their rights" or "provide for their existence in our midst and admit them into our civilization" (*Our Forest Children* 1.1.1), establishing schools as an ethical strategy of coping with this temporal inevitability. The narrative of time in newspapers framed the killing and displacement of Indigenous peoples as unstoppable and not the fault of settlers, who were in fact helping to ameliorate such fates.

Note the difference in an article by Dakota reverend James Garvie, reprinted in Shingwauk Home's newspaper *Our Forest Children*. Garvie's perhaps facetiously titled article, "Why Do Indians Advance So Slowly?" differs markedly from others by non-Indigenous writers. Garvie discusses jealousy, laziness, and gluttony. But buried in the middle of the article is what Garvie labels "the greatest hindrance" – white people. Garvie describes them as trying "every possible way to take away our lands; they run us out of our work; and, if they can, they will hinder us from going to heaven" (2.9:30). He also highlights the limits of the United States' legal system, which harms rather than protects Indigenous men. He concludes: "Who is heartless enough or cruel enough to talk about the Indians not being advanced faster when all these things work against their advancement?" While most schools used their newspapers to deny culpability, Garvie redirected blame from time to white settlers.

Aside from Garvie's article, school newspapers promoted the idea that Indigenous peoples required time to transition from past to present. As one bureaucrat put it, the government should allow Indigenous peoples to "creep for a time before they attempt to walk," as "it is only a few years since they were wild untamed savages" (Benson, 1897, p. 10). Again using wood as a stand in for children, Kitamaat Home's newspaper emphasized that the school could not in short order "bring into perfect cultivation huge tracts of territory which are covered with weeds, noxious herbs, giant trees representing the growth of centuries" (Na-Na-Kwa 8.1). Years later, the same newspaper maintained the metaphor, claiming that "old customs are like the great pines and hemlocks with which our forests abound hard to uproot" (25.8). With this dehumanizing analogy, children/trees could only either die or assimilate, the latter of which was the humane alternative proposed by the newspapers, where settlers would generously allow time for Indigenous peoples to transition from past to present. Edward Francis Wilson, principal of Shingwauk Home, offered a similar compassion. He compared the changes that nations such as England, Sweden, France, and Italy had historically made to the changes expected – of dwelling, livelihood, religion, education – in a short time of Indigenous peoples in North America. Wilson viewed the expectations of change as rushed: "The Indians, I believe, must have time. These changes that we think so good for him, must not be forced upon him too suddenly" (Canadian Indian 1.8: 223). He urged readers to "not expect too much, or too rapid results, from the efforts put forth" (Our Forest Children 4.8:4).

Newspapers established their schools as the salve for a painful present to which Indigenous peoples had to adapt. School newspapers also called attention to the present through the quotidian of the school: picnics, exams, and football matches; visits from inspectors and politicians; buildings built and buildings burnt down. Much of the day-to-day in school newspapers referenced Christmas, Easter, baptisms, and Sunday – Christian markers of time. But the newspapers' present also assumed Indigenous peoples had a problem with time. Rupert's Land School described how time was typically recorded – past tense – using buffalo robes (Aurora 2.22:1). One issue of a Saskatchewan school's newspaper from 1907 explained Indigenous people thought of time differently: "The Indians had no division of time in to weeks before the coming of the missionaries," and the church had "brought Sunday" (Progress 16.11:1), as if the Christian Sabbath existed independent of human creation. A later article claimed, "An Indian has no anxiety for the future" and "observes literally – too literally the command 'take no thought for the morrow'" (18.9:2). Another newspaper believed, "There is no word in the Red Indian language" – importantly, singular – "for the word 'year'" (*Our Forest Children* 3.3:1). Battleford School published an article titled "Prompt People," which advised readers to live every hour doing "exactly what is to be done" (*Guide* 4.11:2), and Rupert's Land School published a poem called "Be in Time!" (*Aurora* 2.22:2). Another article ominously cautioned, "There is no room for drones, sleepyheads and incompetents in the battle of life. They are soon tramped out of sight" (7.12:3). Newspapers offered advice on how best to control time, from lassoing time like a horse (*Progress* 18.5:3) to admonishing students who dream when they should be awake and responding to bells (14.4.8).

Speaking of bells: few twentieth-century survivor memoirs exclude how schools kept strict time with bells and schedules, and nineteenth-century school newspapers reveal a similar concern with time. They would narrate a day in the life for readers, sometimes even in fifteen-minute increments. One issue of *Our Forest Children* provided such an agenda, beginning with the alarm clock that wakes the school captain just before 6:00 a.m. He then rings a bell for everyone else, who get washed and dressed. The agenda then describes how students prayed, ascended the newly unlocked stairwell, and answered roll call, all before 7:00 a.m. At such time, the school captain would sit on a raised seat at the back of the dining hall and watch other students file in. After another bell, students would say grace. Yet another bell would signal when students would sit down and eat.

The reprinted schedule proceeded to describe how a bigger bell would then ring at 8:00 a.m. for morning prayers and chores, and 9:00 a.m. for the start of either work or schooling depending on the particular student's rotation. At 9:05 a.m., the teacher rang a smaller bell to signal the official start of class. A few minutes past noon, students took lunch and switched to the opposite duty (either classroom or work). Tea was at 6:00 p.m., prayers at 7:00 p.m., and self-reporting to the principal on bad behaviour followed. From 7:15 p.m. to 8:15 p.m., depending on their age, students sang, prepared for sleep, or turned in. The outer gates were locked at 9:30 p.m., and then at 11:15 p.m. the principal would go "round of the dormitories to see that all is safe" (*Our Forest Children* 2.10:16). The newspaper also published the reports of dormitory monitors, who noted which children got up on time.

Our Forest Children also reprinted the schedule of Battleford School. The article describes "the daily routine of the pupils, who are in an excellent state of discipline, particularly considering their origin" (3.3:13). The article documents the morning of the school and then continues with the day: "At 12 the large bell rings. Preparations for dinner follow;

and at 12:15 dinner is served, also under charge of an officer; and it is a treat to see the way in which they behave and handle their knives and forks. Recess till 1; trades again till 5; tea at 6; recreation till 7; study till 8, and then prayers. After prayers, each boy as he passes up stairs says, 'Good night, sir,' to the Principal." Other articles discuss the timing of meals, dormitory inspections, and garden recess, the latter a misnomer for building gardens, stonewalls, ditches, and fences (1.4:4). Articles attributed to students in the school newspaper of Rupert's Land School describe each hour and bell from breakfast to reading and writing, and from dinner to face washing and playing (*Aurora* 1.6:4; 1.7:4). One article titled "Day to Day at the Shingwauk" was from the perspective of the principal, Edward Francis Wilson. After the 9:00 a.m. bell rang and students either went to work or to study, Wilson began his day in his "private office, deep in pen, ink, paper and thoughts." The article continues as Wilson evaluated the work of students, attended to sick children in the hospital, and supervised school maintenance, which, in this example, was a road being leveled and graded. By lunch, the mail arrived, but Wilson is pulled away to attend to a boy with a dislocated shoulder, which he pops back in place. After sending the child to the school's nurse, Wilson concludes: "My horse is waiting, and I have to rush the remainder of my lunch, glance hastily through my letters, and then off to the Wawanosh [the girls' school]. Such and such like is our daily life at the Shingwauk" (3.3:6). Not all newspapers included as much detail, but most follow the same pattern of outlining for readers the school's strict adherence to time.

What would these printed agendas in school newspapers have communicated to readers? Like *Our Forest Children*'s title and masthead, agendas included in newspapers would impart there was a problem with time, which the school was remedying. Agendas in the newspapers, whether formal like Wilson's or the description of each school's day-to-day activities, exemplify Foucault's concept of the micropenality: "an area that the laws had left empty" (p. 178). Foucault lists many forms of micro-penality, which Amelia V. Katanski (2005) discusses in relation to American Indian boarding schools: inattention, impoliteness, speech, hygiene, and sexuality. Foucault also highlights time, including lateness, absence, and schedule interruptions. Agendas in school newspapers assured readers such micro-penalities were being corrected.

Basil Johnston's (1989) memoir of an Ontario boarding school in the 1940s demonstrates how students challenged such scripts of time, offering a counternarrative to that found in earlier school newspapers. Johnston printed a sample agenda of his school:

6:15 Rise
6:45–7:25 Mass
7:30–8:00 Breakfast
8:05–8:55 Work
9:00–11:55 Class/work
12:00–12:25 Dinner
12:30–1:10 Sports/games/rehearsal
1:15–4:15 Class/work
4:15–4:30 Collation
4:30–4:55 Work/chores
5:00–5:55 Study
6:00–6:25 Supper
6:30–7:25 Sports/games/rehearsal
7:30–10:00 Study and prepare for bed. (p. 47)

But before listing this detailed agenda, Johnston's memoir annotates it:

6:15 a.m. Clang! Clang! Clang! I was nearly clanged out of my wits and out of bed at the same time. Never had anything – not wind not thunder, awakened me with quite the same shock and fright.
   Clang! Clang! Clang!
   "Come on! Up! Up! Up! What's the hold-up? Not want to get up? Come on, Pius! What's wrong, Henry? You no like get up?"
   Clang! Clang! Clang! Up and down the aisles between the beds Father Buck walked, swinging the bell as if he wanted to shake it from its handle. (p. 28)

Father Buck uses the bell to elicit shock and fright, mocking students' English. Between each bell, Johnston lists the oppression of the clanging, an onomatopoeia he repeats throughout the scene. He also relays the subversions. For Johnston, "Were it not for the spirit of the boys, every day would have passed according to plan and schedule, and there would have been no story" (p. 47). At Johnston's school, the students' spirit and story defied the imposed schedule, agenda, and time of the school. Johnston also describes how flouting the agenda of the school was a method of pushback: "Since the boys could not openly defy authority either by walking out of the school and marching north or south on Highway 17 or by flatly refusing to follow an order, they turned to the only means available to them: passive resistance, which took the form of dawdling" (p. 30). Though school newspapers printed correctives to the problem of time and its micro-penalities, Johnston notes that at least in later boarding school periods, resistance came in the form of spirit, story, and slowness. While dawdling is framed in nineteenth-century school newspapers as a problem, Johnston's work reveals how temporal infractions were in fact forms of defiance.

Beforing and Aftering

Another temporal narrative school newspapers offered is what I am calling "beforing and aftering" – examples of Indigenous peoples in the past alongside examples of them in the present. This proximity of examples served as a foil that could not be accomplished were newspapers to isolate discussions of past and present. This concept is inspired by the work of Jean O'Brien (2010), who observes a similar technique she labels "firsting and lasting." O'Brien describes how early nineteenth-century New Englanders celebrated "firsts," such as birth, death, marriage, and settlement, and "lasts," which highlighted the supposedly last Indigenous person in an area. O'Brien plays on the word "lasting," uncovering ongoing Indigenous presence and resistance. These two turns O'Brien calls a "double act of colonialism," whereby settlers used examples of supposed Indigenous termination to build a story of their own rightful possession of land (p. 94). This double act of firsting and lasting, O'Brien argues, treats Indigenous peoples as only ever victims of historical change, while non-Indigenous people keep for themselves the right to recorded time (p. 107).

Boarding school newspapers, in a later time and different place, share O'Brien's technique of firsting and lasting. Kitamaat Home's newspaper celebrated the first female settler and the first missionaries in the Kitamaat Valley (*Na-Na-Kwa* 12.7; 21.1; 26.9). Other newspapers praised the first reverend to publish a dictionary in Blackfoot (*Our Forest Children* 4.2:179) or the first train in a region. Schools sometimes celebrated the lineage of their press. Methodist missionary Thomas Crosby, who gave the Golding and Company press to the Kitamaat Home in 1894, boasted it was the first press north of Nanaimo in British Columbia, although the claim may be dubious (Fahey and Horton, 2012, p. 47). Battleford School also bragged about the history of its machinery, claiming it was the first press west of Winnipeg and famous for printing the

Saskatchewan Herald, which the school notes was the oldest paper in the Northwest Territories (*Guide* 7.1:1). Yet firsting, when extended to Indigenous peoples, represented death and what readers might view as assimilation. Examples included the first suicide of an Indigenous woman (*Guide* 6.6:3), the first Indigenous woman to work for Indian Affairs (*Our Forest Children* 3.11:141), the first pupil at Shingwauk Home (4.6:254), and the first death of a student at the school (*Na-Na-Kwa* 6.8). In these cases, an Indigenous first was instead a last. School newspapers also celebrated lasting, such as the deaths of a "prominent Mohawk woman" (*Guide* 6.10:4) and "Old Jacob Sasakwamoos" (7.8:1).

Such lasting was particularly acute with reports on the deaths of chiefs. While a thirteen-year-old boy died at Battleford School and received only a classified line in the March 1898 issue of *The Guide* (6.9:1), the passing of Chief Kah-ke-ka-pinais of Fort Alexander three months later occasioned an article on his advanced age, conversion to Christianity, and interest in schools on-reserve (6.12:2). The school newspaper of Rupert's Land School reported on the oldest Indigenous man in British Columbia and on how the Sarcee people "have dwindled away" (*Aurora* 2.23:1–2). It could be argued chiefs received more attention because they lived longer than children, leaving more to write about. But the death of chiefs also represented the passing of a regime, polity, and older generation. The death of a student, on the other hand, represented the failure and horror of the school. School newspapers, often in detailed and mournful strokes, recorded the deaths and legacies of US chiefs Washakie (*Progress* 17.4:4) and Swift Bear (18.5:3), as well as Kitamaat Chief Jessea Morrison (*Na-Na-Kwa* 31.5). Battleford School's newspaper devoted three articles to the death of Chief Ahtahkakoop, "that eminent old chief" (*Guide* 5.7:1; 5.12:3) and the "last surviving real Cree Chief – that is[,] one appointed, or elected, by the Indians themselves under their own old system" (5.6:1). These articles highlighted Ahtahkakoop's Christianity and loyalty during the Riel resistance while flattening the more complicated ways he led his community through unthinkable change (Christensen, 2000; Johns, 2011; J.R. Miller, 1996a, pp. 150–2). In these articles, his delegation to Ottawa is reduced to an excursion (*Guide* 5.6:1; *Progress* 3.70:8). In school newspapers, the death of chiefs served as an opportunity to depoliticize their lives and symbolized the death of Indigenous ways of life more broadly.

Reporting on the death of chiefs also elided the ways Elders hindered or blocked settler colonial encroachments. *Progress* printed an article on Natos-Api (also known as Old Sun) upon his death, focusing on his wife's adventures (*Progress* 3.72:6) rather than that he signed Treaty 7; refused Christian conversion; and how when a missionary asked to live in his camp, Natos-Api marked off a plot of eight feet until he could trust the missionary was not stealing land (Dempsey, 1990). Although not a death, *The Guide* recorded the deposing of the chief at White Bear in the article "The Old Chief Was in the Way" (6.5:1). While the piece acknowledged that many chiefs were what it deemed progressive, it declared that "when the old chiefs oppose schools and keep the young men and woman [*sic*] from advancing they are in the way and should be deposed. Good. The Indian children MUST be educated."[6] Upon the death of Chief Payipwat (also spelled Piapot), one of the most important Plains Cree leaders in the mid-nineteenth century (Tobias, 1994), *Progress* reserved its front page to mourn the loss (17.4:1). Like other chief deaths the article cited his oldness, calling him "an Indian of the old times" who "refused to conform to many of the new ways." The article highlighted his diplomacy and oratory skills, but it also discussed his refusal to convert to Christianity and the "considerable trouble" he brought to the Department of Indian Affairs because "he was a man of forceful character." The article ignored that Payipwat was a signatory to Treaty 4 and devoted his life to exposing its mistakes and broken promises (Tobias, 1994). He held outlawed ceremonies, for which he was arrested and deposed of as chief in 1902. Payipwat also prevented the government from surveying and then parcelling out his land. This attitude to chiefs found in school newspapers, even in their deaths, is unsurprising: as Manitoba's Superintendent of Indian Affairs Ebenezer McColl wrote in 1891, he hoped that as chiefs died that their influence would die too (Lux, 2001, p. 87). Similarly, school inspector Thomas Wadsworth stated that the death of Chief Kamyīstowesit, who fought for Treaty 6 to be honoured (Tobias, 1982), was "hardly to be regretted, as he remained to the last a heathen." School newspapers capitalized on the deaths of chiefs, unlike the deaths of children, to reinscribe larger arguments about settler colonialism and time.

Lasting further occurred when school newspapers mourned the decontextualized "disappearance" of the buffalo. Regina School's newspaper, for instance, noted that in just two years the buffalo population at Yellowstone National Park in the US had gone from two hundred to fifty (*Progress* 3.72:7). "The conditions are not favorable" for the buffalo, the newspaper lamented. Tasha Hubbard connects such laments for buffalo to those for Indigenous peoples, both "the subjects of colonial elegies, which lamented their loss with a pen held in one hand and a gun in the other" (2014, p. 313). The same newspaper documented a settler hunter's encounter with "the last buffalo" in a county of Kansas, complete with details of the killing and the hunter's triumph (*Progress* 4.86:2). Other articles praised settler conservation strategies, replete with Indigenous erasures yet void of settler complicity for the plight of the buffalo. Regina School's newspaper noted the introduction of herds on Antelope Island in Utah and again at Yellowstone. As the article noted, "the future progress of this curious animal colony will be watched with great interest" – similar language the newspaper used to describe educational pursuits (3.83:1). Shingwauk Home's newspaper also praised the domestication of buffalo in Stony Mountain, Manitoba (*Our Forest Children* 2.X:6). While hopeful of preservation efforts, Shingwauk Home's newspaper also predicted that "to the next generation these animals will be almost as great curiosities as the mastodon and the ichthyosaurus are to us" (4.2:189). As Courtney Mason (2014) as well as Tracey Banivanua Mar (2010) uncover, the creation of national parks and spaces of so-called conservation in settler colonies were not departures from earlier nineteenth-century land grabs but continuities and extensions of these thefts. School newspapers' interest in buffalo protection in national parks, then, can be read in this vein.

Hubbard makes the case for the slaughter of buffalo not as disappearance but as genocide (2014, p. 304). Hubbard goes beyond the simpler but important claim that because Indigenous peoples were dependent on buffalo, their slaughter meant destruction. Hubbard instead challenges colonial, human-centric understandings of genocide by extending the term to animals (p. 294; p. 305). Hubbard argues that justifications for and denial of responsibility for buffalo "disappearance" were based in narrative, not unlike depictions of buffalo in school newspapers. What school newspapers were unable to report on is the future of the buffalo, though they predicted museumification. The conservation herd at Stony Mountain was kept by a warden, Samuel Bedson, who worked at the neighbouring penitentiary, the Stony Mountain Institution. Bedson kept the herd as part of his private zoo and got rid of it in 1888 (Gibson, 1990). Today, the Stony Mountain Institution has a 65 per cent Indigenous population of inmates (Macdonald, 2016). Artists today are making these connections clear in their work, including Rebecca Belmore's *The Indian Factory*, Kent Monkman's remix of National Film Board footage titled *Sisters and Brothers* and his exhibition at the Gardiner Museum, and Dana Claxton's film *Buffalo Bone China*, which Hubbard contextualizes (Claxton, 1997; Gilroy and Hubbard,

2015; Hubbard, 2009; L.-A. Martin, 2012; Monkman, 2015). These are artistic interventions into the narratives espoused by publications like school newspapers – narratives such as settler denial of responsibility for genocide and attendant stories of decontextualized "disappearance," claims to innocence through conservation efforts, and fatalism. Unlike school newspapers, as Hubbard states from a Nehiyaw perspective, "our stories, still told and still understood, tell us the buffalo will return one day" (2014, p. 303).

An important part of O'Brien's concept is not only that archives contained firsts or lasts but also that they contained both in tandem. I am borrowing O'Brien's emphasis on simultaneity and extending it to another "double act of colonialism" found in these newspapers: beforing and aftering. In this technique, Indigenous peoples are conceived of before school (in the past) and after, supplying, both visually and textually, a benchmark, a foil, for understanding the many other articles and images. Note how the titles of nineteenth-century Canadian newspapers *Progress* and *Our Forest Children* invoke this concept. Examples of beforing and aftering are well represented in the photography made famous at Carlisle School. The principal, Richard Pratt, would display photographs of students upon their arrival alongside photographs of uniformed children with their hair cut (Malmsheimer, 1985, pp. 55–6). Pratt and reservation agents would use the images in their recruitment pitches to parents and communities. In addition, Pratt included before-and-after photographs in annual reports, materials for the school's benefactors, and Carlisle's school newspapers (pp. 62–3).

Canadian newspapers and reports also used this technique; it was one of the many ways in which Canada modelled itself after the US. The before-and-after images of Thomas Moore have acted as a visual stand in for boarding school history. The original appeared in the 1897 annual report of the Department of Indian Affairs (DIA) and has since been disseminated widely.[7] In this photograph, beforing and aftering goes beyond dress and hair. The images represent a new name and even background, with the civilized stage featuring Moore assertively leaning on a Graeco-Roman post with a tamed potted plant behind him (Brady and Hiltz, 2017; Milloy, 1999, pp. 4–6). Sherry Racette (2009) considers how these photographs were meant to drum up support for schools and paint the government as the benevolent agent of change (p. 56). Such photographs also combined schools' theories on past and present. In one issue, *Our Forest Children* reproduced two photographs of Carlisle students. The photograph on the left rests above the caption

The Old Fashion.

A CORNER IN THE SUMMER VILLAGE — KITAMAAT.

Figure 5.1. "The Old Fashion." *Na-Na-Kwa* 16.6: October 1901.

"Indian pupils as they look on their first arrival to the Carlisle School"
(2.X:10–11). The children are barefoot, with mismatched clothing and
long, untied hair. Importantly, the photograph is shot outdoors, as
if really taken before students stepped into the institution. The photograph on the right features children in uniforms. The boys' hair is
now cut short, the girls' hair tied. The after photograph is indoors,
demonstrating the supposedly civilizing effects of Carlisle. The caption explains, *"This is how the pupils look after a four months training."*
In the after picture, students lose the epithet "Indian" and are simply
"pupils."

One example of beforing and aftering appeared in Kitamaat Home's
newspaper and was not of children, but of homes (see figures 5.1 and
5.2). The newspaper featured an illustration of a traditional coastal home
with the following annotation: "These houses, so fast disappearing from
the Coast villages, here [in the newspaper] remain intact to be a constant
reminder of the tribal system which even at the present time exerts its

The New Fashion.

A GLIMPSE OF THE NEW VILLAGE — KITAMAAT.
(FROM A PHOTO BY MISS MARKLAND.)

Figure 5.2. "The New Fashion." *Na-Na-Kwa* 16.7: October 1901.

influence amongst the natives."[8] According to the newspaper, the traditional houses have "but one door, no windows" and a fire within the home, which the newspaper blames for damaging the eyes of residents. On the opposing page is a cut titled "The New Fashion: Glimpse of the New Village." According to the newspaper, "In outward appearance the houses are 'white man's style,'" symbolizing "an advancing civilization impossible in the old native houses, where two, three, and four families eat, sleep and live together" (*Na-Na-Kwa* 16.6–7). For the newspaper, the difference between before and after is the consequence of old and new *fashion*, which, like time, is offered to readers as an inevitable thing and not the result of colonialism. The old homes exist (though they are "fast disappearing") as a symbol for how far Indigenous peoples have progressed: lightless homes, with threats of sexual deviance due to their mixing of genders and overcrowding, as well as a blinding fire. In this example of beforing and aftering, the home similarly represents what the staged photographs of Thomas Moore attempted to do.

Most times, though, school newspapers depended upon beforing and aftering less overtly. One such example is an image found in Kitamaat Home's newspaper of the "boys at lively play with their bows and arrows." Though there is only one photograph, the caption points out three of the boys in the picture are now at the Coqualeetza Institute and another three are dead (26.1). While a reader might see this photograph and assume the Kitamaat boys were not assimilated because they were playing "lively" with bows and arrows, the caption assures readers that six of the eight are in fact aftering (either with further schooling or death). Rather than concerning readers with such a startling rate of death, as well as the newspaper's disturbing choice to publish the photograph in the first place, such a caption may have assuaged readers concerned by an image supposedly of before (bows and arrows) with no accompanying image of the after. An earlier issue uses similar language, captioning an image of an Indigenous girl from Bella Coola. Her "costume, or lack of it" is labelled as the "old fashion." Though *Na-Na-Kwa* does not present a cut of the new fashion, a student on the same page writes about her ability to read the Bible, bake bread, and sew (8.1). In these instances, rather than presenting before and after images explicitly, readers were invited to draw their own conclusions. Whether the before and after was explicit or implied, the double act of past and present appears to have mattered more than one in isolation.

Another form of past coupled with present found in newspapers included Shingwauk Home's tableau performances, which displayed students past and then present. Tableaux typically exhibit actors frozen in action, sometimes imitating a famous painting or scene. In the nineteenth century, tableaux (often historical, allegorical, or patriotic) were sometimes featured at the end of a play and also served as a popular parlour game (Durham, 1998, p. 76; Glassberg, 1990, pp. 16–20; Pavis, 1998, p. 377). Normally in a tableau, actors delivered a presentation and then remained frozen at the end, attempting to embody the stillness of a painting. In Shingwauk Home's renditions students moved silently and sometimes spoke and sang. Wilson toured tableaux of students on several occasions and wrote about them in *Our Forest Children*.

One tableau routine Wilson described in the school newspaper toured in late 1887 through Western Ontario, with stops in Sarnia, Walpole Island, St Thomas, Kingston, London, and Montreal. The show near Ottawa at Carleton Place attracted an audience of five hundred and required an unexpected second performance (*Our Forest Children*

1.9:4). In the school newspaper, Wilson described the three five-minute sections of the performance:

1. Boys sang as they conducted trades (e.g., blacksmiths; shoesmiths; carpenters; tailors), delivering one speech in Ojibway and one in English on what the white man thinks of the Indian.
2. Boys sang as they conducted their chores (e.g., cutting wood; peeling potatoes), followed by "glee rounds." A Sioux boy then described the history of his life.
3. Girls sang as they worked (e.g., laundry) while boys gave writing, spelling, geography, and drawing lessons.

Rhythm mattered. As Wilson noted about the performance in Ottawa, the sounds from the blacksmith's hammer, the barber's scissors, and girls' irons were all intended to harmonize with the children's song (1.8:3). One local newspaper remarked the children "sang as they worked, regulating their movements to correspond with the measure of the cheerful ditty on their lips" (1.9:4). These tableaux preceded "Indian Singing, by the Sioux Boys from the North West" as well as a debate titled "That the Canadian Government Has Treeted [sic] the Indians Better Than Has the American Government," which lasted for thirty minutes and ended with church music. The entertainment then included a tableau of a typical Sunday evening at Shingwauk Home, where students recited texts and answered questions about the Bible.

One review in a local newspaper and reprinted by *Our Forest Children* cited this final tableau, the only one to feature Wilson with "his entire school about him," as the most interesting. It described Wilson in the tableau as "austere, stately and December-cold in his perpendicular dignity," a coldness thought to be "the secret of his grip on the untutored mind of savages" (1.9:5). This appears to be the only time Wilson or any other teacher was on stage, as one local newspaper explained that "from the beginning of the entertainment to its close, the teachers disappeared, and the Indians were left to run their own show" (1.4:1). Then came what Wilson called the "presentation scene," described as "when the members of each different tribe were presented separately." Students who were Delaware, Sioux, Ojibway, Ottawa, Pottawattamie, and Blackfeet would, nation by nation, step to the front and take a bow. The evening took two and a half hours, concluding with God Save the Queen (1.4:2; 1.8:3). With these tableaux, Wilson explained the purpose was not to raise money but to publicize that each child had "the full capability of taking his place side by side with the white man and emulating him in every branch of industry and civilized occupation" (1.4:2).

If the purpose was to demonstrate assimilation, why did Wilson include the students singing in Sioux and lecturing in Ojibway? Why feature the boy who described his "wild early life" (*Our Forest Children* 1.4:1)? And why bother having the children bow at the end not as a homogenous group but as distinct nations? Brenda Child (1999) notes this phenomenon at Haskell Institute. The school was otherwise devoted to assimilation, yet it still named children's Indigenous nationalities on their tombstones (p. 67). Wilson may have done so because like other techniques, he knew that to exhibit the present did not make sense without also exhibiting what an audience would deem the past.

Not all inclusions of the past were employed to demonstrate how far the schools had brought students into the present. Inclusions of the past may have been what audiences *really* wanted to see. This desire for the past came across in how Wilson pitched his request for volunteers to lodge students while on the tableau tour. Wilson insisted on billeting students, two per host, while on tour to keep expenses down but also to better acquaint Canadians "with our young Indians" (*Our Forest Children* 1.9:1). Like elsewhere in school newspapers, Wilson caricaturizes the children: "Each [billeter] take one Indian to their homes for the night. One could have great tall Snayamani from North West, another can have Charlie Baker from St. Joe's, another little Gracie from Walpole Island for the other. Peter Oshkahboos, the boy who draws so well from Serpent River. The other, Smart, the bootmaker, and little Negaunewenah … another, Jane Samproon, the clever tailoress" (1.4:2). Wilson mentions trades and therefore progress, and the very fact that he advertises lodging the students ("each take one Indian home for the night") asserts his authority, when the children's parents were seldom able to take their children home. But Wilson markets billeting by playing on pastness when he includes students' "exotic" homelands and qualities (e.g., height and artistry). Settler community newspapers reviewing the Shingwauk tableaux also highlighted markers of the supposed present: the thrill of billeting students included seeing that they were clean, neat, and "ate with refinement of manner."

However, one article states that the white hosts enjoyed "consorting with the children of the forest." It seems white billets initially "consented to the proposal with reluctance, some, in fact, with horror; and they began to think whether a bed in the woodshed would not be more satisfying to the spirit of the roving rascals" (*Our Forest Children* 1.8:4).

But "when the electric wires of human nature were strung, and the whites and reds looked into each other's eyes, the fog of misconception dissipated, and there came a feeling of warmth and fraternity." At the same time, the newspaper also delights at recounting how students made bows and arrows for their billets and one particular student hunted a bird during the visit. Present and past are contained in the review of billets, but a thrill also existed in references to the past.

The enjoyment for white audiences of Indigenous pastness was familiar to Wilson. He had reprinted several articles from Pratt's Carlisle publications condemning Buffalo Bill performances on the grounds they exoticized the past and ignored the reformation brought by boarding schools. Wilson became increasingly frustrated, as did Pratt, since audiences desired to see students in what they considered the past rather than present. The frustration continued when Wilson attempted to take the tableaux to England. He wrote in *Our Forest Children* that he had to initially cancel travel plans due to a lack of lodging but also because he received word "a party of Indian boys *in ordinary dress* would create no interest" (2.4:16). Though the tableaux Wilson choreographed for Montreal and Western Ontario included students in what audiences would consider the past through song and language, the primary focus was the present. At some point in Wilson's plans for England, someone may have taken him aside and told him the same show would not work, that his tableaux of students working and wearing uniforms would not be welcomed by British audiences. Two years later, the England trip *did* happen – but with a performance that met such expectations. Wilson's revised trip was scaled down, though, with only two children in attendance. The trip included a tour through Nova Scotia and New Brunswick, where the two boys would "sing hymns, recite a dialogue, and dress up in the costume of wild Indians" (4.2:179), a marked change from Wilson's tours two years prior. Part of the adjustment included a different motivation for the travel: while in his Ontario and Montreal tours Wilson cited his purpose as changing the minds of Canadians, his Maritimes and British tour was to shore up funds for his Canadian Indian Research and Aid Society (4.3:195) and also a new school in Medicine Hat, Alberta. Wilson's new show may have reflected his desperation for funding by giving in to audience expectation, or, maybe he changed his beliefs as well as his involvement as the research society grew.

Wilson wrote in *Our Forest Children* about the two boys who accompanied him on the Maritimes and British tableau trip in late 1890:

twelve-year-old Soney (Pottawatomi from Walpole Island) and eight-year-old Zosie (Ojibway from the north shore of Lake Superior). Indigenous peoples travelling to England has a long history, as the work of Coll Thrush (2016) documents. As Thrush argues, "London has been entangled with Indigenous territories, resources, knowledges, and lives from the very beginning of its experiments with colonization" (p. 15).[9] The newspaper describes the boys using the foil of past and present. *Our Forest Children* recounted how Soney was at first "illiterate," but he learned to read and write in under two years. Zosie is also befored as previously he was "a regular little wild Indian, living in a birchbark wigwam" and knowing "nothing about the English language or ABC." Though an image from the newspaper features Soney and Zosie in what would appear for readers as traditional clothing (see figure 5.3), the accompanying text about their progress in school afters them. During this complicated version of beforing and aftering, the paper lists Soney's and Zosie's "Indian names" and meanings. In this revised show, the two boys began wearing the school's uniform: a navy serge jacket with a scarlet sash. They repeated verses from the Bible, sang hymns, and would then enter a dialogue about where each other came from and how they liked Shingwauk – the answer being "first rate." The beginning of the performance featured the boys' present. Then the performance turned to the boys' imagined past. One boy would ask the other how to say phrases in his language. One phrase was "I like coming here very much," which Zosie would translate as "Ah-peche ne minwandumomaundupe ke-pe ezhahyaun." The boys would then wear Wilson's understanding of traditional Indigenous clothing, which he described as "dress up" (unlike the school uniform). The dialogue would then focus on their clothing:

> ZOSIE: What's that stick in your hand studded with brass nails and two leathern thongs attached to it?
> SONEY: That is the kind of whip the prairie Indians use when they ride their ponies ... It is said they use the lash for their ponies and the stick for their wives.

The performance concluded "with a war dance, accompanied by drum, rattle, and a weird kind of song, to the great amusement of the audience" (4.4:212–13). These two tableaux greatly differ, ranging from a Canadian show exhibiting mostly present with minor past to a British show that concludes with Wilson's imagined past.

212   OUR FOREST CHILDREN.

Two Little Indian Boys.

THE accompanying picture represents two little Indian boys from the Shingwauk Home, who last month accompanied the Rev. E. F. Wilson on a tour through Quebec and the Maritime Provinces, and have now gone with him for a few weeks' visit to England. The eldest boy is named William Soney. He is 12 years old, and is a Pottawatami, from Walpole Island. He has been only 2 years and a-half at the Shingwauk, and when he first came could only read a very little and knew not more than a word or two of English. Now he has made such good progress that he can read in the Third Book. He writes an excellent hand, has advanc'd in arithmetic as far as reduction and compound multiplication, and also learns English grammar and geography. His Indian name is Pah-tah-se-wah, which means " Coming this Way." The little boy is named Zosie Dosum, he is about 8 years old, and is an Ojebway Indian, from the north shore of Lake Superior. When he first came to the Shingwauk, a year and a-half ago, he was a regular little wild Indian, living in a birchbark wigwam, and knew nothing about the Engligh language or A B C. His Indian name is Ah-ne-me-keeus, meaning " Little Thunder." The two little boys are arrayed in the costume of the wild Sioux and Blackfeet Indians in the North-west, and they think it great fun going through their part of the performance at the meetings. When they first appear on the plat-

TWO LITTLE INDIAN BOYS.

form they are in the uniform worn at the institution, consisting of a dark blue navy serge jacket, trimmed with scarlet, ending in a tight band at the waist, around which pass two folds of a netted scarlet sash, the ends of which are tied and fall at the side; the trowsers also are of dark serge. Both the boys repeat texts of Scripture from memory, and know where to find them in their Bibles. The elder boy sings very nicely and gives one or two hymns at each meeting; then they repeat a dialogue, the elder boy asking the younger one where he comes from, etc. In reply to the question, "How do you like being at the Shingwauk?" he answers, with some emphasis, "First-rate." Then Soney says to Zosie, " Say this in our language, Zosie, 'I like coming here very much,'" and Zosie replies, "Ah-peche ne minwan-dumomaunduhpe ke-pe-ezhahyaun." Later on in the proceedings the two boys dress up—as shown in the picture — and by reciting another dialogue explain to the audience the meaning of their various articles of apparel and accoutrements. The rattle in Zosie's hand comes from Indian Territory. It was made by the Cheyenne Indians, and when anyone is sick the medicine man rattles it all day and all night to make him get well. "What's that stick in your hand studded with brass nails and two leathern thongs attached to it?" is asked of Soney, the elder boy. "That is the kind of whip the prairie Indians use when they ride their ponies," answers Soney, "it is said they use the lash for their ponies and the stick for their wives." The little boys then finish up

Figure 5.3. "Two Little Indian Boys." *Our Forest Children* 4.4:212: July 1890. Library and Archives Canada, AMICUS 1292349.

Philip J. Deloria (1998) considers how in a US context, "The fact that native people turned to playing Indian – miming Indianness back at Americans in order to redefine it – indicates how little cultural capital Indian people possessed at the time" (p. 125). Deloria acknowledges that such performances could cement white stereotypes but also had the capacity to shift attitudes and identities unpredictably (pp. 125–6). Such performance is difficult to define. For Deloria, "If being a survivor of the pure, primitive old days meant authenticity, and if that in turn meant cultural power that might be translated to social ends, it made sense for a Seneca man to put on a Plains headdress, white American's marker of that archaic brand of authority" (p. 189). Thrush, too, examines the agency of Indigenous peoples who travelled to London, which happened sometimes by force but other times by choice. But the children in Wilson's tableaux were not the same as Buffalo Bill performers or Deloria's example of a Seneca man donning a headdress. They were not adults, were likely not paid, and perhaps had no choice in the matter. Their tours of Ontario, Montreal, the Maritimes, and England meant children were even more geographically removed from parents than they already were at the school. Families may not have been notified or asked permission. As well, Pratt and Wilson opposed Buffalo Bill shows because they undermined and did not exhibit the progress of schooling; Wilson's tableaux featured the seeming progress of schooling, though this became downplayed during the tour of the Maritimes and England. And it is unclear whether the students enjoyed themselves during these tableaux. Although on the Ontario tour students got to meet celebrity entertainers such as the Count and Countess Magri (Bogdan, 1988, pp. 147–60), students also had to sing on cue under the dome of the National Library during a tour of Parliament led by minister of the interior – also the superintendent general for Indian Affairs in the nineteenth century – Thomas White. During the tour, White "examined carefully the various specimens of [students'] workmanship" (1.8:3). The trip would have included fun, but clearly it was also about business. We do not know how Soney and Zosie felt, nor how readers of *Our Forest Children* were interpreting descriptions of the tableaux.

After the tour of the Maritimes and England concluded, *Our Forest Children* printed Zosie's response when asked how he enjoyed the trip. He answered, "'I was getting a little tired of it'" (4.6:241), a similarly blunt response issued by Gilbert Bear on his experience at the Chicago World's Fair. Upon their return from England, Barbara

Birchbark's column focused on the two boys: "Both [Zosie] and Soney are proud possessors of a watch each. Of course one of first questions asked was, 'Well, Soney, what is the time?' 'I can give you English time,' said Soney, in a most magnificent tone of voice" (4.6.242). What would readers have understood as "English time?" Given the script of Barbara Birchbark's typical column, Soney's response is possibly meant as humorous. The rest of her article catalogues the gifts Soney and Zosie received on their trip to England, suggesting they foolishly and in a "reckless way" gave them to their peers (whom the newspaper refers to, unironically, as "inmates"). Birchbark implies the watches may have followed the same fate, invoking the trope of the Indian who does not understand capital, time, or other markers of the present (an interpretation that ignores generosity as a Christian value). But "English time," said in a "magnificent tone of voice," could have meant something else. Perhaps it meant a trip away from the bells of the school or even a mocking of supposed Indigenous pastness for the complicated reasons Deloria addresses. Regardless, school newspapers used the technique of beforing and aftering in ways that were not always as straightforward as before-and-after photography. Though the tableaux began as a clear example of beforing and aftering on the Canadian tour, Wilson adapted the script for a British audience and wrote about both in the school newspaper.

The Future

While school newspapers wrote about Indigenous people in the past and the present, they rarely located them in the future. And of course, the divisions of past, present, and future are colonially contingent. Instead, these newspapers typically imagined a future free of Indigenous peoples, populated instead by a thriving nation of settlers. As Tuck and Yang (2012) state, "In order for the settlers to make a place their home, they must destroy and disappear the Indigenous peoples that live there" because ongoing Indigenous presence and futurity undermine settlers' claims to land (p. 5). School newspapers participated in Tuck and Yang's definition of destroying and disappearing, both as extensions of the boarding school system as well as in their content of predicting an Indigenous-free future.

But the newspapers' future fantasies are more sophisticated than simply predicting a wipeout or admitting to genocide in any direct way. Instead, the newspapers employ several techniques aimed at describing Indigenous peoples and their relation to time. In the first page of its first issue, *Our Forest Children* explained that "as time goes on and our White population increases we must necessarily come more and more into contact with them" (1.1.1), that "as time goes on [settlers] shall keep advancing more and more. Every year will bring our white population more and more into contact with the wild Indians of the North West." The issue goes on to explain that as "our population increases we must necessarily come more and more into collision with [Indigenous peoples]" through a "gradual aggressiveness" (1.1.2). The newspaper reduces colonial encroachment to *collision* or, even more innocuous, *contact*. The reason for such encounters is chalked up to time. Any admitted violence – aggressiveness – is regarded as gradual and slow and therefore more kind.

Such a future with time as the culprit was painted by Kitamaat Home's newspaper, which went so far as to claim it was "almost an assured fact that the Kitamaat Valley is about to be settled by [the] white population" (*Na-Na-Kwa* 2.2). According to the school's newspaper, "Hitherto the tribe has largely kept to itself and apart from the outside world," but this was a "new era" in which "a number of white men are coming and going, government employees, surveyors, explorers, also civil engineers and prospectors. Thus far all had had a good influence. No word of complaint has been heard by us" (4.3). The newspaper frames Indigenous people as an anti-future (but uncomplaining) group surrounded by an encroaching "new era" of professionals. Regina School's newspaper similarly phrased such inevitability: "History shows a resistless onward march of intelligence, industry and thrift. Races have had to fall in with the tide or perish perhaps in the efforts to escape. The Indian sullenly, stubbornly and often successfully refused to do either. Meantime the vast resources of a productive country could not be developed" (3.70:8). Indigenous peoples in this passage had two choices: they could assimilate or die – "perhaps." The newspaper frames resistance as stubbornness, resulting in a waste of "development."

Cracks in innocence occasionally emerge. Newspapers only thinly veil that these are gestures, not actual innocence: "The United States Government has spent millions of money in trying to reduce the Indians to subjection and compelling them by force not to interfere with the advance of white immigration. But time has made the Americans wiser; they have found that killing the Indians and driving them westward does not pay, the process has been too expensive" (*Our Forest*

Children 1.1.2). It further explained, "Instead of having to fight them, [Indigenous peoples] may join with us in building up this great country" (1.1.1), and "every year will embitter the feelings of jealousy which already exist; the Indians may not perhaps dare to meet us in open warfare, but they will probably be increasingly a terror and an annoyance." Casting settlers, then, as helpers of Indigenous peoples for the future occasionally reveals itself as a way to mitigate warfare, eliminate blockades to development, and save money. More often, though, the future of school newspapers is free of Indigenous peoples because of time, and settlers are the guiltless benefactors.

And the settlers' future? School newspapers forecasted prosperity, progress, and longevity. Regina School was hopeful: "Everything new is coming our way. New Year, a new Province, new Parliament, new settlers, and new resolutions" (*Progress* 15.1:7). This newness – including Saskatchewan's entry into confederation and Laurier's new government – is inevitable, "coming our way" rather than tied to the work of schools. *Our Forest Children* described the future of Sault Ste Marie as "booming"; not only had the school's property appreciated in value twelve times, its newspaper also reported the future construction of a canal and bridge with the US (1.3:3–4). Kitamaat Home's newspaper painted a picture of the proto-resource extraction industries of BC – surveyors, fisheries, and Asian trade (*Na-Na-Kwa* 2.4; 24.10; 22.12). More frequently Kitamaat's newspaper reported on mining potential (20.11). *Na-Na-Kwa*, over the years, covered the activities of prospectors (3.6; 4.7; 22.8; 24.7) and the copper and gold of the region (14.10). It even included a facsimile of a mineral claim because "some of Nanakwa's friends never have seen, perhaps never will see" one. Because the name of the reproduced claim was the "Golden Crown," *Na-Na-Kwa* thought it particularly fitting to include in its coronation special issue (19.8), symbolically connecting for readers the metropole (the crown) and the colony (its resources). *Na-Na-Kwa* would also reprint letters it received from prospectors, who were also likely readers (7.5). The school's newspaper plainly stated, "Many of the readers of Nanakwa are watching the development of this country" (19.2). A new post office also signalled "progress" (9.5), as did a mail route between Kitamaat and Hazelton (22.9) and Indigenous postal workers who brought mail for miners, prospectors, and missionaries (23.9). The newspaper described its vision of "the site of a possible future city": "The site is magnificent, sufficient level land along the water front for a railroad terminus, fine building sites for warehouses and manufactors as well as a large tract of gradually rising ground whereon to build the palatial resident and humble cottage, moreover there are, lumber, stone and iron wherewith to build them" (29.9). Like Richard Scarry children's books of Busytown, newspapers predicted a future full of the signifiers of progress, including government, infrastructure, resource extraction, and mail.

The railway signalled the strongest example of progress. *Our Forest Children* predicted the coming of four lines connecting the US and Canada (1.3:3–4). While its first issue cautioned that the railway's encroachment could trigger open warfare with Indigenous peoples, who might have attributed the lack of buffalo to the construction of the railway (1.1:1), the next issue aimed to contain the narrative: "Our hitherto quiet little village is now all astir in anticipation of the coming railroads ... IT is perhaps a little unfortunate that the railway is to cut through the vestry of ST. Luke's church ... Others of our friends are trembling for their houses, others have their gardens and backyards broken into. Still all are in good humor, and all seem to welcome the advent of the iron horse" (1.2:4). *Na-Na-Kwa* hyped up future railroads, figuring Kitamaat as a "gateway to the interior" (1.4) and reporting on the visit by the deputy minister of railways (2.4). It also reported on the legislation purportedly guaranteeing the coming of a railway (5.7), the proposed railway from Cape Scott to Kitamaat and Hazelton (15.4), the Pacific Northern and Omenica railway (25.11), and the Grand Trunk Railway (30.13). The train had a revolutionary impact on Victorians' understanding of time. As Matthew Beaumont and Michael Freeman (2007) note, the railway was neither just a form of transportation nor "some floating signifier for the spirit of modernity" (p. 7). In the case of nineteenth-century boarding school newspapers, descriptions of the railway served as another example of the natural unfolding of time, which left Indigenous peoples behind despite the supposed benevolence of schools and individual settlers who attempted to mitigate any inevitable devastation.

Conclusion

In his memoir, survivor Augie Merasty (2015) notes how at his Saskatchewan school in the 1930s and 1940s, a particularly cruel teacher and sexual predator named Brother Johannes went to Germany and brought back several cuckoo clocks, which kept time at the school (p. 33). The teacher – a "Hitler worshipper, a complete fascist" – would read German newspapers and tell Augie and his peers, "The Germans were the smartest people in the world, supreme above any other race" (p. 34). The teacher also reminded students that the school's clocks were purchased to contribute to the Nazi regime. Like the temporal narratives of nineteenth-century school newspapers, this memoir also reveals that time is never just time.

What temporal narratives operate today? How do Indigenous peoples continue to resist settler colonial narratives of time? One narrative that persists is the freezing of Indigenous peoples in the past, which came to a head with the Makah whale hunt in 1999. Many non-Indigenous people and media outlets opposed it because hunters appealed to treaty rights and traditional practices while using so-called modern tools (Marker, 2006; R.J. Miller, 2000; Raibmon, 2005b). In my high school on Vancouver Island, I remember the Makah hunt as either an essay prompt or discussion question – something along the lines of "Should Native people be allowed their treaty rights if using modern tools? Should treaty rights and practices from the nineteenth century have any place today?" – as if non-Indigenous students like myself had any right to weigh in. I did not realize it then, but the central point of the debate was time. According to many non-Indigenous media sources, Makah people should not have appealed to a centuries-old treaty and to millennia-old practices. *If* they were going to anyhow, they should not use supposed non-Indigenous markers of the twentieth century such as powerboats and guns. The problem was time.

The *Regina v. Van der Peet* court decision is another example. The case, decided in 1996, found that a Stó:lō woman could not sell salmon acquired through Aboriginal fishing rights. Because selling the fish was not deemed traditional, she could not do it in the present day. John Borrows (2002) argues the *Van der Peet* decision "has now told us what Aboriginal means. Aboriginal is retrospective. It is about what was" (p. 60). For Dale Turner (2013), the *Van der Peet* decision connects directly to Indian boarding school history. Even more so than just the problem of freezing Indigenous peoples in a pre-contact past, "the rights that flow out of Aboriginal 'distinctive practices' are associated with precisely the kinds of practices the boarding schools were designed to eradicate" (pp. 106–7). For Turner, this present-day legal narrative locates Indigenous peoples in the past, co-opting and appropriating such locations as non-Indigenous people see fit. Yet the same technique denies any earlier state-sanctioned attempts to decimate such practices.

Anne McClintock (1995) also correctly notes that "postcolonial" reifies notions of progress, even though both the concept and the theory attempt to disrupt such linearity (p. 10). There is no *post* in a settler colonial context like Canada because its very definition is for settlers to replace Indigenous peoples (Strakosch and Macoun, 2012, p. 41). Indeed, "Settler colonialism has an ongoing, structural temporality, which is generally unacknowledged and contrasts with the linear colonialism–decolonization–post-colonialism narrative" (p. 51). Another word following the conclusion of the Truth and Reconciliation Commission might be reconciliation – that it is a point on a timeline, with a before and an after. Even without using the terms, a present-day example exists in understanding colonialism as "over." Worse, still, is former prime minister Stephen Harper's denial that it ever happened.[10]

These newspapers both constituted and participated in many time-based narratives, assisting the structures of settler colonialism. Reading them carefully helps to denaturalize time by exposing the words, moments, rhetoric, and logic that posit Indigenous peoples as the past and settlers as the future. But much of this future was never realized. Many towns that declared a boom in school newspapers have all but folded today. The certainty of *Na-Na-Kwa* never came to fruition: in 1908 Grand Trunk Pacific decided on Prince Rupert as a terminus station and "Kitamaat slipped into obscurity" (Kelm, 2006, p. xxv). And most importantly, the pastness of Indigeneity that newspapers mostly attempted to both represent and reify never, never happened.

6 Anachronism: Reading the Nineteenth Century Today

My reading of nineteenth-century Indian boarding school newspapers cannot help but be informed by my own time. As I read these documents from over one hundred years ago, I am thinking about former students I have met today or whose testimony I have witnessed. I am reading these newspapers alongside contemporary Indigenous scholarship, art, film, memoir, poetry, and fiction. I am reading these newspapers through my own lens as a white settler woman, and in a post–Truth and Reconciliation Commission (but not post-truth or post-reconciliation) Canada today. The way I encounter these newspapers is inflected by media portrayals of the TRC and official events I attended. My reading is changed by the archives I worked in, by the archivists I encountered and the physical structures that contained and therefore influenced these documents. While the previous chapter considered how school newspapers represent time, this chapter examines concepts in school newspapers highlighted as important today in understanding residential school history.

For some, historical inquiry means mitigating the effects of now, carefully avoiding charges of presentism, which is the problematic imposition of current beliefs or attitudes onto a very different past. Yet others not only acknowledge the effect of their own time on interpretations but also use it as a method. In several places Michel Foucault calls this approach "the history of the present," which is different from searching for origins. Instead, a history of the present seeks historical materials that can help contextualize structures and conditions today (Garland, 2014, p. 373). As Dian Million (2013) states, "the 'past' is always already positioned as the field of our contested now" (p. 70). Lynn Fendler (2008) uses the term "strategic presentism": a recognition of presentism as not only unavoidable but additionally helpful in better understanding today (p. 678).[1] Theories of historical consciousness – not just the study of the past but how we *think* about the past (Laville, 2004; Seixas, 2004; Seixas and Sandwell, 2006) – further call attention to how considering *now* influences readings of before. So, how does the TRC's final report bear on reading these nineteenth-century newspapers?

Centring the final report in this way presents risks. For one, the TRC is not unique but instead part of a longer history of commissions and inquiries, most notably the Royal Commission on Aboriginal Peoples published in 1996. Sara Ahmed (2004), Glen Coulthard (2014), and Million (2013) in different ways demonstrate how state-sanctioned reconciliation can work to soothe settler anxiety, reify the state, pathologize Indigenous peoples, recentre whiteness, and avoid demands for land return. What is more, the Indian Residential School Settlement Agreement (IRSSA) recognized some institutions as residential schools but not others. One thousand claims were denied over what is called the "administrative split," which focuses on where an abuse happened (a classroom, playground, or residence) and who (a provincial government, the federal government, or church) was technically in charge of that space at the time (Galloway, 2015). Many more claims were denied over a lack of archival documentation. The IRSSA required a lot from Indigenous people but little from settlers. It quantified and ranked abuse. And many settlers may consider the TRC an investigation into Canada's past, not its colonial present. Or, they may ignore it altogether.

Yet many survivors fought for the Indian Residential School Settlement Agreement – the commission was never a benevolent gift. The final report documents at least some of what survivors and families shared, what researchers found in archives, and what non-Indigenous people still have to learn. Reading the report provides ways to unsettle what once were and often still are considered self-assured facts. Rather than centring the TRC as unproblematic or as the only lens through which to view colonialism, I am instead acknowledging in this chapter that the TRC cannot help but inform my reading of school newspapers. In this chapter I isolate particular concepts from school newspapers that the TRC consistently highlighted, including issues of ceremony and treaty; the role of parents and oversight; and the realities of fire, health, and death at school. These categories overlap: When does health become distinct from death? Ceremony from family? From treaty? Yet isolating these threads momentarily aids in constructing a history of the present, connecting the nineteenth century to today.

Other concepts highlighted by the TRC could have been taken up here. As just one example, the TRC highlights the importance of sport both in residential schools and today. School newspapers devoted some attention to sport at school. For example, newspapers mentioned cricket matches between students and Canadian Pacific Railway workers (*Aurora* 2.21:4) and football games between students and the Northwest Mounted Police (*Guide* 5.8:1–2).[2] School newspapers expressed concerns that if the school did not provide students with opportunities for play that students would develop their own games, which would likely "counteract instead of accelerate the lessons taught in the schoolroom" (*Aurora* 3.27:1). Newspapers also claimed to have suppressed games invented by the children, such as one that required them to pilfer buttons from each other's pants (2.21:3).[3] Sport and many other categories that the TRC discussed are found in school newspapers. This chapter concentrates on categories the TRC devoted considerable attention to and that all concern ties of kinship and acts of resistance.

Ceremony

School newspapers often described ceremony, seemingly outside the scope of a school's educational mandate. The TRC's final report underscores amendments to the Indian Act that banned Indigenous ceremonies, including the Potlatch and Tamanawas Dance on the Northwest Coast (passed in 1884) and the Sun Dance (also known as the Thirst Dance) on the prairies (which came into effect in 1895) (Pettipas, 1994, p. 3). The Potlatch is traditionally practiced on the Northwest coast by nations including Haida, Tsimshian, Salish, Tlingit, and Makah peoples, and it was banned in Canada from 1884 to 1951. These ceremonies held a variety of spiritual, medical, political, social, and economic purposes.[4] Church and state targeted these ceremonies primarily because they appeared incompatible with agriculture and capitalism. Some settlers also regarded these ceremonies as unsafe (Cole and Chaikin, 1990, p. 20). Yet Indigenous peoples fought bans through the courts, sending delegations to Ottawa, and holding ceremony in secret (pp. 28, 127, 143).

Why was the TRC concerned with ceremonies, seemingly outside its own mandate? For one, these bans were strategies in addition to boarding schools for control over Indigenous land. Furthermore, missionaries running schools applied pressure to government to ban ceremonies, as participation in them allegedly affected school attendance and the ability to Christianize (Cole and Chaikin, 1990, p. 20; Pettipas, 1994, p. 92; TRC of Canada, 2015b, p. 636). Indian Affairs also threatened to enforce the ban on ceremony if parents did not send their children to school; parents in turn threatened to withhold their children from school to protest the ban (Pettipas, 1994, p. 134). Students were also separated from ceremony when at school. In contrast, school newspapers highlighted students' participation in agricultural and regional exhibitions, to which they would submit wares and art for competition. After wares from schools were returned from being submitted for judging at such fairs, it appears in some cases they were further displayed. At Rupert's Land School, for example, "the specimens of drawing and penmanship which comprised our class-room exhibit at the Winnipeg Industrial have been hung in the office for the inspection of visitors" (*Aurora* 2.21:3). Importantly, the 1895 add-on to the Potlatch ban stated, "nothing in this section shall be construed to prevent the holding of any agricultural show or exhibition or the giving of prizes thereat" (qtd. in Bracken, p. 120). Clearly, schools and state carefully delineated *what* forms of ceremony were permissible.

Yet when school newspapers attacked Indigenous ceremonies, they did so for reasons outside of education. *Na-Na-Kwa* was the only newspaper surveyed from territory where people practiced the Potlatch though was not the only newspaper to mention it: the newspaper of Rupert's Land School stated the ceremony included "orgies of the most disgusting character" and featured giving away "large quantities of property" (*Aurora* 3.30:1). *Na-Na-Kwa* devoted more attention. In addition to blaming the Potlatch for the spread of tuberculosis, Raley saw the ceremony as "antagonistic to civilization, Christianity and good government, and is the forerunner of a long list of crimes" (*Na-Na-Kwa* 18.1); he also saw it as a "bete noire" (6.5). Raley stated in the newspaper that at Potlatches it was "very distressing to see the neglected children and the uncared for old on bitterly cold days left without fire, food or friend" (18.1). He even quoted a reverend who "designates the potlatch a thug." Raley further provided for readers the sections of the Indian Act banning the Potlatch and commented on the ban's limits (18.2). The final TRC report reveals that other missionaries in the same time and region approved of a Potlatch ban because of the ceremony's effect on schooling (TRC of Canada, 2015b, pp. 635–41), but in the school newspaper Raley categorized the Potlatch more generally as criminal.

Some newspapers displayed an anxiety over students who returned home and might participate in ceremony. The newspaper of Regina

School, located on the territories of several Plains peoples who practice the Sun Dance, stated that "one of the greatest obstacles in [the] way of industrial and moral progress among Indians is the reversion to the old time dances" and "ancient and vicious festivals" (*Progress* 3.77:4). For the newspaper, ceremonial participation tarnished the school's reputation and brought "open and stinging griefs to Christian workers." *Progress* further proclaimed that "boys and girls who go home on leave of absence, and attend Reserve Dances give a slap on the face to the Institution that has done much for them" (3.81:5). Newspapers printed parables of students who returned home but refused to participate, including one in *Our Forest Children*: Wilson travelled to a Blackfoot community that was preparing for a Sun Dance, which he referred to as "torture" (2.6:18). Wilson wrote he was "anxious about our Shingwauk pupil, James. Would he go to the dance, or would he not?" The story ends with James attending church instead and dissuading three others. Another story from *Progress* portrayed a girl who attended a ceremony but came equipped "with notebook in hand to record notes of the speeches" and set out to prove many superstitions false (3.81:6). A few issues later, *Progress* reprinted an article about White Earth reservation in Minnesota, where community members forfeited a ceremony to build a fence, plow a field, and sow wheat (3.84:5–6). "These White Earth Chippewas have passed the dancing era," the article concluded. Both *Progress* and *The Guide* reported on the same Carlisle student who returned home and was forced to participate (*Progress* 3.81:7; *Guide* 6.6:3). In these examples, ceremony is an era to overcome, participation only permissible as ethnography. But the scare stories of newspapers also reveal communities who continued to hold ceremony and include their children despite the consequences.

Newspapers offered little space for students to counteract schools that vilified ceremony, though a few instances exist. One entry attributed to a former student, who found work after leaving Regina School as an interpreter on Cote reserve in Saskatchewan, described in *Progress* how students on vacation would join ceremony (3.83:8). The entry stated that students on leave would be "jumping in the crowds just for fun, and then they would stop and sit down. They don't mean any wrong, just simply to have some fun." The response continues, stating that these students "are not given to any evil-practices or anything that would bring them down to a low standing. They have not forgotten what they have been, but are going up instead of down." While the former student's defence could be viewed as trivializing ceremony, it also hides the power of ceremony from officials and non-Indigenous readers: If ceremony were mere frivolity, why restrict it? He also insists ceremony is not wrong, evil, or low. And his concluding line is ambiguous: the observation that students still remember could imply the impact of their colonial education or who they were before and after it. The response further shows that ceremonies continued despite sanctions – open enough that a piece attributed to a former student could defend them in a school newspaper.

Treaty

Like ceremony, these newspapers also paid attention to what are seemingly outside of a school's educational mandate – treaties. Harold Cardinal (1999) responded to the government's 1969 White Paper by stating that "to the Indians of Canada, the treaties represent an Indian Magna Carta. The treaties are important to us" because "we entered into those negotiations with faith, with hope for a better life with honour" (p. 24). Several of the TRC's ninety-four calls to action argue for the maintenance, rejuvenation, and creation of treaty relationships (10. VII; 42; 45.III; 46.IV; 51), and the final report outlines how treaties were an extension of long-established political strategies, often initiated by Indigenous peoples. Yet the report states that the Canadian government was often motivated to enter treaty relationships to ease railway construction and resource extraction (TRC of Canada, 2015b, pp. 115–20).

Reading where the numbered treaties discuss education demonstrates how colonial tactics intensified in the nineteenth century. The first two numbered treaties (1871 and 1873) used similar language when it came to schools: "Her Majesty agrees to maintain a school on each reserve hereby made whenever the Indians of the reserve should desire it." But in Treaty 3, the language changes to on-reserve schools when "Her Government of Her Dominion of Canada may seem advisable whenever the Indians of the reserve shall desire it." Treaties 4 (1874) and 7 (1877) promise on-reserve schools, but only for those on-reserve. And then the language changes more drastically:

> Treaty 8 (1899): Her Majesty agrees to pay the salaries of such teachers to instruct the children of said Indians as to Her Majesty's Government of Canada may seem advisable.
> Treaty 9 (1905/1906): His Majesty agrees to pay such salaries of teachers to instruct the children of said Indians, and also to provide such school

buildings and educational equipment as may seem advisable to His Majesty's government of Canada.

Treaty 10 (1906): His Majesty agrees to make such provision as may from time to time be deemed advisable for the education of the Indian children.

Treaty 11 (1921): His Majesty agrees to pay the salaries of teachers to instruct the children of said Indians in such manner as His Majesty's Government may deem advisable.

Increasingly, the written words of treaties turned away from on-reserve, Indigenous-directed institutions to off-reserve, government-controlled schooling. Given these contexts, treaties directly relate to schools in that their existence was enshrined in them. Kitamaat Home's newspaper expectedly remained quiet on treaty given British Columbia's different history of treaty making and the fact that Kitamaat region was not governed by a treaty with the Canadian government at this time;[5] school newspapers from prairies schools, in contrast, often discussed treaty.

School newspapers made appeals to educational treaty obligations (*Progress* 17.11:3; 18.12:1–2; *Guide* 4.2:2), but they also used treaties as ballast for pre-existing narratives. One narrative painted Canada as colonially gentler than the US. For instance, *Progress* cited treaties as evidence of Canada's good relations because "the country was bought from them and not taken by force. Today, the older Indians, speak in kindly terms of the Government[']s commissioner who met them in their encampments and signed treaties" (18.12:1). School newspapers in Canada also cited the seventeenth-century Penn Treaty between the US and the Lenape people as an alternative to American violence (*Our Forest Children* 3.11:141; *Progress* 3.72:3; 3.80:2). As *The Guide* stated, "It is said that the Treaty made by William Penn with the Indians was the only Treaty never sworn to or never broke. I guess the writer didn't know about our Canadian Treaties" (6.7:3).

Less common was a narrative of irrelevance. *The Guide* reported the 1897 scandal of Onondaga chief and wampum keeper Thomas Webster, who was accused of stealing and then selling wampum belts he was entrusted to protect (6.2:4).[6] The article leaves out the possible reasons behind Webster's decision as outlined by Richard W. Hill Sr (2007), long-time fighter for the return to Haudenosaunee people of wampum belts from museums, universities, and collectors. As Hill states, reasons could have included coercion, politics, and profit in desperate times (p. 319). *The Guide* article also ignores who was buying these belts, including a US Indian census agent and a mayor in New York (p. 320). Moreover, the article's title, "The Iroquois Wampum is Gone," and Webster's epithet in the article, "the last of the aged wampum keepers," attempt to diminish the ongoing power of wampum as treaty. In addition, the article aligns with a broader narrative in school newspapers of discounting Indigenous polities and leaving settlers blameless. In contrast, Penelope Myrtle Kelsey (2014) and Lynn Gehl (2014) describe from Haudenosaunee and Algonquin Anishnaabeg perspectives, respectively, how wampum belts – woven blue, white, and purple mussel and clam shells – represent collective memory, literacy, diplomacy, and treaty rights.

Within writing attributed to students there existed space to describe treaties as events rather than relationships. Children's writing instead focused on treaty payment day, an annual event still observed when members of First Nations who signed treaties and government representatives meet to exchange annuities promised in the treaty as well as to contemplate treaty relationships. In some student entries, treaties were limited to opportunities for money (*Guide* 5.4:4). As one entry put it in 1897 from Battleford School, located on Treaty 6 territory, treaty payments were "a good thing, because the weather will soon be getting cold, and we like to see the Indians getting their treaty money, so that they can buy some clothes" (*Guide* 6.3:1). One composition attributed to a student in the newspaper of Rupert's Land School clinically focused on the location of taking treaty and on the "wagons, carts or boats" taken by "the grown-up people" – who were likely kin to students – to travel for treaty (*Aurora* 2.15:4).

More often, student entries described treaty as an opportunity to see parents, who would travel from reserves to towns where schools were located. In the December 1895 issue of *The Guide*, one boy wrote he was "glad to see the Indian people getting treaty payments again, because I like to see them come to Battleford sometimes" (4.6:1). Another student noted, "I am glad to see the Indians get their treaty money. They like to dance when this time comes. I will be glad to see the treaty payments again" (4.6:2). The following year another student wrote, "It is very nice to see the Indians again this winter. I hope they have had a good time in the stores, buying things with their treaty money" (5.5:1). Occasionally, student entries were disparaging. As one student entry observed, "The Town is full of Indians. The Agent paid them their Treaty money, and they came in to spend it and it does not take very long to do so. They should be compelled to buy something usefull" (*Guide* 7.4:1). It is perhaps jarring to read a student entry refer to "the Indians" and "them" rather than relatives. But what space was there otherwise? Most student entries continued to describe treaties as opportunities to reunite with Indigenous relations otherwise blocked or limited by the boarding school. One entry stated the writer was "very very glad to see my brother" on treaty day; another stated he "was very pleased to see some of my friends over town the other day, including my grandfather and grandmother" (*Guide* 5.5:1). One student entry from the newspaper of Rupert's Land School described treaty in more detail:

> On Monday my Father came and saw me and I went home, and when I got home I kissed my mother and all of them. And in the morning we went to the treaty ground and we got to my Aunt[']s house, and we went across and we made the tent up, and I walked about with my sister and we saw the people dancing and my Mother bought a hat for me and she bought a hat for herself, and I bought a handkerchief, and we stayed three days there and on Friday we came back and the girls were glad to see me and the teachers too, and now I am trying to learn all I can and be a good girl, and some day I hope I will go home again for a viset, and this is all of my Composition. (*Aurora* 1.8:4)

In addition to happy scenes of family reunification such as these, student entries also noted how treaty day could be difficult. In an issue following one filled with happy entries of family reunification because of treaty, two entries described students who had hoped to but never saw their parents (*Guide* 5.6:1).

While it is impossible to know if such entries were actually written by children, compare these compositions to an article from the non-student voice of Rupert's Land School: "Numerous friends have visited our children here since treaty time. Boats of all shapes, sizes, and rig on their way to town with berries, skins and all manner of native merchandise, are a never failing source of interest and speculation as they make for shore and land; uncles, cousins or aunts with welcome presents of maple sugar or moccasins for one or another of our pupils" (*Aurora* 3.31:3). This description focuses far more on the event of treaty time rather than the scenes of parent-child reunification that student-attributed entries tend to portray. The year before, the same newspaper wrote a long piece about a school trip with forty students to treaty grounds (*Aurora* 2.19:4). It appears the students stayed in tents with school representatives and were permitted at intervals to wander and "find their friends," even though their parents were also likely there. The article focused on the discipline and schedule that the school continued to enact despite being away from the school, even stating that "we had taken the precaution of bringing the school bell with us – the little one" but that "the conduct of our pupils was exemplary throughout." The article remarked that the treaty trip was the highlight of the students' lives, and that not only did all students return to the school after the trip but the school also recruited four more students during treaty time. There appears to be a great anxiety throughout the article on parent-child reunification and on the threat of not returning after treaty time. Student entries may have been fabricated by schools, but comparisons such as these reveal a clear difference between treaty-as-event from the school's perspective and treaty-as-relationship from the students'.

Treaty time may have also been a chance for parents to check in. The October 1898 issue of *The Guide* included statements about how treaty day was an occasion for Indigenous people to go inside the school. One student entry mentioned, "We were all glad to see the Indians. They went all over the school" (*Guide* 7.4:1). Other entries included how Indigenous visitors – nearly one hundred, estimated one student – ate in the school dining room and watched a concert put on by students after treaty payment. Though one entry conceded "they looked very funny with their faces painted and different coloured blankets some of the men had shells in their ears," it also mentioned "two of the Indians made speeches." What was said? The newspaper summarized speeches by Chiefs Peyasiw-Awasis and Moosomin as showing support for the school. But they, like parents visiting for treaty day "all over the school," may have also been ensuring students had adequate food, clean facilities, or kind teachers. This issue appeared in 1898, following years of inspectors' reports revealing Battleford School's high death rates (Milloy, 1999, pp. 84–5) and sexual violence (J.R. Miller, 1996b, p. 337). This issue of the newspaper appeared only one year after the government confiscated the treaty medal of Peyasiw-Awasis and imprisoned him for holding a ceremony banned by the Indian Act (Pettipas, 1994, pp. 117–18).[7] While these visits may have indeed shown support, treaty day may also have presented an opportunity to remind staff that chiefs and parents were watching.

School newspapers typically quashed Indigenous perspectives on treaty. *Our Forest Children* reprinted the viewpoint that Indigenous people "are not Canadians in the complete sense of the word; but allies of the Canadians" and form "a series of nations living under treaty agreements on friendly terms with their neighbours the whites" (3.9:110); but the newspaper dismissed this belief as "altogether erroneous." One reprinted article in *Progress* described how parents at Round Lake viewed the education of their children in Regina rather than on-reserve as a breach of treaty (3.83:3). Yet the article vaguely concludes, "There is another side to this question, however, which the Indians are not likely to say much about." The other side – that education off-reserve was better – appears to be so well known it was unnecessary to elaborate on. *Progress* also provided a scene of Chief Payipwat consoling someone sick with tuberculosis. The newspaper set up the scene as almost romantic, with the chief "camped in a delightful spot" with "beautiful hills" and "vast fields of hay" earlier mowed by twenty machines that stayed silent for the Sabbath. When addressed as "Chief" by the reverend reporting to *Progress*, Payipwat responded: "A chief indeed! once I was a chief ... I am tired of the white man and of his ways, and I would be delighted if the Government would allow me to go out of the treaty and wander where I please" (3.81:8). Though this passage appears to invite a critique of treaty, the anachronistic portrayal of Payipwat likely added to the scene's pastoralism. Similarly, *Our Forest Children* included an excerpt on the unfulfilled promises of the 1836 Treaty of Washington from Odawa leader Andrew J. Blackbird (*Our Forest Children* 4.5:238); the selected excerpt, however, focused on how Canada welcomed those ripped off by the treaty in the US.

The newspaper of Rupert's Land School included an odd series of responses about Treaty 1, also known as the Stone Fort Treaty, from an anonymous reader of the newspaper who only went by "ONE WHO WAS PRESENT AT THE SAID TREATY." The author does not elaborate on his own role, if any, at treaty signing other than his presence. The first letter to the school newspaper announced he would be subscribing to the school newspaper. The letter then introduces the Stone Fort Treaty for readers by naming the government officials who signed the treaty and clarifying that James McKay was "deeply interested with the Indian population" and a speaker of "all the languages used on both sides" (*Aurora* 2.18:2). The letter writer concludes by stating that "many of the Indians are always harping upon the promises that were made at the Stone Fort Treaty by the Government" but that the letter writer's future communications with the school newspaper will "show who is the gainer or loser by the transaction." In the next month's issue, the "ONE WHO WAS PRESENT" provided a copy of the complete text of the treaty, including the names of all signatories, Indigenous and non-Indigenous (2.19:5–6). In the following issue, the "ONE WHO WAS PRESENT" states that annuity payments, schools, and cattle have all been more than what the treaty promised – ergo, it is "safe to say, an excess has been given to the Indian by the Government" (2.20:2). These understandings of the treaty, printed in the school newspaper, reinforce the written version rather than provide additional contexts. Aimée Craft (2013), in contrast, triangulates sources on the Stone Fort Treaty: written documents, oral history, and Indigenous knowledge. As Craft asks, "Should only one of the systems of law that were relied on for the negotiations of the treaty form the framework of interpretation? Or should Anishinabe legal principles, both procedural and substantive, inform the interpretation and implementation of treaties today?" (p. 14). It is to be expected that the school newspaper would not include the perspectives Craft advocates; what is of note is that the school newspaper actively participated in the unidirectional understanding of treaty that Craft today criticizes. Rarely, school newspapers permitted Indigenous perspectives of treaty to stand on their own. Instead, treaty was an event rather than a relationship with obligations.

Parents

School newspapers discussed parents in relation to treaty as well as more generally. So did the TRC: the commission displayed the following motto on its website and event banners, "For the Child Taken, for the Parent Left Behind." The phrase asks witnesses of the TRC to consider not only children and survivors but also their families, who often endured long periods of separation and who may have attended Indian boarding schools themselves. The final report quotes late nineteenth-century Indian Affairs officials, who painted Indigenous parents as a *problem* and regulated contact between parent and child through a variety of techniques, from denying passes for families to leave the reserve to restricting children's summer holidays and letters exchanged (TRC of Canada, 2015b, pp. 599–613). As the newspaper of Rupert's Land School stated, allowing students to see their parents more frequently would mean greater costs for transportation, but "another reason for retaining the pupils in these institutions for a considerable length of time is, that the influences of the school, which are necessarily cumulative, may have their full force in breaking up the bad habits acquired on the reservation" (*Aurora* 1.3:1). Despite this position of schools, the

TRC's final report also highlights the ways parents resisted – forcefully. Parents kept their children at home by hiding them, removing them when conditions did not meet their expectations, keeping children home when they ran away, and not returning them after a holiday (p. 669). As Sharon Wall (2003) points out, school administrators had to gain and retain parental support (p. 24). One scene in *Our Forest Children* illustrates this point when Shingwauk Home's principal Edward Francis Wilson described how a child died and Wilson had to return to Blackfoot territory to deliver news to the parents. The article emphasizes how the community did not hold Wilson responsible (2.6:17). *The Aurora* similarly explained that "the Indians are greatly pleased to see their children placed in responsible positions" (2.13:1). Rather than completely ignoring parents, it appears important that school newspapers highlighted when parents were supportive of boarding schools.

Yet school newspapers often framed Indigenous parents as incompetent. Kitamaat Home's newspaper stated that "poor neglected babies" existed not because "their parents mean to be unkind, but that they do not know how" to care for their children (*Na-Na-Kwa* 5.4). Regina School's newspaper, too, argued that "young women need to be taught how to care for their children; and for themselves" (*Progress* 17.9:6). Regina School's newspaper also portrayed parents as unable to understand schools as anything but "depots for the distribution of clothing and other creature comforts" (18.9:1–2). Parents could even be killers: *Progress* blamed parents for the death of "little Calvin," a student who left Round Lake School healthy but died, allegedly from drugs or alcohol administered by his parents (3.83:10). "This is not one of the sacred parental ties that we hear so much about," concluded the article. The same newspaper also attempted to dispel the myth of what it called "the sacred home tie" of Indigenous families with the example of "Poor Sadie," who did not receive a Christian funeral upon her death (3.73:7).

It was this tie that school newspapers attempted to contest – a tricky argument considering the fifth Christian commandment to honour thy mother and father. An 1899 issue of *The Guide* presented a scene in which a government official agreed with parents who objected to the removal of their children, and the newspaper labelled him ignorant (7.10:4). Superintendent General of Indian Affairs Frank Oliver highlighted this theological contradiction in 1908, but his point was ignored (Milloy, 1999, p. 28). The same newspapers advocating Indigenous parent-child separation simultaneously printed articles titled "A Tribute to a Mother" (*Guide* 6.2:2) and "A Mother's Love" (7.6:2), representing the largely non-Indigenous readership expected of school newspapers. In these tributes, the mother's lap and smile implied those of white mothers.

Newspapers did not altogether deny a connection. Battleford School suggested parents get over their reluctance to part ways and blamed the failure of day schools on the parent-child bond (*Guide* 4.11:1, 4). But several issues later, the same newspaper stated that "future usefulness should be lifted far above the desires of children and parents to be with each other" (7.1.3): the desire was acknowledged, then swiftly dismissed. The newspaper of Rupert's Land School printed a report on St Boniface School, which claimed that parents "seem unable to control their inclination for unrestricted liberty and their unreasonable fondness of having their children with them" (*Aurora* 2.16:2). Another article in the same publication stated that "it is generally the most difficult thing to persuade their children to go to school, and when they come there is no telling how soon the parents may take them away again" (2.17:1). In 1898, *The Guide* went so far as to question parents' ability to even *protest* being separated: "Are such parents able or rather competent, to form an opinion on this important subject? And why do the parents object? It may be a false love, perhaps the genuine article; but is the cause love in most instances? No! It is merely that the parents may receive the $5.00, which the government gives annually to each child. This may seem harsh but it is too true" (*Guide* 7.6:1). Parents are formulated in this passage as not only unable to care for their children but also further incapable of genuinely loving them or even forming an opinion on their love. The same newspaper reprinted an article from a Carlisle School teacher named Jessie W. Cook, who also admitted she at first considered parent-child separation a mistake after seeing "the grief of the parents when the children left them, and how eagerly they listened to the letters that came from the absent ones, keeping them among their greatest treasures, and how happy they were when the children returned to them" (5.6:4). But Cook changed her mind after witnessing beneficial changes over time, ultimately concluding that "the BEST results have undeniably come from an entire separation of the Indian children from every thing Indian." Newspaper entries attributed to students admitted some children would cry for their parents, but only if the entry ended on a positive note where the child "is getting happy now" (*Aurora* 1.12:3) or "is more of a man now; he never cries" (2.14:4). There was little space in school newspapers to understand parents as capable or even worthy of remaining with their children – one of the most disturbing perspectives offered by school newspapers.

One context for such arguments included the changing compulsory education laws at this time. In 1894, an amendment to the Indian Act made it possible to more strongly enforce attendance (J.R. Miller, 1996b, p. 129). Compulsory attendance in public schools for non-Indigenous children existed as well in the late nineteenth century (Oreopoulos, 2005), though not with the same stated goals of prolonged parent-child separation. The new regulation made it legal for police, school staff, and Indian Affairs officials to enter the homes of Indigenous families and forcibly return students who had left the school, even if parents had voluntarily enrolled their child (TRC of Canada, 2015b, pp. 254–6). In the years immediately following this change, school newspapers showed support for compulsory education and framed opposing parents as barriers. As *The Guide* stated in 1896, "If Indian parents, in their ignorance and paganism, wish to deny a common education to their children, the Department should show itself stronger and wiser than the parents" (4.8:6). *Progress,* too, in 1897 wrote that if parents would not willingly send their children to school, "the right arm of the law ought to come down with power" (3.81:6). Two issues later, the newspaper quoted an Indian commissioner in Manitoba asking children to communicate to their parents that "where the children could not be secured otherwise, the law would be exercised" (3.83:8). *The Aurora* announced an even stronger threat on the front page of an 1895 issue: parents who withheld children could be fined and even imprisoned, and the ultimate right to return children to parents remained in the hands of the superintendent general of Indian Affairs (3.26:1). *The Aurora* also reprinted an excerpt from the amendment to the Indian Act regarding potential repercussions of leaving school early (3.29:1). *Progress* reported the tactics used in the US to enforce compulsory education, such as depriving parents of supplies and arresting families who assisted runaways (3.84:4–5). In these ways, school newspapers contributed to the pro-compulsory debates of the late nineteenth century.

When parents did visit schools, newspapers often displayed how the school was still in control. Student entries sometimes detailed family visits that appear more sporadic, describing activities such as riding horses together or receiving gifts and candy (*Guide* 4.2:4; 4.3:1; 4.6:3; 7.1:1; *Progress* 3.78:7; *Aurora* 2.14:4). But these examples were often followed by an assertion of the school's control over visits. As one entry attributed to a student stated, "I was very glad to see my father and mother the other day; I was in school when they came and I asked Miss Skelton, might I go out and see them and she said yes" (*Guide* 5.6:1). Another form of control over visits appeared in a 1908 issue of *Progress*: "We have quite a lot of Indian vistors *[sic]* these days, and their Tepees look very picturesque on our grounds. It is a pretty sight to see a family group gathered round the fire outside the tent in the twilight of these lovely autumn evenings" (17.8:3). In this example, family reunification is a painting, pacified by lighting and artistic genre, in which parents are temporary and permitted. Kitamaat Home was different from these industrial schools on the prairies: the school was not government funded and was located within the community of many families, unlike Eastern industrial schools often strategically located far from home communities. Kitamaat Home also taught everyone but only boarded girls, so male students returned to their parents at night and left with them seasonally to work. Even with these significant differences, Kitamaat Home's newspaper similarly depicted parental visits as school sanctioned – visits to view the baking and sewing of children (3.5) or to join a two-hour tea, which was thought to "not only [give] pleasure to all but will have a beneficial effect on the Home as well" (15.6). Kitamaat Home's newspaper described children who could see from the top of a hill their parents returning by canoe from their seasonal camp. The newspaper recounted how the children's "faces would light up with pleasure when permission was granted" to approach them (14.6). Students were also able to visit the homes of their grandparents to drop off gifts of clothing and food as an act of Christian charity (30.5–6). That these people were family was unplanned, as the newspaper stated that "it so happened that each old person whom we were to visit had a grand daughter in the 'Home.'" On these visits, students "were commissioned to enter the house first, state the object of [their] visit and present the present." In these ways, newspapers from Kitamaat Home as well as the prairies framed parental contact as controlled – ultimately serving the needs of the school – and unthreatening to its mission.

Despite attempts to dictate the parameters of family, when read contrapuntally school newspapers reveal the ongoing resistance of parents. One issue of *Progress* noted some parents were "very bitter" towards the school and observed how one father from a Saskatchewan reserve stated he "would sooner a man would come, and cut off his head, and take it to school, than that he should take his children to school" (3.83:9): the father would rather die than have his children attend. The newspaper guided readers' interpretations of this story with the headline

"Neglected Children," positioning the father's threat as negligence, not resistance. The minimal framing also suggests readers required little convincing to view Indigenous parents as inept. *Progress* also isolated grandmothers as "a barrier, a real hindrance and obstacle in the way of civilization" because they predicted early deaths and misfortune for children who attended school (3.70:3). Vilifying Indigenous parents in school newspapers helped to justify separating them from their children and deflected from the poor job schools were doing in caring for students.

School newspapers consistently disparaged Indigenous families yet upheld the parent-child relationships of staff as normative. *Progress* for instance would update readers on the life of the principal, R.B. Heron, and his son. The newspaper detailed the baptism of "Little Donald" (17.11:5) as well as the tea party and photographs for his first birthday (18.9:6), his illness and convalescence (18.10:2), and general growth (17.9:3; 18.12:4). While such scenes may sound similar to the caricatures of the Indigenous student "Little Joe," Donald is permitted to grow and belong to a family. Fourteen years later, when no longer principal, Heron addressed the Regina Presbytery with concerns about the separation of parent and child in Indian boarding schools (TRC of Canada, 2015b, p. 319). His concerns were rebuked, but they reveal how even a white settler with somewhat progressive views still served in the newspaper as foil to Indigenous parents.

Kitamaat Home's newspaper also updated readers on the principal George Raley's wife and two children, scenes of settler parent-child relationships that foiled Indigenous ones admonished by the newspaper.[8] One composition attributed to a student and cited as evidence of strong writing skills described the relationship between Raley's new baby Emsley and his mother (*Na-Na-Kwa* 6.7). *Na-Na-Kwa* noted how four-month-old Edith Raley had "decided that to leave her mother is quite an impossibility," requiring Mrs Raley to bring her daughter to school every day and even write the newspaper with the baby on her knee (15.6). An early issue of the newspaper included a cut of Emsley and his mother (see figure 6.1). The penultimate issue before the newspaper ended featured portraits of Raley, his wife, and children spread over three pages (see figures 6.2, 6.3, and 6.4). The brother and sister are in one portrait while the mother and father each has an image, posed and facing the camera. The school newspaper holds all four members of the Raley family intact, while elsewhere the newspaper worked to legitimize the separation of Indigenous families.

MRS. RALEY AND EMSLEY

Figure 6.1. Mrs Raley and Emsley. *Na-Na-Kwa* 9.2: January 1900.

While the raison d'être of Indian boarding schools was to separate parent from child, brother from sister, the Raleys appeared in *Na-Na-Kwa* as an inseparable unit. As well, Edith's middle name was 'Dahlanks to honour a student who died (15.10). But the middle name also reveals how representations of Indigenous and non-Indigenous children at schools tripped over one another, symbolizing how newspapers charted the death of Indigenous children alongside the futures of white settler children. The final issue of *Na-Na-Kwa*, which had recorded the family's growth over its nine-year run, now announced the family's departure from Kitamaat: "[Raley's children] had reached an age when to neglect their intellectual development would be criminal. Emsley

REV. G. H. RALEY.

Figure 6.2. Rev G.H. Raley. *Na-Na-Kwa* 30.1: April 1906.

already ten years of age, had no opportunity for elementary education, Edith nearly six had also to be thought of. It was found necessary
to move in order that they receive the very important primary education before they were too old. At Port Simpson this advantage offered
itself, the place having an exceptionally good public school" (31.6). The
education extended to Indigenous children was seen as neglect and
as criminal for the Raleys, who remained visually and textually a unit
within the pages of the newspaper until its end.

MRS. G. H. RALEY.

Figure 6.3. Mrs G.H. Raley. *Na-Na-Kwa* 30.12: April 1906.

Oversight

School newspapers either did not mention Indigenous parents or sought to vilify them, even though parents in fact deployed a variety of tactics to ensure their children's safety while at school. Such tactics were necessary because, as survivors as well as the TRC have revealed, schools lacked formal oversight on many fronts. How were health, academic standards, and safety monitored? And, how did such oversight compare to non-Indigenous schools of the same era? As the final report states, "Indian Affairs never developed anything approaching the education acts and regulations by which provincial governments administered public schools" (TRC of Canada, 2015b, p. 201). Additionally,

Figure 6.4. Emsley and Edith Raley. *Na-Na-Kwa* 30.16: April 1906.

at non-Indigenous public schools parents typically had nightly contact with children and some proximity to the school – critical opportunities to check in. Policies at Indian boarding schools were mostly developed school by school; no unified, federal guidelines existed (pp. 201–2). In Ontario, Quebec, and the Maritimes, provincial government inspectors were to oversee Indian Affairs schools as of 1885, with British Columbia and New Brunswick following suit the next year. But the TRC reveals some schools went years without inspections, which often focused more on inventories and accounts than on student safety and success. When inspectors did make recommendations, they had no authority to see them through. Of course, even a robust and impossibly objective inspection would never have upended a school's basic premise of separating children from their families and lands to serve a settler colonial future. Still, lack of oversight – viewed as inadequate even contemporaneously by officials within Indian Affairs – made schools more dangerous. Unchecked abuse, unqualified teachers, ineffective fire prevention, food unfit for consumption, dangerous and long hours at a trade – such threats to student life could have at least been mitigated using similar standards of the day found in schools for white settler children.

School newspapers reveal an anxiety on the part of schools over inspections, or at least an awareness they mattered. Shingwauk Home's newspaper admitted that an Inspector McCaig examined the school in October 1889 and declared it overcrowded; the announcement of the critique, though, is couched on the same page by three different updates on new buildings slated for construction (*Our Forest Children* 3.7:77). In June 1900, the inspection of W.J. Chisholm at Battleford School occasioned several comments attributed to students in the school newspaper. One stated, "When the Inspector comes to visit our school he will be surprised how much we have improved since last winter" (*Guide* 7.7:1). Another announced: "Mr Chisholm will be here soon to examine our School. I know he will see many improvements in our work since his last visit. I hope each boy and girl will try his or her best to get a good name for our School." Even three issues after Chisholm's departure appeared another comment: "I hope the Inspector will give us a good name. We are trying to keep up our reputation" (7.10:1). Such remarks reveal an apprehension about the inspection, which may have been directed to a newspaper's governmental readership. The worry exhibited in the school newspaper proved unwarranted: Chisholm's 1900 report was positive (Sessional Paper, volume 11, 14–367). Yet the same cannot be said seven years later, when Chisholm reported negatively on high teacher turnover, poor academics, and a lack of calisthenics (Wasylow, 1972, p. 249).

The school newspaper may have been an avenue for schools to publicly exhibit deference to inspectors. Regina School's newspaper revealed a nervousness regarding a 1905 inspection conducted by W.M. Graham, who judged students' entries to the Regina Territorial Exhibition. The 1905 report was hardly critical, only pointing out that some of the school's horses were old and the building needed repairs (DIA, 1905, 418). Graham also found the younger students "did not speak out so that they could be heard easily," a common denial of children's acquisition of English taken up in chapter 3. Despite the positive report, the school newspaper responded defensively: "As it was nearly four years since the last government inspection of the school there were naturally some few things that did not meet with the Inspector's approval, but on the whole, and especially in the classroom work his comments were favorable. What criticisms Mr. Graham gave were made with the aim of helping us to improve rather than in a fault-finding spirit" (*Progress* 13.3:5). What "did not meet with the Inspector's approval" may have been off the record, not visible today in the final report. Or, the newspaper's comments snidely signalled a lack of oversight desired by the school considering that the article ends by hoping "it will not be four years before he comes again." But Battleford School's newspaper did not list increased safety as a benefit of Chisholm's 1897 inspection. Instead, it highlighted the inspection as an opportunity to hear about former students now living in other communities (6.6:1) and to receive students' academic scores, later published in the newspaper (6.7:1). Kitamaat Home's newspaper, too, framed the visit of school inspector A.E. Green as helpful in promoting "advancement" (*Na-Na-Kwa* 29.7). School newspapers profiled inspections as welcome and respected.

Some inspections appeared, through the window of the school newspaper, as more thorough than others. Inspector T.P. Wadsworth spent one month in 1895 at Rupert's Land School and conducted an "exhaustive examination of the affairs of this Institution" (*Aurora* 3.26:3). Upon Wadsworth's departure, one note attributed to a student even expressed regret at his absence (3.26:4). Wadsworth also inspected Battleford School in 1895, though for a shorter period (*Guide* 4.3:4; 4.4:1). *The Guide* stated the inspector was "always a welcome person around here, and is ever ready to advise and suggest things for the welfare of the work." More often, school newspapers revealed inspections lasted only one day and elicited fanfare and celebration. Chisholm came to Battleford

School in February 1899 as part of "an informal visit" (*Guide* 7.8:1). One of the printers, Louis Laronde, later described in the school newspaper how Chisholm praised the school in a speech and the students marched to "Gathering of the Clans." During the visit, one student was selected to write a motto on the chalkboard: "To the boy or girl leaving this School. Much is expected of you. Go forward, rise higher, and win the place in this new Country which God and your talents enable you to occupy." This was less an inspection of the school than of students.

Besides formal inspections by Indian Affairs officials, school newspapers reveal other opportunities for oversight: informal visits from government officials.[9] J.R. Miller notes that visits to schools from official visitors were common opportunities for publicity, and that schools were often prepared in advance of the visit (p. 145). School newspapers mentioned the visits of treaty signatory and former Manitoba lieutenant-governor Alexander Morris (*Our Forest Children* 3.6:57), the Duke and Duchess of Connaught (4.4:211), and donors from England (3.8:94). Kasota and Washakada Homes in Manitoba welcomed the Governor General Lord Stanley of Preston in 1889 by putting small flags across the veranda and a large Union Jack in the centre, offering a guest book for him to sign (*Progress* 3.8:86). Kitamaat Home's newspaper reported the deputy minister of railways was "very much pleased with the signs of advancement in the village" after a visit (*Na-Na-Kwa* 2.4). When Deputy Superintendent General Hayter Reed visited Rupert's Land School in the fall of 1894, he spent only one day in classrooms (*Aurora* 2.23:3). The school newspaper directed student readers to remember Reed's words of encouragement and "show practical gratitude in the future for the interest he manifested in their welfare" – Reed's visit was framed as evidence of care. A composition attributed to a student detailed the activities of performance required during the visit and a speech Reed delivered, stating that to run away meant a waste of government money (2.23:4). The next year, Reed visited Battleford School accompanied by the Premier of the Dominion Mackenzie Bowell and Minister of the Interior T.M. Daly (*Guide* 4.3:1). Again, according to the school newspaper, the visit evidenced that "the heads of departments [were] taking a hearty interest in the welfare of the institutions under them," which should encourage students since "persons in high and responsible positions [were taking] an interest in them." The newspaper celebrated the visit as a series of firsts: the first visit from a premier of the dominion and in Battleford, dubbed the first capital of the North West. Though the newspaper reported the day as special, it simultaneously claimed the day as typical. It objected to "disarrang[ing] the routine of the School for mere display." Instead, the newspaper claimed Reed, Bowell, and Daly "saw things going on in their every day course, just as they would have been had no visit been paid. Surely this is better than any momentary display under a false face." It is unlikely the school did not prepare for the visit of three dignitaries, who held great power over their institution and whose very presence would have altered activities. Yet it appears important that schools portrayed these visits as evidence of open doors – transparent and consistently recognized as successful.

School newspapers also made it seem doors were open to non-government visitors. Principals, church members, and tourists appear to have visited from near and far. Wilson recorded 143 visitors for July 1889 alone in *Our Forest Children*, many of whom picnicked on the grounds near the school (3.6:57). The next year, Wilson prepared the space for visitors with "tables, benches and rustic seats [which] have been put up for the accommodation of visitors" (4.4:210). Rupert's Land School also printed in its newspaper how steamer boat tours on the Red River gave many from Winnipeg a chance to visit the school (*Rupert's Land Gleaner* 2.8:63) as well as a local snowshoe club (*Aurora* 2.14:3; 3.26:2). *Na-Na-Kwa* printed notes from the Crosby Home in Port Simpson, British Columbia, which claimed it was "open to visitors who wish to look through. We are always pleased to see them and do not find it irksome in any degree to let them know what is being done" (31.12). *The Guide* also stated a visit "helps us a great deal when the pupils ascertain that the visitor really takes an interest in them and their work" (7.3:1). These less official visits may have been ways to attract donations and dispel myths. As one visitor to Battleford School recorded, he was surprised students could dance the Red River Jig, say the Lord's Prayer, laugh, cry, "and emit other evidences of emotion"; he was astonished, in other words, at their humanity. In these instances, schools portrayed themselves not as secret cloisters but as institutions with nothing to hide. As the newspaper of Rupert's Land School stated, "a cordial invitation is extended to visit our institution" (*Aurora* 1.12:1), an invitation, of course, rarely extended to parents. Newspapers were an extension of this seeming openness, which contributed to a veneer of transparency despite what the TRC reveals today.

Yet the doors were not entirely open. Church and state actively attempted to limit the oversight of Indigenous families and communities through forcing students to attend or remain at school, by denying visits home, and censoring correspondence; the geographic distance between a school and reserve also played a role. Other forces prevented parents from being with their children, including the pass system, which restricted Indigenous movement by requiring passes from an Indian agent to leave the reserve (Episkenew, 2009, pp. 39–41). These passes were often denied to parents wishing to leave the reserve to visit their children at school.[10] Despite these barriers, school newspapers reveal that Indigenous adults continued to push the doors open. Battleford School's newspaper listed Chief Ahtahkakoop's brother Jacob Sasakwamoos as a "frequent visitor" to the school, where he counselled students (*Guide* 7.8:1). In June 1906, Regina School's newspaper recorded the visits of Eashappie from Hurricane Hills; Nokahoot from Moose Mountain; Monekan from Piapot's Reserve; Henry French from Crowstand; James Keepness and Alex Maloney from Pasqua; Metaway, Otapiki, Tackwis, and Musjusiwasis from Muscowpetungs; "and several others whose names we were not able to get" (*Progress* 15.6:3). It is not clear whether these were parents or community members passing through. Moreover, newspapers often presented these names as a list rather than with the more robust descriptions of what white settler visitors to schools saw, said, or did. Still, they serve as evidence that schools were not entirely devoid of Indigenous adults and that these visits were important enough to record in the newspaper.

The reasons a school highlighted a visit may not have been the reason the visitor came or the reason a student valued it. *Na-Na-Kwa* thanked "the people" for bringing wood to the school (14.6) and parents who brought the school salmon, halibut, and seaweed (27.5). Unlike other boarding schools, *Na-Na-Kwa* explained that the Kitamaat Home, "while using the necessary white food, strives not to supplant the native foods which are donated generously" and that the students liked, which also saved the school money (20.9). The donations may symbolize more: perhaps they were a way for parents to monitor the school through restricted channels, maintaining a form of oversight despite the larger narratives of them as inept. Regina School's newspaper framed the visits of Chief Payipwat as for himself, not students. On one visit, accompanied by other unnamed Indigenous people, the newspaper reported that Payipwat came to ask for an update on the Greco-Turkish War of 1897 and a map of the conflict (*Progress* 3.78:7). At another point, he had lost one of his children and came to the school "trying, as he says, to rid himself of his sorrow" (3.83:7). The school may well have served as a source of information and comfort, yet shortly after these articles Payipwat was arrested for participating in a Sun Dance and was deposed as chief (Pettipas, 1994, p. 116). What else was Payipwat doing when he would drop by the school? *Progress* also announced the visit of Mohawk writer E. Pauline Johnson in 1897, which it called inspiring (*Progress* 3.83:7). Johnson wrote three short stories about boarding schools: "His Sister's Son (1896); "As It Was in the Beginning" (1899); and "Little Wolf-Willow" (1907), about a boy at boarding school who takes some skills but rejects the assimilationist agenda (Gerson and Strong-Boag, 2000, p. xxxii). These visits may have been opportunities to check in with students and assert a form of oversight.

Chiefs who visited the school often received a write-up in the newspaper and appear to have given speeches for students at the school. *Our Forest Children* wrote about the visit of Chief Brant in 1889 to Shingwauk Home, where his son studied (*Our Forest Children* 3.7:77). Though Plains Saulteaux Chief Louis O'Soup did not deliver his speech at Battleford School, its newspaper reprinted a transcription of one he gave in 1898 at an "Indian Conference" in Winnipeg (*Guide* 6.9:3–4). O'Soup's speech accords with common narratives found elsewhere in *The Guide*: that the government is generous and fair, and that without education Indigenous people "shall become extinct." But he also states that education will lead future generations to do anything white people can do and said he envisions a future with schools on reserves. He alludes to industrial school visits conducted by himself and parents in the crowd, where he saw "that our children are very clever, for it has not taken them very long to learn a good deal." While some of O'Soup's sentiments align with the newspaper, his address also speaks to oversight.

The Guide reported the visit of Chief Peyasiw-awasis in 1898 when he visited Battleford School (6.7:1), which the newspaper frames as support. The newspaper does not go behind the scenes. Peyasiw-awasis, also known as Thunderchild, was, like Payipwat, an important Plains Cree leader. He was a signatory to Treaty 6 in 1876 and throughout his life defended treaty rights (McCullough, 2005). Peyasiw-awasis had clear opinions on education: In 1891, he and supporters tore down a Roman Catholic school on his reserve after it was built without his support. In 1910, he appealed to treaty rights to demand a school for his nation and when the government failed to deliver, his community built it alone. In 1923, Peyasiw-awasis wrote a letter to Duncan Campbell Scott revealing the deplorable conditions he went on to witness at Battleford School, demanding an on-reserve day school (TRC of Canada, 2015b, p. 179). *The Guide* reported another of his visits in 1899, this time accompanied by Chief Moosomin and "a large number of people"

(*Guide* 7.8:4). One student transcribed his speech and reprinted it in the school newspaper, making permanent what the school would consider ephemeral. In the transcription Peyasiw-awasis praises the school and points to how his own children attended. He admits that two students had died but told the crowd the school was not to blame. Yet the transcription reveals other narratives not commonly found within the newspaper's pages. Peyasiw-awasis did not dismantle the bricks and mortar of *this* school as he did on his reserve ten years before; in fact, this speech is deferential to the principal. But unlike an article on the previous page about compulsory education, Peyasiw-awasis disapproves of using force and invites parents into the school instead of barring them from it. Like the school he dismantled the previous decade and the school he built the decade after, the transcription of this speech reveals his ongoing oversight – and invitation for parents to do so as well – of Indigenous education.

School newspapers recorded the visits of parents, siblings, and grandparents as well, but usually through words attributed to students. An exception included the newspaper of Rupert's Land School, which noted that "numerous visits from parents and friends this Christmas Tide, have gladdened the hearts" of students (*Aurora* 3.25:2). Most descriptions of parental visits though were attributed to students, including an entry at Battleford School stating the student was "very much pleased" his brother came from Sturgeon Lake reserve (*Guide* 7.7:1). The printed account of the visit focused on how at school he had never been punished, and that as much as he loved his brother he "would not go home with him" because the school was so good. Yet the entry also reveals the boy took his brother "all around the building"; the brother, in turn, promised to try and get their three younger brothers to attend. This brother travelled two hundred kilometres to visit the school, and, assured by his brother's happiness there only after seeing it for himself, he states he will bring more family members. What newspapers left out were likely the times when Indigenous people were met at the door and ushered away, or the criticisms Indigenous visitors may have had. Newspapers also do not typically mention the visits to school of Indigenous mothers and Indigenous women more broadly.[11] What might have been said off the record to a principal or in another language to the children? What did Indigenous visitors say to their communities when they returned home about the school? Families and chiefs were likely visiting schools for different reasons than white settlers, who came on official inspections with different criteria than a parent; as tourists; as donors checking up on their investments; or as politicians coming for publicity. These visits from chiefs, parents, and communities may have been forms of oversight otherwise prohibited.

Fire! Fire!

Oversight could have prevented some of the most horrific aspects of Indian boarding schools, not the least of which was fire. The October 1889 issue of *Our Forest Children* reported that Shingwauk Home had suffered from a fire the month before. Flames and a "rolling cloud of thick smoke" ravaged the principal's bedroom, some of the dormitory floor, and a partition – damage only mitigated by the school's own fire brigade, consisting of staff and students (3.7:78–9). The fire brigade began in 1877 and consisted of weekly practice and false alarms, where the students practised dumping buckets of river water via a "hoisting apparatus" (Wilson, 1908, p. 49). In addition to assessing the damage, the newspaper described how the 1889 fire originated in the school's "lock-up" where "a refractory boy was at the time confined" (*Our Forest Children* 3.7:78–9). Wilson wrote that "a short examination proved conclusively that the fire was this boy's work," prompting Wilson to send for a constable while the children who helped stop the fire received a holiday and "small gratuity." Wilson also mentioned this fire in a retrospective photo album about his life, where he described the firesetter as a "naughty boy" who "set fire to his prison" (Wilson, 1908, p. 49). Next to this handwritten description is a photograph of the child fire brigade on top of the school's roof (see figure 6.5). Here, admission of resistance (setting "fire to his prison") is coupled with the means of literally throwing water on these attempts. The 1889 fire was not the first deliberately set inferno at Shingwauk Home: six days after first opening in 1873 the school completely burned down and Wilson lost one of his own children in the fire (TRC of Canada, 2015b, p. 465).

Fires threatened any nineteenth-century structure, but especially Indian boarding schools. The TRC's final report devotes an entire chapter to contextualizing fires in schools, which were typically overcrowded, built cheaply, poorly wired, and lacking what even then was considered adequate fire protection. To prevent runaways or the mixing of male and female dormitories, some schools even refused to build fire escapes or would lock them at night, rendering these protection measures futile. Students also set schools afire in protest. The TRC recorded 117 confirmed fires in Indian boarding schools between

Figure 6.5. Fire brigade, 1877. Image and handwritten text taken from Edward Francis Wilson's journal, written from 1908 to 1916. Salt Spring Island Archives, Reverend Edward Francis Wilson Collection, Accession Number Wilson049.

1867 and 1939; of those, at least 26 were likely set deliberately by students (TRC of Canada, 2015b, p. 466). As with other figures in the final report, these numbers may be conservative. As one example shows, the memoir of teacher and Indian agent W.M. Halliday (1935) in Alert Bay, British Columbia, names at least one additional deliberately set fire unrecorded by the TRC (p. 233).

The final report reveals students who warned fellow classmates about their plans and who set fires to get sent home or fight limitations imposed on their time home (TRC of Canada, 2015b, p. 484). Yet, fire starters were criminalized. In the case of Shingwauk Home, Wilson sent the "refractory boy" already being punished to the town constable and rewarded the student members of the fire brigade. The newspaper of Rupert's Land School also reported that its fire brigade was student-run (*Aurora* 1.12:3). School newspapers also framed students who ran away, another common form of protest, as worthy of punishment (*Guide* 1.2:2; 7.11:2). Yet Indian Affairs employee Martin Benson stated in a 1903 letter to the superintendent general that "even an Indian will not set fire to buildings, destroy valuable property and endanger life from pure cussedness. There must have been some real or imaginary grievance which led some of the boys to commit incendiarism" (qtd. in TRC Canada, 2015b, p. 483). Though Benson's understanding assumes an inherent criminality ("even an Indian") and that abuse may be imagined, his letter opens up the possibility that setting boarding school fires might be more than recklessness.[12] Yet publicly, newspapers refused or could not see fire setting as resistance. Several newspapers simply list the fire's facts – the date, damage, and solutions. Students who ran away, whom the TRC's report frames similarly, are rarely mentioned in school newspapers. When they are, the focus is expectedly on their punishment rather than resistance.

In the column next to the article on Shingwauk Home's fire is a seemingly unrelated piece on the construction of Indian boarding school buildings across Canada. Part of the second article discusses new fire protection measures at Battleford School, including a tank of water in the attic, powered by a windmill. Is this placement of the articles coincidental? The newspaper of Rupert's Land School similarly reported Battleford School's fire (*Aurora* 2.17:3) as well as its own fire, carefully sandwiched between news of the sewing room being moved and students practicing hymns (2.24:3). Just a few issues later, the newspaper announced that the school had additional fire pails, extinguishers, fire brigade instructions, and a fire escape platform (3.26:3; 3.30:3–4). Regardless of intentions, readers would have learned of a "criminal" student firesetter next to an ostensibly casual update on fire prevention. Juxtaposing the supposed problem with a solution served to frame fire setting as criminal while it also veiled the stamping out of resistance as innocuous fire protection. The final report also recasts running away as a form of resistance. School newspapers almost never mention students who covertly left the school without permission, and this absence given the frequency the final report uncovers leaves us today with negative evidence. Perhaps the devastation of a fire was too large to omit from a newspaper, while an individual student leaving school could be handled more discreetly and therefore left out. Fire damage also required money to repair, so mentioning it in the newspaper might inspire donations. But running away may have been more sharply viewed as resistance, or at least as a poorer reflection on conditions at the school than a fire. Students who ran away were also criminalized as truants, but newspapers did not openly condemn them the way *Our Forest Children* did with the student who set a fire.

Health

In addition to fire, Indian boarding schools represented extreme risks to student health. Even at the time, Indian boarding schools were known as unhealthy spaces. The TRC repeatedly noted the impact of money-saving measures on the health, safety, and welfare of students, which consistently appeared in various guises in the newspapers. Indigenous students suffered and died from tuberculosis, scrofula, measles, and other diseases more frequently than their non-Indigenous counterparts.[13] Under a per capita system, enrolment – no matter the health of a student – mattered most, so schools would admit children with contagious diseases into classrooms with healthy students (Woolford, 2015, p. 235). Schools were often overcrowded, they served unhealthy food, and they typically lacked medical staff and supplies. Buildings were poorly constructed, regularly without proper ventilation. Students were often overworked and abused. All of these factors contributed to poor health at Indian boarding schools. Disease at school was not inevitable: as both Mary-Ellen Kelm (1999, p. 177) and Andrew Woolford (2015, p. 238) note, disease at schools was not (just) because of agentless bacteria but because of human-created conditions and policies. The TRC's final report outlines how the government's tuberculosis policies for Indian boarding schools in the 1880s were "shamefully inadequate" (TRC of Canada, 2015b, p. 384) and how the government could have established regulations but never did, mostly to save money. The report contextualizes the findings of Peter Bryce, chief medical officer of Indian Affairs, who sounded alarms in 1907 yet was ultimately silenced. Bryce published a damning report after visits to thirty-five boarding schools, signalling high levels of disease and death (A.J. Green, 2006). Newspapers such as the *Ottawa Citizen* and *Saturday Night* summarized Bryce (Milloy, 1999, pp. 91, 101–2) and turned criticism of residential schools into "general knowledge" (J.R. Miller, 1996, p. 134). Bryce was forced to retire, but his report reached wider audiences when he self-published it in 1922 under the title *The Story of a National Crime.*

Disease would have been all around the students and staff writing in school newspapers. Yet topics of disease could not disrupt the general message that everything was going really, really well. School newspapers not only cushioned and explained away poor health but even used illness to justify settler colonialism. Such a move is unsurprising given Kelm's and Woolford's arguments that the imposition of European health practices on Indigenous children in boarding schools was another settler colonial method for attempting to control Indigenous bodies. New research on the twentieth century is emerging on just how far such control extends: F.J. Paul Hackett, Sylvia Abonyi, and Roland F. Dyck (2016) reveal how residential students were mostly healthy before entering school; Ian Mosby's (2013) research exposes the nutritional and human biomedical experimentation at residential schools; and Maureen Lux (2016) examines health care segregation at Indian hospitals. In 2013, residential school survivor Brian Sinclair died in a Manitoba emergency room after thirty-four hours without any help for a treatable infection. The inquest into his death has since been criticized for its refusal to name race as a factor (Geary, 2017). European health care on Turtle Island has never been neutral, and representations of health in these newspapers are no exception.

School newspapers often mentioned disease nonchalantly – that the entire school had "La Grippe" (influenza) or that students enjoyed sleeping in tents instead of the school building (*Progress* 8.13:4; *Guide* 1.2:1–2). These instances decontextualize the use of tents to treat children with tuberculosis, which Lux (2001) states was to save money (p. 193). A newspaper may mention a student had to travel to a hospital for an unnamed operation in which "several glands were removed," but would focus on the student's desire to return to school rather than what necessitated the invasive treatment (*Progress* 18.1:3). Kitamaat Home's newspaper similarly described the school's outbreak of whooping cough by stating that one student, "during a fit of coughing, broke a blood vessel and died in a few hours. Everything possible was done for her, but we could not save her. We are glad to say that all are better now" (*Na-Na-Kwa* 30.4). But not all *was* better since a child had died, left ungrieved by the newspaper. Newspapers inserted these updates of illness casually and infrequently, nearly drowned out by the far more common updates of joy.

School newspapers also managed instances of disease by blaming not conditions at the school but Indigenous people themselves with claims about their biological predisposition to disease as well as their hygienic ignorance. Newspapers suggested Indigenous peoples had "a scrofulous tendency" (*Na-Na-Kwa* 4.1) and lacked immunity (*Progress* 17.11:1). Disease was due to "the tendency of the Indian to consumption" (3.79:4) rather than colonialism, shifting responsibility from schools onto Indigenous peoples. Some articles blamed "the habit of mouth-breathing" and "lazy lungs" (*Indian Leader* 6.8:1) for pulmonary diseases.[14] Other newspapers turned to culture. Regina School's newspaper stated that "moccasins are the mother of consumption" (*Progress* 3.70:1) and presented Indigenous homes as communal and therefore germ ridden (17.11:1). Another article suggested disease was "the natural result of the unnatural neglect of little children" (3.79:4) – at home, not in schools. And Shingwauk Home's newspaper reprinted an article attributing scrofula to "a low state of living" (*Our Forest Children* 3.12:154). The line between nature and culture could blur, as was the case with Kitamaat Home's cover story, "What is Killing the Indians?" Illustrated by a skull and crossbones, the article blamed the Potlatch (*Na-Na-Kwa* 18.1). The article accused the practice of spreading whooping cough, chicken pox, and measles. In this way, biological considerations – the strain of travel and the close proximity of participants – blended with stated and unstated concerns of culture.

School newspapers also attributed disease to Indigenous medicine. As Lux (2001) notes, missionaries fought against Indigenous health care because of its connections to faith (p. 82). Newspapers called traditional healing practices shamanism, black art, and Indian poison (*Na-Na-Kwa* 17.7) and labelled medicine men necromancers and witch doctors (*Progress* 13.3:3) who administered lethal poisons (*Guide* 6.2:4). Regina School's newspaper quoted an Indian agent in Oklahoma, who held medicine men responsible for one-third of Indigenous children's deaths (*Progress* 3.77:3). Rupert's Land School reported that "death has been caused through the assertion of the medicine man" (*Aurora* 2.22:1), and in an earlier issue printed one and a half pages and a picture describing medicine practices (1.5:2). Kitamaat Home's newspaper exhibited a photograph with the caption "An Indian Medicine-Man" with no accompanying text (31.10); however, on the recto side of the photograph was a note on the building of a new hospital at Port Simpson and a plea for donations (31.9). Readers would have encountered the school's hope that it "shall not look in vain for substantial [financial] help" for the hospital on page 9 and the photograph of a medicine man on page 10. The photograph, coupled with the newspaper's earlier articles denigrating Indigenous medicine, may have visually stood in for the dangers of not donating to the hospital.

Though newspapers conceded Indigenous peoples were unavoidably susceptible to disease, they presented schools as the solution rather than cause. Schools, the logic went, should teach hygiene because within Indigenous families "cleanliness means nothing" and "sanitation and hygiene are unknown terms" (*Progress* 17.11:1). Newspapers framed Indigenous people as suspicious "that cleanliness, air, light and sunshine are so many weapons against their hereditary enemy" (3.78:4). *Progress* reprinted the opinion of a Dr Martha Waldon, who believed "positive, explicit directions as to cleanliness, sanitary conditions, and all that pertains to wholesome home life, will give the children a chance to grow up without being poisoned from babyhood." Kitamaat Home's teacher and missionary doctor, Dr Dorothea Bower, perpetuated the belief that Indigenous peoples "do not consider 'Sanitary Science' an important study" (27/28.2). According to school newspapers, such ignorance could be overcome with education (*Progress* 3.79:4; 17.9:6); learning the importance of separate eating utensils, towels, combs, and toothbrushes (*Progress* 17.11:1; 18.1:2); and ventilation (*Na-Na-Kwa* 4.7; 29.10). Rupert's Land School reported that "there has been no case of sickness for more than four months. Dr. Open Air and Dr. Exercise are the best physicians" (*Aurora* 2.20:3). According to school newspapers, biological diseases could be mitigated by the school.

Newspapers also framed schools as sources of medical knowledge. *Na-Na-Kwa* urged "all the Kitamaats to be vaccinated at once" for smallpox because in the US "tribes of Indians in Indian Territory and Arizona have been wiped out" (7.7). Battleford School's newspaper advised sprinkling sulphur to prevent influenza, malaria, rheumatism, and yellow fever (*Guide* 7.8:2). It also reprinted a column called "These Wonderful Bodies of Ours," which offered information on everything from the spine to circulation (5.10:2; 4; 5.12:2; 6.1:3). Regina School used colonial language to matter-of-factly explain germs: "Out from our blood goes a whole army of other little living things and when these begin to fight the other little fellow and kill and eat them up sometimes they have a terrible battle" (*Progress* 18.12:7).[15] *Na-Na-Kwa* described a particularly deadly period in the community, with more deaths in a few weeks than in the whole preceding year and "some times two funerals a day" (17.7). The newspaper attributed this devastation to "superstition and evil," curtailed by drugs shipped from Toronto. It also described an Indigenous man about to treat a cut finger with carbolic acid and amputation had it not been for the intervention of a doctor (7.7). These scenes positioned Indigenous people as medically incompetent and even self-harming, saved by schools.

Another method of containing the taboo topic of disease was to report not on disease but recovery (*Progress* 4.8:1; 19.4:4; *Guide* 5.7:1; 5.11:1). The newspaper of Rupert's Land School reported that "happily, with careful nursing, our patients have now recovered, with the exception of two little girls who contracted influenza in a severe form. They too are on the high road to health, tho' still confined to bed" (*Aurora* 3.26:3). The update reveals students were sick, two severely so and still bedridden; yet it focuses on how sickness was outside the school's control – just the unfortunate consequence of bad weather – and has passed. The same newspaper claimed that "the health of our children has been uniformly excellent since summer began. Life in the open air and plenty of bathing work wonders" (*Aurora* 3.31:3). Underneath this claim, though, was news that two children had to have operations due to "scrofulous swellings" and that another student had died. The April 1897 issue of *The Guide* reported how its school had closed due to quarantine. But the newspaper managed the crisis by highlighting how students could now work more outdoors (5.10:1). The newspaper also recorded a speech by Reverend Matheson on quarantine "not from a physical but from a spiritual point of view," lecturing on how "we all needed quarantining on account of spiritual sickness." As Lux (2001) points out, quarantine was a cheap attempt at stopping the spread of disease, but it wrongly assumed reserves and Indigenous people were always the carriers and ultimately only protected white settler communities (p. 184). While mentioning a quarantined school could undermine a school's broader narrative of safety, newspapers had systems for managing disaster. Other techniques such as painting parents as inept also served to deflect from schools their responsibility for disease, legitimizing the school as otherwise safe and clean.

Such methods of containment did not appear in entries attributed to students, which were sometimes the only mention of sickness, while the rest of the newspaper, coded as authored by the principal and staff, remained silent (*Guide* 4.10:3; 7.7:1). In two 1897 issues of *The Guide*, students alluded to several classmates with prolonged sore eyes (5.7:1; 5.8:1). The reason was likely trachoma, an infectious condition that can lead to permanent visual impairment. Caused by overcrowding, lack of water, and poor medical care, trachoma was rampant at Indian boarding schools (TRC of Canada, 2015b, p. 446). The TRC's final report reveals how Indian Affairs downplayed the risks of trachoma and ignored medical advice. Despite the student entries signalling sore eyes, the larger newspaper declared the school was entirely healthy (*Guide* 5.7:1; 5.8:1). The following issue contained a student entry about a classmate: "The girls are all very sorry for Mary Ann Black because she is very sick, but we hope she will get well and strong again" (5.9:1); in the next issue, readers learned the seventeen-year-old had died (5.10:1). While newspapers repackaged illness for readers and renarrated the health-related horrors of these institutions, students continued to remember their friends and punctured the silence.

Death

Like health, school newspapers also had methods for framing student death. Of the six volumes of the TRC's final report, one is entirely dedicated to missing children and unmarked burials. In addition, the TRC created two registers for the deaths of named and unnamed residential school students. The final report confirms the deaths of 3,200 deaths – likely an underrepresentation (TRC of Canada, 2015b, p. 376). The TRC found that children at schools "died at a far higher rate than school-aged children in the general population" (TRC of Canada, 2015a, p. 1). For instance, from 1891 to 1897, at Regina School 48 students died from tuberculosis (TRC of Canada, 2015b, p. 394). The final report also details death from measles, smallpox, diphtheria, typhoid, pneumonia, fire, suicide, abuse, whooping cough, trachoma, and accidents. Deaths were poorly recorded, parents were poorly informed, and school gravesites today are poorly maintained.

Newspapers presented disease and death as anomalous and controlled interruptions to the school, not constitutive of it. One front-page article on the Queen's birthday celebration at Shingwauk Home reported the day's weather, flags, and music; nestled in the middle was the news of a student's death: "We had intended at first to have the picnic on the 24th, but the death of a little Indian girl on the 23rd, necessitated its being postponed until the 26th" (*Our Forest Children* 4.4:209). Though the newspaper featured the student's obituary two pages later, the article continues on with the celebration, just as the school did, by listing the food, sports, and music of the day. Similarly, Kitamaat Home's newspaper stated that "owing to so much sickness at the Home we have not been able to do as much of our regular work, but amongst other things we have managed pinafores of the same material, they look nicely in their uniform. Preparations for Xmas will soon commence" (*Na-Na-Kwa* 4.6). In these ways, death and disease for readers only temporarily forced schools to change their plans.

One way school newspapers managed death in their pages was by cushioning bad news with happier topics. A close look at one issue can stand in for the same technique in many. Page 6 of an 1897 issue of *Progress* featured the regularly occurring section "School Matters," composed of short updates on day-to-day operations (3.70:6). This particular issue contained four updates in the following order: a teacher's departure; Bible verse memorization; a student – importantly labelled as *former* – who had died at home in Muscowpetungs and had been sick for years; and the school's literary society and football team. The quotidian of an otherwise lively school cushions the news of the student's death, contextualized by the fact that he died at home and was ailing a long time. This softening extends before and after the "School Matters" section as well: the preceding pages featured a poem titled "Departure of the Indians" (3.70:2); a scathing critique of Indigenous women (3.70:3); praise for former student farming colonies; an anthropological article on Tuscarora political structures (3.70:4); and missionary updates from Cairo, India, and Uganda (3.70:5). In this issue, both before and after the two sentences on a student's death, readers would have encountered articles on Indigenous life in demise, frozen in time, and related to the "Indian Problem" elsewhere in the world. While jarring on its own, the two sentences of student death – missed entirely by a skimming reader – were nestled among explanations.

The November 1897 issue of *Progress* did not have the luxury of spacing out death and disease because there was just too much of it. The "School Matters" section in this issue featured no less than ten entries on health, death, and disease (3.84:6–7). The section detailed students sick with measles, diphtheria, and scrofula, as well as two deaths: the former shoe- and harness-making instructor by coal gas as well as a student. Even in this exceptional issue, in which death and disease remain unpadded, readers would have also encountered articles on solving the "Indian Problem" (3.84:2), a vanishing Indigenous population in Greenland (3.84:3), an Indian execution (3.84:3), and statistics on student assimilation (3.84:4). Readers, in other words, had by page 6 already confronted explanations and context for Indigenous death at school. As well, one of the "School Matters" entries stated that the carpentry boys were working on a new hospital – the problem of death was being managed, according to the newspaper.

Some newspapers did not so much bury bad news as put it front and centre. *The Guide* listed deaths on the front page like classifieds, along with marriage and birth announcements directly under a list of staff names and subscription information (4.6:1; 5.1:1; 5.6:1; 5.10:1; 6.1:1; 6.3:1; 6.8:1; 6.9:1; 7.5:1; 7.9:1; 7.11:1). These entries included the name, student number, date of death, and relationship to the school (e.g., student, former student, chief, or child of staff). *Na-Na-Kwa* listed student deaths as classifieds on the last page, along with the deaths of community members. Some write-ups on death in *Progress* and *Na-Na-Kwa* also featured a thick black border. When three students died in a short span of time, *The Aurora* also marked off a section of its front page with thick black lines (1.4:1). While these ways of making death more prominent may signal transparency or mourning, these lists were sometimes the only attention directed to someone's passing. They also serve to routinize or even normalize death at school. The same cannot be said of white settlers' deaths. When the infant daughter of the principal (*Guide* 6.8:1) or a reverend died (6.12:3), school newspapers often expended space memorializing them.

While newspapers typically reserved few lines for the sickness and death of students, there were notable exceptions. Students who received an article about their death or an obituary were listed as special. For one student who died at Regina School, the newspaper called him "one of the brightest and most promising boys in the school" as well as a skilled engineer-in-training and artist (*Progress* 15.1:4). The article reminisced how an English banker visited the school and was so taken by the late student's art he commissioned some of his work. When two students died three years later, *Progress* memorialized them in an obituary outlined by a black border (18.4:3). These students were called "two of our most promising boys" and strong athletes and farmers. One had passed a provincial examination for steam engineering and both were said to have followed school rules. *Our Forest Children* called one of its students who died "one of the best girls at Wawanosh Home, and last summer [she] received the Bishop's prize for general good behavior" (3.7:77). Other students received attention after their deaths for their devotion to Christianity (*Guide* 7.9:1; *Progress* 3.84:7; *Na-Na-Kwa* 31.4). Kitamaat Home's newspaper reported the drowning death of one boy: "Indian children are fearless and skillful in both boats and canoes" so therefore "when an accident happens it is invariably the result of play" (*Na-Na-Kwa* 24.8), meaning that the boy was to blame for his own death. Just three issues later, the same newspaper reported the drowning of a reverend on Vancouver Island and noted his death as peculiar given his superior ability to command a sailboat (27.10). But while *Na-Na-Kwa* acknowledged the skills of both people, the newspaper extends the possibility of a rogue gust – an external force – to the reverend but not the child.

Those whose deaths received attention in school newspapers were perhaps viewed as *grievable*. Jodi Byrd, informed by Lauren Berlant and Judith Butler, distinguishes between life lamentable – sad, but inevitable and in the past – and life grievable, which requires people to stop and consider what led to such suffering (p. 38). While church and state justified high death rates in Indian boarding schools by self-serving Darwinist logic that Indigenous people were transitioning from wild to civilized (Lux, 2001, p. 150), school newspapers may also reveal that schools did not consider Indigenous children as fully human before supposed assimilation (Woolford, 2015, p. 238). This belief may help to explain why students deemed exceptionally talented or devout received more lines in the newspaper concerning their illness or death.

While school newspapers inconsistently memorialized students who died at school, they appear more forthcoming when students died at home. It was common practice to discharge sick students (Lux, 2001, p. 107), which permitted families to spend more time with their children and seek traditional health care but also meant less perceived responsibility on the part of the school (Kelm, 1999, p. 75). The practice meant student deaths happened off school rolls and at least superficially off the hands of administrators. A 1909 issue of *Progress* reprinted a lecture US Indian Commissioner Frank Leupp gave at the International Congress on Tuberculosis. In the article, he stated that government advice had been to return sick children home because they tend to improve, "though the physical environment there is far worse than at the school" (18.1:2). The likely reason for improvement, Leupp argued, was "the child is released from confinement and is with his own people; for homesickness plays a large part in the emotions of an Indian child." But leaving school also meant fresh air, escape from other sick students and abuse, a better diet, less stress, a loving environment, and access to traditional health care.

Did newspapers consider returned students as students? This remains unclear. The *Guide* announced when a student was "allowed to go home on sick leave" (5.1:1) or was "allowed to leave with her father and mother on account of ill health" (4.1:3). But these announcements positioned the school as in control of who could leave and why.

With little follow-up on the fate of these discharged students – who if sick enough to be discharged may have later died – the newspaper had no need to report the death, leaving its narrative of health and wellness intact. One issue of *Progress* announced that "all have recovered from the measles," but it also listed in the next sentence two boys who "have gone to their homes to recover from scrofula. We hope they will soon be back" (18.4:5). The next issue confirmed that "the pupils have all recovered from the measles and are enjoying the bright sunshine and the outdoor life" (18.5:6–7); no announcement followed, though, about the two boys with scrofula who left for home. Did they return? Did they die? Did the newspaper no longer consider them students? For one Battleford School student, the October 1897 issue of the newspaper announced he was "granted his discharge" and headed home because of poor health. The March 1899 issue briefly announced that the "expupil" died. It appears newspapers wished for it to seem they were *doing* something about the health of their students: in Leupp's reprinted address he stated that "the Indian Office, though maintaining the necessity of giving the Indian child an education has no intention of making him pay for it by sacrificing his health. If at any point it has failed in this it is not through intention" (*Progress* 18.1:2). Years earlier, the newspaper strategically placed a notification that the school was building a hospital beneath the announcement of the death of a former student as well as the message from "one of our absentees," who presumably was a sick, discharged child (3.81:5). Sending sick children home was one measure of preventing the spread of illness, but it also wiped responsibility off the school's hands and onto communities.

Na-Na-Kwa gave more consistent attention to student deaths than other newspapers. As a mission school rather than an industrial school, it was smaller and many of the children came from within the same community as the school. And because the institution educated boys but only boarded girls, Kitamaat Home was in some ways a day school, at least for boys. Months before a student named Flora passed away, the newspaper announced she was sick (*Na-Na-Kwa* 14.7). Her achievements and writing appeared in other issues, and her obituary acknowledged for readers that "to many of you her name has become quite familiar." Rather than a generic obituary, it specifies how Flora was adept at the mechanical work of the newspaper and at needlework. She was very smart and was a helper. The newspaper even announced how the principal George Raley honoured her in the middle name of his newly born daughter (15.7). Another student several years later, Minnie, also received a long write-up (31.4). But outside of *Na-Na-Kwa*, the death of Indigenous people who consistently received attention were chiefs. As the previous chapter argues, their deaths represented O'Brien's (2010) concept of lasting and therefore did not undermine larger narratives of Indian boarding school the way students' deaths did.

School newspapers were more likely to report on the funeral rites of Indigenous peoples (*Progress* 4.86:4; *Our Forest Children* 4.3:206; 3.7:79; *Na-Na-Kwa* 5.7; 19.10). Some articles highlighted the specific funeral rites of parents, often in overtly disparaging ways unlike the more anthropological profiles. One missionary contributed a full-page account of a family's funeral for a recently discharged student. He labelled their customs "barbarously, pagan, ceremonies performed over the body of a christian girl" and "earthly foolishness" (*Progress* 3.73:11). Just a few issues later, another article even blamed Gros Ventre funeral rites – "a performance and not a true outburst of grief" – on accelerating death (3.80:2–3). The unnamed missionary did not label his Christian songs, readings, and reciting of the Lord's Prayer three times as performance. *Na-Na-Kwa* also provided examples of staff attempting to control funerary customs (4.5). One teacher policed a family's grief at the bedside of a sick student:

> I found two old women there doing their "cry sing," I touched one of them on the should and said "hush," they stopped for a while then started again, so I gave another tap, and they stopped again, then an old blind woman came in they got her a place at the foot of the bed, she had a little talk with them and they all three started, it was dreadful, but I stopped them again … In a few minutes the room was full of people making a frightful noise, the death wail. I went out to tell Mr. Raley, he came and persuaded them to go away.

The teacher went on to explain that grief was particularly inappropriate when supposedly performed for money: "This is what they do. The friends of the parents get the most pay." This custom justified for the teacher why the school should "begin with the children and take them while young." In these instances, Indigenous responses to death were monitored and interpreted by the school newspaper.

Conclusion

The TRC may have, for some settlers, made some facts that were unthinkable in the nineteenth century more thinkable today. Some of these facts – which Indigenous people knew and communicated all along – may include that parents were the best form of care for their children, that freedom includes practicing health care and spirituality, that acts deemed criminal were in fact forms of resistance, or that Indigenous people were always already wholly human regardless of state recognition or eighteenth-century European concepts of humanness. Suggesting these as perhaps previously unthinkable does not let church and state off the hook or presume settlers know better now with new facts. (We don't.) Instead, Michel-Rolph Trouillot's (2012) concept of thinkable and unthinkable facts offers ways to hold these institutions and the people comprising them even more responsible when unthinkable facts are plainly stated.

But other facts were already thinkable by settlers in the nineteenth century, yet school newspapers omitted them. Though newspapers held Indigenous people rather than church and state responsible for the spread of disease, this was a thinkable fact by Bryce in at least 1907. It was also thinkable by the authorities who silenced Bryce for speaking out and by settler readers of his research. Government staff and missionaries had to actively suppress the thinkable fact that children and parents have a sacred relationship. Treaties for white settlers were thinkable in the nineteenth century as more than just events, payment, or antiquities, as evidenced by·oral history as well as the diaries of treaty commissioners, which reveal what was said versus written (Long, 2010). And school newspapers never mention abuse, which was thinkable in the government shadow texts that privately condemned or attempted to hide it. But these silences in school newspapers on topics today highlighted loudly in the TRC's final report prevented punctures in many settler colonial narratives. Rather than anachronistic, tracing topics that today appear in the final report and are therefore currently being discussed to the nineteenth century helps to paint a history of the present, acknowledging Dian Million's point that thinking about the past is always already about the now.

7 Layout: Space, Place, and Land

Recently, 'Namgis First Nation off the coast of what is currently known as Northern Vancouver Island hosted a survivor ceremony prompted by the demolition of the former St Michael's School. Indigenous leaders, community members, and survivors gathered to witness and participate in the destruction of the old school's brick building (Hyslop, 2015; Stueck, 2015). Nineteenth-century boarding school newspapers often depicted the physical space of education, though in ways that directly contradict the counternarrative this ceremony tells. School newspapers erased and printed over Indigenous concepts of and claims to land, mirroring colonial spatial practices outside of schools and their printed pages in the late nineteenth century.

Indigenous Studies scholars such as Glen Coulthard (2014) conceive of place as a way to know, experience, and relate to the world (p. 61). Sandra Styres, Celia Haig-Brown, and Melissa Blimkie (2013) challenge space and place as property by instead emphasizing the spirit, emotion, intellect, and sentience of land (pp. 37–8). School newspapers overwrote such definitions, using spatial practices that included positioning, naming, locating, and mapping. Scott Lyons (2010) describes the spatial practice of romanticism, where "Indian space … is circular, communal, and never near a cosmopolitan center. (Even when it is, it's not.) It is always pungent: smoky and sagey in a manner that evokes the past" (pp. 15–16). When the principal, Edward Francis Wilson, of Shingwauk Home in Sault Ste Marie travelled to Indian Territory,[1] he used his school's newspaper to similarly romanticize place: "There is no mistake about Indian land. The change is noticeable directly [after] a stranger enters it. The train goes rattling along as before, – but there is a quiet, a peace, a calm, an absence of rush and bustle, – the prairie rolls away to the horizon, without a village, a house or even a hut in sight; the soil is unbroken, it is one great unfenced field, a few trees here and there, a solitary rider perhaps" (*Our Forest Children* 3.7:73). Wilson's observation, that space in and out of Indian Territory differed, reifies Indigenous land as only limited to that which *settlers* designate as such. This spatial practice reconceptualized land as property, romanticizing as well as commodifying it.[2] When school newspapers did acknowledge Indigenous land, they depicted it as wastefully unpeopled and unfilled. Some school newspapers converted supposedly wild space into settled place for readers by referencing Canada; others overtly borrowed from the place of England and the US. School newspapers used a variety of spatial practices to re-place Indigenous land – the ultimate goal of settler colonialism. Yet entries attributed to students offer breaks in this narrative. As Mishuana Goeman (2013) notes, "Colonial spatial construction is not unidirectional, and Native people have mediated these spatial constructions with the best tools at their disposal – storytelling, writing, and sense of place" (p. 36). School newspapers provide examples of such mediations.

The Place of Canada in School Newspapers

Inside the pages of school newspapers emerged a story of Canada as a site of conversion from a barren landscape devoid of culture to a site of civilization, a distinction Jo-Anne Fiske (2009) makes using the terms colonial space (figured as empty) and colonial place (figured as filled). The first issue of Shingwauk Home's publication *Our Forest Children* informed readers that Indigenous peoples were "scattered throughout the Dominion of Canada" (1.1.2), framing them as *within* Canada (rather than the reverse) and as *scattered* (rather than as organized nations). Newspapers also documented how schools were teaching the conversion of space into place. *The Aurora* stated that each of Rupert's Land School's classrooms had maps of Canadian railways on the walls and that students learned geography from the Canadian Pacific Railway timetable (3.25:2–3). Other geography lessons included drawing the school's buildings and grounds (3.25:3) as well as answering what were "the chief uses of Mountains and rivers" (2.19:1). Another question asked students to plot a railway trip "from Halifax to Vancouver, naming the province and chief towns passed through on the way," as well as to identify "the boundaries of the Dominion, and its principal lakes, mountains, and rivers." These classroom practices positioned

Indigenous land as under colonial rule, in service to the railway and extractive resource industries. Such questions asked students to conceive of land in English that they may have known differently in their own languages. These questions assume mountains and rivers only exist to offer uses. *Our Forest Children* published the following questions from a geography exam:

1. Where and what are Queen Charlotte, Charlottetown, Fraser, Assiniboine?
2. Name each Province of the Dominion, with its capital or chief city?
3. Through what Provinces and what principal cities does the C.P.R. pass, and what are its termini? (2.9:31)

Other exams asked students to locate Ecuador and Santiago (3.6:55) or to define a lagoon, a glacier, and the first meridian (3.13:162). In these examples, Indigenous children were being asked to reformulate understandings of space, place, and land. Sometimes the creation of place was abstract. As Tracey Banivanua Mar and Penelope Edmonds (2010) state, "It was never enough just to acquire legal title to Indigenous land. Instead it needed to be reimagined and shaped by the colonial eye" (p. 5). Today, Indigenous people are continuing to undo these colonial place names and toponymies.[3]

Even the place of Saskatchewan changed as its newspapers unfolded. While originally the tagline of Regina School's newspaper beneath its title read "Regina, Assiniboia," by the year 1905 when the territory "became" a province it had changed to "Regina, Saskatchewan." Its newspaper documented how students marked the change with a visit to the city's inauguration celebration. Students listened to then Prime Minister Wilfrid Laurier speak and watched a procession of bands, labour organizations, "the chiefs," and "the Indians," who according to the newspaper "looked fine and called forth cheer after cheer" (*Progress* 14.4:2). Students also saw a circus with camels and an elephant. At night they watched fireworks depicting the likenesses of Governor General Albert Grey and Laurier while everyone sang "God Save the King." Though the newspaper titled this article "Our Holiday," the original scene and its later representation in the paper were more than frivolity: these acts – from the political speech to the British anthem; from the procession of unions, notorious for blocking would-be Indigenous membership, alongside chiefs; from the fireworks, which literally overwrote place onto a celestial canvas, to the importing of "exotic animals," connecting British imperialism throughout the world – these acts were tools in creating the place of Canada, which was made with more than just maps, patrolled borders, and boundary markers.

But some notes attributed to students within school newspapers troubled such colonial place-making. One student at Regina School defined Canada as "a place where Whitemen and Indians and other tribes live" (*Progress* 18.2:7). The entry continued, stating, "The Canadian girls and boys go to school and read of the History about Canada and other parts of the world, and also read out of the Alexandra readers and do arithmetic and write compositions [and] also write in the copybooks."[4] This passage mentions that Canada includes "Indians and other tribes" despite the homogenizing thrust of school newspapers. And notwithstanding the school's assimilative attempts, this entry distinguishes Indigenous people from white men. The thorough description of what "Canadian girls and boys" do at school contrasts the common experience at boarding schools, which were academically inferior, with a focus on labour and domestic training. Another student entry described home:

> My home is near a lake and near it are many trees around it; some poplar and fir trees and all mixed trees in the great woods. My home is just forty miles from the town; but there is a store near w[h]ere we get our mechewin and clothing; also there is a school: not an Industrial school nor a boarding school, and there is a church where all my friends go ... I lived in it till my mother died and I came here. There were seven of us children besides mother and father; but six died and I am the only one living and five years ago I came to this school. When I went home to visit I went no more in that home, my father had given it away when my mother died. We had a new house when I went back and I missed the old one very much. (*Progress* 17.4:5)

Unlike schools' attempts to denigrate Indigenous family life, this composition provides a warm picture of home. The student continues to use the Cree word mechewin instead of food, and also – importantly – describes her earlier home as having an on-reserve day school and church. Her description of home is in present tense, even though she reveals her family died. These examples insist on presence.

School newspapers often highlighted the place of schools themselves. Despite survivor reports describing the inside of schools as clinical, *The Guide* reprinted an article answering "how can the dormitory be made cheerful and homelike" (5.6:3). Suggestions included mottos written over every window and door as well as decorating with "a judicious use of cheese cloth." The article even recommended hanging lithographs of "eminent women" such as Lucretia Mott and Harriet Beecher Stowe. How mottos, cheesecloth, and portraits of white abolitionists from the US would create a home for children separated from their families went unstated. As for the outside of schools, Geoffrey Paul Carr (2011), Sarah de Leeuw (2007), K. Tsianina Lomawaima (2014), and Andrew Woolford (2014) all formulate ways a school's architecture continued the colonizing agenda of the classroom. The often lavish design of schools attempted to envelope and disorient students from markers of places they originally knew. Richard Wagamese's (2012) novel *Indian Horse* portrays this disorientation when the character Saul first sees the cupola, balustrade, and frosted glass of his new four-storey school (pp. 43–4).

While school newspapers would sometimes describe the inside of their schools – a new wing or room, new furniture, or a repurposed industrial building – they more often showcased how the school was taming its outdoor spaces. Regina School's newspaper described how the school received nearly five thousand boxes of elder, cottonwood, elm, and ash trees from the federal forestry department. The newspaper boasted that although the trees were small, "in a few years when the ones being set out now have grown, our grounds ought to be very beautiful" (*Progress* 13.3:7). Battleford School's newspaper, too, bragged that its "large acreage has been put under cultivation, and the prospects of a bountiful yield of wheat, oats and barley are good. The gardens are also coming on splendidly" (4.1:1). *Our Forest Children* reprinted a description of Carlisle School: "It would hardly be possible to find a better location for an Indian School than here ... In fact, there is nothing here to remind the Indian of his aboriginal condition, except the Indian trail from Gettysburg Junction – across the green, through two brick-yards, over fences, across a field, through mud, shoe deep ... Then there bursts upon the view the commodious buildings, arranged around a lovely lawn, the trees, the flowers, everything to make a school attractive" (4.3:204–6). The article admits that a trace of Indigenous space – a trail – may remain, but only beneath layers of lawn and fence and tree. *Our Forest Children* also described the grounds of Shingwauk Home as newly tamed, though from the perspective of a resort on a nearby island. The newspaper states that the island "has been nicely cleared – that is to say a good deal of the thick underbrush has been cleared away, and delightful little paths made, twisting and winding by a signboard pointing to 'Readers' Retreat,' 'Bay View,' 'Shingwauk View,' etc." (4.5:225). The newspaper paints for readers a vantage point of an idyllic home among an outdoors tamed by paths, tourist signs, and constructed views. Such descriptions contrast with entries attributed to students about outdoor play at Rupert's Land School. The students appear to have created a teepee outside of their school using sticks and rags. One entry describes how when work and sanctioned leisure such as walks were done, the students would "all run into the teepee and we start to play again" (*Aurora* 3.30:3). Inside, students would prepare pretend feasts and drink tea during the months when it was not too windy. Such a play place, albeit known to teachers and safely contained as "play" by the school newspaper, may have been a reprieve from the school and its grounds and may have remade signifiers of home for some students. Notice, though, that the intimacy of such moments is often left exposed by the newspaper. Survivor testimony is helpful in learning of such moments that went unnoticed by teachers and staff.

Some newspapers' descriptions combined buildings and grounds. *Our Forest Children* reprinted a "visit," conjugated in first-person plural, to Battleford School: "We turn off the road at the top of the hill and pass through a large gate in a neat wire fence (put up, as we are informed, by the boys) and enter the school grounds, passing a compact vegetable garden surrounded by palisading and trees planted last spring. We find the boys playing football on our left, and see farther on the lawn tennis court and swings for the girls. The front of the building faces the north-east, and on entering we find ourselves in a lofty hall." This article, which begins with "let us pay a visit," asks readers to think of themselves as guests, who move from the road to the grounds to the inside of the school. *Our Forest Children* also printed the experiences of a visitor to its own school:

> The Home is about two miles east of the Sault, and is one of the prettiest spots in the world. On the way down we passed a group of small picturesque islands, near the shore, covered with tamarac, spruce and birch, and looking like so many large bouquets in the clear blue river. A little further on, we reached the Home, – a massive stone building, somewhat like an hospital, with a fenced area in front. A little to the right side was the Chapel – a unique little stone building, standing in a beautiful native grove on rising ground, facing the river, and a model place of worship in every way. Over the front gate, a rustic archway is built, with a gabled roof; and the church-yard has a very neat dry stone wall around it. (1.10:1)

The visitor's impressions – of not only the school's structure but also its grounds, chapel, and surrounding area – graced the newspaper's front page, accompanied by a sketch of the school in the snow (see figure 7.1).

OUR FOREST CHILDREN,

PUBLISHED IN THE INTEREST OF INDIAN EDUCATION AND CIVILIZATION.

| Vol. I. | SHINGWAUK HOME, CHRISTMAS, 1887. | No. 10. |

A Visit to the Shingwauk.

A RECENT visitor to the SHINGWAUK HOME, says: One day last week, in company with a lady who takes great interest in Missionary work, I visited the Indian boys' school here, or Shingwauk Home—which means a Pine Tree, and was so named in honor of an old Indian Chief. The Home is about two miles east of the Sault, and is one of the prettiest spots in the world. On the way down we passed a group of small picturesque islands, near the shore, covered with tamarac, spruce and birch, and looking like so many large bouquets in the clear blue river. A little further on, we reached the Home,—a massive stone building, somewhat like an hospital, with a fenced area in front. A little to the right side was the Chapel—a unique little stone building, standing in a beautiful native grove on rising ground, facing the river, and a model place of worship in every way. Over the front gate a rustic archway is built, with a gabled roof; and the church-yard has a very neat dry stone wall around it. The Church itself has fine stained-glass windows, a hardwood floor, excellent pews, chancel, vestry, and baptismal font—the latter made of grey granite—base, pedestal and bowl out of one block—The walls are decorated with scripture mottoes, cut in wood scrolls. Too many of our grand city churches have become mere social clubs for the higher classes to spend a pleasant hour or two on Sunday, and see each other; but in this modest little chapel half hid in the tall trees, like a Druid temple, a strangely devout feeling comes irresistibly over one, excluding all worldly thoughts, and you leave it with a strengthened heart for the duties and responsibilities of life. Coming to the Institution we entered the school room and found the teacher and a number of the boys busily engaged doing some exercises in arithmetic on the blackboard. The

SHINGWAUK HOME.

WAWANOSH HOME.

Figure 7.1. Shingwauk Home. *Our Forest Children* 1.10:1: December 1887.

Figure 7.2. Shingwauk chapel and buildings, 1880. Edward F. Wilson Fonds, Shingwauk Indian Residential School Photograph Series, 2011-016-001 (001), Shingwauk Residential Schools Centre, Algoma University.

Wilson even sent photographs of his schools to the Colonial and Indian Exhibition in London in 1886, which won awards (1.4:3). He advertised a photograph of the school for thirty-five cents (see figure 7.2). In this image, left to right, are the hospital, Shingwauk Home, the chapel, the bandstand, and the drill hall. The dock is also visible, as is the rail line from the dock to the school.[5] Importantly, the cemetery for children who died at school is not visible in this photograph.

These scenes broadcasted to readers the school's assimilative envelopment, but in painterly strokes. The "picturesque" in the nineteenth century was a popular way of taming or containing land and reframing it as landscape, a representational practice seen in these views. Tourists could gaze onto the school like any other pastoral scene. It would not have been a far leap for readers to understand these scenes of control over land – converting colonial space into place – as a stand-in for the attempted assimilation and control over children. These examples interpellate readers as part of the conversion, offering impossible, omnipresent perspectives – from the water or from both in and outdoors.

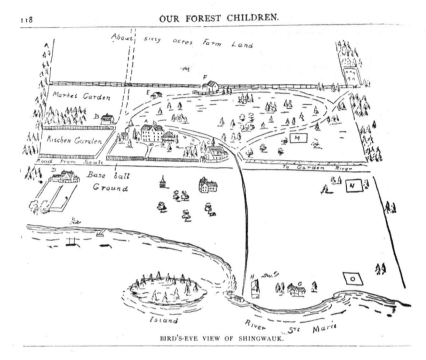

BIRD'S-EYE VIEW OF SHINGWAUK.

Figure 7.3. Bird's-eye view of Shingwauk. *Our Forest Children* 3.10:118: January 1890.

Readers were granted visual power over place through newspaper depictions. Though school newspapers do not profile this power as diminishing, the novel *Indian Horse* (2010) offers a helpful counternarrative. When Saul returns as an adult, the once enveloping structure has been defaced by smashed windows, bullet holes, graffiti, and shit (pp. 195–8), possibly by other former students who also returned.

Images of school grounds could also act as what Lorenzo Veracini (2010b) calls "anticipatory geographies," which foresee a place that does not yet exist (p. 179). The very act of describing it, though, is an attempt to will a place into being. One example exists in a bird's-eye view printed in *Our Forest Children*. The sketch (see figure 7.3) depicts Shingwauk Home's entire grounds in existence at the time, including parts newly developed such as the beachfront and a new field for the school band and baseball team (named the Buckskins). But the bird's-eye view also *imagines* place: a new central building with a dining hall, kitchens, and officers' quarters as well as schoolrooms; a new girls' school that would be closer to the boys'; and a new laundry facility. The text accompanying the bird's-eye view pleas for readers to donate money so that imagined parts of the sketch may be realized (3.10:118–19). Parts of this bird's-eye view were pure fantasy yet printing them coaxed readers into donating money so that plans could materialize. In this way, the imagined space became a realized place. A document among George Raley's collection deposited with BC Archives includes a 1904 pamphlet advertising the sale of lots in Kitamaat before what was imagined to be the coming of the Grand Trunk Railway terminus. The pamphlet boasts of the area's "great mineral wealth" and ideal harbour for transporting goods to Asia. In addition to text, the pamphlet features maps of the lots for sale as well as the train and its wharf (see figure 7.4). It is unsurprising that Raley had this pamphlet in his collection, as he owned adjacent land and could have profited if the railway had come to Kitamaat (Kelm, 2006, p. xxv). Yet Kitamaat did not ultimately become Grand Trunk's terminus, despite the anticipatory geography of Raley's pamphlet and self-assuredness of its existence in *Na-Na-Kwa*.

Newspapers did not only promote their own schools but also others in Canada, forming a loose spatial support network. Schools promoting one another in newspapers may appear at odds with evidence that many schools competed for limited funds and were rivalrous along denominational lines (J.R. Miller, 1996b, p. 132). For instance, *Our Forest Children* warned readers that the gains Jesuits had made in boarding schooling could prove disastrous and urged all Protestants to put aside their differences and unite against Roman Catholic schools (2.7:21). The newspaper occasionally acknowledged the work of Catholics in boarding schooling (1.8:1; 3.1:46) and advocated working "harmoniously together, sink[ing] all petty feelings of rivalry and jealousy" (3.11:140). At the same time, it appears Wilson's understanding of "opening arms" meant to other Protestant denominations. Wilson suggested having a common uniform among Protestant schools, "so that whether at school or at home, traveling by steamboat or traveling by rail, they would always be known and recognized" (2.8:27). Wilson also proposed "Our Indian Homes" monograms on all uniforms and a flag (2.11:38). He recommended himself as "chief" and constructed "general rules which are to govern all the Homes." He had hoped to institute a local superintendent for each school, with reports and financial statements sent back to him in Sault Ste Marie.

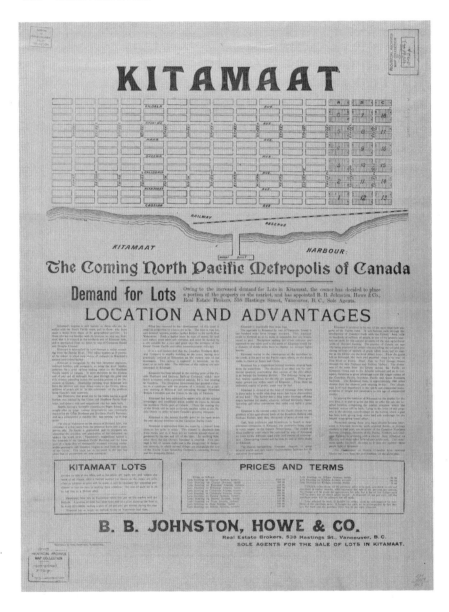

Figure 7.4. "The Coming North Pacific Metropolis of Canada," 1904. George Raley Fonds (PR-0465), BC Archives, Reg # 3113, old cat. # S615.6 (46) J72p, recatalogued as CM/A129: Johnson (B.B.), Howe & Co.

Despite such tensions, school newspapers often reveal collaboration among Canadian boarding schools. The principal of Rupert's Land School paid Wilson a visit when he first began so Wilson could go "thoroughly into the matter, showing him our book of rules, our various publications, printed forms, slips, &c, and explained all our plans and system of management" (*Our Forest Children* 2.8:27). Newspapers would also provide updates on other Canadian schools. *Our Forest Children* apprised readers on the progress at Elkhorn and in Medicine Hat, but it also described schools with which Wilson had no formal ties: Battleford, Mohawk, Mount Elgin, Rupert's Land, and Qu'Appelle Schools. Battleford School's newspaper mentioned schools in Calgary and the Pas. It also reported a fire at Washakada and the appointments of principals at St Paul's and Middle Church schools. Regina School's newspaper described the particulars of other schools, from the ventilation system of Mt Elgin's School to the garden at Brandon Industrial School. An 1898 issue of Battleford School's newspaper reveals a deeper connection: at the opening of a new school at the Pas in Manitoba, the school laid the foundation stone and sang in both English and Cree, with speeches from clergy, politicians, and teachers. The ceremony also included burying newspapers in a time capsule, including Battleford School's newspaper. The quotidian of Canadian schools mattered little in and of itself. But put together, such items projected for readers not individual schools but a larger *system* extending across the newly forming place of Canada, a depiction strengthened by school newspapers.

Some newspapers depicted the place of the reserve. Articles designed a future in which Indigenous peoples moved away from the reserve, conclusively conceived of by newspapers as a place that undid all the work of the schools. Newspapers depicted reserves as dirty and disease-ridden; for instance, *Progress* claimed that "the log cabin and reservation life have produced the tubercular diathesis" (3.78:4). Although the argument was that graduates who returned to the reserve could exert influence over those back home, as *Progress* put it the graduates "may be too small a quantity of leaven to leaven the whole lump on the reserve" (3.70:4). Newspapers instead promoted the idea of reserving farmland for students upon graduation near the school or securing them positions with farmers, "with less cost of the country" and offering an "incalculable benefit to the Indian race, and to the country at large, for the future" (3.70:4). Newspapers suggested that surveillance over students ("supervision") should extend to students during their work life after graduating from the school (18.9:3). *Na-Na-Kwa* depicted "the old Indian houses" as containing families "herded together in a miserable den, a filthy dwelling, a single room where all ages, and both sexes slept, ate and dwelt together" (2.2). The article implied that Indigenous homes lacked necessary separations between ages, genders, activities, and the clean from the dirty. It used these kinds of scenes as justification for the removal of children from their parents: "If we want the future of the people to be Christian, we must remove the children from such demoralizing surroundings." Many articles used the place of the reserve as foil for the school.

One article in *Progress* profiled reserves as places of containment. It stated, "A good old chief on one of the Reserves has his mind bent on visiting the school. He has never been in a train and scarcely out of the Reserve. The only difficulty in his way is how to get hold of a pass" (3.73:7). The newspaper leaves unsaid who the chief was or why he had his "mind bent" on coming to visit the students. It is unlikely, though, that this proposed visit was welcome considering that the pass system, an attempt to contain Indigenous people on-reserve, required permission to move. If the school wished to facilitate this visit, it likely could have intervened, as the previous chapter discussed. The pass system routinely restricted parents from visiting their children at school, and this context frames this newspaper's anticipation of unlikelihood as almost boastful of the reserve as a powerful place of containment. Within these newspapers, empty space and the filled space of schools and reserves operated together to justify the existence of Indian boarding schools.

The Place of England

School newspapers converted supposedly "vacant" space into Canadian place for readers, unsurprisingly referencing British place in the process. The nation-state of Canada of course began as several British colonies, many of the school principals were British-born, and some of the school newspapers had a British readership. Even after immigration from England decreased, immigrants from outside England often understood themselves as British (Buckner, 2008; G. Martin, 2011). But school newspapers also represented British place because *the schools* represented British place. Important to note here is Adele Perry's (2003) point that "colonies were not simply venues where Europeans applied their notions of civilized household space; they were one of the spaces where such ideas were produced and honed" (p. 590).

Newspapers frequently mentioned their schools' devotion to Queen Victoria, praising her at picnics, the close of summer holidays, and graduation. Most school celebrations described by school newspapers would include singing "God Save the Queen" or "Queen, Flag, and Country." School newspapers ran articles praising Queen Victoria's longevity and the growth of Christianity under her reign. Newspapers further commented on the Queen in the curriculum: a teacher from Battleford School composed a song praising her, and Regina School's newspaper reported that "A large book of 498 pages, entitled *Queen Victoria. Her Life and Rign [sic]* has been in great demand by both boys and girls for the past month" (*Guide* 3.80:8). In these instances, schools imported the ultimate symbol of England.

Newspapers also praised Victoria through image. Upon the visit of an inspector to Battleford School in 1899, one student created an oil painting of the Queen. Its newspaper remarked that the school "felt proud" and thought the painting should be given to the Queen (*Guide* 7.8:1). Communities also received images. The newspaper of Kitamaat Home relayed how Chief Shakes of Kitkatlah received "a life sized picture of [the Queen] in oils set in a very magnificent massive gilt frame" (*Na-Na-Kwa* 14.2). The cover of this issue featured a photograph of the Queen, though the community learned late of her death in their "isolated corner of her wide domain." Regina School also received a portrait and a note from the lieutenant governor of the Northwest Territories, who was sure "no artificial stimulus is necessary, to awaken sentiments of love and loyalty in the breasts of all true Canadians" on the occasion of her diamond jubilee (*Progress* 3.80:9). The portrait was an important part of the jubilee, yet the lieutenant governor denies its artifice and extends the identity of "true Canadians" to Indigenous boarding school students.

Victoria's image also entered Shingwauk Home. To celebrate the Queen's jubilee, members of the school collectively wrote a letter accompanied by a watercolour sketch Wilson made of the school with, symbolically, "some Indian wigwams in the back ground." The letter read:

We the pupils of the Shingwauk and Wawanosh Homes desire to congratulate our Queen on her Jubilee. We wish to relate your Majesty about our procession this morning; we took your picture, and above it the bible to indicate that always to put first God whatever we do in this world; our teacher had told us before you gave a present to a prince from Africa,

Figure 7.5. *The Secret of England's Greatness*. Queen Victoria presenting
a Bible in the Audience Chamber at Windsor. Thomas Jones Barker c. 1863.
Asset number 4969, National Portrait Gallery, London.

and you said "This is the secret of England's greatness." You so love the
bible and we love you. When we got [to] the town we all turned to the
people and [sang] the Jubilee hymn.

The letter concludes with student names and nationalities: Ojibway,
Ottawa, Sioux, Pottawatomie, Blackfoot, and Delaware. Below the letter, *Our Forest Children* printed the Queen's acknowledgment of the
student letter, less than one month later (1.6:2). The newspaper reveals
no less than three images associated with the school's jubilee event:
the picture of Victoria held under a Bible as the children marched; Wilson's watercolour, featuring the trinity of school, hospital, and church
and signifiers of being Indigenous ("some Indian wigwams") in the
background; and the 1863 oil painting *The Secret of England's Greatness*
by Thomas Jones Barker (see figure 7.5), with which the children were

familiar. The painting depicts Victoria presenting a Bible to a bowing East African ambassador and is based on the legend that when an African or Indian prince asked Victoria what the secret behind her powerful empire was, she passed a Bible and proclaimed the book "the secret of England's greatness." The phrase itself was commonplace in the latter half of the nineteenth century, particularly among Protestants, and the image was widely circulated (Barnes, 2013, pp. 2–3). Here, image mattered in both preparing for and celebrating the jubilee.

Not all jubilee events were imaged based. Battleford School's newspaper reported how its event began at the barracks with a speech from a major, with dinner and games back at the school (*Guide* 6.1:2). Regina School students listened to a reverend lecture on "her Majesty's Canadian Realm," and the newspaper made sure to mention that students listened attentively for one and a half hours and even asked for more (3.80:8–9). The newspaper transcribed part of the speech, which predicted that in another sixty years "the Indian of Canada would no longer represent the teepee" but would instead join "the customs of civilization, and imbued with the spirit of Christianity, equal in the sight of their sovereign and equal in intelligence and loyalty with their white brethren" (3.80:9). The school newspaper's reporting of the celebration offered a bleak forecast: sixty years of Victoria's reign was a halfway mark to a future of total assimilation, where Indigenous people and land was re-placed by England.

But the jubilee celebration at Battleford School may also have been a chance for families to reunite. The school's newspaper reported that "between 1100 and 1200 Indians were camped near the race course to take part in the 'Diamond Jubilee' proceedings." The school newspaper framed their visit as ephemeral upon their departure: "Nothing is now seen of their 'Canvas Town' but the old fire places" (*Guide* 5.12:1). But entries attributed to students tell a different story. Many of them remarked how students were able to see friends and family. One letter noted this student "was very glad to see all my friends yesterday." Another explained his "father came here on 17th of June and I was very glad because I have not seen him for two years." One letter noted the student "was very glad to see my father and mother when they came here to see us." And one student admitted he was "very glad to see one of my friends from Stony Lake"; this friend delivered word the student's "father is sick so that he couldn't come and see" him. Another letter mentioned the student "went over to the tents and I saw my parents." These entries focus not on celebrating the Queen and her longevity but on maintenance of family in spite of her longevity.

Some student entries in the newspaper more guardedly mentioned jubilee visits. One passage attributed to a student explained, "During this month several visitors have arrived for the purpose of seeing their children and I am sure they felt happy to see them in a healthy state." This excerpt is unlike others attributed to students in its distancing. Maybe this student's family did not come, or perhaps this student distanced himself from the events to fulfil the style of reportage expected of him. It is possible that this entry was not actually written by a student. This student entry aligns more with the newspaper's non-student reportage on the jubilee celebrations. According to the non-student voice, a "company of others from the surrounding country, were among the visitors who came to see their children, nieces, nephews, brothers and sisters, grandchilldren [sic] and other 'relatives' during the month." The newspaper's voice, as opposed to most of the statements attributed to students, speaks in the third person and puts "relatives" in scare quotes, as if doubting their relation.

Though student entries also mentioned the weather of the celebrations and the prizes won, most make far more mention of the opportunity to see family. The jubilee brought Indigenous families back together despite the school's goal of separation. In this way, the jubilee represented more than what the school intended. Vine Deloria Jr (2003) describes how this phenomenon was not unique. When Indigenous peoples' ceremonies in the US came under attack, they would choose an American or Christian holiday and fulfil "their own religious obligations while white bystanders glowed proudly to see a war dance or rain dance done on their behalf" (p. 240). Deloria called this strategy a form of seeking "subterfuge." Brenda Child (2014a) provides an example of how Red Lake people in Minnesota held their powwow on the Fourth of July to evade bans and suppressions on their traditional gatherings (p. 125). Oblate missionaries in the late nineteenth century would record how Secwepemc chiefs held political meetings and prepared for potential war against settlers during settler-sanctioned festivals and horse races (Ignace and Ignace, 2017, p. 464). Celebrations for Queen Victoria's birthday were also political opportunities for Stó:lō political strategizing (Carlson, 2010, pp. 211–31). Similarly, it appears from school newspapers that parents and children at Battleford School used Christian and colonial celebrations such as the jubilee for their own purposes. When children recounted their reunions in the school newspaper, they highlighted happiness that the larger editorial voice of the newspaper missed or ignored.

Shingwauk Home's golden jubilee celebration was the most elaborate, with a visit to Montreal for the Jubilee Sunday School Demonstration. Wilson announced in *Our Forest Children* that twenty boys and ten girls at his school had been invited to join twelve thousand other Sunday schoolers, including those from the "blind and deaf and dumb Institutions, also Chinese, Japanese" (1.7:2). The children were to gather in a parade beginning at McGill, followed by religious services at the Victoria Skating Rink. The Fisk Jubilee Singers also performed (*Canada Presbyterian* 16:41:657), an African-American a cappella group from Fisk University, a historically Black college in Tennessee. The singers toured the world, introducing slave hymns to primarily white audiences (Ward, 2001, pp. xii, xiv). When the group travelled to Canada they did not find refuge from the racism they faced in the southern US – in Toronto, four hotels denied the Fisk Jubilee Singers accommodation. The fifth accepted but overcharged them (p. 387). These diverse groups – Shingwauk students, the hearing impaired, African-American university students, and Chinese and Japanese groups – performed for white settlers who came to celebrate that the sun never set on the British Empire. But when the Fisk Jubilee Singers had previously sung for Indigenous peoples in Australia and New Zealand, it resulted in a "major emotional, crying exchange" of mutual understanding (pp. 390–1). How did Shingwauk students react to hearing such songs of survival? While reactions are speculative, Wilson outlined his own motivations for participating. For him, the trip "afforded us the opportunity of bringing our Indian Children face to face with a vast concourse of white people and white children. They will see what our pupils look like and be able to judge a little of their capabilities" (*Our Forest Children* 1.7:2–3). At least in his statements in the newspaper, Wilson's motivations for the trip were less about the jubilee or opportunities for cross-student contact than showcasing assimilation.

Our Forest Children relayed for readers how inclement weather forced the demonstration indoors. Still, each Sunday school carried a flag and a banner, and when the Shingwauk children crossed the platform "an immense cheer went up" (1.8:2). The program included readings of scripture and the Lord's Prayer by children. Shingwauk students also performed tableaux. The students each received "a jubilee cup – each cup being [a] *simile* of those given in Hyde Park, London, in the last. They will be highly prized by our young Indians."

Figure 7.6. "A Beautiful Photograph of the Shingwauk Pupils Who Went with Mr Wilson to Montreal and Ottawa," 1887. Edward F. Wilson Fonds, Shingwauk Indian Residential School Photograph Series, 2011-016-001 (021), Shingwauk Residential Schools Centre, Algoma University.

Two years after the trip, Wilson advertised two photographs in *Our Forest Children*: one titled "JUBILEE DAY PROCESSION – Wild Horses on Horseback" and the second a group portrait of the children who went to Montreal (see figure 7.6). Wilson sold this photograph in a 7.5" × 10.5" format for fifty cents, or for free if readers would send three dollars and the names and addresses of six new subscribers. The secretaries of the Colonial and Continental Church Society donated the engraved block of the original photography to Wilson, allowing Wilson to print the images for profit (3.4:22–3).

The photograph features twenty-nine students, some standing and some lying down or sitting. In the centre sits Wilson with his daughter on his left. Students hold several props, including a wheel, chain and hook, and a picture stand – metonyms for the school's industries.

Wilson names every student and his or her nationality and home territory (e.g., "Ojebway, from Walpole Island"). The article also informs readers where, two years after the jubilee trip, students are now. Some were still Shingwauk students and bookmakers or weavers or telegraph operators in training. Some students from the jubilee trip were now employed: two were teachers and one was a blacksmith. A few students had transferred schools. The newspaper listed other students as simply having left the school or that they were "back among [their] people," leaving it unclear whether Wilson lost track or whether he deemed their post-jubilee lives unworthy of reporting. Two students were listed as dead. One was very sick. Though Wilson used the photograph two years after the jubilee to highlight assimilation and gain subscribers, it captures devastating statistics: three out of twenty-nine young people were gravely sick or dead. The entire celebration – from the flags and the tableaux and the cups to the photograph two years later – worked to establish the place of England within the place of Canada. Though *Our Forest Children* presents the jubilee one way, we do not know how the variety of groups who assembled in Montreal, differently experiencing and surviving colonialism, considered the experience.

The place of England was also poured into the seeming void of space with other celebrations of the monarchy. Schools celebrated the Queen's birthday by flying flags, holding processions, and races. Battleford School opened its annual celebratory picnic in 1896 by electing two girls as May Queens. Children skipped, tug-of-warred, played cricket, and danced around the maypole (*Guide* 4.12:1). Newspapers also commemorated Victoria's death. Kitamaat Home observed it with a purple wreath of flowers made by the children. The community held a procession starting from the school, where everyone was given "a memento in the form of a linen badge with a picture of the Queen" (*Na-Na-Kwa* 15.2). At King Edward's coronation celebration, Kitamaat Home's newspaper remarked, "The native races of the British Empire are loyal, and take great interest in such an event," relating how the community celebrated with memento badges, a procession, picnic, firecrackers, and "God Save the King" (19.2). One student even wrote a composition (19.4). Kitamaat Home's newspaper insisted, "Indians as a nation are just as loyal to the great totemic symbol of the Empire the British Lion, as they are, individual tribes, to their particular crests" (24.5). Such purported enthusiasm can be read in multiple and often contradictory ways: on the one hand, that the supposed emptiness of the space of Canada was being filled by notions of empire (the preferred reading of the newspaper); on the other hand, that Indigenous people in Kitamaat saw themselves as participating in a nation-to-nation relationship with the Queen, bypassing Canada.

The Place of the United States

But more than England, Canadian school newspapers consulted with and compared themselves to the place of the US. Comparative attention must be paid to Canada and the US. For one, both countries share a border, which divided and divides Indigenous families and communities. In the late nineteenth century, some Indigenous peoples called the border the "medicine line," a term likely first used by Dakota people at the end of the 1870s when Sitting Bull and others escaped the US cavalry by crossing to Canada after the battle of Little Bighorn (Rees, 2009, p. 5). The Blackfoot, too, considered the seemingly magical boundary to hold political power, which they used to their advantage (LaDow, 2002). Although the Canada–US border attempted to delineate for Indigenous peoples in the nineteenth century where and if they could hunt, trade, join treaty, and vote, they also used the border to undermine the Hudson's Bay Company (Hogue 2015). Richard Wagamese (2010) speaks of how "there were no straight lines in Ojibwa culture" and "land could not be divided. It was whole, as defined by the Creator" (p. 53). The border between Canada and the US began and continues to separate traditionally connected communities, moving away from Wagamese's concept of wholeness.

When studies do consider Indigenous peoples and the Canada–US border (S. Evans, 2006; McCrady, 2006; McManus, 2005), as Andrew Woolford (2014, 2015) points out boarding schools are rarely compared. An exception includes the hemispheric comparisons of Brenda J. Child and Brian Klopotek (2014), which bring together Canadian and American Indian boarding schools along with those in Peru and Venezuela. But usually, studies on boarding school history discuss schools in Canada *or* in the US. One barrier in comparing the US and Canadian systems is their significant differences. The US system formally wound down earlier, so fewer generations of families attended. As well, Canadian schools never experienced a reform period like the US, where challenges to the assimilationist agenda (at least on paper) began in the 1930s. Children also entered school at a younger age in Canada, and US parents theoretically had more input as to what school their children would attend. Furthermore, American boarding schools had more of a military rather than religious foundation. In addition, there was less administrative turnover and therefore fewer new ideas and people in Canada's Department of Indian Affairs than in the US (Woolford, 2015, p. 77). These differences, of course, did not necessarily mean major differences in terms of student experience. Kiera L. Ladner (2014) acknowledges the variations in the two systems but insists that in both countries Indigenous peoples "were extirpated from their lands, and their territories were occupied" (p. 228); the differences do not change this fundamental similarity.

Comparisons between boarding schools for Indigenous children in the US and Canada matter as well because these newspapers reveal sustained consultation. Indian boarding school newspapers suggest the two systems did not operate on parallel tracks but were in conversation, keenly interested in each other. Formal comparisons between Canada and the US on Indian boarding schools began in 1879, when John A. MacDonald commissioned Nicholas Flood Davin to conduct research in the US on its form of "aggressive civilization." Based on his American travels, Davin outlined how schools might be funded through church-government partnerships. Some of Davin's recommendations were followed, such as preference for industrial over day schools and compulsory attendance. Other recommendations were not followed, such as regular inspections and teachers hired directly by government and paid well. John S. Milloy (1999) cautions that we cannot think of the Davin report as *the* text authoring boarding schools (p. 52). Still, when Davin lectured at Regina School in 1897 its newspaper noted that the beginning of boarding schools for Indigenous children in Canada was because of him (*Progress* 4.8:8). So, if we can conceive of colonial comparisons on schools beginning with Davin, what do school newspapers reveal about later cross-border consultations?

Canadian school newspapers often printed American understandings of issues, such as allotments or the legacy of Sitting Bull. The newspaper of Washakada School in Manitoba even had a column titled "From over the Line: Interesting Items from the United States." Commonly, Canadian newspapers zeroed in on American Indian educational news by summarizing conferences, policies, and reports. Often, these inclusions began with a preface about how American contexts had relevance for Canada. Battleford School's newspaper, for instance, relayed perspectives from the El Reno Indian Teachers' Convention, which pushed for compulsory education and separation of parent and child (*Guide* 4.9.2). Newspapers also reported on the mundane aspects of American boarding schools – a fire or the trend of elaborate graduation ceremonies, for instance. They occasionally profiled opportunities for Indigenous students in Canada to study in the US, like one pupil of Regina School who went on to attend Hampton Institute in Virginia (*Progress* 17.8:3). But the practice was disputed when Regina School noted, "It would be better if any of our pupils who desire to take a more advanced course than can be given in the present system of Indian schools, would go to the High Schools, Universities, and Colleges that are available in our own land" (18.9:1).

A common refrain of Canadian school newspapers was that the US was "doing" colonialism better. Veracini (2010a) describes such critical comparisons as settler colonial "peer reviewing" (p. 24). One of Wilson's biggest critiques of Canada was its lack of money for boarding schools. The first page of the first issue of *Our Forest Children* predicted that Canadians had "in all probability the same troubles in store for us that they have been suffering for so long in the United States" (1.1:1). In a letter to the founder of Carlisle School in Pennsylvania, Richard Pratt, Wilson explained he wanted "our government to take up the Indian cause the same way that your government is doing in the States." Wilson praised American philanthropy, implying Canada should follow suit. Although Wilson conceded "all that has been said of [the US'] cruel and unjust treatment of the Indians, they have some 32 large Institutions for Indian children," which receive ample money from government and public donations (1.6:1). Wilson espoused the still common myth that colonialism in Canada was or is less violent than in the US, but with a twist: America may have had a violent past, but its government and public now pay for schools. Wilson's argument that the government should pay ran counter to the larger belief of the day that Canada should not fund non-Indigenous schools so parents could better control education. Wilson's argument also reveals how inadequate he viewed Indigenous parents of making decisions about their children's education.

Such comparisons were not always financial. Though *Our Forest Children* remarked Canadians and Americans were "*all one* in our work for God," it believed the US had more "good people championing the Indian cause" (3.1:1). Wilson praised the US for its split day between labour and academics as well as its outing system, where students would spend their summers employed by a white family. The newspaper also lauded the small ratio of Catholic-run schools in the US and praised groups such as the Women's National Indian Association, the

Syracuse Indian Association, and the Pittsburg Indian Association, asking "why have we nothing of the kind in Canada" (3.1:47; 3.13:176). Wilson further asked why the US but not Canada employed special police to retrieve school runaways (2.11:38). Battleford School's newspaper also praised the US for providing education to children who had a white father and an Indigenous mother (*Guide* 4.11:2). Regina School's newspaper, too, saw Americans as more invested in "their Indian population" than were Canadians (*Progress* 3.77:10).

Occasionally, newspapers featured Indigenous perspectives on the border. When Wilson shared with Chief Buhkwujjenene his findings on American spending, the chief was "gratified to hear that the Americans had so completely turned round in favour of the Indians" but doubted the Canadian government "cares enough" (*Our Forest Children* 1.2.3). In stark contrast, one Regina School article quoted writer E. Pauline Johnson: "The Indians are so handicapped in the United States, by ill government and erroneous methods introduced by the white people, that I fear it will be many years before they accomplish what the Canadian Indians have done. You see, we Canadians are respected by our government, and so considerately used that we advance much more rapidly than when we had the set-backs that the unfortunate American Indians suffer" (*Progress* 3.83:2). Unlike the chief, in this passage Johnson viewed the US as restraining Indigenous peoples, setting them behind those in a country whose government respected them. Johnson made a similar point in an interview three years earlier, though with context the school newspaper did not include. In the interview, Johnson stated that Canada respected Indigenous people but also discussed land theft, white misconceptions of Indigenous people and art, Iroquois political strategy, and how the whole continent belongs to Indigenous people "by right of lineage" ("Fate of the Red Man" 1894). In comparison to the frequent and near-unanimous support Canadian school publications had for US policy, the scant inclusion of Indigenous perspectives remained more varied.

US publications only occasionally mentioned Canada. The newspaper of Rupert's Land School reprinted an article from the newspaper of a school in Nebraska, which detailed the tour of Charles Eastman to Canada (*Aurora* 2.24:2). An 1885 article from Carlisle School devoted several pages to Canada and Louis Riel (*Morning Star* 5.10:2–4). The newspaper advised the US to look to Canada for "how it should be done." But according to the newspaper, Canada was never morally superior; instead, its climate merely allowed "relations between the original and incoming inhabitants [to] have more time to adjust." Other articles attributed Canada's "greater quiet" to the low turnover of Indian Affairs employees (5.10:4), less impact of the whiskey trade, and Canada's perceived fairness. The newspaper of Rupert's Land School reprinted an article from *Harper's*, which stated that "the Dominion Government appears to have come a good deal nearer than we [the US] to the solution of the Indian problem" through "the arts of peace" rather than war (*Aurora* 1.12:2). But the praise was not consistent: another issue of Carlisle School's newspaper declared the Canadian government negligent when it came to Indigenous people in the Mackenzie basin (*Morning Star* 9.10:7). Most praise in school newspapers flowed north to south.

Canadian schools kept informed of the goings-on of US institutions in one way by reading newspapers. Most Canadian reportage on the US was not original but clipped directly from US publications, though was not always credited. Both *Our Forest Children* and *Progress* had whole sections devoted to US school clippings. Other Canadian newspapers simply blended these with their own content.[6] Canadian newspapers especially extracted from Carlisle School's many publications, to which even Canada's Department of Indian Affairs subscribed (DIA, 1899, p. 695). Canadian schools accessed US newspapers through paper exchanges – one school would trade its newspaper with another. Some of these exchanges remained within Canada; Battleford School swapped with Regina School, for instance. However, Canadian schools were more likely to excerpt from and exchange with a US publication. Regina School boasted of having fifty exchanges (1895, p. 176), which included newspapers from a whopping eighteen states (*Progress* 3.84:6–7). In 1888 alone, Shingwauk Home's exchange list included Santee School and Genoa School (Nebraska), Hampton Institute (Virginia), Sisseton School (South Dakota), Muskogee Mission (Oklahoma), two newspapers from Carlisle, and more (*Our Forest Children* 2.8:28). Though a Canadian newspaper's clipping of a US article typically meant endorsement, there were exceptions. One student entry from Battleford School disagreed with a Nebraska newspaper's claim that Indigenous children were incapable of comprehending math. It stated, "Most white teachers go the wrong way about their work in teaching mathematics. The Indian's head is every bit as good as the white man's" (*Guide* 7.9:1). But more often, Canadian schools reprinted US articles with which they agreed.

Canadian schools were likely interested in US school newspapers for several reasons. First, they provided free reading material in under-funded institutions promoting English literacy. Wilson thought US exchanges meant he could relay the superior work being done south of Canada (*Our Forest Children* 1.5:3–4). He advised readers to "subscribe for some of these little papers published in the States so that they may see how wide awake people are across the border in dealing with the vexed Indian question," offering the titles and prices of his recommendations (1.7:4). Exchanges were also a form of mutual praise. A Canadian newspaper might applaud a US newspaper for printing or content. Battleford School's newspaper, for instance, called *Indian News* from Nebraska "one of our highly valued exchanges" (*Guide* 7.9:1) and the *Indian Helper* from Carlisle "one of our exchanges [that] is always read with great interest" (7.2:1). Regina School's newspaper called Carlisle's *Red Man* "always brimful of encouragement for the Indian" (*Progress* 3.80:3). Mentioning these exchanges accomplished several things: It boasted to Canadian readers the breadth and worldliness of a school's reading material. As well, it was a plug – Canadian readers might have subscribed after reading these pseudo-advertisements. These "shout-outs" also demonstrated the I-scratch-your-back mentality of the exchange since schools reading the praise may have wished, too, to subscribe. Sometimes praising a US exchange was an underhanded form of self-promotion, as was the case in *Our Forest Children*: "We know of no other periodical in Canada that is undertaking this work. In the United States there are numbers of papers published in their interests, societies in operation for maintaining their rights; but in Canada we look in vain for anything of this kind. Not one paper is there, so far as we are aware, except our humble little FOREST CHILDREN, published in behalf of the Indians" (3.1:45). Here, Wilson's praise for a US newspaper is also self-aggrandizing. Commending American Indian boarding school newspapers also reinforced the image of schools on both sides of the border as a network. Listing how many US publications a Canadian school was reading offered the impression that schools were not operating in isolation.

Canadian newspapers were being read south of the border, too. As *Our Forest Children* explained, American Indian school newspapers "have nearly all of them from time made mention of our work here at the Sault St. Marie, and the pupils of these Institutions in the States correspond with our pupils" (1.7:3). The newspaper of Haskell Institute in Kansas also mentioned how Regina School's newspaper "contains many items of interest about Indians both of the United States and Canada" (*Indian Leader* 1.3.2). It even reprinted a graduation address from Regina School's newspaper (1.6:3). Canadian schools typically reprinted any praise offered by a US school. Battleford School's paper reprinted when a Nebraska School called it "one of the brightest of Indian school papers" (*Guide* 7.5:4). Shingwauk Home, too, reprinted a Carlisle shoutout: "Boys and girls! Wouldn't you like to have a little paper called OUR FOREST CHILDREN, printed at an Indian School, away up in Canada, by Rev. EF Wilson, Principal of the Shingwauk Home? It is only ten cents a year, and Dr. Given is getting up a club. Give him your name and ten cents and let us keep up a brotherly feeling between the two schools" (*Our Forest Children* 1.10:12). Because this praise was in *Indian Helper* (Carlisle's student publication), naming Wilson was likely less important than for Wilson to read that Pratt had levied praise publicly. Similarly, Battleford School's newspaper reprinted a letter from Carlisle. After reading in an earlier issue of Battleford School's eighteen honour students, one printer at Carlisle wanted to send eighteen copies of the *Indian Helper* personally addressed to them. Battleford School thanked Carlisle for its "fraternal action." Such "brotherly feeling" or "fraternal action" is complicated seeing that Indigenous relations pre-exist the colonial border; additionally, these schools actively sought to disrupt relations, separating children from parents, siblings from one another, and students who spoke the same language. These feelings are also figured as male, furthering the imposition of white settler understandings of gender. And yet, through exchanges, both school systems claimed to cultivate colonial relations.

Some articles hinted at relationships that predated the border. One issue of Battleford School's newspaper reprinted an article presumably from Chemawa Indian School in Oregon. The reprint explained that the US Chemawa students had read that there was also a Chemawawin in Canada: "Chemawa sends greetings to Chemawawin its Northern neighbor and hopes that it will succeed in all its noble undertakings" (*Guide* 7.9:1). Rather than interrogate the unnaturalness of the colonial border, these greetings guise themselves as gratitude to the newspapers that such relations were uncovered. Articles also asked whether Indigenous people on either side of the border were related. *Our Forest Children* profiled a lecture given by ethnologist Arthur Chamberlain, who argued, "The question of the relation of the Canadian aborigines to those of the United States was pointed out as being of very great importance" (3.12:155). Some of Wilson's ethnographic work attempted to uncover these connections, for instance the similarity between Apache people in the Southwestern US and Sarcee people in the Canadian Northwest (4.3:209). In another issue Wilson appeared surprised Ojibway nations were "in" the states of Michigan and Minnesota yet also Lake Winnipeg (1.12:1).

Out of all American Indian institutions, Canadian newspapers most closely kept tabs on Carlisle School in Pennsylvania. The fascination may have stemmed from Carlisle's reputation as the first federally funded, off-reservation school in the US. But Canadian schools may have also heard more about it: Carlisle had eight newspapers filled with Carlisle-related news,[7] and many Canadian schools subscribed. Canadian newspapers followed Carlisle's policies, attendance statistics, English-only rules, and funding. Canadian schools even reported the quotidian, from Carlisle's choir and football team to the death of the school's doctor. *Our Forest Children* even mentioned when a dove took residence in Carlisle's hospital (3.12:159). Battleford School argued that the Carlisle way "can be, and is being, accomplished in our Schools" (*Guide* 6.7:3).

Such fascination is no more evident than in *Our Forest Children*, where Wilson would list the ways Carlisle and its founder Richard Pratt influenced him. The Onward and Upward Club seems to have begun with Pratt. As well, Wilson may have been inspired by Pratt in his travelling tableaux, which with Pratt also included troubling debates such as whether "the Indian [should] be exterminated" (*Our Forest Children* 1.2:1–2; 4.2:177). Wilson credited Carlisle with inspiring his choice for an enlarged and illustrated newspaper (DIA, 1890, p. 22). He also likely copied his rhetorical technique of beforing and aftering in text and image from Pratt, who employed it extensively. Wilson wrote in his journal that he even had a photograph of Carlisle students hanging in his study (p. 81).

Wilson also shared news about Pratt. *Our Forest Children* ran Pratt's biography, from birth to military career and Carlisle. It also printed an article on Pratt's answer to the "Indian question" (1.10:4). Wilson and Pratt occasionally corresponded by mail, and Wilson would sometimes reprint the letters. One such letter from Pratt praised Wilson's "heroic work." Though Pratt denied Wilson's request for help in securing accommodations for his trip to England, Wilson still felt Pratt's response was worth reprinting in *Our Forest Children*: "I wish I could help you big and strong, like you need and deserve, but I can do little more than pray for your success in every way" (1.10:16). Pratt went on to request the latest issues of *Our Forest Children*. In another letter published from Pratt, he advised Wilson as one boarding school head to another to not "do less than you started to do. Go farther and do more. Start the secular press at work in your favor, and the church and clergy will fall into line very soon. You and I see that the field is ripe, and if we can't make others see it and help, then the Lord has made a mistake in selecting us" (2.4:16). These published letters reveal at least two things: First, Wilson and Pratt's relationship was in many ways professional. As the head of an institution widely regarded as the best of the best at this time, Pratt provided strategic advice. Pratt also highlighted the role of the press in their shared vision of Indigenous education. Second, these letters reveal Wilson's pride in them. The content offered little to readers of *Our Forest Children*; instead, publishing them reinforced to readers a big name like Pratt had faith in Wilson.

Sometimes, Wilson's fascination with Pratt stepped beyond professional lines. In one article, Wilson reported on his visit to Pratt's private residence:

[Pratt's living room] was interesting on account of the Indian pictures, curiosities and ornaments which adorned it on every side. Parts of the carpet were covered with handsome Navajo blankets, of bright colors, and clear, sharp patterns. On the mantel-piece and over the bookcases were specimens of Pueblo pottery, large white clay jars of globular shape, standing fifteen or eighteen inches high, and covered with curious Indian devices in red and black paint. On one wall was a large collection of curious Indian weapons and articles of bead-work, forming quite a trophy, and from the corner of a bookcase hung suspended a splendid Sioux head-dress, consisting of a crown of eagle feathers, and eagle feathers pendant from a long strap, which extended from the back of the head to heels. The captain [Pratt] put this head-dress on to show us how it looked. (3.4:26)

In this less official scene, Wilson deviates from his professional interests in the curriculum and pedagogy of Carlisle School. We see here Pratt's own ethnographic leanings, best symbolized by his donning of a headdress. Wilson's second visit, this time accompanied by his wife Frances Wilson, further focuses on Pratt-the-man: "We heard the captain's voice within, and in another minute he appeared at the doorway and extended us a warm welcome. Captain Pratt is a tall, powerful-looking man ... stooping a little, as though he were accustomed to pass through doorways a little too low for him, wearing a black sack coat on his back, and a kindly smile on his face; he won our affection at once, and we soon became fast friends" (3.4:26). Wilson depicts the physical space of Carlisle as unable to contain Pratt's body, which he further describes as "great, tall, towering." Though Wilson and his wife expected for Pratt to have "a big voice," Pratt "spoke rather low, but very clearly, and everybody listened" (3.4:27). Here, Wilson is less concerned with content than delivery. Some of Wilson and Pratt's interactions remained professional, and Carlisle clearly influenced Wilson's policies and pedagogy. But Canadian newspapers in places also glorified Pratt-the-man.

Settler colonial comparisons occurred not only through newspapers but also face-to-face. The future principal of Rupert's Land School in Manitoba first prepared for his role with visits to Carlisle School and Hampton Institute in Virginia (*Our Forest Children* 2.8:27). The commissioner of Indian Affairs for the Northwest Territories, Hayter Reed, also visited Carlisle in 1889 (3.3:14). Carlisle's newspaper praised Canada's consultative approach and printed, "Every moment of [Reed's] five hours' stay was spent in industriously looking through our school, asking questions and discussing the Indian problem" (*Morning Star* 9.5:1). Reed (1889) wrote up his findings on Carlisle (as well as the Mohawk and Mount Elgin Institutes in Ontario) in a report. Reed particularly focused on language, and he noted how at Carlisle it was easier to "put down entirely the use of the native tongue" because students spoke forty different so-called "dialects" and therefore orders, teaching, and books were all in English (p. 5). Though Reed admitted he believed in "the sole use of the English language" before his visit to Carlisle (p. 9), his experiences in the US bolstered his appeal to government to adopt the policy more widely: "I am aware that the Department has not yet adopted these views; and while I have of course only to bow to its ruling in this, as well as in all other matters, I none the less feel it to be my duty to express my conviction to be, that it will, in the long run, be found best to rigorously exclude the use of Indian dialects" (p. 10). School newspapers were avenues to publish and facilitate settler colonial comparisons.

But by far the most prolonged consultation was Wilson's seven-thousand-mile trip through the US. In total, Wilson visited thirteen schools during his trip. On 20 October 1888 Wilson stood on a platform of Shingwauk's schoolroom and prepared teachers, friends, students, and the bishop of Algoma for his trip with a map (see figure 7.7): "It is an Indian map, and its object is to shew the location of all the Indian

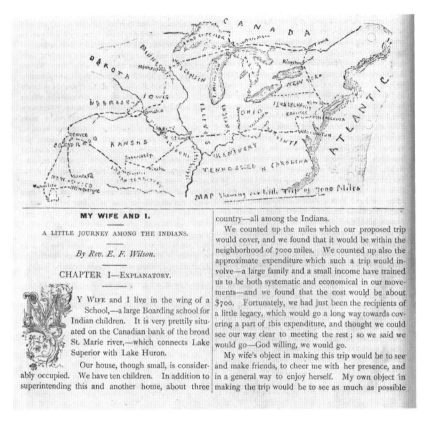

Figure 7.7. Map of Wilson's trip. *Our Forest Children* 3.3:8: June 1889.

tribes still existent in Canada and in the United States. The figures denote the number of Indians in each State of the United States and in each Province of Canada. The crosses indicate institutions for training Indian children: one hundred and nine in the States, but as yet only ten in Canada. After giving these particulars, I point to a dotted line on the map which marks our intended tour" (2.10:1). As Yi-Fu Tuan (2011) states, "Drawing maps is indubitable evidence of the power to conceptualize spatial relations" (p. 76). This map communicated three things: Wilson's locating of Indigenous nations, the lack of schools in Canada compared to the US, and his planned trip. As Wilson stood on the platform, his map played into the "vanishing Indian" paradigm by pointing out the "still existent" nations and charting the growth of schools. This map helped to prepare his school and his readers for the trip.

But oddly, he begins discussion in *Our Forest Children* of his US trip with the image of England instead, from where he and his wife Frances Wilson first came:

> We have not always lived among Indians. Our home is England. We were married in a dear old ivy-clad church, with a great old Norman tower, in Gloucestershire, and thence, while the bells were clanging, we walked together as bride and bridegroom, amid a throng of smiling villagers to the dear old Rectory, mantled with clematis and Jessamine and honeysuckle; and within the Rectory walls we had our wedding breakfast, and cut our wedding cake; and then we bade adieu and went to Chepstow, and Clifton, and Cheltenham for our honeymoon. (3.3:9)

Sherene Razack's (2002) work clarifies why Wilson begins an article about life in the "wilds" of North America by describing England, which he rarely mentioned in the rest of Shingwauk Home's newspaper. Razack explains how white settlers come to know themselves through journeys "into the wild" in three steps: they first establish the place from which they come as civilized, they transgress from this place to degenerate space, and then assert themselves as in control of the journey "through individual practices of domination" (pp. 13–14). Wilson relished his life "in the wild" and was consumed with his side career as an amateur ethnographer. But Razack's point is critical: before Wilson can engage in these fantasies, he must first establish, for himself and readers of his newspaper, that the initial space he inhabited was "civilized," from the ivy-clad church and its Norman tower to his wedding breakfast. Only after establishing these details can he transition from "respectable to degenerate" space, ultimately exerting control over it.

Wilson emphasized exchange between US and Canadian schools on his trip. Wilson began his trip in Washington, where he met with a commissioner of the Indian Bureau. The commissioner asked Wilson "several questions about the Canadian Indians, [and] the prospects for their education and civilization, etc." The commissioner also asked Wilson, once he completed his trip, to write him "some account of [Wilson's] impressions as a stranger" (*Our Forest Children* 3.5:43). This interaction reveals the two-way, cross-border exchange Wilson desired. The meeting in Washington was also strategic, as Wilson asked the commissioner for a formal letter to smooth his movement through the US.

Wilson brought with him more unofficial documents to help facilitate his travels: letters written by Shingwauk students, which he read aloud at American Indian schools. One letter Wilson read was addressed "*To our Unknown Brothers and Sisters:* Dear Relations," and explains the place of Shingwauk Home as "beautifully situated on the banks of the River St. Mary" (3.4:25). In turn, Wilson received responses from US students that he later published in *Our Forest Children*. In these formalized exchanges students wrote nothing private, perhaps because they knew what they wrote would be both read aloud by Wilson and later published in his newspaper. In a letter to Pratt, Wilson explained how once home he had students "from both homes collected in the school room and I told them all about you and showed them the photographs and pictures and read to them the letters which you sent; and now there are two or three boys busy in the school room writing to you. All our pupils were very much astonished at the photograph of the Carlisle group, it looks such an immense number and the faces are all so plain. My boys and girls were much pleased too to see the specimens of your school work and drawing." Here, the cross-border exchange continued long after the trip concluded. Wilson sustained his correspondence with Pratt, who continued to send letters, photographs, and schoolwork from his students. Wilson then published some of these in his newspaper for an even larger audience. Students on both sides of the border may have valued the exchanges with one another. But Wilson also positioned himself as the one "reuniting" relations rather than disrupting them. Also, reading Shingwauk letters to American Indian children, like the commissioner's letter, smoothed Wilson's movement in the US.

Wilson continued with his emphasis on exchange beyond student letters. After his first trip to Carlisle, Wilson visited Indigenous people in Sarnia, where he had "two meetings with them and told them all about my visit" to Carlisle. Wilson showed several objects he collected on the way – Cheyenne moccasins from Carlisle, a doll and pottery from Hampton Institute, and many photographs. Wilson wrote to Pratt, "The Indians were very much interested in seeing all the things." Wilson also shared what he learned in the US with Indian Affairs officials back in Canada. Rarely, Americans visited Canada to trade notes. Pratt's assistant, A.J. Standing, paid a visit to Shingwauk while on a trip to recruit students in Michigan (3.7:77). Regina School also reported a visit from the superintendent of Phoenix School in Arizona, who "took some photographs of our boys and girls, and left us a handsome book of pictures of his own school" (*Progress* 17.8:3). But largely, face-to-face exchange was initiated north of the border.

For Wilson, the US was an exercise in comparison and an extended practice in classifying races. Wilson wrote the following of his trip in *Our Forest Children*: "The Mexican men are dark-skinned, have black hair and eyes and generally short stubby beards; the women wear shawls, generally dark ones, over their heads and drawn up round the lower part of the face; the children look much like those of the French half-breeds in Canada. The people are generally quiet, well-disposed, industrious and happy, but seem to be slow-moving and old-fashioned" (3.12:158). Wilson's racist categories encompass physical features as well as where on a continuum of progress someone lies. Wilson found himself on the other end when he was described, by an interpreter, as "an Americano from a long way off up north and had been twenty years among the Indians" (4.3:201). In this reversal, where someone else classified Wilson based on looks and speech, he is converted into an American but also an almost-Indigenous person. The categories of English or Canadian – how Wilson self-identified – are not available. But this rare reversal of the power to classify had no consequence for Wilson, unlike the categories he typically administered.

In Shingwauk Home's newspaper Wilson also classified the Black men he met. He would mention when his waiter was "superior" or, on the other end of the spectrum, ignorant. When Wilson went to a cotton field in Oklahoma and encountered a Black man shovelling cottonseed, Wilson claimed the man was unaware of the purpose of his job (3.8:89). Wilson further described Black men as a looming hazard for his wife, invoking long-standing tropes of sexuality and supposed white innocence. Wilson mentioned when a Black man assisted in hoisting his white wife on the train (3.4:24). When a train-scheduling error separates Wilson and his wife, a porter delivers his wife the message (3.6:61), as if to heighten the potential danger of the mix-up. After a railway accident, another porter answered Wilson "ambiguously," declining to tell Wilson the full story (3.11:139). One reason Wilson may have chosen to highlight Black men in his articles was to further offer a "different" territory for white readers. Though Rinaldo Walcott (2004) importantly reminds those who forcefully choose to ignore that Black Canada has "an almost five-hundred-year past" (p. 280), perhaps the inclusion of Black men in Wilson's newspaper highlighted a not-Canada for readers, participating in a broader erasure of ongoing Black presence and resistance to white supremacy in Canada as well as diminishing any sense of Black geographies (McKittrick and Woods, 2007). And as Sarah-Jane Mathieu's (2010) research reveals, Black porters in both the Canada and the US have a long history of resistance.[8]

Representations within school newspapers of Black people in Canada seldom appeared outside of Wilson's scenes in the US. Disturbing exceptions exist, including an anti-Black joke in Regina's School newspaper (*Progress* 3.83:7), Battleford School's production of *Uncle Tom's Cabin* (*Guide* 5.7:1), and the same school's performance of a "Negro Show" (1.2:1). In his scenes of US travel, Wilson subordinates Blackness to inflate whiteness, which Toni Morrison (1992) observes more generally in the US. For her, these images are how white Americans come to know themselves as "not enslaved, but free; not repulsive, but desirable; not helpless, but licensed and powerful; not history-less, but historical; not damned, but innocent; not a blind accident of evolution, but a progressive fulfillment of destiny" (p. 52). Though Aileen Moreton-Robinson (2015, p. xix) and Iyko Day (2015, p. 113) importantly note that settler colonialism is not only built on Indigenous land theft but also enslaved Black labour, Lisa Lowe (2015) also makes the point that despite similarities white settlers justify these processes differently, "however much these processes share a colonial past and an ongoing colonial present" (pp. 10–11). Wilson's ethnographies of Indigenous people in the US therefore required different tools than his depictions of Black people, though he exhibits both in the same column.

The biggest source of anxiety with respect to racist categories for Wilson was in Indian Territory, where his usually dependable classifications fail. Wilson had heard the Cherokee territory Vinita was a "civilized Indian town," with its own insurance offices, parliament, and judges. Relevant to Wilson, he even heard they ran a newspaper:

> [The *Vinita Chieftain* is] owned, as we had been led to suppose, by an Indian proprietor, and edited by an Indian editor; and in this newspaper we had seen advertisements of lawyers and doctors and dentists and butchers and milliners and hotel-keepers – all Cherokees … [It] seemed to us to smack so very much of the American, – indeed it was a marvel to us – knowing as we did so well the Indian character – that Indians of whatever tribe could have been led so far to forget their ancient traditions as to adopt not only the dress and the language, but also the swagger and the greed of the white race. (*Our Forest Children* 3.7:73)

Wilson described himself reading the *Chieftain* as his train arrived in Vinita, aghast at Indigenous people capable of white "swagger." Wilson even published advertisements from the Vinita newspaper in *Our Forest Children*, as if to share the disbelief.

But Wilson was confounded because Vinita was, according to Wilson, white. He observed most of the teachers and students at the school "seemed to be entirely white, and shewed their white character by their behavior; some few were partly Cherokee; of full blood Cherokees there were none" (*Our Forest Children* 3.7:74). The shops, Wilson realizes, were all kept by white men, and the governor "was not very much Cherokee" (3.8:90). Even the newspaper "was owned by a man who had one-fourth part Cherokee blood in him, but it was edited by a white man" (3.7:74). Wilson learns why from a Cherokee professor he meets. The professor explains that "all the land on which [the] town is built is Indian property; it belongs to the Cherokee Nation." The professor also elaborates for Wilson that "these blue-eyed, golden-haired children, which you see about are, in fact, Cherokees, members of the great Cherokee Nation; entitled to hold Cherokee property, and to have a vote in the Cherokee elections." The professor states that these rights are less about blood than about family relations (3.7:74).

However, Wilson is not satisfied. As he explains, "It would have been more satisfactory to have found a veritable Indian community, unmixed with whiteblood, casting off, voluntarily and determinately, the old Indian way of living, and adopting the customs and the mode of living of white men" (3.8:88). The professor points to a field: "'There are the Indians,' he said contemptuously pointing to a wagon load of those individuals, just come in from the country. Yes, there they were, – blankets over their shoulders, long black straggling or plaited hair, moccasins on their feet. – Yes, those were Indians, they were full-bloods unmistakably" (3.8:88). Later, Wilson sees another group of Cherokee people: "I took a good look at the motley throng assembled under the trees. I was glad to see so many dark faces, and so much of the pure Indian element among them. True, there were a good many American-looking beards and American-looking eyes and noses, but the great bulk of the assembled throng was Indian, or at least half-breed; a goodly proportion might even have passed for full-bloods" (3.8:90). His reaction is at first confusing considering that Vinita ostensibly appears to represent Wilson's proposed future for Indigenous peoples. What leaves him so unsatisfied?

Daniel Heath Justice (2006) helps to historicize Wilson's reaction. For Justice, Cherokee identity "is often seen as conveniently porous and easily appropriated, diluted from an ideal Indigenous purity" (p. 6). He views these tropes as a "variant of the 'vanishing Indian'; the Indians aren't necessarily gone, but they exist only as dislocated and washed-out halfbreeds" (p. 212). Wilson arrived at Vinita with his suitcase and these narratives. Justice distinguishes between assimilation – "the wholesale rejection of Indigenous values and their replacement with Eurowestern values, either through choice, coercion, or violence" – and acculturation, "the adaptation of certain Eurowestern ways into a larger Cherokee context, thus changing some cultural expressions while maintaining the centrality of Cherokee identity and values" (p. xvi). Wilson's disappointment is twofold: While he encounters acculturation, and hears its definition from the professor, Wilson desires assimilation. Acculturation – what Wilson encounters in Vinita – is not on white terms, unlike the assimilation he strives for at Shingwauk. As Renisa Mawani (2002) states, "Many feared that mixed-race people, if assimilated into the white population, would claim land as easily as white settlers could"; but if seen as Indigenous, they would be a burden on the government (p. 50). Such fears manifest in Wilson's disappointment in Vinita, when his typically dependable categories are out of his control.

Conclusion

An issue of Regina School's newspaper reported on the Zayante Indian Conference, held annually in California by the Northern California Indian Association (a white-led charity devoted to assimilation). It invited Indigenous speakers to indicate what they thought their needs were, and (unsurprisingly) the first named need was land. The newspaper did not reprint details of this conference to contemplate the speakers' demand for land, for to do so would undermine the settler colonial goals of both the Regina School that reprinted the newspaper as well as the Northern California association. Instead, the article dismissed this clear demand, focusing on what *the association* deemed were the immediate needs of Indigenous peoples: protection from liquor traffic, industrial education, and on-reserve physicians – in other words, needs that supported settler colonial goals. The article admitted the Zayante conference had relevance for Canada, though in Canada "our's have plenty of land; more than they need" (17.9:3, 6). If the violent displacement of Indigenous peoples from their land was arguably at its height at the end of the nineteenth century, why do both the Zayante conference and Regina School's newspaper deny it? Because to accept the demand – land – undermines the number one settler colonial desire. For the Zayante conference or Regina School to take this demand seriously (rather than state that Indigenous peoples "have plenty of land") would require interrogating the very existence of settlers on Turtle Island.

This chapter does not focus on Indigenous demands for land or the primacy of land in Indigenous epistemologies because school newspapers actively erased these realities, substituting their own conceptions of space and place. Newspapers promoted the idea of seemingly nebulous space converted into the place of Canada. *Na-Na-Kwa* reprinted how two government land reserves in the Kitsilas Canyon were "cancelled" and now for sale (29.8) – notice, with impunity, that Indigenous land could be converted by the whim of the state into settler place and that Indian boarding schools, through their publications and other means, aided the idea of these supposed conversions.

Less officially, school newspapers also documented the colonial conversion of space into place through holidays and geography exams. They discussed the place of schools themselves as enveloping institutions, with outdoors that tamed the "wild" space surrounding them. A place did not even yet have to exist for a newspaper to describe it for readers, as the anticipatory geographies of *Our Forest Children* and the pamphlet in Raley's fonds illustrates. Newspapers also referenced England through image and celebration, helping to convert supposedly empty space into place, as did the comparisons between Canada and the US. Similar comparisons that happen today obfuscate the fact that both nations violently dispossess Indigenous peoples from their land and waterways, overwriting them with colonial place and space. Campaigns and advertisements during Canada's sesquicentennial in 2017 capitalized on such fictions, portraying the country as hokey, peaceful, and profusely polite in comparison to the US. As with previous national myth-making projects such as Expo 67 (Griffith, 2015), many Indigenous people challenged the narratives of Canada 150 celebrations (Ladner and Tait, 2017). Newspapers' comparisons reified the naturalness of the border, locating power with schools (not Indigenous families and nations) to establish "brotherly" and "fraternal" relations.

Individual boarding schools in Canada were not isolated aberrations but instead components of a system; these newspapers reveal the system is larger still. Treating US and Canadian boarding schools as distinct muddies the fact that these are settler colonial institutions with minor differences that were in consultation much more than has been previously considered and downplays the borrowing, affirmation, and ideological consolidation that comprised such exchanges. This network among schools within Canada (albeit along denominational lines) as well as between the US came in the form of rare face-to-face consultations and the more sustained contact of school newspapers. Wilson's trips demonstrate the deference Canadian schools had to US ones, found particularly in their glorification of Carlisle and Pratt; US sources occasionally praised Canada.

But resistance – ways "Indigenous people have been able to subvert that system of spatial control, transgressing its numerous finely drawn boundaries" (Byrne, 2010, p. 103) – peeks out. The jubilee celebrations at Battleford School may have been established to reinforce the place of England, but families used the jubilee to reunite. Students defied the taboo of discussing their parents in newspapers by highlighting the visits of their families among trivial details about the jubilee races and prizes. Resistance as well comes from the Cherokee professor Wilson meets in Vinita. But it is not in the newspapers' interest to document the resistance to spatial control and land dispossession at the end of the nineteenth century that was alive and well; newspapers instead profiled spatial subjugation, an erasure that continues today. While the place-making of Canada, England, and the US can be read as distinct, they are also variations of the same settler colonial end goal. The newspapers emphasized these differences, which reinforced their own particularity and therefore blurred their shared purpose of land dispossession.

8 Concluding Thoughts

In 2012, a student was suspended from her parochial school in Wisconsin for speaking Menominee. When the twelve-year-old girl (whose grandmother directed the Menominee Language Program) was found teaching a friend how to say "hello" and "I love you," her non-Indigenous teacher retorted: "You are not to speak like that! How do I know you're not saying something bad? How would you like it if I spoke in Polish and you didn't understand?" (ICTMN Staff, 2014). In this response the teacher imposed an English-only rule, assumed what the student said was bad, proposed English as a lingua franca, and equated a European language with an Indigenous one.

One year after this news story, I was struck by graffiti on the backside of a university building in Toronto. It read: "english broke my father's confidence. We will break English" (see figure 8.1). The first "english" is triply defiant: not only does it begin both a proper noun and a sentence with a lowercase "e," the double underline (a copy editor's notation for "make lowercase") insists the grammatical transgression is not a typo. The father may have been a former residential school student. Perhaps he was a newcomer to Canada facing employment barriers. Maybe he had been offered problematic "accent training." Or, the father was a university student, written off by professors for his "non-standard" English. The child is determined to "break" the language, but this second use of "English" is capitalized, as if to say the breaking hasn't happened yet. It is as if English had not yet been dethroned, but the intention had been noted.

In the summer of 2014, a three-year exhibit opened on the thirty-four Indigenous languages within the borders of what is currently called British Columbia at the provincial museum. The "Our Living

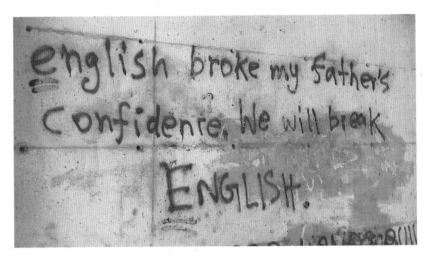

Figure 8.1. University graffiti. Author's photograph, 2014.

Languages" exhibit highlights the beauty and complexity of these languages through audio and visual and includes a language forest and
language cocoon (see figure 8.2). In addition to showcasing the successes
of communities, the space also describes what it labels "disruptions": separation from land, bans on ceremonies, and theft of children. The exhibit
names specific government acts and policies that directly impacted the
ability for Indigenous languages to thrive. The space also displays latch-
keys made from sardine cans by students of Kamloops and Kuper Island
Schools, used to access otherwise restricted food. This exhibit reframes
Indigenous languages not as inexplicably disappearing but as stolen
through concrete, nameable actions. It highlights the immense resistance
of Indigenous peoples and pushes against the museum's larger narratives (like other provincial museums) of settler colonialism outside of
this exhibit – the "our" in the exhibit's title is different from the same
pronoun in the title of Shingwauk Home's newspaper. This museum
shares the same physical structure as BC's provincial archives, where I
accessed Kitamaat Home's newspaper and learned of the school's efforts
to enforce the English language and promote the very disruptions this
exhibit now condemns. In a review of the exhibit, the local newspaper
quotes Mike Willie, Kwak'wala language teacher, who explains how his
language unlike English is verb based and action oriented – that to translate "child" means "my reason for breathing" (Watts, 2014).

Figure 8.2. *Our Living Languages* exhibition. Royal BC Museum (http://learning.royalbcmuseum.bc.ca/pathways/our-living-languages/).

In June 2015, Indigenous languages again made headlines with the release of the Truth and Reconciliation Commission's ninety-four calls to action six months before the final report. The calls include that the federal government acknowledge language as an Aboriginal right and that it develop an Aboriginal Languages Act. Another call included that post-secondary institutions develop programs in Indigenous languages. The report ties these calls to rights and treaties, insisting on the need for adequate funding and for Indigenous peoples to lead these language programs. As of early 2019, the so-called Act Respecting Indigenous Languages had just undergone its first reading in parliament under the Minister of Canadian Heritage and Multiculturalism, naming residential schools as contributing to language erosion but also emphasizing fiscal management. How will invoking Canadian heritage inflect such an act? Citing international examples of language legislation, many are advising that any language act in Canada must go beyond aspirations and symbols (L. Fontaine, Leitch, Nicholas, and de Varennes, 2017).

That same summer the national chief of the Assembly of First Nations, Perry Bellegarde, called for the nearly sixty Indigenous languages spoken within what is called Canada to be national languages. Responses were swift, as settler commentators became bogged down by the feasibility of what Bellegarde proposed. As one journalist in the *Calgary Herald* wrote, "If languages are dying out and remaining unlearned despite the millions of dollars spent annually on teaching and preserving them," then "at some point, people have to take advantage of the opportunities offered" (Lakritz, 2015). This response invokes the trope of the unappreciated handout, leaves out that government funding is woefully inadequate, and ignores the colonial contexts of English literacy that this book discusses. Similarly, Canadian Broadcasting Corporation (CBC) radio aired a program with the polemic title, "Do First Nations Have a Right to Indigenous Language Schools?" (*The 180*, 2015). The guest host asked:

- "What would an entire education, though, in a First Nations language accomplish that could not be accomplished with classes teaching that language?"
- "In Canadian society … there's an expectation that people will be fluent and competent in either French or English. Would an education purely in a First Nations language – would that prepare a student for life in Canada?"
- "How does broader society benefit over this?"
- "What is in it for English and French Canada if First Nations have this right?"

Not all of the host's questions were this pointed, but these four are telling. The host's biggest concerns are how Indigenous children will participate in "modern" society without English and how non-Indigenous people will benefit. These reactions ignore the history of why Indigenous languages are under threat. Focusing on feasibility and cost ignores Indigenous languages as a right. And, these questions recentre white settler language rights and elide the broader entanglement of English and colonialism, leaving alone the history of how the English language (and, though outside of this book's scope, French) was naturalized as official.

Over a year later, a senator named Lynn Beyak stood in the chamber and attempted to highlight the happier side of residential school (Senate, 2017). She appealed to the fact that some missionaries used

Indigenous languages, citing this evidence of bilingualism as positive. In addition to other problematic ways of framing residential schooling, the transcript of her comments reveals she twice requested further time to elaborate on her position. After this second extension, fellow senator Murray Sinclair (and former chair of the TRC) expresses his shock and asks a pointed question. At this point Beyak's time again expires and when asked by the speaker for the third time if she wishes for a longer period to respond, this time she says no: saved by the bell. The transcript of the entire senate session uncovers more language-related issues discussed that day: access to French immersion schools in British Columbia, gendered pronouns in the national anthem, a lack of English language classes for newly arrived Syrian refugees, and a government report on housing now published in Inuktitut syllabics. The same day, when Murray Sinclair spoke in support of amending the criminal code to prevent child-rearing violence, he provided the context of children in residential schools who were punished for speaking their languages.

Simon Fraser University recently began a partnership with Kwi Awt Stelmexw, an adult immersion program for Squamish language learners. The program offers an intensive, immersive two-year program with the goal of producing fifteen fluent speakers in its first year (Gallop, 2016). Khelsilem, the founder and programming director of Kwi Awt Stelmexw, states that his purpose is not to initially produce language teachers, unlike the focus of other language programs: "That goal is too limited. Our focus shouldn't be to increase the number of teachers. Our goal should be to increase the number of homes speaking the language as their primary mode of communication, and raising their children with intergenerational language support" (Vowel, 2016). Khelsilem insists this work is urgent and outside of the work of linguists. "I'm not interested in putting my dead language on a wall for future generations to talk about [how] interesting it is that it has a 'feminine and non-feminine pronoun structure,'" he states.

Above is a selective scan of both the legacies and failures of nineteenth-century language practices and policies today. Indigenous languages did not "disappear": they were stolen and disrupted, as the museum exhibit shows. They can *still* be forbidden in school, as the Wisconsin school's punishment reveals. Today Indigenous languages are misrepresented but also championed. And English continues to command a capital letter even when people fight its supremacy, as the graffiti exposes. In the example of the radio host, non-Indigenous people focus on feasibility, on how Indigenous languages *belong* to or can benefit Canada. Even scholars who discuss the violence of English and literacy in North America sometimes neglect this history entirely.

This book reads school newspapers as a way to "excavate the colonial terrain," treating them as repositories and propaganda but also sites of resistance. School newspapers do not overtly display what survivors reveal: the corporal punishment, rewards, humiliation, surveillance, and other linguicidal tactics used to police Indigenous languages. Instead, school newspapers packaged these manoeuvres as a civilizing foundation and a lingua franca for mutually unintelligible and supposedly deficient Indigenous languages. Newspapers framed methods of English instruction as innocent and neutral – the reading material, telegraph lessons, magic lantern shows, literary societies, student letters, compositions, and of course the newspapers themselves. But schools elided the violence of English, naturalizing its acquisition by students who "preferred" English and "forgot" how to speak the language with which they were raised. As Verna St Denis (2004) notes, framing language as loss instead of theft blames Indigenous peoples instead of settler colonialism (p. 43).

Though schools promoted English they seldom conceded student mastery, criticizing enunciation and labelling students diffident and slow, occasionally along gendered lines. Schools were not devoid of Indigenous languages, and schools did not treat North America as a *lingua nullius* (Phillipson, 2014) – a land with no language. Students, at young ages with threats of grave consequences for doing so, sought spaces to maintain their languages to evade the same fate as Latin. Schools and their newspapers promoted Indigenous languages, but as a gateway to English and Christianity through bilingual programs, syllabics, and sign language. Indigenous languages also acted as entertainment, as was the case with the *Boys' Own* how-to guide on sign language or the Cree "God Save the Queen" gift for the prime minister. School newspapers located authority for Indigenous languages with principals, who "saved" languages they also attempted to decimate. Shingwauk Home's Edward Francis Wilson went to great lengths to "get Indian words" by using force to extract language, not unlike oil or copper. I read this seeming contradiction not as lament for the linguicidal mission of the schools but as a continuation of other settler colonial tactics. Schools, through their newspapers, attempted to dictate who did and did not get to know Indigenous languages.

In addition to language, school newspapers constructed time and place for readers. Boarding schools established Indigenous peoples as foil to the speed, success, and industry of non-Indigenous peoples. They constructed time – not the settler – as the unavoidably geno-cidal culprit. The primary authors of these newspapers – principals and teachers – wrote themselves into the position of temporal helper rather than as directly complicit. Schools used micro-penalities, daily agendas, techniques of firsting and lasting (O'Brien, 2010), and befor-ing and aftering to construct a settler future. But as Wilson's tableaux indicate, *what* timeline could be directed by audience desire and expec-tation. Like time, schools imagined colonial space as empty, wild, and otherwise wasted. Place, in contrast, was modelled after England and the US, to the exclusion of Indigenous land. These techniques included geography exams, the architecture of the school and its grounds, and anticipatory geographies. School newspapers helped form a network of boarding schools across North America. While research on boarding schools in the US and Canada (and other settler colonial states) is often separated, the US and Canada in fact engaged in colonial comparisons. Such consultations reified the border, obfuscating each country's shared purpose of land dispossession. In turn, schools and their newspapers actively ignored Indigenous demands for land or the primacy of land in Indigenous epistemologies.

Conflating experiences of white supremacy flattens the specificities of genocide in North America. Yet attacks on Indigenous peoples repre-sented in school newspapers is not unrelated to the anti-Asian rhetoric on the prairies, which emerged alongside the perceived threat of board-ing school print shops; the casual invocation of disability to describe English language learners; the Black train porters Wilson used as foil; and the Fisk Jubilee Singers, whose music resonated with Indigenous peoples in Australia and New Zealand but who could not rent a hotel room in Toronto. Some school newspapers also provided missionary reports from Africa and Asia. The colonial practices of Indian boarding schools did not operate in isolation from (yet are also not the same as) larger histories of white supremacy, heteropatriarchy, capitalism, chat-tel slavery, indentured labour, and ableism.[1]

At the same time school newspapers also reveal printers who appear to have thrived. Schools remarked on the "dilapidated" condition of their libraries and students who voraciously read in English. It appears students in turn narrated how they used English for their own purposes and in addition to Indigenous languages. But these experiences do not justify the barriers Gilbert Bear faced. They do not erase that schools bestowed upon their newspapers childlike personae while simultaneously denying the same humanity to students. Robert Warrior's (2005) speculations on the "Indian boys" newspaper bylines are instructive; students may have fought to include this line proudly. Or, they may have laughed. Printers may have been signing Lyons's concept of the x- mark in their excitement over and desire to write, edit, and print in English. Students learned and parents promoted English as a means of survival and a focus on the future. School newspapers reveal scenes of students and parents adapting English as their own tool.

School newspapers reveal resistance throughout, such as the debate club whose members did not unanimously agree that "Indians were happier before the coming of the white man" or James Garvie's article on "why do Indians advance so slowly," which blamed the government. Reports of fire, runaways, and the girls who "played grandmother" all exemplify resistance, as does Gilbert Bear, who refused ill treatment at his printing job and answered "no" when asked if he enjoyed being on display. Children and their families used jubilee celebrations and treaty time to reunite, defying school intentions. Basil Johnston and his peers dawdled while their teachers rang bells in their ears. Wilson consistently faced resistance to his ethnographies, from the Cherokee professor in Vinita who challenged Wilson's racist classifications to his interlocutors, who would mumble, remain silent, and dodge his "instantaneous photographs." Newspapers did not broadcast that students maintained their languages, which survivor testimony and the sheer fact that Indigenous languages exist today disprove; however, annual reports leak out the difficulties in (i.e., resistance to) enforcing English-only policies.

One wonders why such strictly censored newspapers would even permit fissures in the narrative. In documents heavily guided by expectations of principals, teachers, and readers – where bylines insisted students could provide labour but not content – why not excise all challenges to the script? Michel-Rolph Trouillot (2012) contends that "to acknowledge resistance as a mass phenomenon is to acknowledge the possibility that something is wrong with the system" (p. 84). Schools may have safely acknowledged resistance in their newspapers by reframing them as isolated cases or as anything other than resistance. Examples of this technique included falsely framing students who learned English as assimilated or those who continued to speak Indigenous languages as slow. For a school to acknowledge these examples as sustained defiance would have required acknowledging the children's humanity.

If a teacher were to type "residential school lesson plans" on the internet, she may find the Canadian Broadcasting Corporation's Digital Archives website. It offers three lesson plans on residential schooling: write a diary from the perspective of a survivor, brainstorm the "challenges and opportunities" of residential school, and write a letter to parents. All three lessons problematically ask present-day students to put themselves in the role of a residential school student. Lesson plans such as these ask everyone – including settlers – to identify with residential school students rather than promote a space to bear witness to survivor testimony. Moreover, the examples here are inaccurate because residential school students were not normally permitted private spaces like a diary to write, abuse is more than a challenge, and letters home were often censored and written only in English. Settler colonial narratives from the nineteenth century – of text, labour, language, time, place, land – inform violence and pedagogy today.

Settler education must move away from the role-playing these lesson plans represent. John Willinsky (1998) suggests teaching English by considering how the language "marks the flow of power through history" (p. 211). Markers of such flows include Eve Haque's (2012) work on how the Royal Commission on Bilingualism and Biculturalism (1963–9) forcefully insisted on the *bi-* of French and English languages despite petitions from a variety of language communities.[2] Learning these language histories *and* reading Indigenous literature and testimony all offer ways of learning anew.

But little work among fellow settlers has been devoted to moving beyond denial, guilt, voyeurism, and satisfaction in banking "the facts."[3] Settler goals of tolerance, shame, empathy, and multiculturalism will only serve to centre settlers such as myself, affirm the legitimacy of the state, and distract from returning land. Nineteenth-century school newspapers help to highlight critical histories of language and may help initiate methods for stopping everyday practices that directly take from Indigenous languages and literary production (different from only asking how much to give instead of how much less to take).[4] Indigenous peoples and communities already have language nests, immersion programs, books, intergenerational transmission, podcasts, place-renaming projects, and writers' residencies – both inside and outside of state-sanctioned channels. And as this book demonstrates, Indigenous peoples have always shaped languages and literary

Figure 8.3. Wilson's cairn, with Shingwauk Home (now Algoma University and Shingwauk Kinoomaage Gamig) in the background. Stephanie Matchiwita, 2018.

practices on their own terms. This book insists on the responsibility that all settlers have for the attempted eradication of Indigenous languages and the theft of land that such attempts helped to facilitate, urging that such responsibility translates into tangible and concrete restitution in ways that Indigenous peoples determine.

The physical structure of Shingwauk Home still exists in Sault Ste Marie, Ontario. Like other Indian boarding schools still standing, it has been converted into a new school – Algoma University and Shingwauk Kinoomaage Gamig, realizing the dream Chief Shingwauk had for education in 1850. In front of the school, if facing it from the road, is a cairn dedicated to the school's founder Edward Francis Wilson (see figure 8.3). This cairn is not where Wilson is buried: his final resting place is

Figure 8.4. Survivors' side of Wilson's cairn. Stephanie Matchiwita, 2018.

in a cemetery on xʷənenə̓č (Salt Spring Island) in British Columbia, a stone's throw away from my own white settler grandma's ashes. On the other side of the cairn in Sault Ste Marie, if looking at the cairn with the school behind, is a plaque and garden dedicated to residential school survivors (see figure 8.4). The school behind the cairn now teaches the Anishinaabemowin language. These two sides symbolize much: the cairn's recto and verso are worlds and times apart, and both must still be thought of on the same page.

Tables

Table 1. Newspaper Profiles

Newspaper Title and School	Location	Denomination	Frequency	Dates	Format	Circulation (self-reported)	Price
The Aurora **Rupert's Land Indian Industrial School**	Middlechurch, Manitoba	Church of England	Monthly	1893–5(?)	4 pages	?	25 cents/year
The Canadian Indian **Shingwauk Industrial Home**	Sault Ste Marie, Ontario	Church of England	Monthly	1890–1	26 pages	?	20 cents/year
The Guide **Battleford Indian Industrial School**	Battleford, Saskatchewan	Church of England	Monthly	1891–9	4 pages	?	50 cents/year
Na-Na-Kwa: Or, Dawn on the Northwest Coast **Kitamaat Home**	Kitamaat, British Columbia	Methodist	Quarterly	1898–1907	4–18 pages	3000	By donation
Our Forest Children: And What We Want to Do with Them **Shingwauk Industrial Home**	Sault Ste Marie, Ontario	Church of England	Monthly	1887–90	4–16 pages	2000	10 cents/year
Progress **Regina Industrial School**	Regina, Assinaboia/ Saskatchewan	Presbyterian	Semi-monthly	1894–?	8 pages	1000	25 cents/year

Table 2. Edward Francis Wilson's American Indian School Visits, 1888

School Name	Location	Reference in Shingwauk Home Newspapers
Albuquerque School	Albuquerque, NM	*Our Forest Children*, 4.4:218–19
Araphoe Mission School	Darlington, Indian Territory	*Our Forest Children*, 3.9:108–9
Carlisle School	Carlisle, PA	*Our Forest Children*, 3.4:25–8
Cherokee Seminaries	Indian Territory	*Our Forest Children*, 3.8:91
Cheyenne Mission School	Darlington, Indian Territory	*Our Forest Children*, 3.9:108; 310:123
Chilocco School	Indian Territory	*Our Forest Children*, 3.11:138
Genoa School	Genoa, NE	*Canadian Indian*, 1.6:176–7; 1.7:208–13
Lincoln Institute	Philadelphia, PA	*Our Forest Children*, 3.4:24–5
Mennonite Mission School	Darlington, Indian Territory	*Our Forest Children*, 3.9:108
Ponca School	"?"	*Our Forest Children*, 3.11:137–8
Ramona School	Sante Fe, NM	*Our Forest Children*, 4.1:172–3
Worcester Academy	Vinita, Indian Territory	*Our Forest Children*, 3.7:73–4
Zuni Protestant School	Zuni Territority, NM	*Canadian Indian*, 1.2:51

Notes

1. Bury the Lede: Introduction

1 I use "boarding schools" to designate any school that both housed and taught Indigenous children. While the term "residential school" is more common in Canada, it does not accurately represent schools in the late nineteenth century. Beginning in the 1880s, Canadian schools were classified as industrial (for older students who learned an industry) and boarding (for younger students who learned basic farming or domestic skills), in addition to other classifications such as day and mission schools (J.R. Miller, 1996, p. 135). The distinction of boarding and industrial meant different funding from government and also a division in class, as industrial schools were considered more prestigious. By the close of the century, though, the distinction had dissipated as both systems raced to the bottom. In 1923, the difference was officially collapsed, and all schools were from then on known as residential (pp. 134–41). In the US, the term "residential" was typically not used. For these reasons, unless a school is a day school, I refer to schools that housed students as "boarding schools" no matter what time period, country, or technical designation they originally had. When I drop the word "Indian" before the name of a school and simply call it "boarding school," I am always referring to Indian boarding schools.

2 The term "settler" is commonly used as a noun in Canada to denote a non-Indigenous person and as an adjective to denote a particular type of colonialism shared by states such as Australia, New Zealand, and the United States. The term is also slippery, as its etymology reveals: according to the *Oxford English Dictionary*, the verb "settle" originated from the Old English word "setl," meaning "place of rest." But the word was commonly

confused with the similar sounding but distinct Middle English word "saȝtle," which means "to appease" or "to reconcile." Broadly using the term "settler" risks collapsing distinctions amongst all non-Indigenous peoples and evading both the whiteness and the violence of settlerhood that much of these school newspapers represent. See Scott Morgensen (2014), Paulette Regan (2010), and Eve Tuck and K. Wayne Yang (2012) for more on the term.

3 The term "Indigenous" is used throughout this book to refer to Native American, First Nations, Métis, and Inuit peoples in North America. Where possible, I specifically name the nation a person belongs to instead of the generic term "Indigenous." With regards to school newspapers, though, their very point was to homogenize and flatten these distinctions (which this book discusses), so such specificity is often not possible. As Gerald Vizenor (1999) argues, "The word *Indian*, however, is a colonial enactment, not a loaned word, and the dominance is sustained by the simulation that has superseded the real tribal names. The Indian was an occidental invention" (p. 11). When a school newspaper *does* name the specific nationality of someone, I sometimes use the term the school employed in the nineteenth century for this nation, which may not have been how that nation referred to itself then or now.

4 Citations for school newspapers are as follows: newspaper title, volume, issue (though not all include issue numbers), page number.

5 See chapters in *Colonial Genocide in Indigenous North America* (Woolford, Benvenuto, and Hinton, 2014) for articulations on using the term "genocide" with regards to Canada. Article II of the United Nations Genocide Convention names forcibly transferring children from one group to another, though exclusively sticking to the UN definition is complicated, since an earlier draft in 1948 also named the prohibition of language, but this was struck out of the final version due to pressure from settler colonial nations including Canada (Woolford, 2015, p. 25).

6 See Glen Coulthard (2014), Jennifer Henderson and Pauline Wakeham (2013), Dian Million (2013), and Paulette Regan (2010) for more on cultures of redress and state-sponsored reconciliation.

7 Examples of scholarship that engages with individual newspapers of Indian boarding schools in Canada in some capacity include work by Kathleen Buddle (2002, 2001), Alicia Fahey and Chelsea Horton (2012), David Nock (1988), Sharon Wall (2003), and Walter Wasylow (1972).

8 This book frequently refers to people who formally attended boarding schools as "survivors." The term was used by people in organizations formed in the 1990s (Niezen, 2013, p. 19) and then later by the TRC. The

term is not universally accepted; Theodore Fontaine (2010), for instance, prefers to identify himself as a victor (p. 121). In 2008, journalist Wab Kinew faced opposition for using the term with the Canadian Broadcasting Corporation to describe his own father (Shea, 2015). As well, many students did not survive. Some scholarship instead uses terms such as "alumni" or "former student."

9 For more on the archive and colonialism, see Camille Callison, Crystal Fraser and Zoe Todd (2016), Griffith (2018), Achille Mbembe (2002), Loriene Roy and Gretchen Alice LeCheminant (2016), Ann Laura Stoler (2009), and Michel-Rolph Trouillot (2012).

10 Sample issues (but not complete series) of some of these newspapers can also be accessed through *Early Canadiana Online*. For more on digitization and the nineteenth-century press, see James Mussell (2012).

11 Alberni, Ahousaht, Christie, St Michael's, and Kuper Island Residential Schools. These five are in addition to Indian day schools and other institutions not officially recognized by the Indian Residential School Settlement Agreement. For more on day schools in British Columbia, see Helen Raptis (2016). For more on Kuper Island School, see Christine Welsh (1997).

12 For international and comparative perspectives on truth and reconciliation commissions in settler states, see Jeff Corntassel and Cindy Holder (2008) and Sheryl Lightfoot (2015).

13 Two exceptions of published work by survivors who attended Indian boarding schools in the nineteenth century include the 1933 memoir of Luther Standing Bear (2006), who attended Carlisle School in Pennsylvania beginning in 1879, and interviews conducted by Walter Wasylow (1972) with students who attended Battleford School in Saskatchewan in the 1880s and 1890s.

14 See Rosemary Nagy and Emily Gillespie (2015) for analysis of newspaper coverage of Canada's Truth and Reconciliation Commission.

15 See Cheryl Suzack (2006) for more on the history of Indigenous peoples and publishing in Canada.

16 Jim Crow laws, formally in place from the late nineteenth century until 1965 in the US, mandated the segregation of Black peoples in a variety of public spaces and institutions. See Robin D. G. Kelley (1993) for resistance and Jim Crow laws. See Michelle Alexander (2012) for contemporary iterations of Jim Crow laws and Barrington Walker (2009) for more on Jim Crow laws and Canada. For context on the Papaschase, see Dwayne Donald (2004) and Jaimy L. Miller (2011).

17 Battleford School in Saskatchewan, which had a newspaper, brought students to witness the hanging as a field trip (Cuthand, 2007, p. 35).

18 See An Act Respecting Indians, Statutes of Canada 1894, chapter 32, section 11.
19 See volume II of *History of the Book in Canada* (Fleming, Lamonde, and Black, 2005) for more on early print culture in Canada.
20 Though I occasionally mention the French language because of French-speaking missionaries, this project exclusively focuses on newspapers written in English. There were not to my knowledge Indian boarding school newspapers in Canada from the nineteenth century written in French. While the French language is outside of this book's scope, it is of course, like English, a colonial language.
21 See table 1 for all six newspapers and their frequency, dates, format, circulation, and prices.
22 The five schools that are the main focus of this book do not represent all regions or all peoples, even though schools operated throughout Canada for First Nations, Métis, and Inuit students alike. New research is emerging on the distinct histories of residential schooling in the North. Such schools began later than residential schools elsewhere in Canada, and the final TRC report includes an entire volume, *The Inuit and Northern Experience,* to begin unpacking these distinctions. See also Anthony Di Mascio and Leigh Hortop-Di Mascio (2011) and Heather McGregor (2015). Chooutla School in Carcross, Yukon, had a student newspaper titled *Northern Lights,* though it existed decades after the period that is the focus of this book. See as well the TRC's final report volume on Métis experiences in residential school in addition to Jonathan Anuik (2006) and Larry N. Chartrand (2006).
23 Shingwauk Home was dubbed an industrial school but initially was funded as a boarding school (TRC of Canada, 2015b, p. 218).
24 Most references throughout the book focus on these five schools and their six newspapers. I frequently turn, though, to other schools in Canada and other newspapers from Indian boarding schools in the US for comparisons and for context.

2. Printer's Devil: The Trade of Newspapers

1 See also Mindy J. Morgan (2009).
2 I thank Gordon Goldsborough for this information.
3 Although this particular speech praised white printers such as Benjamin Franklin, Indigenous printers were celebrated in school newspapers, too. One issue of Carlisle School's newspaper printed an article titled "The First Indian Printer" (10.1:6). School newspapers also praised Indigenous-led newspapers such as the *Cherokee Advocate.*

4 See J.R. Miller's (1996b) chapter, "Work and Play" for a detailed assessment of labour in schools.

5 The Gordon press has a printing bed on two legs hinged at the floor. A large, rotatable shaft supports the platen, while a crank hinges the bed back and forth. To ink, three rollers were used, moving from an ink disc above the bed and then down, powered by pumping a treadle (F. Williams, 1985).

6 Exceptions included Birtle and Wikwemikong Schools, which had printing programs but no newspaper. Shingwauk Home in Sault Ste Marie, Ontario, had a school newspaper but no printing program. Instead, proofs of the newspaper were sent to a printer in Owen Sound. Despite not printing on-site, Shingwauk Home offered typewriter, cyclostyle stencil copying, and photography lessons, but perhaps only (as one article indicates) to children too sick for other trades (*Our Forest Children* 2.7:21). The principal of Shingwauk Home offered a printing program in 1876, but it seems to have only lasted one year.

7 The File Hills Colony in Saskatchewan was one such example, where many of Regina School's former students went to farm after ending their studies (Bednasek, 2009; Poitras, 2001).

8 The phrase in nineteenth-century school newspapers predates Duncan Campbell Scott, deputy superintendent of Indian Affairs, in 1920: "I want to get rid of the Indian problem ... to continue until there is not a single Indian in Canada that has not been absorbed into the body politic and there is no Indian question." The "Indian problem" is a not unrelated variation on the "Negro problem," which W.E.B. Du Bois's *The Souls of Black Folk* famously confronted by asking, "What does it feel like to be a problem?" See José Esteban Muñoz (2007) for discussion of the phrase in Du Bois; see Paulette Regan (2010) for the *settler* problem (p. 230) and Lisa Monchalin (2016) for the *colonial* problem; and see Warrior (2005) for Du Bois and boarding school.

9 The Davin Report (1879) tried to counter this widespread belief, clarifying that the *race*, not the people, was in its childhood (p. 10).

10 Written by Elizabeth Long, a teacher at Kitamaat and frequent contributor to *Na-Na-Kwa*, the story was reprinted by the United Church of Canada in 1907 under the title *How the Light Came to Kitamaat*.

11 The seeds of Carlisle School are found in the history of Hampton Institute. After the Red River War (1874–5), the US army transferred seventy-two Indigenous prisoners to Fort Marion in Florida. Richard Pratt, who founded Carlisle School in 1879, oversaw their imprisonment and developed an educational program. Upon release, some prisoners went on to study at Hampton and later at Carlisle. For more on the Hampton Institute, see Donal F. Lindsey (1995).

12 For a first-hand description of injuries in schools because of operating machinery, see Isabelle Knockwood's *Out of the Depths*. See also the TRC's final report, vol. 1 pp. 347–50.

13 Though the Kitamaat Home taught both girls and boys, it only housed girls. Boys only attended school for half the year typically, working with their families for the rest.

14 Carlisle's printing program was run by a woman, Marianna Burgess. See Fear-Segal (2004).

15 Children were generally aged seven to sixteen at schools, though much younger children such as Joe were not infrequent. The newspaper was unclear whether Joe was young or just small for his age.

16 Subscription incentives were not unusual during the nineteenth century. As Rutherford (1982) explains, the *Montreal Witness* motivated new subscribers with skates, gold lockets, magic lanterns, and chromos of Lady and Earl of Dufferin (p. 97).

17 After the First World War, school newspapers were typically addressed to parents.

18 Though "Stray Leaf" began as free for Sunday schools already donating money to Shingwauk and Wawanosh Homes (3.11:129), several issues in the principal began charging one dollar per year for ten copies, which would offset costs and do away with the "labor and anxiety" of managing the "free list" (3.13:175).

19 See *Troubling Tricksters*, especially the preface and Kristina Fagan's introduction, for more on tricksters used out of context (Reder and Morra, 2010).

20 For an interrogation of the canoe within discourses of Canadian nationalism, see Misao Dean (2013).

21 By 1920, attendance of seven-year-olds was mandatory, though younger children also attended.

22 See Timothy J. Stanley (2011) for more on Chinese student resistance in early twentieth-century Canada.

3. Indigenous Languages Did Not Disappear: English Language Instruction

1 Gerald Vizenor's use of the term connotes an ongoing, active survival that opposes the subject position of victim (1999).

2 Niezen (2013) interviewed an Oblate priest who felt that while teaching in an Indian boarding school "there was even a sense of *French* being illicit and repressed" (p. 141) rather than Indigenous languages. Sellars (2013),

too, notes how at her boarding school in the 1960s students resented the nuns who enforced English yet spoke French (p. 45).

3 English studies at the end of the nineteenth century in Canada conflated many distinctions we make today: English as an Additional Language (sometimes referred to as English as a Second Language), English literature, grammar, pronunciation, elocution, rhetoric, composition, literacy, and phonetics were all often grouped together as "English." This remained true at most boarding schools, where the subject English meant many of these categories.

4 See Tanya Titchkosky (2007) for contemporary ways in which disability is metaphorized in print and in everyday life, not unlike this nineteenth-century example.

5 It appears the same loss of status for women who learned English did not apply; however, under the Indian Act a woman lost status if she married a white man (and a white woman gained Indian status by marrying an Indigenous man). This distinction was repealed in 1985 (Lawrence, 2003; Palmater, 2011), though the Indian Act still contains forms of gender discrimination.

6 For more on the subject of English, see Jory Brass (2011, 2013, 2016), Bill Green, Phillip Cormack, and Annette Patterson (2013), Peter Medway and Ivor Goodson (1990), and Annette Patterson, Phillip Cormack, and William Green (2012). For introductions to histories of the English language in Canada, see Charles Boberg (2010) and John Edwards (1998). For critical takes on language policies in Canada and the US, see Bruce Curtis (1990), Eve Haque (2012), Matthew Hayday (2015), Monica Heller and Bonnie McElhinny (2017), Malathi Michelle Iyengar (2014), and Jennifer E. Monaghan (2005).

7 For just one example of a contemporary English-only movement, see Barker, Giles, Noels, Duck, Hecht, and Clément (1998).

8 Niezen's (2013) reading of the National Film Board's *PowWow at Duck Lake* (1967) may shed further light on this consistency in Wasylow's interviews, which focus on language rather than other abuses. In a scene from the documentary, former students confront a priest; they do not mention abuse other than that connected to language. Perhaps, then, language denigration was the earliest harm that could be heard at this time (though not in this case: the priest laughs at the group and leaves the scene). The fourteen-minute film (available online) is well worth watching, combatting the myth that resistance to residential schooling is a recent phenomenon. The film shows Indigenous academics, politicians, and youth condemning the system forty-five years ago. Of course, parents and children fought from the beginning.

9 I have used the spellings/names in this manuscript from the original sources.

10 John A. Macdonald believed proximity to reserves was one of *the* barriers to assimilation. He told the House of Commons in 1883 that "when the school is on the reserve, the child lives with his parents who are savages; he is surrounded by savages, and though he may learn to read and write, his habits and training and mode of thought are Indian. He is simply a savage who can read and write" (qtd. in Truth and Reconciliation Commission of Canada, 2012a, p. 6).

11 The essay prompt was likely informed by the many debates in the US on the place of Indigenous languages in boarding schools at this time – recall the funding tied to English instruction in 1881 and then the ban in 1887.

4. "Getting Indian Words": Representations of Indigenous Languages

1 Compare this note to a scene in Cherie Dimaline's *The Marrow Thieves*, when the narrator asks a stranger what language he dreams in (pp. 227–8).

2 New Zealand made English mandatory in all schools earlier, in 1867 (Grenoble and Whaley, 2006, p. 54).

3 Several bilingual non-school newspapers existed in the nineteenth century. In the US, the *Cherokee Phoenix* was a newspaper arguing for sovereignty (Littlefield and Parins, 1984, p. xii). Canada had the *Kamloops Wawa*, published from 1891 to 1904 (P. Petrone, 1990). Prior to *Our Forest Children*, Edward Francis Wilson also published a bilingual newspaper, *Pipe of Peace*, from 1878–9 (J.R. Miller, 1996b, p. 7). Thomas Hurlburt in Sarnia, Ontario, also published *Petaubun* beginning in 1862 (Buddle, 2001, p. 61).

4 For a detailed description of Standing Bear and English, see Spack (2002, pp. 101–7) and Warrior (2005).

5 The newspaper does not specify which national anthem, as the phrase in 1895 could have meant "The Maple Leaf Forever" *or* "God Save the Queen"; however, the newspaper printed a version of "God Save the Queen" in Cree two issues later. Though the newspaper does print "The Maple Leaf," it is not for another two years and is only in English (*Guide* 6.1:3).

6 In the series *Prayer Language*, artist Kent Monkman explores the tangled histories of syllabics, representation, religion, colonialism, language, and sexuality (Francis 2011, pp. 148–55; R.W. Hill 2002). See Kent Monkman: http://www.kentmonkman.com/.

7 For more on Evans and syllabics, see Roger Burford-Mason (1996). For more on Evans and his trial over the abuse, see Raymond Morris

Shirritt-Beaumont (2001) and Gerald M. Hutchinson (1977). His guilt remains unclear, as many Indigenous people supported Evans, and his accusers later admitted that another missionary, who later went on to take credit for the syllabics after Evans' death named William Mason, was in fact the perpetrator (Francis, 2011, pp. 190–1). Whatever the case, the history of syllabics is embroiled in the history of Hudson's Bay, the law, and sexual violence – far more complicated than the school newspaper makes it out to be.

8 The term "syllabics" is typically used in Canada to indicate that similar sounds use the same symbol; the term "syllabary," which is used more in the United States, usually denotes different characters for different sounds, no matter how similar.

9 See also Steven Conn (2006) for US histories of linguistics and colonialism in the nineteenth century.

10 For more on Indigenous peoples, missionaries, and print culture see Cornelius J. Jaenen (2006)

11 Wilson "collected" Indigenous languages with pencil and paper, which is unsurprising. When he left for his trip in 1888, the phonograph for ethnographic research was not yet viable and wax cylinders were unreliable, expensive, and unwieldy (Hochman, 2014, p. xi).

5. Ahead by a Century: Time on Paper

1 See Elizabeth Edwards (2006), Brian Hochman (2014), and Christopher Pinney (2011) for more on settler photographers and colonialism. Edward Sherriff Curtis is perhaps the most well-known white settler photographer of "vanishing" Indigenous peoples (B. Evans and Glass, 2014; Gidley, 2003), but there were other photographers such as H. H. Bennett (Hoelscher, 2008) and Frank Rinehart (Ortiz, 2004).

2 As Ann Stoler (2016) asks, "Is it possible to dispense with the sharply defined temporalities that past, present, and future invoke as discrete time frames? Can we use these terms but still understand that they are not sequential ways of living time and colonial duress, but they can exist simultaneously, recessed and seized on, with different weightings?" (p. 33).

3 See also Sarah Sharma (2014) for connections between time and labour.

4 Fleming was also a member of Edward Francis Wilson's Canadian Indian Research and Aid Society.

5 See Kenton Storey (2016) and Patrick Brantlinger (2003) for more on humanitarian language and settler anxiety in the nineteenth century.

6 See Arthur J. Ray, J.R. Miller, and Frank Tough (2000, pp. 192–5) for more on the deposing of Chief Wahpeemakwa and his son.

7 At the 2014 conference for the International Association of Genocide Scholars, which used the image of Thomas Moore in its promotional material, a discussion ensued surrounding the ethics of disseminating images such as these. As Susan Sontag (2003) writes: "Perhaps the only people with the right to look at images of suffering of this extreme order are those who could do something to alleviate it" or "those who could learn from it. The rest of us are voyeurs, whether or not we mean to be" (p. 42). See Miranda J. Brady and Emily Hiltz (2017) for a detailed "archaeology" of the Thomas Moore photographs.

8 For more on Indigenous architecture and planning, see K. Tsianina Lomawaima (2014) and David C. Natcher, Ryan Christopher Walker, and Theodore S. Jojola (2013).

9 See also Jane Carey and Jane Lydon (2014).

10 For a transcript of Harper's comments in 2009, in which he stated that Canada had no history of colonialism despite the year before apologizing for residential schools, see Aaron Wherry (2009).

6. Anachronism: Reading the Nineteenth Century Today

1 See also a special issue on presentism in the journal *Past and Present* (Walsham, 2017)

2 Given Jeffrey Monaghan's (2013) research on the role of the North-West Mounted Police in the late nineteenth century, such football matches are further troubling and may shed historical light on current debates about police officers in public schools.

3 See Janice Forsyth and Michael Heine (2017) and Janice Forsyth and Braden Te Hiwi (2017) for more on sport and residential schooling.

4 See Dean Neu and Richard Therrien (2003) and Shiri Pasternak (2016, 2017) for more on fiscal control and colonialism.

5 British Columbia also has treaties, though a different history of them. See J.R. Miller (1996a, pp. 146–8) and Alexandra Harmon (2008).

6 This article in the *Guide* was likely paraphrased from a longer piece published one month earlier in the *New York Tribune* (Krehbiel, 1897).

7 Peyasiw-Awasis would later go on to appeal to treaty rights in his continued fight against Section 114 of the Indian Act, which banned ceremonies (Pettipas, 1994, pp. 128–9).

8 See Kristine Alexander (2016) for ways in which colonialism informs depictions of settler childhoods.

9 See Brian Titley (1986, 2009, 2011) for more on the history of Indian Affairs and individual Indian commissioners.

10 The pass system was administered by Indian agents but was never actually made legal. For further context, see the documentary *The Pass System* (A. Williams, 2015).

11 See Victoria Freeman (2003) for more on parental interventions.

12 See also Sean Carleton (2016, pp. 319–20).

13 Recent work by Ian Mosby and Tracey Galloway (2017) uncovers health effects such as diabetes of survivors of residential school *after* they left as well.

14 Sherene Razack (2015) exposes how the claim that Indigenous people are "shallow breathers" continues to justify death, this time of Indigenous people in custody in the twenty-first century (pp. 124–6).

15 Susan Sontag's *Illness as Metaphor* (2003) draws attention to how descriptions of cancer originate from the military (p. 63) – words like "invasive," "colonize," and "defenses" (as in the body's). While school newspapers do not discuss cancer, they similarly borrow from colonial and military language (e.g., "outbreak").

7. Layout: Space, Place, and Land

1 A shifting area of land in the south central United States marked off by government for Indigenous peoples whose land was allegedly ceded. More often, Indigenous groups were forcibly, violently removed and sent to live in Indian Territory. Many groups continued to live there despite forced relocation until Indian Territory "became" Oklahoma in 1907 (Justice, 2006).

2 See Eve Tuck and Marcia McKenzie (2015) for more on critical place inquiry.

3 See for instance Dylan Robinson's (2016) discussion of the Ogimaa Mikana Project (pp. 64–7) and Leanne Simpson's (2017) discussion of PKOLS (pp. 240–2).

4 *Alexandra Readers* were texts commonly assigned in elementary school. See Amy von Heyking (2006, pp. 15–24).

5 I thank Adam Stewart for his knowledge of Shingwauk Home's grounds.

6 *Our Forest Children* also reprinted excerpts from the serialized fiction of Carlisle School's newspaper *Indian Helper*, which was called *Stiya* (4.2:190). Like MOTBS, Marianna Burgess likely wrote *Stiya* (though under a pseudonym). Katanski (2005) and Fear-Segal (2007) view the narrative of *Stiya* as an extension of MOTBS – a warning of what happens to children

when they return to their family and reservation. The *Aurora* also reprinted what appears to be serialized fiction titled *The Banished Chief* (1.12:2; 1.13:2), and so did *Progress* in a series titled *Yellow Shield* (18.2:1; 18.3:3).

7 Carlisle's eight newspapers existed at various points in Carlisle's history, beginning in 1880. Some publications were intended just for children while others were for a wider, adult audience. Topics included the day-to-day of Carlisle as well as American Indian policy more broadly. The eight newspapers were *Eadle Keatah Toh, Morning Star, Indian Helper,* the *Red Man, Red Man and Helper,* the *Arrow,* the *Carlisle Arrow,* and the *Carlisle Arrow and Red Man* (Fear-Segal, 2007, p. 206). Some of these publications were distinct; others were just new names for a repackaged newspaper.

8 Being a porter on a sleeping car was one of the better paying jobs available to African-American men after the American Civil War for nearly one hundred years. In 1925, "Pullman Porters," as they were known, established the first union exclusively for Black people – the Brotherhood of Sleeping Car Porters (Bates, 2001).

8. Concluding Thoughts

1 For more context, see the special issue of *Social Identities* (Grech and Soldatic, 2017), Tiffany King (2014), Lisa Lowe (2015), and Iyko Day (2015, 2016).

2 See also John Long's (2006) work on Indigenous language policy in the 1980s.

3 Important exceptions include Paulette Regan (2010), Roger Simon (2005), and many others.

4 A distinction informed by the work of Vandana Shiva.

References

Correspondence

Wilson, E.F. (1887–8). [Letters from Edward Francis Wilson to Richard J. Pratt]. Letter book series. Shingwauk Residential School fonds, 2013-112/004 (001). Shingwauk Residential Schools Centre. Algoma University, pp. 233, 425, 436, 437, 462, 578.

Government Reports

Benson, M. (1897, July 5). Report from the records of the Department of Indian Affairs, RG10 Volume 6039, File 160-1, Part 1, Microfilm reel C-8152. Microfilm pages 1468, 1470, 1471.

Department of Indian of Affairs (DIA) Annual Reports, 1880–1936: http://www.bac-lac.gc.ca/eng/discover/aboriginal-heritage/first-nations/indian-affairs-annual-reports/Pages/search.aspx.

School Newspapers

Aurora of Rupert's Land School. 1893–5 (incomplete). E 96.65 R87 Aur O.S. Manitoba Legislative Library.

Canadian Indian of Shingwauk Home. 1890–1 (complete). 8_06250_. Early Canadiana Online. http://eco.canadiana.ca/view/oocihm.8_06250.

Elkhorn Advocate of Washakada Home. October 1892–September 1910. De 14 1893–Oc 13 1910. Manitoba Legislative Library.

Guide of Battleford School. 1895–9. R-E1632. Saskatchewan Archives Board.

Indian Leader of Haskell Institute. 1887–1997. Haskell Indian Nations University Museum and Cultural Center.

Moccasin Telegram of Blue Quills School. 1930s and 1940s (incomplete). 133
71.220/5772. Provincial Archives of Alberta. HR6651.C73R15: Deschâtelets
Archives.

Morning Star of Carlisle School. 1882–7. Cumberland County Historical
Society Archives. Call number PI-023.

Na-Na-Kwa of Kitamaat Home. 1898–1907. NW 970.7 N175. British Columbia
Archives.

Our Forest Children of Shingwauk Home: 1887–90 (incomplete). 8_06666, Early
Canadiana Online. http://eco.canadiana.ca/view/oocihm.8_06666 1887–90
(incomplete). Ayer 1.09, Newberry Library; 1889–90 (incomplete). 2009–
081–001. Engracia de Jesus Matias Archives and Special Collections.

Progress of Regina School. 1897–1910. R-2.40. Saskatchewan Archives Board.

Rupert's Land Gleaner of Rupert's Land School. July 1890–December 1892. Jy
1890, Fe 1892–De 1892. Manitoba Legislative Library.

Treaties

"Numbered Treaties": Treaty Texts. *Aboriginal Affairs and Northern
Affairs Canada*. Retrieved from https://www.aadnc-aandc.gc.ca/
eng/1370373165583/1370373202340

Treaties 1 and 2 between Her Majesty the Queen and the Chippewa and
Cree Indians of Manitoba and Country Adjacent with Adhesions.

Treaty No. 3 between Her Majesty the Queen and the Saulteaux Tribe of
the Ojibbeway Indians at the Northwest Angle on the Lake of the Woods
with Adhesions.

Treaty No. 4 between Her Majesty the Queen and the Cree and Saulteaux
Tribes of Indians at the Qu'appelle and Fort Ellice.

Treaty No. 5 between Her Majesty the Queen and the Saulteaux and Swampy
Cree Tribes of Indians at Beren's River and Norway House with Adhesions.

Treaty No. 6 between Her Majesty the Queen and the Plain and Wood Cree
Indians and other Tribes of Indians at Fort Carlton, Fort Pitt and Battle
River with Adhesions.

Treaty and Supplementary Treaty No. 7 between Her Majesty the Queen
and the Blackfeet and Other Indian Tribes, at the Blackfoot Crossing of
Bow River and Fort Macleod.

Treaty No. 8 Made June 21, 1899 and Adhesions, Reports, etc.

The James Bay Treaty – Treaty No. 9 (Made in 1905 and 1906) and
Adhesions Made in 1929 and 1930.

Treaty No. 10 and Reports of Commissioners.

Treaty No. 11 (June 27, 1921) and Adhesion (July 17, 1922) with Reports, etc.

Secondary Sources

Adams, D.W. (1995). *Education for extinction: American Indians and the boarding school experience, 1875–1928*. Lawrence, KS: University Press of Kansas.

After the rebellion. (2012). Retrieved from https://www.heinsburg.ca/after-rebellion

Ahmed, S. (2004). *The cultural politics of emotion*. New York, NY: Routledge.

Alexander, K. (2016). Childhood and colonialism in Canadian history. *History Compass, 14*(9), 397–406. https://doi.org/10.1111/hic3.12331

Alexander, M. (2012). *The new Jim Crow: Mass incarceration in the age of colorblindness*. New York, NY: The New Press.

Allen, G. (2014). *Making national news: A history of Canadian Press*. Toronto, ON: University of Toronto Press.

Anderson, B.R.O. (1991). *Imagined communities: Reflections on the origin and spread of nationalism*. London: Verso.

Anderson, M.C., and Robertson, C. (2011). *Seeing red: A history of Natives in Canadian newspapers*. Winnipeg, MB: University of Manitoba Press.

Anuik, J. (2006). Forming civilization at Red River: 19th-century missionary education of Métis and First Nations children. *Prairie Forum, 31*(1), 1–15.

Arfken, G.B., and Pawluk, W.S. (2006). *A Canadian postal history 1897–1911*. Ottawa, ON: British North American Philatelic Society.

Armstrong, J. (1998). Land speaking. In S.J. Ortiz (Ed.), *Speaking for the generations: Native writers on writing* (pp. 174–95). Tucson, AZ: University of Arizona Press.

Banivanua Mar, T. (2010). Carving wilderness: Queensland's national parks and the unsettling of emptied lands, 1890–1910. In T. Banivanua-Mar and P. Edmonds (Eds.), *Making settler colonial space: Perspectives on race, place and identity* (pp. 73–94). Houndmills, UK: Palgrave Macmillan.

Banivanua Mar, T. and Edmonds, P. (Eds.). (2010). *Making settler colonial space: Perspectives on race, place and identity*. Houndmills, UK: Palgrave Macmillan.

Barber, X.T. (1989). Phantasmagorical wonders. *Film History, 3*(2), 73–86.

Barker, V., Giles, H., Noels, K., Duck, J., Hecht, M.L., and Clément, R. (2001). The English-only movement: A Communication analysis of changing perceptions of language vitality. *Journal of Communication, 51*(1), 3–37. https://doi.org/10.1111/j.1460-2466.2001.tb02870.x

Barnes, J. (2013). "The secret of England's greatness": A note on the anti-imperialism of *Such Is Life*. *Journal of the Association for the Study of Australian Literature, 13*(1), 2–11.

Barrera, J. (2013a, May 1). Ottawa fears admission it purposely destroyed Indian residential school files would lead to court fights: Documents. *Aboriginal Peoples Television Network*. Retrieved from http://aptnnews. ca/2013/05/01/ottawa-fears-admission-it-purposely-destroyed-indian-residential-school-files-would-lead-to-court-fights-documents/

– (2013b, May 15). Residential school survivor challenges Valcourt to review archival document destruction record. *Aboriginal Peoples Television Network*. Retrieved from http://aptnnews.ca/2013/05/15/residential-school-survivor-challenges-valcourt-to-review-archival-document-destruction-record/

Bates, B.T. (2001). *Pullman porters and the rise of protest politics in Black America, 1925–1945*. Chapel Hill, NC: University of North Carolina Press. https://doi.org/10.5149/uncp/9780807849293.

Battiste, M. (2000). Maintaining Aboriginal identity, language, and culture in modern society. In *Reclaiming Indigenous voice and vision* (pp. 192–208). Vancouver, BC: UBC Press.

– (2011). Micmac literacy and cognitive assimilation. In M.J. Cannon and L. Sunseri (Eds.), *Racism, colonialism, and Indigeneity in Canada: A reader* (pp. 165–73). Don Mills, ON: Oxford University Press.

Battiste, M., and Barman, J. (1995). *First nations education in Canada: The circle unfolds*. Vancouver, BC: UBC Press.

Bear Nicholas, A. (2011). Linguicide: Submersion education and the killing of languages in Canada. *Briar Patch, 40*(2), 5–8.

Beaumont, M. and Freeman, M.J. (Eds.). (2007). *The railway and modernity: Time, space, and the machine ensemble*. Oxford, UK: Peter Lang.

Bednasek, C.D. (2009). Remembering the File Hills farm colony. *Historical Geography, 37*, 53–70.

Bender, M.C. (2002). *Signs of Cherokee culture: Sequoyah's syllabary in Eastern Cherokee life*. Chapel Hill, NC: University of North Carolina Press.

Blackstock, C. (2007). Residential schools: Did they really close or just morph into child welfare? *Indigenous Law Journal at the University of Toronto Faculty of Law, 6*(1), 71–8.

– (2014, June 21). The government spied on me without a warrant. *Toronto Star*. Retrieved from https://www.thestar.com/opinion/commentary/2014/06/21/the_government_spied_on_me_without_a_warrant.html

Boberg, C. (2010). *The English language in Canada: Status, history and comparative analysis*. Cambridge, UK: Cambridge University Press. https://doi.org/10.1017/CBO9780511781056.

Bogdan, R. (1988). *Freak show: Presenting human oddities for amusement and profit*. Chicago, IL: University of Chicago Press.

Borrows, J. (2002). *Recovering Canada: The resurgence of Indigenous law*. Toronto, ON: University of Toronto Press.

Brady, M.J., and Hiltz, E. (2017). The archaeology of an image: The persistent persuasion of Thomas Moore Keesick's residential school photographs. *Topia, 37*, 61–85. https://doi.org/10.3138/topia.37.61

Brantlinger, P. (2003). *Dark vanishings: Discourse on the extinction of primitive races, 1800–1930*. Ithaca, NY: Cornell University Press.

Brass, J. (2011). Historicizing English pedagogy: The extension and transformation of "the cure of souls." *Pedagogy, Culture and Society, 19*(1), 153–72. https://doi.org/10.1080/14681366.2011.548997

– (2013). Re-reading the emergence of the subject English: Disrupting NCTE's historigraphy. *Journal of Curriculum Theorizing, 29*(1), 102–16.

– (2016). English teaching and the educationalisation of social problems in the United States, 1894–1918. *Paedagogica Historica, 52*(3), 221–35. https://doi.org/10.1080/00309230.2016.1151056

Brooks, L.T. (2008). *The common pot: The recovery of Native space in the Northeast*. Minneapolis, MN: University of Minnesota Press.

Buckner, P.A. (Ed.). (2008). *Canada and the British empire*. Oxford, UK: Oxford University Press.

Buddle, K. (2002). Shooting the messenger: Historical impediments to the mediation of modern Aboriginality in Ontario. *Canadian Journal of Native Studies, 22*(1), 97–160.

– (2001). *From birchbark talk to digital dreamspeaking: A history of Aboriginal media activism in Canada* (Unpublished doctoral dissertation). McMaster University, Hamilton, ON.

Burford-Mason, R. (1996). *Travels in the shining island: The story of James Evans and the invention of the Cree syllabary alphabet*. Toronto, ON: Natural Heritage Books.

Byrne, D. (2010). Nervous landscapes: Race and space in Australia. In T. Banivanua Mar and P. Edmonds (Eds.), *Making settler colonial space: Perspectives on race, place and identity* (pp. 103–28). Houndmills, UK: Palgrave Macmillan. https://doi.org/10.1057/9780230277946_8.

Callison, C., Roy, L., and LeCheminant, G.A. (Eds.). (2016). *Indigenous notions of ownership and libraries, archives and museums*. Berlin: De Gruyter Saur. https://doi.org/10.1515/9783110363234.

Canadian Press (2013, January 30). Ottawa ordered to provide all residential schools documents. *CBC News*. Retrieved from http://www.cbc.ca/news/politics/ottawa-ordered-to-provide-all-residential-schools-documents-1.1345892

Cardinal, H. (1999). *The unjust society.* Vancouver, BC: Douglas and McIntyre.

Carey, J., and Lydon, J. (2014). *Indigenous networks: Mobility, connections and exchange.* New York, NY: Routledge.

Carleton, S. (2016). *Colonialism, capitalism, and the rise of state schooling in British Columbia, 1849–1900* (Unpublished doctoral dissertation). Trent University, Peterborough, ON. Retrieved from http://digitalcollections.trentu.ca/islandora/object/etd%253A373

Carlisle Indian Industrial School. (1915). *The Carlisle Indian School: Catalogue and synopsis of courses.* Carlisle, PA: Carlisle Indian Press.

Carlson, K. (2010). *The power of place, the problem of time: Aboriginal identity and historical consciousness in the cauldron of colonialism.* Toronto, ON: University of Toronto Press.

Carr, G.P. (2011). *"House of no spirit": An architectural history of the Indian residential school in British Columbia* (Unpublished doctoral dissertation). University of British Columbia, Vancouver, BC.

Carter, S. (1990). *Lost harvests: Prairie Indian reserve farmers and government policy.* Montreal, QC: McGill-Queen's University Press.

Chartrand, L.N. (2006). Métis residential school participation: A literature review. In *Métis history and experience and residential schools in Canada* (pp. 5–55). Ottawa, ON: Aboriginal Healing Foundation.

Cheyfitz, E. (1997). *The poetics of imperialism: Translation and colonization from The Tempest to Tarzan.* Philadelphia, PA: University of Pennsylvania Press.

Child, B.J. (1999). *Boarding school seasons: American Indian families, 1900–1940.* Lincoln, NE: University of Nebraska Press.

– (2014a). *My grandfather's knocking sticks: Ojibwe family life and labor on the reservation.* St Paul, MN: Minnesota Historical Society Press.

– (2014b). The boarding school as metaphor. In B.J. Child and B. Klopotek (Eds.), *Indian subjects: Hemispheric perspectives on the history of Indigenous education* (pp. 267–84). Santa Fe, NM: School for Advanced Research Press.

Child, B.J. and Klopotek, B. (Eds.). (2014). *Indian subjects: Hemispheric perspectives on the history of Indigenous education.* Santa Fe, NM: School for Advanced Research Press.

Cho, L. (2013). Redress revisited: Citizenship and the Chinese Canadian head tax. In J. Henderson and P. Wakeham (Eds.), *Reconciling Canada: Critical perspectives on the culture of redress* (pp. 87–99). Toronto, ON: University of Toronto Press.

Chrisjohn, R.D., and Young, S.L. (1997). *The circle game: Shadows and substance in the Indian residential school experience in Canada.* Penticton, BC: Theytus.

Christensen, D. (2000). *Ahtahkakoop: The epic account of a Plains Cree head chief, his people, and their struggle for survival, 1816–1896.* Shell Lake, SK: Ahtahkakoop.

Chrystos. (1994). Savage eloquence. In *Not vanishing* (pp. 40–1). Vancouver, BC: Press Gang.

Claxton, D. (1997). *Buffalo bone China.* Video Out.

Cobb, A.J. (2000). *Listening to our grandmothers' stories: The Bloomfield Academy for Chickasaw Females, 1852–1949.* Lincoln, NE: University of Nebraska Press.

Cobham Brewer, E. (1892). *Character sketches of romance, fiction and drama* (Vol. 1). In Marion Harland (Ed.), *A revised American edition of the reader's handbook.* New York, NY: Selmar Hess.

Cole, D., and Chaikin, I. (1990). *An iron hand upon the people: The law against the Potlatch on the Northwest coast.* Vancouver, BC: Douglas and McIntyre.

Conn, S. (2006). *History's shadow: Native Americans and historical consciousness in the nineteenth century.* Chicago, IL: The University of Chicago Press.

Corntassel, J., Chaw-win-is, and T'lakwadzi. (2009). Indigenous storytelling, truth-telling, and community approaches to reconciliation, *35*(1), 137–59.

Corntassel, J., and Holder, C. (2008). Who's sorry now? Government apologies, truth commissions, and Indigenous self-determination in Australia, Canada, Guatemala, and Peru. *Human Rights Review)*, *9*(4), 465–89. https://doi.org/10.1007/s12142-008-0065-3

Coulthard, G. (2014). *Red skin, white masks: Rejecting the colonial politics of recognition.* Minneapolis, MN: University of Minnesota Press. https://doi.org/10.5749/minnesota/9780816679645.001.0001.

Coward, J.M. (1999). *The newspaper Indian: Native American identity in the press, 1820–90.* Urbana, IL: University of Illinois Press.

Craft, A. (2013). *Breathing life into the Stone Fort Treaty: An Anishinabe understanding of Treaty One.* Saskatoon, SK: Purich.

Creet, M. (1998). Fleming, Sir Sandford. In *Dictionary of Canadian Biography* (Vol. 14). Toronto, ON: University of Toronto/Université Laval. Retrieved from http://www.biographi.ca/en/bio/fleming_sandford_14E.html

Curtis, B. (1990). Some recent work on the history of literacy in Canada. *History of Education Quarterly, 30*(4), 613–24. https://doi.org/10.2307/368949

Cushman, E. (2011). *The Cherokee syllabary writing the people's perseverance.* Norman, OK: University of Oklahoma Press.

Cuthand, D. (2007). Askiwina: A Cree world. Toronto: Coteau Books.

Daschuk, J.W. (2013). *Clearing the Plains: Disease, politics of starvation, and the loss of Aboriginal life.* Regina, SK: University of Regina Press.

Davin, N.F. (1879). *Report on industrial schools for Indians and half-breeds*. Ottawa, ON. Retrieved from http://eco.canadiana.ca/view/oocihm.03651/1?r=0&s=1

Davis, J.E. (2010). *Hand talk: Sign language among American Indian nations*. New York, NY: Cambridge University Press.

Day, I. (2015). Being or nothingness. *Critical Ethnic Studies, 1*(2), 102–21. https://doi.org/10.5749/jcritethnstud.1.2.0102

– (2016). *Alien capital*. Durham, NC: Duke University Press. https://doi.org/10.1215/9780822374527.

Dean, M. (2013). *Inheriting a canoe paddle: The canoe in discourses of English-Canadian nationalism*. Toronto, ON: University of Toronto Press.

de Leeuw, S. (2007). Intimate colonialisms: The material and experienced places of British Columbia's residential schools. *Canadian Geographer. Geographe Canadien, 51*(3), 339–59. https://doi.org/10.1111/j.1541-0064.2007.00183.x

Deloria, P.J. (1998). *Playing Indian*. New Haven, CT: Yale University Press.

– (2004). *Indians in unexpected places*. Lawrence, KS: University Press of Kansas.

– (1988). *Custer died for your sins: An Indian manifesto*. Norman, OK: University of Oklahoma Press.

– (2003). *God is red: A native view of religion*. Golden, CO: Fulcrum.

Dempsey, H.A. (1990). *Natos-Api. Dictionary of Canadian biography* (Vol. 12). Toronto, ON: University of Toronto/Université Laval. Retrieved from http://www.biographi.ca/en/bio/natos_api_12E.html

Diabo, R., and Pasternak, S. (2011, June 7). First Nations under surveillance. *Media Co-op*. Retrieved from http://www.mediacoop.ca/story/first-nations-under-surveillance/7434

Dillon, G.L. (Ed.). (2012). *Walking the clouds: An anthology of Indigenous science fiction*. Tucson, AZ: University of Arizona Press.

Dimaline, C. (2017). *The marrow thieves*. Toronto, ON: Cormorant.

Di Mascio, A., and Hortop-Di Mascio, L. (2011). Residential schooling in the Arctic: A historical case study and perspective. *Native Studies Review, 20*(2), 31–49.

DiNova, J. (2012). *Spiraling webs of relation: Movements toward an Indigenist criticism*. London: Routledge.

Dion, S.D. (2009). *Braiding histories*. Vancouver, BC: UBC Press.

Di Paolantonio, M. (2000). Loss in present terms: Reading the limits of post-dictatorship Argentina's national conciliation. In R.I. Simon, S.

Rosenberg, and C. Eppert (Eds.), *Between hope and despair: Pedagogy and the remembrance of historical trauma* (pp. 153–86). Lanham, MD: Rowman and Littlefield.

Donald, D. (2004). Edmonton pentimento: Re-reading history in the case of the Papaschase Cree. *Journal of the Canadian Association for Curriculum Studies, 2*(1), 21–53.

Donaldson, L.E. (1998). Writing the talking stick: Alphabetic literacy as colonial technology and postcolonial appropriation. *American Indian Quarterly, 22*(1/2), 46–62.

Dumont, M. (1996). *A really good brown girl.* London, ON: Brick.

– (2007a). *That tongued belonging.* Wiarton, ON: Kegodonce.

– (2007b). That tongued belonging. In *That tongued belonging.* Wiarton, ON: Kegodonce.

Dunae, P.A. (1980). Boys' literature and the idea of empire, 1870–1914. *Victorian Studies, 24*(1), 105–21.

Dunbar-Ortiz, R. (2014). *An Indigenous peoples' history of the United States.* Boston, MA: Beacon.

Durham, S. (1998). *Phantom communities: The simulacrum and the limits of postmodernism.* Stanford, CA: Stanford University Press.

Eastman, E. (1935). *Pratt: The red man's Moses.* Norman, OK: University of Oklahoma Press.

Edwards, B. (2005). *Paper talk: A history of libraries, print culture, and aboriginal peoples in Canada before 1960.* Lanham, MD: Scarecrow.

Edwards, E. (2006). *Raw histories: Photographs, anthropology and museums.* Oxford, UK: Berg.

Edwards, G. (2001). *Creating textual communities: Anglican and Methodist missionaries and print culture in British Columbia, 1858–1914* (Unpublished doctoral dissertation). University of British Columbia, Vancouver, BC.

Edwards, J. (Ed.). (1998). *Language in Canada.* Cambridge, UK: Cambridge University Press. https://doi.org/10.1017/CBO9780511620829.

Eisenstein, E.L. (2005). *The printing revolution in early modern Europe.* Cambridge, UK: Cambridge University Press. https://doi.org/10.1017/CBO9780511819230.

Elkhorn and District Historical Society. (1982). *Steel and grass roots.* Elkhorn, MB: Elkhorn and District Historical Society.

Ellis, C. (1996). *To change them forever: Indian education at the Rainy Mountain Boarding School, 1893–1920.* Norman, OK: University of Oklahoma Press.

Emery, J. (2012). Writing against erasure: Native American students at Hampton Institute and the periodical press. *American Periodicals: A Journal*

of History. Criticism, and Bibliography, 22(2), 178–98. https://doi.org/10.1353/
amp.2012.0017

Episkenew, J.-A. (2009). *Taking back our spirits: Indigenous literature, public policy,
and healing.* Winnipeg, MB: University of Manitoba Press.

Esmail, J. (2013). *Reading Victorian deafness: Signs and sounds in Victorian
literature and culture.* Athens, OH: Ohio University Press.

Evans, B., and Glass, A. (2014). *Return to the land of the head hunters: Edward S.
Curtis, the Kwakwa̱ka̱'wakw, and the making of modern cinema.* Seattle, WA:
University of Washington Press.

Evans, S. (Ed.). (2006). *The borderlands of the American and Canadian Wests:
Essays on regional history of the forty-ninth parallel.* Lincoln, NE: University of
Nebraska Press.

Fabian, J. (2014). *Time and the other: How anthropology makes its object.* New
York, NY: Columbia University Press. https://doi.org/10.7312/fabi16926.

Fahey, A., and Horton, C. (2012). "The iron pulpit": Missionary printing
presses in British Columbia. Retrieved from http://rbsc.library.ubc.ca/
files/2013/09/Iron_Pulpit_Exhibition.pdf

Fanon, F. (2008). *Black Skin, White Masks.* New York: Grove Press.

Fear-Segal, J. (2004). Eyes in the text: Marianna Burgess and The Indian
helper. In S.M. Harris and E.G. Garvey (Eds.), *Blue pencils and hidden
hands: Women editing periodicals, 1830–1910* (pp. 123–45). Boston, MA:
Northeastern University Press.

– (2007). *White man's club: Schools, race, and the struggle of Indian acculturation.*
Lincoln, NE: University of Nebraska Press.

Fee, M. and Nason, D. (Eds.). (2015). Introduction to *Tekahionwake: E. Pauline
Johnson's writings on Native North America.* Peterborough, ON: Broadview.

Fendler, L. (2008). The upside of presentism. *Paedagogica Historica, 44*(6), 677–
90. https://doi.org/10.1080/00309230802486150

Fetherling, G. (1990). *The rise of the Canadian newspaper.* Toronto, ON: Oxford
University Press.

Fiske, J.-A. (2009). Placing violence against First Nations children: The use
of space and place to construct the (in)credible violated subject. In L.J.
Kirmayer and G.G. Valaskakis (Eds.), *Healing traditions* (pp. 140–59).
Vancouver, BC: UBC Press.

Fleming, P., Lamonde, Y., and Black, F.A. (2005). *History of the book in Canada:
Vol. 2. 1840–1918.* Toronto, ON: University of Toronto Press.

Fontaine, L., Leitch, D., Nicholas, A.B., and de Varennes, F. (2017). *What
Canada's new Indigenous languages law needs to say and say urgently.* National
Observatory on Language Rights. Retrieved from http://odl.openum.ca/
files/sites/68/2017/06/DavidLeitch_notes.pdf

Fontaine, L.S. (2017). Redress for linguicide: Residential schools and assimilation in Canada. *British Journal of Canadian Studies, 30*(2), 183–204. https://doi.org/10.3828/bjcs.2017.11

Fontaine, T. (2010). *Broken circle: The dark legacy of Indian residential schools.* Surrey, BC: Heritage House.

– (2014, July). Eleventh Conference of the International Association of Genocide Scholars. Winnipeg, Manitoba. Quoted with permission.

Forbes, W. (2012). Print industry. In *Canadian Encyclopedia.* Retrieved from https://www.thecanadianencyclopedia.ca/en/article/print-industry

Forsyth, J., and Heine, M. (2017). "The only good thing that happened at school": Colonising narratives of sport in the Indian school bulletin. *British Journal of Canadian Studies, 30*(2), 205–25. https://doi.org/10.3828/bjcs.2017.12

Forsyth, J., and Te Hiwi, B. (2017). "A rink at the school is almost as essential as a classroom": Hockey and discipline at Pelican Lake Indian Residential School, 1945–1951. *Canadian Journal of History, 52*(1), 80–108. https://doi.org/10.3138/cjh.ach.52.1.04

Fournier, S., and Crey, E. (2006). "Killing the Indian in the child": Four centuries of church-run schools. In R. Maaka and C. Andersen (Eds.), *The Indigenous experience: Global perspectives* (pp. 141–49). Toronto, ON: Canadian Scholars' Press.

Francis, M. (2011). *Creative subversions: Whiteness, Indigeneity and the national imaginary.* Vancouver, BC: UBC Press. Retrieved from http://search.ebscohost.com/login.aspx?direct=true&scope=site&db=nlebk&db=nlabk&AN=434736.

Fraser, C., and Todd, Z. (2016). Decolonial sensibilities: Indigenous research and engaging with archives in contemporary colonial Canada. *L'Internationale.* Retrieved from http://www.internationaleonline.org/research/decolonising_practices/54_decolonial_sensibilities_indigenous_research_and_engaging_with_archives_in_contemporary_colonial_canada

Freeman, V. (2003). Voices of the parents: The Shoal Lake Anishinabe and Cecilia Jeffrey Indian Residential School 1902–1929. In J.E. Oakes (Ed.), *Native voices in research* (pp. 71–81). Winnipeg, MB: Aboriginal Issues Press.

Gallop, T. (2016, January 18). New initiative launched at SFU to save Squamish language. *SFU News.* Retrieved from https://www.sfu.ca/sfunews/stories/2016/new-initiative-launched-at-sfu-to-save-squamish-language.html

Galloway, G. (2015, July 8). AFN asks Ottawa to declare all Aboriginal languages official. *The Globe and Mail.*

Garland, D. (2014). What is a "history of the present"? On Foucault's genealogies and their critical preconditions. *Punishment and Society, 16*(4), 365–84. https://doi.org/10.1177/1462474514541711

Geary, A. (2017, September 18). Ignored to death: Brian Sinclair's death caused by racism, inquest inadequate, group says. *CBC News.* Retrieved from https://www.cbc.ca/news/canada/manitoba/winnipeg-brian-sinclair-report-1.4295996

Gehl, L. (2014). *The truth that wampum tells: My debwewin on the Algonquin land claims process.* Halifax, NS: Fernwood.

General Synod Archives. Call number MM29.7 G59. Retrieved from https://www.anglican.ca/archives/

Ghaddar, J. J. (2016). The spectre in the archive: Truth, reconciliation, and Indigenous archival memory. *Archivaria, 82,* 3–26.

Giasson, P. (2004). *The typographic inception of the Cherokee syllabary.* (Unpublished master's thesis), University of Reading, United Kingdom.

Gibson, L. (1990). Bedson, Samuel Lawrence. *Dictionary of Canadian Biography* (Vol. 12). Toronto, ON: University of Toronto/Université Laval. Retrieved from http://www.biographi.ca/en/bio/bedson_samuel_lawrence_12E.html

Gidley, M. (2003). *Edward S. Curtis and the North American Indian project in the field.* Lincoln, NE: University of Nebraska Press.

Gidney, R.D. (2003). Ryerson, Egerton. In *Dictionary of Canadian Biography* (Vol. 11). Toronto, ON: University of Toronto/Université Laval; Retrieved from http://www.biographi.ca/en/bio/ryerson_egerton_11E.html.

Glassberg, D. (1990). *American historical pageantry: The uses of tradition in the early twentieth century.* Chapel Hill, NC: University of North Carolina Press.

Goeman, M. (2013). *Mark my words: Native women mapping our nations.* Minneapolis, MN: University of Minnesota Press. https://doi.org/10.5749/minnesota/9780816677900.001.0001.

Goodburn, A. (1999). Literacy practices at the Genoa Industrial Indian School. *Great Plains Quarterly, 19*(1), 35–52.

Goutor, D. (2011). *Guarding the gates: The Canadian labour movement and immigration, 1872–1934.* Vancouver, BC: UBC Press.

Graff, H.J. (1987). *The legacies of literacy. Continuities and contradictions in Western culture and society.* Bloomington: Indiana University Press.

Grech, S., and Soldatic, K. (2015). Disability and colonialism: (Dis)encounters and anxious intersectionalities. *Social Identities, 21*(1), 1–5. https://doi.org/10.1080/13504630.2014.995394

Green, A.J. (2006). Telling 1922s story of a national crime: Canada's first chief medical officer and the aborted fight for Aboriginal health care. *Canadian Journal of Native Studies, 26*(2), 211–28.

Green, B., Cormack, P., and Patterson, A. (2013). Re-reading the reading lesson: Episodes in the history of reading pedagogy. *Oxford Review of Education*, *39*(3), 329–44. https://doi.org/10.1080/03054985.2013.808617

Grenoble, L.A., and Whaley, L.J. (2006). *Saving languages: An introduction to language revitalization*. Cambridge, UK: Cambridge University Press.

Griffith, J. (2015). One little, two little, three Canadians: The Indians of Canada pavilion and public pedagogy, Expo 1967. *Journal of Canadian Studies. Revue d'Etudes Canadiennes*, *49*(2), 171–204. https://doi.org/10.3138/jcs.49.2.171

– (In press). Settler colonial archives: Some Canadian contexts. *Settler Colonial Studies*, 1–21. https://doi.org/10.1080/2201473X.2018.1454699

Hackett, P., Abonyi, S., and Dyck, R.F. (2016). Anthropometric indices of First Nations children and youth on first entry to Manitoba/Saskatchewan residential schools – 1919 to 1953. *International Journal of Circumpolar Health*, *75*(30734), 1–9.

Haig-Brown, C. (1988). *Resistance and renewal: Surviving the Indian residential school*. Vancouver, BC: Tillacum.

Hall, D. (2009). Clifford Sifton and Canadian Indian administration, 1896–1905. In G.P. Marchildon (Ed.), *Immigration and settlement, 1870–1939* (pp. 183–212). Regina, SK: University of Regina.

Hall, S. (2007). Encoding/decoding. In Simon During (Ed.), *The cultural studies reader* (pp. 90–103). London, UK: Routledge.

Haller, B. (1993). The little papers: Newspapers at nineteenth-century schools for deaf persons. *Journalism History*, *19*(2), 43–51.

Halliday, W.M. (1935). *Potlatch and totem*. London, ON; Toronto, ON: J. M. Dent and Sons.

Hancock, R.L.A. (2006). Toward a historiography of Canadian anthropology. In R. Darnell and J.D. Harrison (Eds.), *Historicizing Canadian anthropology* (pp. 30–40). Vancouver, BC: UBC Press.

Haque, E. (2012). *Multiculturalism within a bilingual framework: Language, race, and belonging in Canada*. Toronto, ON: University of Toronto Press.

Hare, J. (2009). To "know papers": Aboriginal perspectives on literacy. In J. Anderson, M. Kendrick, T. Rogers, and S. Smythe (Eds.), *Portraits of literacy across families, communities, and schools: Intersections and tensions* (pp. 243–64). New Jersey, NJ: Taylor and Francis.

Harjo, J., and Bird, G. (1997). *Reinventing the enemy's language: Contemporary native women's writing of North America*. New York, NY: Norton.

Harmon, A. (Ed.). (2008). *The power of promises: Rethinking Indian treaties in the Pacific Northwest*. Seattle, WA: University of Washington Press.

Harris, V. (2002). The archival sliver: Power, memory, and archives in South Africa. *Archival Science*, *2*(1–2), 63–86. https://doi.org/10.1007/BF02435631

Hayday, M. (2015). *So they want us to learn French: Promoting and opposing bilingualism in English-speaking Canada.* Vancouver: UBC Press.

Heller, M., and McElhinny, B. S. (2017). *Language, colonialism, capitalism: Towards a critical history.*

Henderson, J. and Wakeham, P. (Eds.). (2013). *Reconciling Canada: Critical perspectives on the culture of redress.* Toronto, ON: University of Toronto Press.

Higham, C.L. (2000). *Noble, wretched and redeemable: Protestant missionaries to the Indians in Canada and the United States, 1820–1900* (1st ed.). Albuquerque, NM: University of New Mexico Press.

Hildebrandt, W. (1994). Laurie, Patrick Gammie. In *Dictionary of Canadian Biography* (Vol. 13). Toronto, ON: University of Toronto/Université Laval. Retrieved from http://www.biographi.ca/en/bio/laurie_patrick_gammie_13E.html

Hill, R. W. (2002, September). The unreadable present: Nadia Myre and Kent Monkman. *C Magazine.*

Hill, R.W., Sr. (2007). Regenerating identity: Repatriation and the Indian frame of mind. In S.E.R. Watson (Ed.), *Museums and their communities* (pp. 313–23). London, UK: Routledge.

Hochman, B. (2014). *Savage preservation: The ethnographic origins of modern media technology.* Minneapolis, MN: University of Minnesota Press. https://doi.org/10.5749/minnesota/9780816681372.001.0001.

Hoelscher, S.D. (2008). *Picturing Indians: Photographic encounters and tourist fantasies in H.H. Bennett's Wisconsin Dells.* Madison, WI: University of Wisconsin Press.

Hogue, M. (2015). *Metis and the medicine line: Creating a border and dividing a people.* Chapel Hill, NC: University of North Carolina Press. https://doi.org/10.5149/northcarolina/9781469621050.001.0001.

Houston, R. (2014). *Literacy in early modern Europe.* London, UK: Routledge.

Hubbard, T. (2009). "The buffaloes are gone" or "return: buffalo"? – The relationship of the buffalo to Indigenous creative expression. *Canadian Journal of Native Studies, 29*(1 and 2), 65–85.

– (2014). Buffalo genocide in nineteenth-century North America: "Kill, Skin, and Sell." In A. Woolford, J. Benvenuto, and A. Hinton (Eds.), *Colonial genocide in indigenous North America* (pp. 292–305). Durham, NC: Duke University Press. https://doi.org/10.1215/9780822376149-014.

Huebener, P. (2016). *Timing Canada: The shifting politics of time in Canadian literary culture.* Montreal, QC: McGill-Queen's University Press.

Hutchinson, G.M. (1977). James Evans' last year. *Journal of the Canadian Church Historical Society, 19*(1–2), 42–56.

Hyslop, K. (2015, February 18). Marking the end of a "dark era." *The Tyee.*

Ignace, M., and Ignace, R.E. (2017). *Secwépemc people, land, and laws*. Montreal, QC: McGill Queens University Press.

Iozzo, A. (2015). *"Silent Citizens": Citizenship education, disability and d/Deafness at the Ontario Institution for the Education of the Deaf, 1870–1914* (Unpublished doctoral dissertation). University of Ottawa, Ottawa, ON.

Iyengar, M.M. (2014). Not mere abstractions: Language policies and language ideologies in US settler colonialism. *Decolonization, 3*(2), 33–59.

Jaenen, C.J. (2006). Aboriginal communities. In Y. Lamonde, P. Lockhart Fleming, and F.A. Black (Eds.), *History of the book in Canada/Histoire du livre et de l'edition au Canada* (Vol. 2, pp. 33–40). Toronto, ON: University of Toronto Press.

Joe, R. (1989). I lost my talk. *Canadian Women's Studies, 10*(2/3), 28.

Johns, D. (2011). Merging the private past with public perception: John Hines's missionary journals and the Red Indians of the Plains. *Journal of Canadian Studies. Revue d'Etudes Canadiennes, 45*(3), 109–36. https://doi.org/10.3138/jcs.45.3.109

Johnson, E.P. (1894, June 21). Fate of the red man. *Ottawa Daily Free Press*, p. 3.

– (2015). As it was in the beginning (pp. 193–200); His sister's son (p. 201); Little wolf-willow (p. 201–12). In M. Fee and D. Nason (Eds.), *Tekahionwake: E. Pauline Johnson's writings on Native North America*. Peterborough, ON: Broadview.

Johnston, B. (1989). *Indian school days*. Norman, OK: University of Oklahoma Press.

Justice, D.H. (2006). *Our fire survives the storm: A Cherokee literary history*. Minneapolis, MN: University of Minnesota Press.

Katanski, A.V. (2005). *Learning to write "Indian": The boarding-school experience and American Indian literature*. Norman, OK: University of Oklahoma Press.

Kelley, R.D.G. (1993). "We are not what we seem": Rethinking Black working-class opposition in the Jim Crow South. *Journal of American History, 80*(1), 75–112. https://doi.org/10.2307/2079698

Kelm, M.-E. (1999). *Colonizing bodies: Aboriginal health and healing in British Columbia, 1900–1950*. Vancouver, BC: UBC Press.

– (Ed.). (2006). *The letters of Margaret Butcher: Missionary-imperialism on the North Pacific Coast*. Calgary, AB: University of Calgary Press.

Kelsey, P.M. (2014). *Reading the wampum: Essays on Hodinöhsö:ni' visual code and epistemological recovery*. Syracuse, NY: Syracuse University Press.

King, T. (2014). Labor's aphasia: Toward antiblackness as constitutive to settler colonialism. *Decolonization*. Retrieved from https://decolonization.wordpress.com/2014/06/10/labors-aphasia-toward-antiblackness-as-constitutive-to-settler-colonialism/

Knockwood, I. (1992). *Out of the depths: The experiences of Mi'kmaw children at the Indian Residential School at Shubenacadie, Nova Scotia.* Lockeport, NS: Roseway.

Krehbiel, H. E. (1897, July 11). The Iroquois wampum: An ancient treasure that has disappeared. *New York Tribune*, p. 31.

Ladner, K.L. (2014). Political genocide: Killing nations through legislation and slow-moving poison. In A. Woolford, J. Benvenuto, and A.L. Hinton (Eds.), *Colonial genocide in Indigenous North America* (pp. 226–45). Durham, NC: Duke University Press. https://doi.org/10.1215/9780822376149-011.

Ladner, K.L. and Tait, M. (Eds.). (2017). *Surviving Canada: Indigenous peoples celebrate 150 years of betrayal.* Winnipeg, MB: ARP Books.

LaDow, B. (2002). *The medicine line: Life and death on a North American borderland.* New York, NY: Routledge.

Lakritz, N. (2015, July 11). More money won't save Aboriginal languages. *Calgary Herald.* Retrieved from https://calgaryherald.com/opinion/columnists/lakritz-more-money-wont-save-aboriginal-languages

Latour, B. (1993). *We have never been modern.* Cambridge, MA: Harvard University Press.

Laville, C. (2004). Historical consciousness and historical education: What to expect from the first for the second. In P.C. Seixas (Ed.), *Theorizing historical consciousness* (pp. 165–82). Toronto, ON: University of Toronto Press.

Lawrence, B. (2003). Gender, race, and the regulation of Native identity in Canada and the United States: An overview. *Hypatia, 18*(2), 3–31. https://doi.org/10.1111/j.1527-2001.2003.tb00799.x

Lightfoot, S. (2015). Settler state apologies to Indigenous peoples: A normative framework and comparative assessment. *Native American and Indigenous Studies, 2*(1), 15–39. https://doi.org/10.5749/natiindistudj.2.1.0015

Lindsey, D.F. (1995). *Indians at Hampton Institute, 1877–1923.* Urbana, IL: University of Illinois Press.

Littlefield, D.F., and Parins, J.W. (1984). *American Indian and Alaska Native newspapers and periodicals* (Vol. 1). Westport, CT: Greenwood.

Lomawaima, K.T. (1995). *They called it Prairie light: The story of Chilocco Indian School.* Lincoln, NE: University of Nebraska Press.

– (2014). "All our people are building houses": The civilization of architecture and space in federal Indian boarding schools. In B.J. Child and B. Klopotek (Eds.), *Indian subjects: Hemispheric perspectives on the history of Indigenous education* (pp. 148–76). Santa Fe, NM: School for Advanced Research Press.

Long, J. (2010). *Treaty No. 9: Making the agreement to share the land in Far Northern Ontario in 1905.* Montreal,QC: McGill-Queen's University Press.

– (2006). Making Native language policy in Ontario in the 1980s. *Historical Studies in Education, 18*(2), 135–62.

Lowe, L. (2015). *The intimacies of four continents.* Durham,NC: Duke University Press. https://doi.org/10.1215/9780822375647.

Lowman, E.B. (2017). Mamook Kom'tax Chinuk Pipa / Learning to write Chinook jargon: Indigenous peoples and literacy strategies in the south central interior of British Columbia in the late 19th century. *Historical Studies in Education, 29*(1), 77–98.

Lux, M.K. (2001). *Medicine that walks: Disease, medicine, and Canadian Plains Native people, 1880:1940.* Toronto, ON: University of Toronto.

– (2016). *Separate beds: A history of Indian hospitals in Canada, 1920s–1980s.* Toronto, ON: University of Toronto Press.

Lyons, S.R. (2009). The fine art of fencing: Nationalism, hybridity, and the search for a Native American writing pedagogy. *Journal of Advanced Composition, 29*(1/2), 77–105.

– (2010). *X-marks: Native signatures of assent.* Minneapolis, MN: University of Minnesota Press. https://doi.org/10.5749/minnesota/9780816666768.001.0001.

Mabel Harry-Fontaine. (n.d.). Retrieved from wherearethechildren.ca/en/stories/#story_7.

Macdonald, N. (2016, February 18). Canada's prisons are the "new residential schools." *Maclean's.* Retrieved from https://www.macleans.ca/news/canada/canadas-prisons-are-the-new-residential-schools/

Mackay, C. (1892). There's a good time coming. In C. Fiske Bates (Ed.), *The Cambridge book of poetry and song* (p. 363). New York, NY: Thomas Y. Cromwell.

Mackey, E. (2013). The apologizers' apology. In J. Henderson & P. Wakeham (Eds.), *Reconciling Canada: Critical perspectives on the culture of redress* (pp. 47–62). Toronto: University of Toronto Press.

Malmsheimer, L.M. (1985). "Imitation white man": Images of transformation at the Carlisle Indian School. *Studies in Visual Communication, 11*(4), 54–75. https://doi.org/10.1111/j.2326-8492.1985.tb00135.x

Marker, M. (2006). After the Makah whale hunt: Indigenous knowledge and limits to multicultural discourse. *Urban Education, 41*(5), 482–505. https://doi.org/10.1177/0042085906291923

Martin, G. (2011). *Britain and the origins of Canadian confederation.* Vancouver, BC: UBC Press.

Martin, L.-A. (2012, March 6). Out in the cold: An Interview with Rebecca Belmore. *Canadian Art,* 78–81.

Mary Battaja. (n.d.). Retrieved from http://wherearethechildren.ca/en/stories/#story_3

Mason, C.W. (2014). *Spirits of the Rockies: Reasserting an Indigenous presence in Banff National Park.* Toronto, ON: University of Toronto Press.

Mathieu, S.-J. (2010). *North of the color line: Migration and Black resistance in Canada, 1870–1955.* Chapel Hill, NC: University of North Carolina Press. https://doi.org/10.5149/9780807899397_mathieu.

Mawani, R. (2002). In between and out of place: Mixed-race identity, liquor, and the law in British Columbia, 1850–1913. In S. Razack (Ed.), *Race, space, and the law: Unmapping a white settler society* (pp. 47–70). Toronto, ON: Between the Lines.

Mbembe, A. (2002). The power of the archive and its limits. In C. Hamilton, V. Harris, J. Taylor, M. Pickover, G. Reid, and R. Saleh (Eds.), *Refiguring the archive* (pp. 19–27). Dordrecht: Springer Netherlands. https://doi.org/10.1007/978-94-010-0570-8_2.

McCall, S. (2011). *First person plural: Aboriginal storytelling and the ethics of collaborative authorship.* Vancouver, BC: UBC Press.

McCarthy, T. (2010). Dę'ni:s nisa'sgao'dę?: Haudenosaunee clans and the reconstruction of traditional Haudenosaunee identity, citizenship, and nationhood. *American Indian Culture and Research Journal, 34*(2), 81–101. https://doi.org/10.17953/aicr.34.2.yv6n3n601523m65k

McClintock, A. (1995). *Imperial leather: Race, gender, and sexuality in the colonial contest.* New York, NY: Routledge.

McCrady, D.G. (2006). *Living with strangers: The nineteenth-century Sioux and the Canadian-American borderlands.* Lincoln, NE: University of Nebraska Press.

McCullough, A.B. (2005). Peyasiw-awasis. *Dictionary of Canadian Biography* (Vol. 15). Toronto, ON: University of Toronto/Université Laval. Retrieved from http://www.biographi.ca/en/bio/peyasiw_awasis_15E.html

McGregor, H.E. (2015). Listening for more (hi)stories from the Arctic's dispersed and diverse educational past. *Historical Studies in Education, 27*(1), 19–39.

McKegney, S. (2007). *Magic weapons: Aboriginal writers remaking community after residential school.* Winnipeg, MB: University of Manitoba Press.

McKittrick, K. and Woods, C.A. (Eds.). (2007). *Black geographies and the politics of place.* Toronto, ON: Between the Lines.

McLaren, K. (2008). "We had no desire to be set apart": Forced segregation of Black students in Canada West public schools and myths of British egalitarianism. In B. Walker (Ed.), *The history of immigration and racism in Canada: Essential readings* (pp. 69–80). Toronto, ON: Canadian Scholars' Press.

McLean, J. (1890). *James Evans: Inventor of the syllabic system of the Cree language.* Toronto, ON: William Briggs.

McManus, S. (2005). *The line which separates: Race, gender, and the making of the Alberta-Montana borderlands.* Lincoln, NE: University of Nebraska Press.

Medway, P., and Goodson, I. (1990). *Bringing English to order: The history and politics of a school subject.* London, UK: Taylor and Francis.

Merasty, J.A. (2015). *The education of Augie Merasty.* Regina, SK: University of Regina Press.

Metatawabin, E. (2014). *Up Ghost River.* Toronto, ON: Vintage.

Miller, J.L. (2011). The Papaschase band: Building awareness and community in the city of Edmonton. In C. Proulx and H.A. Howard (Eds.), *Aboriginal peoples in Canadian cities: Transformations and continuities* (pp. 53–68). Waterloo, ON: Wilfrid Laurier University Press.

Miller, J.R. (1996a). *Compact, contract, covenant.* Toronto, ON: University of Toronto Press.

– (1996b). *Shingwauk's vision: A history of Native residential schools.* Toronto, ON: University of Toronto Press.

– (2003). Reading photographs, reading voices: Documenting the history of Native residential school. In J.S.H. Brown and E. Vibert (Eds.), *Reading beyond words: Contexts for Native history* (pp. 461–81). Peterborough, ON: Broadview.

– (2000). Exercising cultural self-determination: The Makah Indian tribe goes whaling. *American Indian Law Review, 25*(2), 165–273.

Million, D. (2011). Intense dreaming: Theories, narratives, and our search for home. *American Indian Quarterly, 35*(3), 313–33. https://doi.org/10.5250/amerindiquar.35.3.0313

– (2013). *Therapeutic nations: Healing in an age of Indigenous human rights.* Tucson, AZ: University of Arizona Press.

Milloy, J. (1999). *A national crime: The Canadian government and the residential school system, 1879 to 1986.* Winnipeg, MB: University of Manitoba Press.

Milroy, S., and Hubbard, T. (2015). *Kent Monkman: The rise and fall of civilization.* Toronto, ON: Gardiner Museum.

Monaghan, J. (2013). Mounties in the frontier: Circulations, anxieties, and myths of settler colonial policing in Canada. *Journal of Canadian Studies. Revue d'Etudes Canadiennes, 47*(1), 122–48. https://doi.org/10.3138/jcs.47.1.122

Monaghan, J.E. (2005). *Learning to read and write in colonial America.* Amherst, MA: University of Massachusetts Press.

Monchalin, L. (2016). *The colonial problem: An Indigenous perspective on crime and injustice in Canada.* Toronto, ON: University of Toronto Press.

Monkman, K. (2015). *Sisters and brothers.* National Film Board of Canada. Retrieved from https://www.nfb.ca/film/sisters_brothers/

Moreton-Robinson, A. (2015). *The white possessive*. Minneapolis, MN: University of Minnesota Press. https://doi.org/10.5749/minnesota/9780816692149.001.0001.

Morgan, L.H (1877). *Ancient society*. New York, NY: Henry Holt.

Morgan, M.J. (2009). *The bearer of this letter: Language ideologies, literacy practices, and the Fort Belknap Indian community*. Lincoln, NE: University of Nebraska Press. https://doi.org/10.2307/j.cttldfnv7d.

Morgensen, S. (2014, May 26). White settlers and Indigenous solidarity: Confronting white supremacy, answering decolonial alliances. Retrieved from https://decolonization.wordpress.com/2014/05/26/white-settlers-and-indigenous-solidarity-confronting-white-supremacy-answering-decolonial-alliances/

Morrison, T. (1992). *Playing in the dark: Whiteness and the literary imagination*. Cambridge, MA: Harvard University Press.

Mosby, I. (2013). Nutrition research and human biomedical experimentation in Aboriginal communities and residential schools, 1942–1952. *Social History, 46*(91), 145–72.

Mosby, I., and Galloway, T. (2017). "The abiding condition was hunger": Assessing the long-term biological and health effects of malnutrition and hunger in Canada's residential schools. *British Journal of Canadian Studies, 30*(2), 147–62. https://doi.org/10.3828/bjcs.2017.9

Mosher, J.S. (2016). The Protestant reading ethic and variation in its effects. *Sociological Forum, 31*(2), 397–418. https://doi.org/10.1111/socf.12250

Muñoz, J.E. (2007). "Chico, what does it feel like to be a problem?": The transmission of brownness. In J. Flores and R. Rosaldo (Eds.), *A companion to Latina/o studies* (pp. 441–51). Malden, MA: Blackwell.

Mussell, J. (2012). *The nineteenth-century press in the digital age*. New York, NY: Palgrave Macmillan. https://doi.org/10.1057/9780230365469.

Nagy, R., and Gillespie, E. (2015). Representing reconciliation: A news frame analysis of print media coverage of Indian residential schools. *Transitional Justice Review, 1*(3), 3–41.

Natcher, D.C., Walker, R.C., and Jojola, T.S. (2013). *Reclaiming Indigenous planning*. Montreal, QC: McGill-Queen's University Press.

Neu, D., and Therrien, R. (2003). *Accounting for genocide: Canada's bureaucratic assault on Aboriginal people*. Black Point, NS: Fernwood Publishing.

Neylan, S., and Meyer, M. (2006). "Here comes the band!": Cultural collaboration, connective traditions, and Aboriginal brass bands on British Columbia's North Coast, 1875–1964. *BC Studies* (152): 35–77.

Ngugi wa Thiong'o. (2005). *Decolonising the mind: The politics of language in African literature*. Oxford, UK: Currey.

Niezen, R. (2013). *Truth and indignation: Canada's Truth and Reconciliation Commission on Indian residential schools.* Toronto, ON: University of Toronto Press.

Nock, D.A. (1976). The Canadian Indian Research and Aid Society: A Victorian voluntary association. *Western Canadian Journal of Anthropology, 6*(2), 31–48.

– (1988). *A Victorian missionary and Canadian Indian policy: Cultural synthesis vs. cultural replacement.* Waterloo, ON: Wilfrid Laurier University Press.

Norman, A. (2017). "Teachers amongst their own people": Kanyen'kehá:ka (Mohawk) women teachers in nineteenth-century Tyendinaga and Grand River, Ontario. *Historical Studies in Education, 29*(1), 32–56.

O'Brien, J.M. (2010). *Firsting and lasting.* Minneapolis, MN: University of Minnesota Press. https://doi.org/10.5749/minnesota/9780816665778.001.0001.

The 180. (2015, July 10). *CBC Radio.* Retrieved from https://www.cbc.ca/radio/the180/wildfires-fight-or-flight-are-referendums-bad-for-democracy-the-lost-art-of-parallel-parking-1.3143601/do-first-nations-have-a-right-to-indigenous-language-schools-1.3143926

Oreopoulos, P. (2005). *Canadian compulsory school laws and their impact on educational attainment and future earnings.* Ottawa, ON: Statistics Canada.

Ortiz, S.J. (2004). *Beyond the reach of time and change: Native American reflections on the Frank A. Rinehart photograph collection.* Tucson. AZ: University of Arizona Press.

Palmater, P.D. (2011). *Beyond blood: Rethinking Indigenous identity.* Saskatoon, SK: Purich Publishing.

Pasternak, S. (2016). The fiscal body of sovereignty: To "make live" in Indian country. *Settler Colonial Studies, 6*(4), 317–38. https://doi.org/10.1080/2201473X.2015.1090525

– (2017). *Grounded authority: The Algonquins of Barriere Lake against the state.* Minneapolis, MN: University of Minnesota Press.

Patterson, A., Cormack, P.A., and Green, W.C. (2012). The child, the text and the teacher: Reading primers and reading instruction. *Paedagogica Historica, 48*(2), 185–96. https://doi.org/10.1080/00309230.2011.644302

Pavis, P. (1998). *Dictionary of the theatre: Terms, concepts, and analysis.* Toronto, ON: University of Toronto Press.

Pearson, P.D., Barr, R., and Kamil, M.L. (Eds.). (1996). *Handbook of reading research.* Mahwah, NJ: Lawrence Erlbaum.

Pennycook, A. (2002). *English and the discourses of colonialism: The politics of colonialism.* London, UK: Routledge.

Perry, A. (2003). From "'the hot-bed of vice'" to the "'good and well-ordered Christian home'": First Nations housing and reform in nineteenth-century British Columbia. *Ethnohistory, 50*(4), 587–610. https://doi. org/10.1215/00141801-50-4-587

Petrone, P. (1990). *Native literature in Canada from the oral tradition to the present.* Toronto, ON: Oxford University Press.

Petrone, S.P. (1998). Brant-Sero, John Ojijatekha. In *Dictionary of Canadian Biography* (Vol. 14). Toronto, ON: University of Toronto/Université Laval. Retrieved from http://www.biographi.ca/en/bio/brant_sero_john_ojijatekha_14E.html

Pettipas, K. (1994). *Severing the ties that bind: Government repression of Indigenous religious ceremonies on the prairies.* Winnipeg, MB: University of Manitoba Press.

Pfister, J. (2004). *Individuality incorporated: Indians and the multicultural modern.* Durham, NC: Duke University Press. https://doi. org/10.1215/9780822385660.

Phillipson, R. (2013). *Linguistic imperialism continued.* New York, NY: Routledge.

– (2014). Linguistic imperialism of and in the European Union. In H. Behr & Y. A. Stivachtis (Eds.), *Revisiting the European Union as an empire* (pp. 134–64). New York, NY: Routledge.

Pinney, C. (2011). *Photography and anthropology.* London, UK: Reaktion Books.

Poitras, E. (2001). *To colonize a people: The File Hills Indian farm colony.* Blue Thunderbird Productions.

Pokiak-Fenton, M., and Jordan-Fenton, C. (2010). *Fatty legs: A true story.* Toronto, ON: Annick.

Povinelli, E.A. (2010). The crisis of culture and the arts of care: Indigenous politics in late liberalism. In J.C. Altman and M. Hickson (Eds.), *Culture crisis: Anthropology and politics in Aboriginal Australia* (pp. 17–31). Sydney, AU: University of New South Wales Press.

Powell, J.W. (1880s and 1890s). Published varies studies in the Smithsonian Institution's Bureau of Ethnology.

PowWow at Duck Lake. (1967). National Film Board of Canada. Retrieved from https://www.nfb.ca/film/powwow_at_duck_lake

Pratt, R.H. (2003). *Battlefield and classroom: Four decades with the American Indian, 1867–1904.* Norman, OK: University of Oklahoma Press.

Prendergast, C. (2003). *Literacy and racial justice: The politics of learning after Brown v. Board of Education.* Carbondale, IL: Southern Illinois University Press.

Proulx, C. (2014). Colonizing surveillance: Canada constructs an Indigenous terror threat. *Anthropologica, 56*(1), 83–100.

Quan, D. (2015, May 15). "This is somebody's young kid": The unmarked graves of Brandon's residential school. *National Post.* Retrieved from http://news.nationalpost.com/news/canada/the-secret-graves-of-brandon-residential-school-773123

Qureshi, S. (2011). *Peoples on parade: Exhibitions, empire, and anthropology in nineteenth century Britain.* Chicago, IL: University of Chicago Press. https://doi.org/10.7208/chicago/9780226700984.001.0001.

Racette, S.F. (2009). Haunted: First Nations children in residential school photography. In L.R. Lerner (Ed.), *Depicting Canada's children* (pp. 49–84). Waterloo, ON: Wilfrid Laurier University Press.

Raible, C. (2007). *The power of the press: The story of early Canadian printers and publishers.* Toronto, ON: Lorimer.

Raibmon, P. (1996). "A new understanding of things Indian": George Raley's negotiation of the residential school experience. *BC Studies, 110,* 69–96.

– (2005a). Theatres of contact: The Kwakwaka'wakw at the fair. In *Authentic Indians: Episodes of encounter from the late-nineteenth-century Northwest coast* (pp. 50–73). Durham, NC: Duke University Press. https://doi.org/10.1215/9780822386773-004.

– (2005b). *Authentic Indians: Episodes of encounter from the late-nineteenth-century Northwest coast.* Durham, NC: Duke University Press. https://doi.org/10.1215/9780822386773.

Raptis, H. (2016). *What we learned: Two generations reflect on Tsimshian education and the day schools.* Vancouver, BC: UBC Press.

Ray, A.J., Miller, J.R., and Tough, F. (2000). *Bounty and benevolence: A history of Saskatchewan treaties.* Montreal, QC: McGill-Queen's University Press. Retrieved from http://www.deslibris.ca/ID/400325

Razack, S. (2002). When place becomes race. In S. Razack (Ed.), *Race, space, and the law* (pp. 1–20). Toronto, ON: Between the Lines.

– (2015). *Dying from improvement: Inquests and inquiries into Indigenous deaths in custody.* Toronto, ON: University of Toronto Press.

Reder, D. and Morra, L.M. (Eds.). (2010). *Troubling tricksters: Revisioning critical conversations.* Waterloo, ON: Wilfrid Laurier University Press.

Reed, H. (1889). *The following Indian industrial schools in Canada and the United States: Mount Elgin or Mohawk, the Muncey and the Carlisle* (No. 2060682). Library and Archives Canada (57500 R216-245-8-E Black Series, RG10, File 57799), Ottawa, ON.

Rees, T. (2009). *Arc of the medicine line: Mapping the world's longest undefended border across the Western Plains.* Vancouver, BC: Douglas and Mcintyre.

Regan, P. (2010). *Unsettling the settler within: Indian residential schools, truth telling, and reconciliation in Canada.* Vancouver, BC: UBC Press.

Rhodes, J. (1999). *Mary Ann Shadd Cary: The Black press and protest in the nineteenth century.* Bloomington, ID: Indiana University Press.

Rifkin, M. (2017). *Beyond settler time: Temporal sovereignty and Indigenous self-determination.* Durham, NC: Duke University Press. https://doi.org/10.1215/9780822373421.

Robinson, D. (2016). Intergenerational sense, intergenerational responsibility. In D. Robinson and K. Martin (Eds.), *Arts of engagement: Taking aesthetic action in and beyond the Truth and Reconciliation Commission of Canada* (pp. 43–66). Waterloo, ON: Wilfrid Laurier University Press.

Robinson, E. (2001). *Monkey beach.* Toronto, ON: Vintage.

Rutherford, P. (1982). *A Victorian authority: The daily press in late nineteenth-century Canada.* Toronto, ON: University of Toronto Press.

Ryerson, E. (1847). Report by Dr. Ryerson on industrial schools, appendix A. In *Statistics respecting Indian schools* (pp. 73–7). Ottawa, ON: Government Printing Bureau.

Sadowski, E.G. (2006). *Preliminary report on the investigation into missing school files for the Shingwauk Indian Residential School.* Retrieved from http://archives.algomau.ca/main/sites/default/files/2010-046_003_048.pdf

Said, E.W. (1994). *Culture and imperialism.* New York, NY: Vintage.

Samuel Ross. (n.d.). Retrieved from http://wherearethechildren.ca/stories/#story_25

Seixas, P.C. (2004). *Theorizing historical consciousness.* Toronto, ON: University of Toronto Press.

– (2006). What is historical consciousness? In R. Sandwell (Ed.), *To the past: History education, public memory, and citizenship in Canada* (pp. 11–22). Toronto, ON: University of Toronto Press.

Sellars, B. (2013). *They called me number one: Secrets and survival at an Indian residential school.* Vancouver, BC: Talonbooks.

Senate. (2017). 1st Session, 42nd Parliament, *150*(102). Retrieved from https://sencanada.ca/en/content/sen/chamber/421/debates/102db_2017-03-07-e#80

Sharma, S. (2014). *In the meantime: Temporality and cultural politics.* Durham, NC: Duke University Press. https://doi.org/10.1215/9780822378334.

Shea, C. (2015, March 15). Kinew owes success in broadcast by marching to the beat of his own drum. *The Globe and Mail.* Retrieved from https://www.theglobeandmail.com/arts/books-and-media/kinew-found-success-in-broadcast-by-marching-to-the-beat-of-his-own-drum/article23453469/

Shirritt-Beaumont, R.M. (2001). *The Rossville scandal, 1846: James Evans, the Cree, and a mission on trial* (unpublished master's thesis). University of Manitoba/University of Winnipeg, Winnipeg, MB.

The sign language of the American Indians. (1890a). *The Boys' Own Paper* (590), 492–5.

The sign language of the American Indians. (1890b). *The Boys' Own Paper* (591), 508–11.

Simon, R.I. (2005). *The touch of the past: Remembrance, learning, and ethics.* New York, NY: Palgrave Macmillan. https://doi.org/10.1007/978-1-137-11524-9.

Simpson, A. (2007). On ethnographic refusal: Indigeneity, "voice" and colonial citizenship. *Junctures, 9,* 67–80.

– (2014). *Mohawk interruptus.* Durham, NC: Duke University Press. https://doi.org/10.1215/9780822376781.

Simpson, L. (2011). *Dancing on our turtle's back: Stories of Nishnaabeg re-creation, resurgence and a new emergence.* Winnipeg, MB: Arbeiter Ring.

Simpson, L.B. (2017). *As we have always done: Indigenous freedom through radical resistance.* Minneapolis, MN: University of Minnesota Press. https://doi.org/10.5749/j.ctt1pwt77c.

Skutnabb-Kangas, T. (2013). *Linguistic genocide in education – or worldwide diversity and human rights?* New York, NY: Routledge.

Smith, L.T. (2012). *Decolonizing methodologies: Research and Indigenous peoples.* London, UK: Zed.

Snelgrove, C., Dhamoon, R.K., and Corntassel, J. (2014). Unsettling settler colonialism: The discourse and politics of settlers, and solidarity with Indigenous nations. *Decolonization, 3*(2), 1–32.

Sontag, S. (2003). *Regarding the pain of others.* New York, NY: Picador.

Sotiron, M. (2005). *From politics to profit: The commercialization of Canadian daily newspapers, 1890–1920.* Montreal, QC: McGill-Queen's University Press.

Spack, R. (2002). *America's second tongue: American Indian education and the ownership of English, 1860–1900.* Lincoln, NE: University of Nebraska Press.

Spencer, P.L. (1895a). The camera in the missionary field. *Canadian Photographic Journal, 4*(2), 36–9.

– (1895b). The camera in the missionary field. *Canadian Photographic Journal, 4*(3), 68–70.

Staff, I.C.T.M.N. (2014, February 7). Student suspended for speaking Native American language. *Indian Country Today Media Network.* Retrieved from https://newsmaven.io/indiancountrytoday/archive/student-suspended-for-speaking-native-american-language-f_5s-jHxAkuGfgKtnG_N-w/

Standing Bear, L. (2006). *Land of the spotted eagle.* Lincoln, NE: University of Nebraska Press.

Stanley, T.J. (2011). *Contesting white supremacy: School segregation, anti-racism, and the making of Chinese Canadians.* Vancouver, BC: UBC Press.

St Denis, V. (2004). Real Indians: Cultural revitalization and fundamentalism in Aboriginal education. In *Contesting fundamentalisms* (pp. 35–47). Halifax, NS: Fernwood.

Steel, D. (2012, April 15). Marks left by the children communicate a difficult time past. *Ha-Shilth-Sa*.

Sterzuk, A. (2011). *The struggle for legitimacy*. Bristol, UK: Multilingual Matters.

Stevenson, W. (1999). Calling Badger and the symbols of the spirit language: The Cree origins of the syllabic system. *Oral History Forum, 19–20*, 19–24.

Stoler, A.L. (2009). *Along the archival grain: Epistemic anxieties and colonial common sense*. Princeton, NJ: Princeton University Press.

– (2016). *Duress: Imperial durabilities in our times*. Durham, NC: Duke University Press. https://doi.org/10.1215/9780822373612.

Storey, K. (2016). *Settler anxiety at the outposts of empire: Colonial relations, humanitarian discourses, and the imperial press*. Vancouver, BC: UBC Press.

Strakosch, E., and Macoun, A. (2012). The vanishing endpoint of settler colonialism. *Arena, 37/38*, 40–62.

Strong-Boag, V., and Gerson, C. (2000). *Paddling her own canoe: The times and texts of E. Pauline Johnson (Tekahionwake)*. Toronto, ON: University of Toronto Press.

Stuckey, J.E. (1991). *The violence of literacy*. Portsmouth, NH: Boynton/Cook.

Stueck, W. (2015, February 18). Alert Bay residential school survivors gather for demolition ceremony. *Globe and Mail*. Retrieved from https://www.theglobeandmail.com/news/british-columbia/alert-bay-residential-school-survivors-gather-for-demolition-ceremony/article23067233/

Styres, S., Haig-Brown, C., and Blimkie, M. (2013). Toward a pedagogy of land: The urban context. *Canadian Journal of Education, 36*(2), 34–67.

Suzack, C. (2006). Publishing and Aboriginal communities. In C. Gerson and J. Michon (Eds.), *History of the book in Canada/histoire du livre et de l'edition au Canada* (Vol. 3, pp. 293–7). Toronto, ON: University of Toronto Press.

Terrance, L.L. (2011). Resisting colonial education: Zitkala-Sa and Native feminist archival refusal. *International Journal of Qualitative Studies in Education: QSE, 24*(5), 621–6. https://doi.org/10.1080/09518398.2011.600265

Thompson, J.H. (1994). Davin, Nicholas Flood. In *Dictionary of Canadian Biography* (Vol. 13). Toronto, ON: University of Toronto/Université Laval. Retrieved from http://www.biographi.ca/en/bio/davin_nicholas_flood_13E.html

Thrush, C. (2016). *Indigenous London: Native travelers at the heart of empire*. New Haven, CT: Yale University Press.

Titchkosky, T. (2007). *Reading and writing disability differently: The textured life of embodiment*. Toronto, ON: University of Toronto Press.

Titley, B. (1986). *A narrow vision Duncan Campbell Scott and the administration of Indian Affairs in Canada*. Vancouver, BC: UBC Press.

– (2009). *The Indian commissioners: Agents of the state and Indian policy in Canada's prairie West, 1873–1932*. Edmonton, AB: University of Alberta Press.

– (2011). *The frontier world of Edgar Dewdney*. Vancouver, BC: UBC Press.

Tobias, J.L. (1982). *Kamīyistowesi. Dictionary of Canadian Biography* (Vol. 11). Toronto, ON: University of Toronto/Université Laval. Retrieved from http://www.biographi.ca/en/bio/kamiyistowesit_11F.html

– (1994). *Payipwat. Dictionary of Canadian Biography* (Vol. 13). Toronto, ON: University of Toronto/Université Laval. Retrieved from http://www. biographi.ca/en/bio/payipwat_13F.html

Tomalin, M. (2011). *And he knew our language: Missionary linguistics on the Pacific Northwest Coast*. Amsterdam, PA: John Benjamins. https://doi. org/10.1075/sihols.116.

Traill, C.P. (1987). *The Canadian settler's guide*. Toronto, ON: McClelland and Stewart.

TRC of Canada. (2015a). *Canada's residential schools: Missing children and unmarked burials* (Vol. 4). Montreal, QC: McGill-Queen's University Press.

– (2015b). *Canada's residential schools: The history, part 1 origins to 1939* (Vol. 1). Montreal, QC: McGill-Queen's University Press.

Trouillot, M.-R. (2012). *Silencing the past*. Boston, MA: Beacon.

Troutman, J.W. (2009). *Indian blues: American Indians and the politics of music, 1879–1934*. Norman, OK: University of Oklahoma Press.

Truth and Reconciliation Commission of Canada (2012a). *They came for the children: Canada, Aboriginal peoples, and residential schools*. Winnipeg, MB: Truth and Reconciliation Commission of Canada. Retrieved from http:// publications.gc.ca/collections/collection_2012/cvrc-trcc/IR4-4-2012-eng.pdf

– (2012b). *Truth and Reconciliation Commission of Canada interim report*. Winnipeg, MB: Truth and Reconciliation Commission of Canada. Retrieved from http://www.myrobust.com/websites/trcinstitution/File/ Interim%20report%20English%20electronic.pdf

– (2015). *Honouring the truth, reconciling for the future: Summary of the final report of the Truth and Reconciliation Commission of Canada*. Retrieved from http://www.trc.ca/websites/trcinstitution/File/2015/Findings/Exec_ Summary_2015_05_31_web_o.pdf

Tuan, Y.-F. (2011). *Space and place: The perspective of experience*. Minneapolis, MN: University of Minnesota Press.

Tuck, E. (2009). Suspending damage: A letter to communities. *Harvard Educational Review, 79*(3), 409–28. https://doi.org/10.17763/haer.79.3.n0016675661t3n15

Tuck, E., and McKenzie, M. (2015). *Place in research.* New York, NY: Routledge.

Tuck, E., and Yang, K.W. (2012). Decolonization is not a metaphor. *Decolonization, 1*(1), 1–40.

Turner, D. (2013). On the idea of reconciliation in contemporary Aboriginal politics. In J. Henderson and P. Wakeham (Eds.), *Reconciling Canada: Critical perspectives on the culture of redress* (pp. 100–14). Toronto, ON: University of Toronto Press.

Venne, S. (Ed.). (1981). *Indian acts and amendments: 1868–1975: An indexed collection.* Saskatoon, SK: Native Law Centre, University of Saskatchewan.

Veracini, L. (2010a). *Settler colonialism: A theoretical overview.* New York, NY: Palgrave Macmillan. https://doi.org/10.1057/9780230299191.

– (2010b). The imagined geographies of settler colonialism. In T. Banivanua Mar and P. Edmonds (Eds.), *Making settler colonial space: Perspectives on race, place and identity* (pp. 179–97). Houndmills, UK: Palgrave Macmillan. https://doi.org/10.1057/9780230277946_12.

Vizenor, G.R. (1999). *Manifest manners: Narratives on postindian survivance.* Lincoln, NE: University of Nebraska Press.

von Heyking, A. J. (2006). *Creating citizens: History and identity in Alberta's schools, 1905–1980.* Calgary, AB: University of Calgary Press.

Vowel, C. (2016, March 19). That our languages thrive, not merely survive: Skwomesh immersion. Retrieved from http://apihtawikosisan.com/2016/03/that-our-languages-thrive-not-merely-survive-skwomesh-immersion/

Vučković, M. (2008). *Voices from Haskell: Indian students between two worlds, 1884–1928.* Lawrence, KS: University Press of Kansas.

Wagamese, R. (2010, August). Walking by the crooked water. *Canadian Geographic, 130*(4), 52–3.

– (2012). *Indian Horse.* Vancouver, BC: Douglas and McIntyre.

Waite, P.B. (1998). Bowell, Sir Mackenzie. In *Dictionary of Canadian Biography* (Vol. 14). Toronto, ON: University of Toronto/Université Laval. Retrieved from http://www.biographi.ca/en/bio/bowell_mackenzie_14E.html

Walcott, R. (2004). "A tough geography": Towards a poetics of Black space(s) in Canada. In C.C. Sugars (Ed.), *Unhomely states* (pp. 277–88). Peterborough, ON: Broadview.

Walker, B. (2009). Finding Jim Crow in Canada, 1789–1967. In *A history of human rights in Canada: Essential issues* (pp. 81–98). Toronto, ON: Canadian Scholars' Press.

Walker, C. (1997). *Indian nation: Native American literature and nineteenth-century nationalisms*. Durham, NC: Duke University Press.

Wall, S. (2003). "To train a wild bird": E.F. Wilson, hegemony and Native industrial education at the Shingwauk and Wawanosh residential schools, 1873–1893. *Left History, 9*(1), 7–42.

Walsham, A. (2017). Introduction: Past and … presentism. *Past and Present, 234*(1), 213–17. https://doi.org/10.1093/pastj/gtw054

Ward, A. (2001). *Dark midnight when I rise: The story of the Fisk Jubilee Singers*. New York, NY: Amistad.

Warley, L. (2009). Captured childhoods: Photographs in Indian residential school memoir. In M. Kadar, J. Perreault, and L. Warley (Eds.), *Photographs, histories, meaning* (pp. 201–21). New York, NY: Palgrave.

Warrior, R.A. (2005). *The people and the word: Reading Native nonfiction*. Minneapolis, MN: University of Minnesota Press.

Wasylow, W.J. (1972). *History of Battleford Industrial School for Indians* (Unpublished master's thesis). University of Saskatchewan, Saskatoon, SK.

Watts, R. (2014, June 19). Royal BC museum exhibit immersed in Native languages. *Times Colonist*. Retrieved from http://www.timescolonist.com/news/local/royal-b-c-museum-exhibit-immersed-in-native-languages-1.1137363

Welsh, C. (1997). *Kuper Island: Return to the healing circle*. Gumboot Productions.

Weston, M.A. (1996). *Native Americans in the news: Images of Indians in the twentieth century press*. Westport, CT: Greenwood.

Wherry, A. (2009, October 1). What he was talking about when he talked about colonialism. *Maclean's*.

Whitney, W.D. (1867). *Language and the study of language*. London, UK: N. Trübner.

Williams, A. (2015). *The pass system*. V-Tape.

Williams, F. (1985, Fall). George Gordon's "dream" press. *Type and Press*.

Willinsky, J. (1998). *Learning to divide the world: Education at empire's end*. Minneapolis, MN: University of Minnesota Press.

Wilson, E.F. (1874). *The Ojebway language: A manual for missionaries and others employed among the Ojebway Indians*. Toronto, ON: Rowsell and Hutchison.

– (1908). *The Reverend Edward Francis Wilson: His illustrated family journal, 1868–1908*. Accession Number: Wilson001, Salt Spring Island Archives, Retrieved from http://saltspringarchives.com/wilson/Journal/pages/Wilson001.htm

Wolfe, P. (1999). *Settler colonialism and the transformation of anthropology: The politics and poetics of an ethnographic event*. London, UK: Cassell.

Womack, C.S. (2008). Theorizing American Indian experience. In J. Acoose, C.S. Womack, D.H. Justice, and C.B. Teuton (Eds.), *Reasoning together: The Native critics collective* (pp. 353–410). Norman, OK: University of Oklahoma Press.

Woolford, A. (2014). Discipline, territory, and the colonial mesh: Indigenous boarding schools in the United States and Canada. In A. Woolford, J. Benvenuto, and A.L. Hinton (Eds.), *Colonial genocide in Indigenous North America* (pp. 29–48). Durham, NC: Duke University Press. https://doi.org/10.1215/9780822376149-002.

– (2015). *This benevolent experiment: Indigenous boarding schools, genocide, and redress in Canada and the United States.* Lincoln, NE: University of Nebraska Press.

Woolford, A., Benvenuto, J., and Hinton, A. (Eds.). (2014). *Colonial genocide in Indigenous North America.* Durham, NC: Duke University Press. https://doi.org/10.1215/9780822376149.

Zembylas, M. (2008). *The politics of trauma in education.* New York, NY: Palgrave Macmillan.

Index

Page numbers in *italic* refer to figures or tables.